The Shortest Way with Defoe

*Winner of the Walker Cowen Memorial Prize
for an outstanding work of scholarship
in eighteenth-century studies*

The Shortest Way with Defoe

Robinson Crusoe, Deism, and the Novel

Michael B. Prince

University of Virginia Press / Charlottesville and London

University of Virginia Press
© 2020 by Michael B. Prince
All rights reserved
Printed in the United States of America on acid-free paper

First published 2020

9 8 7 6 5 4 3 2 1

LIBRARY OF CONGRESS CATALOGING-IN-PUBLICATION DATA

Names: Prince, Michael (Michael B.) author.
Title: The shortest way with Defoe : Robinson Crusoe, deism, and the novel / Michael B. Prince.
Description: Charlottesville : University of Virginia Press, 2019. | Includes bibliographical references and index.
Identifiers: LCCN 2019014011 | ISBN 9780813943640 (cloth : alk. paper) | ISBN 9780813943657 (pbk. : alk. paper) | ISBN 9780813943664 (ebook)
Subjects: LCSH: Defoe, Daniel, 1661?-1731 Robinson Crusoe. | Deism in literature.
Classification: LCC PR3403.Z5 P75 2019 | DDC 823/.5—dc23
LC record available at https://lccn.loc.gov/2019014011

Cover art: Plate no. 93, Friday and the bear on the Limb. (From François Aimé Louis Dumoulin, *Collection de cent-cinquante gravures représentant et formant une suite non interrompue des voyages et aventures surprenantes de Robinson Crusoé* [(1810) 1962]; courtesy of Harvard University, Houghton Library)

Ralph Cohen, 1917–2016
In memory and application

Contents

Acknowledgments   ix

1   Lessons of the Pillory: Defoe's *The Shortest Way with the Dissenters*, 1702   1

The Puzzle and a Clue • Defoe's Nemesis • An Absurd and Abusive Title Page • Defoe's Irony • Defoe's Accomplices • "Quaker" Defoe

2   Defoe's Lunar Voyage: *The Consolidator*, 1705   46

A Literary Slough of Despond • Failure before Success • The Artistic Battle between Defoe and Swift • The Lucian Revival, 1620–1720 • Defoe's Feathery Craft • A Lunar Theory of the Novel?

3   Cosmopolitan Defoe: *A Continuation of Letters Written by a Turkish Spy at Paris*, 1718   90

Defoe's Spy Novel • The Secret History of the *Turkish Spy* • Orientalism and Literary Deism • Aesthetic Problems in the *Turkish Spy* • The *Hayy Ibn Yaqzān* of Ibn Tufayl and *Robinson Crusoe*

4 Defoe's Deist Masterpiece: *The Life and Strange Surprizing Adventures of Robinson Crusoe* and *The Farther Adventures of Robinson Crusoe*, 1719   134

Robinson Crusoe's First Critics • Two Jonahs and the Genres of *Robinson Crusoe* • Our Man Kreutznaer • The Footprint in the Sand • A "Coining of Providences" • Suspect Conversions • Sweet Revenge

5 Defoe, Deism, and the Novel: *Serious Reflections during the Life and Surprising Adventures of Robinson Crusoe*, 1720   208

Erich Auerbach and the *Ansatzpunkt* • Defoe's Religion • *A Vision of the Angelick World* • "A Strange Capitalist" • The Disappearing Author

Notes   235

Bibliography   295

Index   317

Acknowledgments

Ralph Cohen read the beginning of this book and let me know, in his inimitable way, that the idea had promise. He taught me how to read early modern texts and to ask good questions about them. James Anderson Winn read and offered meticulous comments on the Crusoe chapter shortly before his death, a generosity of spirit and intellect for which I shall be forever grateful. Paula Backscheider was generous with her extensive knowledge of Defoe and alerted me to the challenges of this study. Robert Folkenflik also supported this investigation at an early stage. Throughout the writing of this book, I have benefited from conversations with Christopher Ricks, who read and commented on several chapters. For his generous response to an early study of Auerbach's deist philology, I thank Sacvan Bercovitch, of blessed memory. Marshall Brown encouraged my study of deism and the novel and published a portion of the underlying research in *Modern Language Quarterly*. Allegra Goodman brought a novelist's intuition to the review of each chapter. For help with translations from F. A. L. Dumoulin's graphic novel version of *Robinson Crusoe,* I am grateful to my friend and colleague James Johnson and to Sophia Mizouni. I thank Susan Mizruchi for her steadfast friendship and encouragement. The Boston University Center for the Humanities supported this book early with a Jeffrey Henderson Senior Research Fellowship and late with a Humanities publishing stipend. For her precise work creating the index, I thank Ms. Katherine Hastie. The staff of the Houghton Library at Harvard University provided excellent assistance, as did the reference staff at Yale's Beinecke Library. J. William Frost and the staff of the Friends Historical Library at Swarthmore College introduced me to research on the Quakers, and my Quaker friend and colleague, the late Martin Fido, helped me understand Defoe's relation to the Quakers. I am especially grateful to Angie Hogan, my editor at the University of Virginia Press, for her immediate receptivity to the proposal and her openness and professionalism throughout the publishing process. It is indeed an honor to publish this book with the University of Virginia Press. Finally, I thank my family—my wife and fellow scholar, Abigail Gillman, and our children, Jacob, Ellen, and Livia, as well as my father, David Prince; my mother, Reva Scheinbaum Prince, of blessed memory; my sister, Erica, and brother, Paul; and my wife's parents, Neil Gillman, also of blessed memory, and Sarah Gillman. I am grateful for the many ways they have enriched my life and supported the writing of this book.

The Shortest Way with Defoe

1   Lessons of the Pillory
Defoe's *The Shortest Way with the Dissenters*, 1702

The Puzzle and a Clue

In the space of about two decades, the son of a candlemaker transforms himself from a brick merchant and political pamphleteer, "a Man of great Rashness and Impudence," as one enemy called him, "a mean Merceneries Prostitute, a State Mountebank, an Hackney Tool, a Scandalous Pen, a Foul-Mouthed Mongrel, an Author who writes for Bread, and Lives by Defamation," into an artist who launched the English novel.[1] How did this happen? The oddity of the situation has led reputable scholars to call *Robinson Crusoe* an accident.[2] Assuming it was not a freak occurrence, how are we to explain Defoe's remarkable breakthrough?

Many have been the attempts to solve this puzzle, and any new effort must rely on the work of preceding generations of biographers, editors, and literary historians. However, the sheer multiplicity of historical information—deattributions of the voluminous Defoe canon notwithstanding—has posed a great challenge, which Paula Backscheider acknowledges in her exasperated chapter titles "Four Hundred Thousand Words" and "Six Hundred Thousand Words."[3] It is not that Defoe left too few clues; he left too many. A short way from early to late, from bankrupt merchant and topical satirist to the immortal author of *Robinson Crusoe,* has eluded us.

Yet one clue, ignored until now, takes us immediately to the angry heart of the matter. The year is 1720, the triumph of *Robinson Crusoe* secure. Defoe nevertheless takes what appears to be a parting shot at someone he despises. His *Serious Reflections during the Life and Surprising Adventures of Robinson Crusoe* begins with the narrator's assurance that "The Fable is always made for the Moral, not the Moral for the Fable."[4] One might expect Crusoe to say next what the moral is and how the fable serves it. No such luck. Instead, the narrator adds the following paragraphs, which I quote here in full and refer to throughout this investigation:

> I have heard, that the envious and ill-disposed Part of the World have rais'd some Objections against the two first Volumes, on Pretence, *for want of a better Reason;* That (*as they say*) the Story is feign'd, that the Names are borrow'd, and that it is all a Romance; that there never were any such Man or Place, or Circumstances in any Mans Life; that it is all form'd and embellish'd by Invention to impose upon the World.
>
> I *Robinson Crusoe,* being at this Time in perfect and sound Mind and Memory, Thanks be to God therefore; do hereby declare, their Objection is an Invention scandalous in Design, and false in Fact; and do affirm, that the Story, though Allegorical, is also Historical; and that it is the beautiful Representation of a Life of unexampled Misfortunes, and of a Variety not to be met with in the World, sincerely adapted to, and intended for the common Good of Mankind, and designed at first, *as it is now farther apply'd,* to the most serious Uses possible.
>
> Farther, that there is a Man alive, and well known too, the Actions of whose Life are the just Subject of these Volumes, and to whom all or most Part of the Story most directly alludes; this may be depended upon for Truth, and to this I set my Name.
>
> The famous History of *Don Quixot,* a Work which thousands read with Pleasure, to one that knows the Meaning of it, was an emblematic History of, and a just Satyr upon, the Duke *de Medina Sidonia;* a person very remarkable at that time in *Spain:* To those who knew the Original, the Figures were lively and easily discovered themselves, as they are also here, and the Images were just; and therefore, when a malicious, but foolish Writer, in the abundance of his Gall, spoke of the *Quixotism of R. Crusoe,* as he called it, he shewed evidently, that he knew nothing of what he said; and perhaps will be a little startled, when I shall tell him that what he meant for a Satyr, was the greatest of Panegyricks.[5]

On the face of it, the passage might signal the autobiographical nature of *Robinson Crusoe.* Crusoe is Defoe in disguise. These lines have also sent scholars searching for historical individuals—Selkirks and Dampiers—who could have served as the real-life models for Defoe's story of a twenty-eight year castaway who lived to write about it. The lines also appear to affirm the value of historical truth through the odd expedient of a fictional character swearing an oath by his fictional name. None of this accounts for what comes next: a seeming *non sequitur* to *Don Quixote* and its reputation as a disguised satire, written against one man, the Duke *de Medina Sidonia,* the commander of the Spanish Armada at the time of its destruction.[6]

If one were to paraphrase the final paragraph, it might run something like this: a few specialists know that *Don Quixote* was a satire aimed at one man, but that did not keep Cervantes from writing the book in such a way that thousands would read it with pleasure even without knowing the historical key. There is a malicious critic out there whom I shall not name.[7] This scoundrel dares to suggest that my book, *Robinson Crusoe,* is quixotic in the same way. This critic is a fool, and I reject, vehemently, any suggestion, such as the one I am not now making, that *Robinson Crusoe* is a satire targeting one person. Even granting the case, since "the Figures [in *Don Quixote*] were lively and easily discovered themselves, as they are also here [in *Robinson Crusoe*]," this idiot will be startled to find that his criticism is my praise, because satire has been transformed, by the alchemy of genius, into panegyric—which can be said of both books, Cervantes's and mine.

The moment is tantalizing. Is Defoe prepared to identify this individual, this English Duke *de Medina Sidonia,* and thereby reveal the human forces that motivated his masterpiece? Of course not. This final insult, *Robinson Crusoe,* will be all the more final for being deeply disguised—as popular entertainment, "a Work which thousands read with Pleasure, to one that knows the Meaning of it." Having raised the possibility of a nemesis, Defoe's narrator promptly drops the subject: "Without letting the Reader into a nearer Explication of the Matter, I proceed to let him know, that the happy Deductions I have employ'd myself to make from all the Circumstances of my Story, will abundantly make him amends for his not having the Emblem explained by the Original."[8] Defoe could have explained the emblem (*Robinson Crusoe*) by the original (naming his enemy and all he represents), but he omits any "nearer Explication of the Matter." Instead, we get a consolation prize, those "amends" or "happy Deductions . . . from all the Circumstances of my Story" that so annoy modern readers and, judging from this passage, served even at the time as a smokescreen for something else. Defoe has Crusoe nearly admit that those moral bromides are meant to distract the reader from motives the author wishes to keep secret.

Defoe's evasions worked. *Robinson Crusoe* does not read as satire, and no one has looked to the war that broke out between Defoe and this unnamed adversary for a biographical, intellectual, and aesthetic account of the genesis of the novel.⁹ He covered his tracks so well that the whole notion of a *personal* explanation seems outlandish. Yet Defoe points the way to a reading of *Robinson Crusoe* as an act of literary revenge. The question then becomes: to whom does Defoe steadfastly *not* refer when he invites comparison between Cervantes's nemesis and his own? Since nothing so petty as a personal grudge could have issued in a work as great as *Robinson Crusoe,* how did this confrontation operate on Defoe to produce a work of lasting interest not just to this or that nation or religion or race, but, apparently, to the whole world? Three hundred years have passed since Defoe added this postscript comparing *Robinson Crusoe* to *Don Quixote.* It is time to test the hypothesis that for once he was telling something like the truth: find my nemesis, Defoe suggests; figure out what he meant to me, and what I did to him; and by that means you will arrive at the origin and meaning of *Robinson Crusoe.*

Defoe's Nemesis

In search of Defoe's nemesis it is safe to assume he would have had something to do with the greatest calamity in a calamity-filled life. Sure enough, we find this enemy who became more than an enemy in the shadow of the pillory (see fig. 1). Turn therefore from the triumph of 1720 to the dark winter and spring months of 1702–1703, the famous episode of "the pillory'd Author" that finds Defoe fleeing London, Queen Anne's exorbitant bounty on his head; captured and incarcerated in Newgate Prison; questioned as to motive and accomplices; put on trial for seditious libel (the original charge was treason, punishable by death); and sentenced, despite his ill-advised guilty plea, to the ignominy and danger of being pilloried in three different parts of London, as well to a potentially interminable jail sentence, a hefty fine that bankrupted him and cost him his brick- and tile-making factory—with the addition of a paid surety for seven years' good behavior—all for publishing, on December 1, 1702, a thirty-page pamphlet titled *The Shortest Way with the Dissenters.*[10]

Historians and biographers find this chapter of Defoe's life irresistible, as did Defoe himself. The pillory was a turning point, for this was the moment, Backscheider writes, that Defoe the speculative businessman and polemicist became Defoe the man of letters: "By the time Defoe stood in the pillory, everyone knew Defoe and his story. He had gone from Luttrell's unknown 'La Foe' to 'Daniel Foe, author.'"[11] "Defoe was an author," observes John Richetti, "whose life was changed by one piece of writing."[12] "It may be allowed," writes Maximillian Novak, "that Defoe felt deeply enough the anguish of these times in prison to have felt some imaginative empathy with Crusoe's

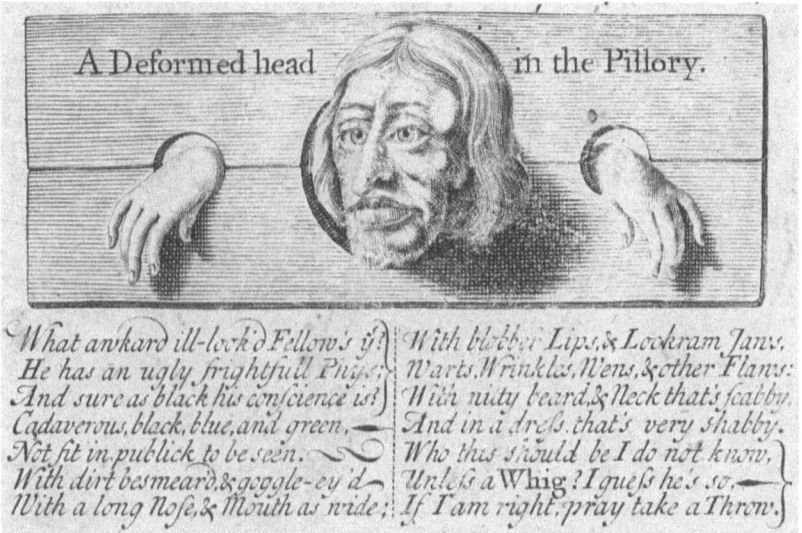

Figure 1. Defoe in the pillory. From George Bickham, *The Whig's Medley*, 1711. (Courtesy of Harvard University, Houghton Library)

island experience."¹³ John Robert Moore quotes E. M. Forster to the effect that "something occurred to him in prison, and out of its vague, powerful emotion Moll and Roxana are born."¹⁴ Moore poses a rhetorical question to which he assumes the answer is no: "If Defoe had continued to flourish as a pantile manufacturer, and if he had become a great force in politics, would he have been likely to write *Robinson Crusoe?*"¹⁵ These are tremendous claims. They suggest a direct line from *The Shortest Way with the Dissenters* to *Robinson Crusoe*. Only no one has filled in the historical basis for this scholarly intuition. It has been left at Forster's "vague, powerful emotion."

Returning to the scene of Defoe's crime, we discover something odd. Some basic questions remain unanswered and even unasked. Why did Defoe take such a huge risk with his *Shortest Way with the Dissenters?*¹⁶ Explanations range from the animal (he had irrepressible energy and just could not help himself) to the political (he sought to influence parliamentary deliberations on a bill hostile to the dissenters). We also have the non-explanation that the whole thing was a mistake: Defoe blundered badly and almost got himself killed.¹⁷ Who was the immediate target of *The Shortest Way?* Scholarly consensus coheres around one suspect, a fiery preacher named Henry Sacheverell, but that solution ignores obvious clues pointing to a more profound and consequential enemy. Did Defoe act alone, or, despite his repeated denials, did he have accomplices beyond the Whig agent who carried the manuscript to the publisher? There is evidence, long known to scholars, that Defoe had two powerful accomplices, one deceased under suspicious circumstances, and another alive and influential. Then there is the most curious feature of all: the outsize impact this brief pamphlet had on the reading public. There are several detailed studies of the reception of Defoe's *The Shortest Way* and the immediate political context that gave rise to it, but there is no clear answer to the question, Why did the little missile carry such a vast payload? And if, as so many biographers and critics assert, *The Shortest Way* somehow jump-started Defoe's career as a novelist, how and why did this happen? This chapter proposes answers to these questions, assembling new and old information into a profile of Defoe's motives and strategies.

Who, then, was Defoe's prime object of attack? *The Shortest Way* is usually viewed as a skillful interweaving of ventriloquized albeit unattributed passages from works by a number of High Church zealots, principally Roger L'Estrange (1616–1704), Henry Sacheverell (1674–1724), and Charles Leslie (1650–1722). Defoe encouraged this interpretation. In an early attempt to exonerate himself, he assured the public that his purpose was not political. The work was not written to influence any "Publick Bills in Parliament, now depending; or any other proceedings of either House, or of the Government relating to the Dissenters, whose Occasional Conformity the Author has constantly opposed."[18] Instead, he wrote to denounce the writing of poisonous religious invective drawn from well-known Tory-Jacobite-High Church sources. Naming their publications, Defoe claimed that nothing in his *Shortest Way* was more violent or seditious than passages in "the Sermon preach'd at *Oxford* [by Sacheverell], the *New Association* [by Leslie], [or] the *Poetical Observator* [by L'Estrange]."[19]

Past attempts to locate the target of Defoe's undetected satire have focused on the first named individual: Sacheverell. Howard D. Weinbrot states that, "for Defoe, the final of final straws was Henry Sacheverell's 1702 *Political Union*."[20] Novak also observes that "Defoe issued an 'Explanatory Preface' in a second edition of his work which noted the imitation of passages from Sacheverell and claimed that he had employed 'an *Irony not unusual.*'"[21] It is easy to see why historians arrived at this conclusion: Defoe appears to confirm it. In self-defense, he claims he might have avoided trouble by citing his source texts, Sacheverell's foremost among them: "Some People have blam'd the Author of the aforesaid Pamphlet, called *The Shortest Way*, &c. for that he did not quote either in the Margin, or otherwise the Sermon of *Sacheverell*, aforesaid, or such other Authors from whom his Notions were drawn."[22] In *The Present State of the Parties in Great Britain* (1712), Defoe adds further evidence that Sacheverell was the trigger:

> The Violences of the Day . . . may be a little guess'd at, by the famous Expression of that known Malefactor *Sacheverell,* who first made himself remarkable to the World on this Occasion, by a Sermon preach'd at *Oxford,* in which he had an Expression to this Purpose, *That he could not be a True Son of the Church of* England *who did not lift up the Banner of the Church against the* Dissenters. . . . This was the Sermon upon which an Author, till then not much known, wrote that unhappy Book called, *The shortest Way with the* Dissenters.— In which, seeming to fall in with the Times, he urg'd, with the most pungent Reasons, and with the utmost seeming Eagerness, the Absolute Necessity of Rooting out the *Dissenters* from the Nation. The Wisest *Church-men* in the Nation were deceiv'd by this Book; those whose Temper fell in with the Times hugg'd and embrac'd it; applauded the Proposal; fill'd their Mouths with the Arguments made Use of therein; and an eminent *Church-man,* in the Country, wrote a Letter to his Friend in *London.*[23]

I do not deny that Sacheverell is *a* target. I assert, however, that he is not *the* target, also alluded to at the end of this passage. Many churchmen wrote letters to their friends in London, but only one eminent churchman's letter had fast become the most sought-after antidote to the perceived deist threat overtaking England. Defoe placed only one churchman's title under bold attack with his title, which mimicked and mocked its victim. That churchman was Charles Leslie, whose *A Short and Easie Method with the Deists . . . in a Letter to a Friend* "was frequently reprinted, hailed as a polemical classic, and finally given the accolade of inclusion in both versions of *The Scholar Armed* (1780; 1795, 1800), the orthodox compendium of political conservatism."[24] Mary Astell has no doubt who Defoe's prime antagonist is. She reveals his initials on her own title page, echoing Defoe's title: *A Fair Way with the Dissenters and Their Patrons. Not Writ by Mr. L——y, or Any Other Furious Jacobite, whether Clergyman or Layman; but by a Very Moderate Person and Dutiful Subject to the Queen* (1704).[25] In Leslie we have the mastermind of the rival operation, a far more important *thinker* than Sacheverell, and just as scurrilous. J. C. D. Clark describes him as "one of the ablest intellects in the Stuart cause."[26] Leslie's *Short and Easie* was still being published in Lancaster, Pennsylvania, in 1797, in Dublin and London in 1799, and at Oxford in 1832.[27] Defending himself in 1703,

Defoe insisted that all he did was follow Leslie's spiteful lead: "Any Gentlemen who have the Patience to peruse the Author of the *New Association* will find Gallows, Galleys, Persecution and Destruction of the Dissenters are directly pointed at."²⁸ Defoe may have woven several sources of High Church diatribe into the fabric of his undetected hoax; he may even have singled out Sacheverell's bloody flag as immediate provocation, but Leslie was Defoe's nemesis—a man whose politics and theology were diametrically opposed to Defoe's; a man who, after 1702, would never tire of reminding the public of Defoe's disgrace. Leslie set up his own weekly magazine to rival Defoe's *Review* (Leslie's was called *The Rehearsal* [1704–1709]), and in 1710, Leslie called on the government to inflict corporal punishment on Defoe.²⁹ Even when they agreed, as on the topic of occasional conformity, they did so for opposite reasons: Leslie opposed occasional conformity as a dangerous practice that would imperil church and crown by allowing heretics to infiltrate the government. Defoe opposed occasional conformity because he wanted dissent to remain pure in its principles, thus forcing a more profound confrontation with the theocratic state.³⁰

Although his reputation had declined by the end of the eighteenth century, Leslie was a major figure when Defoe challenged him. With a ten-year head start (he was born in 1650), Leslie was the champion—meaning the most prolific, wily, and combative author—of the Anglican, nonjuring, Jacobite contingent.³¹ "He took his place in the front rank of the Jacobite body, and remained there stedfastly [*sic*], through all the dangers and vicissitudes of three and thirty troubled years," Macaulay writes in *The History of England*.³² Richetti calls Leslie the "most ferociously able of High Church polemicists," someone "riotously immoderate and scurrilous . . . defiant, unappeasable, and uncompromising."³³ In a quip reported by Boswell, Samuel Johnson captured this quality of violent intelligence: "Johnson made a remark this evening which struck me a good deal. 'I never (said he) knew a nonjuror who could reason.'" At this point, Boswell shunts the main line of thought—what did Johnson mean by this?—into a footnote, where he reports a dialogue between Johnson and a Mr. Henderson conveyed back to Boswell by a Reverend Agutter. The speaker challenges Johnson's statement that he never met a nonjuror who could reason, and Johnson dismisses candidate after candidate until he gets to Leslie: "He said, but, Sir, What do you think of Lesley? JOHNSON. 'Charles Lesley I had forgotten. Lesley *was* a reasoner, and a reasoner who was not to be reasoned against.'"³⁴ Since Johnson shared many of Leslie's religious views, the line could be read as praise: Leslie was not to be out-reasoned because he was right. J. C. D. Clark reads the lines in this unironic way: "Johnson was an admirer of Charles Leslie, to whom he paid tribute as 'a reasoner who was not to be reasoned against.'"³⁵ However, Johnson's quip also exposes Leslie's weakness: his hatred for his enemies could never be concealed for long. In that sense, as well, there was no reasoning with him or against him. "But you are Proof against Argument," Defoe wrote in response to Leslie's *The Wolf Stript of Its Shepherd's Cloathing* (1704), "and without taking notice of these things, or of anything else that stands against you, you *Repeat and Repeat* your Railings, and suffer your Tongue to Launch out in a senseless and insignificant Manner, *In Infinitum*."³⁶ The *Oxford Dictionary of National Biography* calls Leslie "the violentest Jacobite in the Nation."³⁷ Yet he possessed a powerful mind and resourceful pen. Johnson's witticism suggests that both accounts are true.

The antipathy that developed between Defoe and Leslie was both personal and public. Swift gives us an idea just how public it had become by 1710:

> We are unhappily divided into two Parties, both which pretend a mighty Zeal for our Religion and Government . . . *The Evils we must fence against are, on the one side Fanaticism and Infidelity in Religion; and Anarchy, under the Name of a Commonwealth, in Government: On the other Side, Popery, Slavery, and the Pretender from* France. . . . Here on one side [are] two stupid illiterate Scribblers, both of them Fanaticks by Profession; I mean the *Review* [Defoe] and the *Observator* [John Tutchin, 1660/64–1704]. On the other Side we have an open *Nonjuror*, whose Character and Person, as well as good Learning and Sense . . . do indeed deserve Respect and Esteem; but his [Charles Leslie's] *Rehearsal*, and the rest of his Political Papers, are yet more pernicious than those of the former two.³⁸

To out-pernicious Defoe was quite a feat, but the criticism is richly deserved. Leslie was a worthy adversary with a gift for bare-knuckles polemic, and he was determined to block Defoe at every turn. His stated purpose in *The Rehearsal* was to protect the public from contamination by Defoe: the "People must be Antidoted, their Judgments rectified, concerning Persons and Things. And this is the only Design (and I hope a good one) of my present Writing."³⁹ He carried out this design religiously, constantly abusing Defoe in print, as Defoe abused him. Leslie's *Rehearsal* asks, "But what will Foreign Countries think of our *Church* . . . when they shall hear, That this Man is not *Punish'd* but Continues still to Write on *Reviews* three times a *Week*, in the Face of the *Church* and *Government*, Encreasing every Day in these *Black Characters* of the *Church* and *Clergy*."⁴⁰

An Absurd and Abusive Title Page

In *A Political Biography of Daniel Defoe*, F. N. Furbank and W. R. Owens note that Defoe draws the title of his *Shortest Way* from Leslie's previous writings against the deists and the Jews, but they do not explore the significance of this decision.[41] Leslie's late nineteenth-century biographer, Robert Joshua Leslie, assumed that Defoe's *The Shortest Way* was written against his great forebear. He explains: "Thirteen years after publication of the 'Short Method with the Deists,' appeared a treatise in reply, which he [Leslie] was inclined at first to dismiss with contempt . . . on account of its absurd and abusive title-page. . . . Finding, however it was boasted of among the Deists as a very clever performance, he resolved to answer it."[42] Although feared by the dissenters and despised by Anglicans, *The Shortest Way* delighted the deists, a fact that has never received sufficient attention.

What made Defoe's title absurd and abusive? It punned on Leslie's title to exaggerate the violence of his entire way of thinking about politics and religion. Leslie's title promised two contradictory things. The phrase conjured seventeenth-century pedagogical works such as Edward Burles's *Grammatica Burlesa; or, A New English Grammar Made Plain and Easie for Teacher and Scholar* (1652) and William Mason's *Arts Advancement; or, The Most Exact, Lineal, Swift, Short, and Easy Method of Short-Hand-Writing* (1682). These works offered common readers important lessons delivered in a systematic and familiar way. Leslie's *Short and Easie* would provide a short course in defeating the deists by rational means. The course would be easy because written in the style of a letter to a friend. The work begins, "Sir, In Answer to yours, of the Third Instant, I much condole with you your Unhappy Circumstances of being placed amongst such Company, where, as you say, you continually hear the Sacred *Scriptures*, and the Histories therein contain'd, and all Reveal'd Religion turn'd into Ridicule by Men who set up for *Sense* and *Reason*."[43] Under siege, the friend asks for "some short Topic of *Reason*, if such can be found, whereby, without running to *Authorities*, and the intricate Mazes of *Learning*, which breed long Disputes . . . [the writer would] Demonstrate the Truth of the *Christian* Religion; and at the same time distinguish it from the *Imposters* of *Mahomet*, and the old *Pagan* World: That our *Deists* may be brought to this *Test, and* be either oblig'd to Renounce their *Reason*, and the common *Reason* of *Mankind*, or to submit to the clear Proof, from *Reason*, of the *Christian* Religion."[44] So the title promises a friendly, rational way of staving off irreligion.

Readers at the time would have heard a second, snarling meaning implied by the title, for according to the well-known pun, the shortest and easiest method of dealing with heretics was to hang them, behead them, or ignite them. Unable to resist augmenting rational cures with violent threat, Leslie observed, "By a prudent Compliance with *Popularity* and *Laws*, [the deists] preserve themselves from *Outrage* and legal *Penalties;* for none of their Complexion are addicted to *Sufferings* or *Martyrdom.*"[45] If the deists are reluctant to martyr themselves, however, the state should step in and do the job for them: "Therefore if the *Deists* would avoid the *Mortification* (which will be very uneasie to them) to *yield* and *submit* to be *subdu'd* and *Hew'd* down before the *Priests,* whom of all Mankind, they *Hate* and *Despise;* if they would avoid this let them confess, as the Truth is, that *Religion* is no Invention of *Priests,* but of *Divine* Original: The *Priests* were Instituted by the same *Author* of *Religion;* and that their *Order* is a *Perpetual and Living Monument* of the *Matters of Fact* of their *Religion.*"[46] Leslie and Defoe would have known the case of Thomas Aikenhead (1676–97), the University of Edinburgh medical school student who was tried and executed by hanging at age twenty-one merely for speaking deist ideas to classmates who turned him in.[47] Leslie's threats were not idle. They endow his *Short and Easie* with a sinister second meaning. And they reveal why Leslie's biographer hears Defoe's title as absurd and abusive: Defoe exposed the sadist behind the theologian, and he did so through a magnificent act of literary imposture that fooled everyone, including its intended victim.

Defoe's Irony

Having identified Defoe's target, it is time to take a closer look at his weapon: the brief first-person narrative that caused such an uproar. Defoe writes:

> Nothing was more strange than to see the Effect upon the whole Nation which this little Book, a contemptible Pamphlet of but three Sheets of Paper, had, and in so short a Time too. . . .
>
> The severe Usage of the Author encreas'd this Turn; they Find him, Imprison'd him, Pillory'd him, and, indeed, Ruin'd him: But his Contempt of them, even under all his Sufferings, his *Hymn to the Pillory,* which he made in Derision of them, and publish'd the very Day they expos'd him; the Shouts of the People when he was taken down, and the general Abhorrence shown, as well by *moderate Church-men* as *Dissenters,* at the Severities used against him, all testify'd, that the whole Nation had receiv'd a New Tincture, and the furious Spirit, aforesaid, received a visible Check from this Accident.[48]

Defoe is not exaggerating when he refers to "the Effect upon the whole Nation which this little Book, a contemptible Pamphlet of but three sheets of Paper, had, and in so short a Time too." Here is direct evidence that Defoe has done something new and disconcerting—surprising, perhaps, even to himself. Whether the immediate reception was right or wrong, ignorant or just self-deceived, the mere fact of such consternation confirms Novak's conclusion that Defoe's "audience was ill-equipped to read Defoe's text."[49] But what was it that confused them, and why were reactions seemingly disproportionate to the cause?

Fortunately, this aspect of the case—the immediate reception of *The Shortest Way with the Dissenters*—is one of the most fully analyzed topics in all of Defoe. Critics then and since have tried to explain the pamphlet's strange effect. This has not been easy. To begin with, there is a difficulty naming its genre. "Is it possible to classify it?" asks Bonamy Dobrée. "Purposeful parody, yes: but of what sort? Can you call irony what is so nearly burlesque? If it is ironical, it is irony carried so far that it ceases to be itself. Yet what are you to call it? For it isn't satire, which attacks frontally; it isn't invective, except perhaps inversely, which might constitute a branch of the ironic; nor is it sardonic."[50] Any confident naming of the genre fails to capture the confusion of Defoe's first readers. To them *The Shortest Way* read as James Sutherland describes it: "*The Shortest Way*, in fact, seemed a genuine utterance to almost everyone who read it."[51] Readers took it as a sincere, unsatiric, unparodic expression of a character's state of mind, charged by events—anticipating, in other words, the narrative mode of Defoe's later fictions. Satire would seem incompatible with such narrative sincerity, yet Defoe managed to combine them. By an ingenious modulation of first-person narrative, he impersonated not Leslie or Sacheverell but a vital and vibrant character who shared their views, and then some. Defoe amps up the High Church rhetoric without himself being heard, revealing the author behind the hoax. Leslie's short becomes Defoe's shortest; Leslie's deists become Defoe's dissenters; Leslie's method becomes Defoe's way. Defoe gives us a narrator who blurs the line between reason and violence; yet this figure, taken as a character, never seems like a fall guy or obvious satiric mouthpiece for ideas the true author hates. Through this narrator, Defoe constructs the outlines of a character—enraged, yes, but also witty, impetuous, far-reaching in his associations, and fluid in his command of biblical and historical analogies.[52] Choose any passage, and this persona shines through:

> BUT, says another Hot and Cold Objector, this is renewing Fire and Faggot, reviving the Act *De Heret. Comburendo:* This will be Cruelty in its Nature, and Barbarous to all the World.

I answer, 'TIS Cruelty to kill a Snake or a Toad in cold Blood, but the Poyson of their Nature makes it a Charity to our Neighbours, to destroy those Creatures, not for any personal Injury receiv'd, but for prevention; not for the Evil they have done, but the Evil they may do.⁵³

Why not believe that the narrator and the author are the same? And why not believe that the author is someone like Sacheverell or Leslie, whose faith justifies violence against the religious other? As in one of Charles Morton's dialectical school exercises taken to its extreme, the narrator weaponizes the entire catalog of rhetorical appeals—to logos (we outnumber the dissenters now and such was not always the case, so killing and banishing them will be easy); to ethos (I am your true guide, now that "their *Monmouths*, and *Shaftsburys*, and *Argiles* are gone, their *Dutch-Sanctuary* is at an end"); to pathos (the blood of your children be on your hands if you fail to act); and to kairos ("Heaven has made way for their Destruction, and if we do not close with the Divine occasion, we are to blame our selves").⁵⁴ An all-too-believable tone of justified grievance permeates *The Shortest Way*, as the narrator, speaking directly to his enemy in the second person, names past atrocities in England and Scotland, rising to the memorable lines, "You have Butcher'd one King, Depos'd another King, and made a mock King of a Third."⁵⁵ The constant refrain is, "And now the tables are turned on you." Once the identity of the author became known, the statement was doubly true.

The confused reception of Defoe's *The Shortest Way* suggests just how new and threatening this mode of narrative was to early modern readers. So they dissected its rhetoric, hoping to expose its underlying politics. Defoe's enemies put themselves in the unenviable position of defining and defusing a profound ironist. *The Shortest Way with Whores and Rogues*, published while Defoe was still on the run, takes aim first at Defoe's punning title, running it into the ground through repetition ad nauseam. "*Sir*," it begins, "(to *convert the* Dissenters), *you teach us the* SHORT DOCTRINE *of Fire and Faggot* . . . *If God will not give you the* GRACE *to follow this Advice, I recommend you to that* SHORT WAY *of burning you* (so Ironically) *design'd for the* Dissenters, *only adding the Experiment of a String to it;* and no Question but God in his Providence has designed something like that for you." The author provides details of Defoe's physical description, hoping the reader will turn vigilante: "*every Man . . . thinks you a scandalous and seditious Author . . . and for this Reason our* Gracious Queen *has promis'd fifty pounds to anyone that shall seize you; and 'tis not doubted (if you are not tripp'd to* Holland), but your long Chin, and Mold in your Face *will* (SHORTLY), *put a* Preternatural *Hook in your Roman Nose."* These lines are not the worst the author has to offer. He proceeds to challenge Defoe to a duel, anywhere, anytime: "*Accept* this Gentle Dedication *(and seasonable Warning) from one that neither Loves nor Fears you, (and were it Lawful) dares meet you at any Time with a brighter Weapon than a Pen.*"[56]

The true author of *The Shortest Way* was nowhere to be found. That was just the problem—not only literally, in that the work appeared anonymously and Defoe was hiding, but also figuratively in that Defoe's irony upset the usual expectations, concealing the author where the first-person narrator appeared most vehement. *The Shortest Way* lacked the proper generic markers for satire and was therefore deemed faulty on rhetorical grounds. Had Defoe "not forgot his *Farnaby,*" one critic chides, referring to a popular seventeenth-century school rhetoric, he would have observed the rules of satire and not fooled anyone: "for Satyrs, tho' they have some humane shape above, are known by their Tails or Cloven-feet below: And if our Author had been bred a Scholar instead of a Hosier, he would have found another kind of Figure *for making other Peoples Thoughts speak in his words.*"[57] Is there any clearer indication of Defoe's awareness of a distinction between prose satire and some other genre of fiction that is not yet named? No wonder Defoe later repeated this charge in a tone of mock bewilderment: "Thus a poor Author has ventur'd to have all Mankind call him a Villain and Traytor to his Country and Friends, for making other Peoples thoughts speak in his Words."[58]

If born of ignorance, this style of ventriloquized first-person narrative was hardly innocent. Defoe's enemies assigned treasonous motives to the rhetorical fault. They held him to political account not just for *what* he wrote, but for for *how* he wrote. The author of *The Fox with His Fire-Brand Enkennel'd and Ensnar'd* (1703) thought he had Defoe cornered:

> To be short and brief with him: It is granted him that he is a very *Ironical* Gentleman all over: That he has a very *Ironical* Name, but is still more Knave than Fool: That he has a very *Ironical Style,* but what abounds with more malice than Wit: But that he is free from any *seditious Design,* is such an *Irony,* that it must move Laughter more than Attention or Belief, and make a Jest of himself and the Government together. . . . Mr. *Foe,* with a *Shorter Way* indeed, paums his [irony] upon the whole Government and Constitution at once; and very *Ironically* dresses up the Church and State in the Lions and Bears Skin, and such *Ironical Figures* as are not to be found in the *Tropes* of our Modern Rhetorick, but a barbarous *Irony* that was much

practiced by the Old *Romans* on the Primitive Christians, the better to bring their Dogs to worry them."⁵⁹

Defoe's irony violates the rules of "our Modern Rhetorick." Seeking a generic parallel, the critic reaches back to Roman satire of the most decadent and irreligious variety. Immoral and lewd, Defoe's satire is also politically toxic: it implicates "Government and Constitution at once . . . Church and State." These perceptions of public danger from a mere literary device help explain why the ruse almost cost Defoe his life. Defoe's enemies discovered the religious and political radical behind the literary hoax: "his *plain English*, 'tis plain, was not *without Design*. It plainly told them, That God's peculiar People were to have their *Tryals again of Mockings and Scourgings, Bonds and Imprisonments, of the Gallies and Gallows:* And come, my Brethren, *come up and help the Lord against the Mighty,* **was the darker English of it.** If this were *Irony* too, so was *Guy Faux's* dark Lanthorn, when it came to blow up the Government!"⁶⁰ The witty substitution of Faux/Foe for Guy Fawkes (1570–1606) paints Defoe as an instrument of would-be regicide, bent on torching church and state with one blast. Leslie adds powder to the charge, likening Defoe's text to the 1683 Rye House Plot to assassinate Charles II and his brother James, Duke of York: "And the *Design* of that *Shortest Way with the Dissenters,* was as *Wicked* as can be imagin'd, notwithstanding all the *Fig-leaves* he has sew'd before it. It was like that of the *Rye-House-Plot* before mentioned, after they had *Murther'd* the *King,* to lay it upon others, and Cause a General *Massacre* of them through the *Kingdom.* For what other End could it be, to make the *Dissenters* believe, that the *High-Church* were for the *Shortest Way* of *Cutting* all their *Throats;* but to prompt the *Dissenters* for their own *Preservation,* to begin with us!"⁶¹ Here is an enemy reading past Defoe's narrative trickery—"notwithstanding all the *Fig-leaves* he has sew'd before it." Whether or not the reading captures the "real" Defoe may be irrelevant. Leslie and Defoe's enemies were responding to his texts. They did not care whether Defoe was "really" a republican revolutionary or "really" a deist. They cared about what his texts implied once the fig leaves of fiction were stripped away. If they were reading against the grain, they thought they were reading him accurately.

These accusations of radical religious and political ties are frequent. In another work that provides the title of this study, *The Reformer Reform'd; or, The Shortest Way with Daniel D'Fooe* (1702), the author concludes: "In short, the Book from the beginning to the latter end, is a scandalous malicious Libel, and seems purely to have its Rule and Beginning at the Calves'-Head Club, of which Mr. D Fooe is a worthy Member."⁶² The Calves'-Head Club, although possibly a hoax, is thought to have met every January 30 between about 1703 and 1734 to celebrate the day of Charles I's execution. An elaborate and possibly made-up description of the club's rituals appeared in *The Secret History of the Calves Head Club, or the Republican Unmask'd* (1703).⁶³ To Defoe's enemies, the purpose of *The Shortest Way with the Dissenters* was abundantly clear. He "assumes the character of an *Elevated High Churchman*, and takes all opportunities under false Colours, to abuse and asperse the Church; his Design was to alarm the *Whiggish* Party in *England*, and by his furious Discourse, would make it seem as though a Persecution could follow Occasional Conformity. While under his seeming Zeal for the Church of *England*, there lurk'd a Poison, to have infected the whole Nation."⁶⁴ This poison was also a literary feat.

Friend and foe alike marveled at Defoe's ability to create *personae*, in dramatic fashion, within the context of first-person narrative. In 1720 Charles Shadwell described Defoe as the writer who transformed heroic drama into popular narrative. Troubled by his own felt inadequacies as a modern dramatist, Shadwell looked about for a model of a writer who had dealt with the same burden of the past:

> Th' Exploits, of mighty Men and fighting Kings,
> Were Sounds too big for humble trembling Strings.
> What need you, for a Tale, so high to go,
> Said I, have you not *Robinson Crusoe?*
> There Incidents in full Perfection flow,
> (Such a Dramatick is the fam'd *De Foe*.)⁶⁵

This sense of the dramatic within narrative justified comparisons to Homer; it also provoked comparisons to a bedroom trick: "*Sir* (a word in your Ear) . . . *I must say your Writing* for, and against the Dissenters, *shews you to be one of the greatest*——&c, *that ever talk'd fine and tender things to a Woman.*"⁶⁶ While attacking *Robinson Crusoe,* Charles Gildon has to admit that if Defoe's works "should happen to live in to the next Age, there would in all probability be a greater Strife among the several Parties, whose he really was, than among the seven Grecian Cities, to which of them Homer belonged: The Dissenters first would claim him as theirs, the Whigs in general as theirs, the Tories as theirs, the Non-jurors as theirs, the Papists as theirs, the Atheists as theirs, and so on to what Sub-divisions there may be among us."⁶⁷ Even Charles Leslie allowed a character in one of his dialogues to observe, "*The World has not in any Age produc'd a Man beyond Mr.* DE FOE, *for his Miraculous Fancie, and Lively Invention in all his Writings, both Verse and Prose.* . . . For was it not a *Miraculous Fancie,* and *Lively Invention, which the World has not in any Age produc'd,* to write that *Shortest Way* in a Strain to be taken for a *Church-man?*"⁶⁸

Leslie does not mean to celebrate Defoe's genius. He aims to point out a public menace: "And tho' it is much *Beneath* him [i.e., Leslie] to enter the *Lists* with *De Foe*, as of any man of *Character* to answer the *Observator* (i.e., Tutchin); yet where the *Mischief* is *Great* and *Spreading*, the putting a *Stop* to it *is not* Unworthy *of the* Greatest Man, tho' he *Stoop* Below *Himself*, when that becomes *Necessary*."⁶⁹ Leslie has to stoop below himself *as a writer* because Defoe has broken through with the mob: "To propagate these Wicked Suggestions, and gain them a popular Reception, the Mob's Favourite and Solicitor General Mr. *Foe*, took his Clamorous Pen in Hand, which Spawn'd *The Shortest Way with the Dissenters*. . . . [T]he Government took notice of [Defoe], who was made an Example of, to deter others from the like Insolence, and Fin'd, Pillory'd, and Bound over to his good Behaviour for Seven Years."⁷⁰ Leslie cannot resist reminding the public of Defoe's humiliation. Clearly, though, what bothers him is that Defoe is winning the battle for hearts and minds. It galls him that Defoe revels in his victory, where the purpose of the pillory had been to shame him:

> Of a Piece in this Consummated *Wickedness,* was D'*Foe's Shortest way with the Dissenters*. And the *Party* causing his Books to be *Hauk'd* and Publickly *Sold* about the *Pillory,* while he stood upon it (in *Triumph!*) for *Writing* them. And *Writes* on still. And the *Advertisements* in our *New Papers* are fill'd with new *Editions* of his *Works,* among which this *Shortest way,* for which he was *Pillory'd,* still bears the Bell. For he has since Publish'd another *Shortest way* (as he calls it) *to Peace and Union* . . . and puts upon it, by the *Author* of *The Shortest way with the Dissenters,* he *Glories* in the *Title*. . . . So far is he or the *Party* from thinking the *Pillory* a *Shame,* in such a *Cause!*⁷¹

Leslie imagines the struggle with Defoe in political terms, to be sure, and Defoe, when contemplating Leslie, does the same. But Tory and Whig, High Church and Low Church, Jacobite and Williamite do not capture the politics of form in this case. Charles Leslie's biographer helps in this regard. He points out that Leslie "was inclined at first to dismiss [*The Shortest Way*] with contempt. . . . He thought it might fairly be left to sink of its own weights of nonsense and contradiction. Finding, however, it was boasted of among Deists as a very clever performance, he resolved to answer it."⁷² The only group that approved of *The Shortest Way* was the deists. How did they read *The Shortest*

Way with the Dissenters? Why did the deist John Toland (1670–1722) involve himself, with or without Defoe's knowledge, as principal distributor of *The Shortest Way* throughout Holland in 1703?[73] They heard an attack on religious zealotry pure and simple. They inferred from the irony a capacity to stand aloof from religious passions and see them for what they are: manifestations of *character* and the psychological needs that drive character. They were privy to a part of Defoe's literary biography that dropped out of the account because it does not accord with the view of him as a religious moderate, a Trinitarian dissenter.

Defoe himself commented frequently on *The Shortest Way*, at first in self-defense, later in self-praise, and his thoughts revert to the experience of the pillory and Newgate quite often in subsequent years. In 1703, still under threat of capture and punishment, Defoe tried to exonerate himself this way: "If any man take the Pains seriously to reflect on the Content, the Nature of the Thing, and the Manner of the Stile, it seems impossible to imagine it should pass for anything but an Irony."[74] While the *Oxford English Dictionary* provides instances of the word irony used as a genre label—"An Irony is a nipping jest, or a speech that hath the honey of pleasantnesse in its mouth, and a sting of rebuke in its taile"[75]—very few works in Defoe's day or since advertise themselves as ironies. Such labeling defeats the purpose of irony, as Defoe well knew. Defoe may claim that his readers should have seen through it, but the purpose of irony is not to be seen through—at least, not at first.

Defoe's subsequent explanations grow bolder: "And as to the excepted Piece, since the general Vogue has Condemn'd it, I submit to the Censure, but must enter a Protestation that my Intension was not Seditious. I avoid Vindicating the Measures I took in the Method of the Argument, and rather acknowledge my self in the wrong than dispute it, but, however, I might by my ill Conduct draw a Picture which shew'd a Face, I did not design to Paint; yet, I never designed such a Face as should scare Mankind, and make the World think me Mad."[76] Despite the mea culpa, the phrase "the Measures I took in the Method of the Argument" suggests a conscious strategy, which Defoe chooses not to divulge. Notice that he feels under no pressure to justify the political dimension of the text—its intervention in the debate over Occasional Conformity. What Defoe feels compelled to explain is a method. Instead of describing that method, however, he only confesses to his "ill Conduct" in too realistically painting a "Face" that would scare Mankind. The lesson? Keep the ironic method of ventriloquized first-person narration, but lose the angry face—transform Satyr into Panegyrick.

By 1712, the passage of time permitted greater openness about the narrative trick he had performed: "The Case of the Book pointed at was to speak in the first Person of the Party, and then, thereby, not only to speak their Language, but make them acknowledge it to be theirs, which they did so openly, that [it] confounded all their Attempts afterward to deny it, and to call it a Scandal thrown upon them by another."[77] Defoe both states the effect he intended on his audience and confirms that the effect took place. He claims victory by means of a narrative device, a first-person narrative delivered with such proximity to the consciousness of the protagonist, that author and narrator might be thought to coincide. They both do and do not. The shortest way mode presents the reader with a built-in ambiguity. The author maintains the reader in a state of indecision between equal alternatives. The authority of the narrator wavers, switching, like an optical illusion played out linguistically. Some readers may take the relation of author to narrator to be close, if not identical, and approving; others, or even the same reader in the next instant, may take the relation to be detached and disapproving. *The Shortest Way*'s effect of sustained narrative irony might be pictured along the lines of the "Figure-Ground" illusion of Gestalt psychology (i.e., "Rubin's Vase").

Reaching forward to Gestalt psychology to explain *The Shortest Way*'s effect suggests the difficulty critics have had in accounting for Defoe's irony. To sustain an irony as Defoe does over thirty pages, while impersonating a character he hates, reveals a strong admixture of what the ancient skeptics called equipoise, or skeptical indifference, in the writer, and equipollence, or equal alternatives, in the text.[78] The effect is more than one of dissimulation. Defoe is more than what William Minto called him: "a great, a truly great liar, perhaps the greatest liar that ever lived."[79] Truth and lies are not the issue here, any more than assumptions about Defoe's personal theology and political convictions disprove the possibility of irony as a structural constant *in his texts*. Instead, he is an artist achieving on the small scale of a pamphlet an aesthetic quality to which he would continue to aspire in longer and more complex prose fictions. L. S. Horsley emphasizes Defoe's aesthetic achievement in *The Shortest Way*, which he describes as a work of consummate literary skill: "When irony was not merely a brief taunt but the very basis for an extended piece of satire, the writer addressing a wide audience was generally willing to sacrifice formal consistency for intelligibility, and the structure of substantial satires, such as the ironic defence, often suffered from the pamphleteer's reluctance to refrain from direct attack or to rely upon his audience to see his real meaning without having it pointed out to them. Most popular propagandists were half-hearted in sustaining irony."[80] Not Defoe. *The Shortest Way with the Dissenters* is a thoroughgoing irony. It differs fundamentally from Swift's *A Tale of a Tub* and *A Modest Proposal* in not relinquishing the possibility that its protests and proposals are sincere.

Weinbrot and Novak have argued that Defoe's irony was easily penetrated, and those who did not penetrate it were either willfully ignorant or incompetent readers.[81] These conclusions run counter to historical information—most dramatically, the case of Charles Leslie himself, which reveals how a smart and competent reader was taken in by Defoe's ruse. Defoe himself delights in this effect. In *The Dissenter's Answer to the High-Church Challenge*, he introduces part of a letter supposedly sent from one High Church friend to a fellow Tory who had given him a copy of Defoe's *The Shortest Way:* "SIR, *I Received yours, and enclosed the Book, call'd,* The Shortest Way with the Dissenters, *for which I thank you; and, next to the Holy Bible, and Sacred Comments, I place it as the most Valuable Thing I can have. I look upon it as the only Method, and I pray God to put it into the Heart of our most Gracious Queen to put what is there propos'd in Execution.'"* To which Defoe adds, "Here is the Character of a High-Churchman drawn to the Life."[82] To undergo the shame of self-exposure in this way, Defoe's enemy had to identify with a singular character, a fascinating stew of intolerance. Defoe discovered his strange facility for this narrative feat in the process of trying to shame Leslie and his fellow churchmen. It is as if Defoe field-tested the eventual narrative mode of his novels with complete success. One short way to describe Defoe's emergence as a novelist is to suggest that over the next seventeen years, he discovered ways to scale up this narrative invention from pamphlet to novel length.

Defoe's Accomplices

The comparison of Defoe to Guy Fawkes helps explain why Queen Anne's agents grilled him for the names of his collaborators. Novak observes that "Nottingham must have believed that Defoe was privy to many of the transactions by the Whig Junto during the reign of King William, and probably shared with Charles Leslie and others the notion that some sinister, secret group of plotters had put Defoe up to writing *The Shortest Way.*"[83] A court spy in Holland, reporting home in January 1703, immediately after the publication of *The Shortest Way,* revealed that the notorious deist "Mr. Toland hath been very Industreus [*sic*] to disperse these Books [*The Shortest Way with the Dissenters*] in every Town all over Holland. He rails at our Government & Governours to every Body, in every Place where he is. He said the Printer and Author were both Dissenters, that that unworthy Book was certainly contriv'd & hatch't by Stronger heads than the pretended author Danl Fooe, tho he believed him capable.... If Dissenters contriv'd that Book, Toland calls himself agent for them."[84] Armed with such information, Defoe's interrogators pressed him to name names. He steadfastly refused.

Defoe liked to dwell on this heroic part of his story (as opposed to begging to be spared the pillory).[85] In his *A Hymn to the Pillory*, he alludes to accomplices he might have revealed in exchange for leniency: "Tell them he stands Exalted there, / For speaking what we wou'd not hear; / And yet he might ha' been secure, / Had he said less, or wou'd he ha' said more."[86] Defoe returns to this theme in *A Dialogue between a Dissenter and the Observator* (1703), in which a confused dissenter and a Tutchin stand-in take up the question of accomplices:

> Dissenter: Pray who do you reckon is the Author of this Devilish Book, call'd, *The Shortest Way?*
> Observator: I shall answer most of your Questions with a Question, I believe, and begin with you here. Do you think my name is Mr. *Bellamy* that you take me for *an Informer?* Read the *Gazett.* There you have the Man with the *Sharp Chin,* and a *Dutch Nose.*
> Dissenter: Ay, but Sir, we begin to doubt that is not the true Author, that he has been only made the Tool of some other party, who now they find the World Exasperated at it, have slipt out of the Noose, and left him it; we begin to be afraid the thing is a Reality, and there is such a design on foot.
> Observator: Your Answer, like Parson *Jacob's* Text, ought to be taken a pieces and Explain'd.
>
> 1. If you are not sure he is the Author, you *Dissenters* have done him a great deal of wrong, for you have rail'd at him more than all the rest of the World, and charg'd him with more Crimes than 'tis well possible for one Man to be Guilty of.
> 2. And yet supposing him not to be the Author, you suppose him to be very Honest to his friends, that he bears all this without discovering them.
> 3. As for your fears of a real design, to put the *Shortest way* in practice upon you, no Question there are abundance of People in the World, who would be glad there was not one of you left; I believe no body doubts it.

Dissenter: Pray who do you think they are?
Observator: Sir your Humble Servant; no *Bellamy, I* tell you not *I* Sir; If I were in a Plot with the Devil, I'le never turn Evidence, *besides Sir, I* have no Mind to have my Nose and Chin describ'd.⁸⁷

Why restage the whole thing unless Defoe is hinting that he did indeed have accomplices and is proud of himself for not betraying them? Yet those who have looked into the matter have generally accepted Sutherland's conclusion that "it is probable that on this occasion Defoe was playing no hand but his own."⁸⁸ It has been hazarded that Whig ministers of King William's court, displaced in 1702 by the king's deathly fall from a horse and the Tory Queen Anne's ascension, might have put Defoe up to it, but no evidence has surfaced to support these claims.

Defoe had at least two important accomplices: one deceased but very much alive through his controversial writings, and the other living and quite famous. We find a hint of the dead accomplice in a scorching poem written against Defoe shortly after his release from prison. In *The True-Born Hugonot; or, Daniel de Foe, a Satyr* (1703), the Tory polemicist William Pittis calls our author,

A true Malignant, Arrogant and Sour,
And ever Snarling at Establish'd Pow'r;
More Famous for *ill-Nature,* than for *Wit,*
And like a *Bull-dog* lik'd, because he Bit.⁸⁹

The poet attacks Britain for somehow allowing Defoe to flourish:

Britain, 'tis true, thou'rt Scandalously low,
That could'st stretch out thy *Arms* to a *De Foe;*
Lend him those *Aids,* which none but *Thou* wou'dst give,
And raise a poys'nous Plant that shou'd not live.⁹⁰

These interesting lines raise a question. What if, in addition to suggesting that Defoe is foreign to England, the word "arms" alludes to a rhetorical weapon that only Britain could supply. Well then, which British author supplied Defoe with the model for his *Shortest Way?*⁹¹ The poet is being coy, not naming names, lest others raid the same arsenal. Yet Pittis leaves a broad hint when associating Defoe with

> Those Interloping Jugglers of the *Town*,
> Who live by others Wit and not their own,
> That act like Hounds to smell out Men of Sense,
> And wriggle into Company for Pence;
> That follows *Authors* just as Carrion Crows,
> And treat *L'Estrange's* equal with *De Foe's;*
> Lay Traps and Snares, and bait the tempting Gin
> With Gold, to catch our Understandings in.[92]

We have had the information needed to decipher these lines since 1974, when Miriam Leranbaum published her detailed study of the textual history of *The Shortest Way with the Dissenters*. Defoe's rhetorical arms, the principal model for *The Shortest Way*, she concluded, was a pamphlet written by the notorious deist Charles Blount:

> If we describe the *Shortest Way* as a hoax whereby Tory extremists were to be trapped into acknowledging as sound and laudable an imitation of their own extremist views, we discover a precedent so like Defoe's deception as to raise the serious possibility that Defoe had it in mind as a model for his banter. Almost exactly a decade earlier, in January 1693, the printer Richard Baldwin brought Edmund Bohun, the Tory licenser, an anonymous pamphlet entitled *King William and Queen Mary Conquerers*, which, Bohun writes, he read over "with incredible satisfaction; finding it well written, close argument, modest and full of reason." . . . It was published a few days later with Bohun's enthusiastic approval. . . . It was a deliberately contrived imitation by Charles Blount to victimize Bohun.[93]

Pittis's reference to "L'Estrange's equal" likely refers both to the man who succeeded L'Estrange as licenser of the press, Edmund Bohun, and to the man who bettered them both, Charles Blount. While there is some disagreement as to what Blount's intentions were in writing *King William and Queen Mary Conquerors*, there is no doubt about the effect his pamphlet had on Bohun.[94] Macaulay's description of the case is so apt that it is worth repeating in full:

> [Bohun] was requested to authorize the publication of an anonymous work entitled *King William and Queen Mary Conquerers*. He readily and eagerly complied. For there was between the doctrines which

he had long professed and the doctrines which were propounded in
this treatise a coincidence so exact that many suspected him of being
the author; nor was this suspicion weakened by a passage in which
a compliment was paid to his political writings. But the real author
was that very Blount who was, at that time, labouring to inflame
the public both against the Licensing Act and the licenser. Blount's
motives may be easily divined. His own opinions were diametrically
opposed to those which, on this occasion, he put forward in the most
offensive manner. It is therefore impossible to doubt that his object
was to ensnare and to ruin Bohun. It was a base and wicked scheme.
But it cannot be denied that the trap was laid and baited with much
skill. The republican succeeded in personating a high Tory. The atheist
succeeded in personating a High Churchman. . . . The censor was in
raptures. In every page he found his own thoughts expressed more
plainly than he had ever expressed them. Never before, in his opinion,
had the true claim of their Majesties to obedience been so clearly
stated. . . . From these pleasing dreams Bohun was awakened by
learning, a few hours after the appearance of the discourse which had
charmed him, that the title-page had set all London in a flame, and
that the odious words, 'King William and Queen Mary Conquerors',
had moved the indignation of multitudes who had never read further.
Only four days after the publication he heard that the House of
Commons had taken the matter up, that the book had been called by
some members a rascally book, and that, as the author was unknown,
the Sergeant at Arms was in search of the licenser.[95]

Word for word, this sounds like an uncanny forecast of what Defoe would do
to Leslie and the High Church ten years later, in 1702–3. "Laid and baited with
much skill," Blount's impersonation of an extreme Tory view of the revolution
of 1688–89 deceived the very reader who should have been most on guard.
Macaulay and others hold that Parliament was likely to continue the Licensing
Act beyond 1694–95, but Blount's pamphlet changed minds. He showed that
ingenious writers and courageous publishers would always find ways to evade
the censor. Blount accomplished this three times previously, in 1678–80, with
philological works approved by the Tory licenser, Roger L'Estrange, which
were immediately banned and burned once their implicit deism and republicanism became clear. Blount was also the author of two previous works attacking press censorship. Failing to achieve his purpose by means of direct polemic,
the resourceful deist adopted a more devious approach, which carried the

day.⁹⁶ Prepublication licensing, though obviously not post-publication prosecution and punishment, ceased after 1695. "Little as either the intellectual or the moral character of Blount may seem to deserve respect," wrote Macaulay with Victorian disdain, "it is in a great measure to him that we must attribute the emancipation of the English press."⁹⁷

Unfortunately, *King William and Queen Mary Conquerors* was to be Blount's last work. He died the same year, at thirty-nine, an apparent suicide, caused either by a stab wound to the arm that festered (Alexander's Pope's account) or by a bullet to the brain (the more approved version).⁹⁸ Here is the man the poet refers to as L'Estrange's equal, who taught Defoe to "Lay Traps and Snares, and bait the tempting Gin / With Gold, to catch our understandings in." Blount made a career of popularizing the most republican and deistical portions of Milton, Hobbes, Herbert, Spinoza, and others, offering them to the public in accessible miscellanies, essays, and translations. Pittis likens this work to "Carrion Crows" feasting on dead meat. "Carrion Crows" may also refer to Leslie's full-throated celebration of Blount's suicide at the start of his *Short and Easie*.

In a letter to the Earl of Halifax dated April 5, 1705, Defoe describes himself as "this despicable thing who scorn'd to Come out of Newgate at the Price of betraying a Dead Master."⁹⁹ In *An Appeal to Honour and Justice* (1715), Defoe refers to William III as "the King my Master," and the assumption has always been that the dead master he is protecting refers to William and possibly his ministers.¹⁰⁰ Yet Defoe was aware of Blount; he had fought beside him in support of Monmouth's Rebellion, had escaped the Bloody Assizes with him, and had observed the remarkable effect his ventriloquizing pamphlet had on church and state. There was an accomplice to protect, not so much out of concern for Blount's body, since he was already dead, but out of concern for his own, since it would not do to draw attention to the fact that the weapon he had deployed against Leslie and his allies bore a strong resemblance to the deist's weapon that took down the Tory licenser in 1693. Nevertheless, Defoe found a devious way to acknowledge Blount. He begins *The Shortest Way with the Dissenters* with a tribute to L'Estrange, an irony we are now in a position to appreciate: "Sir Roger *L'Estrange* tells us a Story in his Collection of Fables, of the Cock and the Horses." There is nothing to keep the reader from recognizing the logic of a High Church zealot praising the Royalist Roger L'Estrange. The fable of the chicken daring to roost among horses' hooves, then asking for room to feather, would apply to upstart dissenters, who must be trampled underfoot, just as L'Estrange had "suppressed 600 sorts of seditious pamphlets" in his capacity as surveyor of the press between 1679 and 1685.¹⁰¹ Notice, however, how easily this interpretation flips once Defoe's irony is taken into account. Now the fable of a cock suggests not the impertinent dissenters, but the vainglorious religious bigots, who try to stifle publication but are trampled underfoot by ingenious writers.

Defoe's nod to Blount had to be subtle because Leslie's condemnation of him at the start of his *Short and Easie* had been so loud and violent. Leslie received criticism for the way he handled Blount in the first edition, so he made as if to apologize at the start of the second, delivering these chilling lines:

> *I find myself oblig'd to account for what I have said of him. I have been told (since the* First Edition *of this Part against the Deists) That it has Disoblig'd some* Friends *(far from my Intention) who for* Relation *or* Acquaintance *had a Regard to the* Person *of Mr.* Blount, *tho' not to his* Principles; *and think that I have us'd him too* Coursely, *he being a* Gentleman. *But when it is Consider'd, how he treated our Blessed* Lord *and* Saviour, *like the* Soldiers *who* Bow'd *the* Knee *to Him and* Spit *in His* Face; *who cry'd Hail, King of the Jews! to Mock* Him the more Outragiously. *That not only in his* Comments *upon this* History *of* Apollonius, *but in his* Great Diana, *his* Oracles of Reason, *and in all his* Works, *he set himself, with his whole Might, to* Oppose *and* Ridicule *the* Birth, Passion, Resurrection, Ascension, *and all that is said of our* Christ *and* God *in the* Holy *Gospel, and all* Reveal'd Religion. . . . *Considering that his* Blasphemous Works *(many of which were well nigh Lost) are of late carefully* Collected *and* Re-Printed *(to the Scandal of a* Christian *Country) and* Dispers'd *to* Poison *the* Nation . . . *I have no* Apology *to make, for calling this man* Execrable: *Nor can I Retract or Compound it. Seeing it is come to this, that either his* Memory *(who set himself at the head of the* Deists, *and after whom they now* Copy*) or else the* Memory *of Our* Lord Jesus Christ, *must remain for Ever* Accursed![102]

The either-or between deism and Christianity plays out over the body of the suicide; the passion of Leslie's rhetoric gives ample testimony to what contemporaries thought was at stake. Referring darkly to Blount's demise, Leslie thunders, "The Hand of that Scorner, which durst write such outrageous Blasphemy against his Maker, the Divine Vengeance has made his own Executioner." Christ and Leslie emerged victorious over Apollonius's "New Editor" (Blount). Now let us see who dares step forward to replace him: "I Invite them, I Provoke them."[103]

Defoe rose to this challenge ten years later with a literary hoax that does to Leslie what Blount did to Bohun and L'Estrange. Leslie himself had warned his readers to be on guard against another Blount. He wants first of all in his preface to the *Short and Easie* to defuse a controversy that Blount started with his translation of *The First Two Books of Philostratus* (1680), in which is told the story of Apollonius of Tyana, a miracle worker who lived at the time of Christ—a rival messiah, in other words.[104] "The Pains that Philostratus took," Leslie writes, "was upon the relations of Apollonius that were in the Commentaries of Damis. And to fit them for the Ear of an Empress, who lov'd Rhetorick, alias Romancing and fine Stories. So that we are not sure we have one Word of the Commentaries of Damis. But this we are sure of, That we have them only as they were New-Drest, and Vampt by an Orator, to please the Fancy of a Rhetorical Lady."[105] That is, do not be seduced by a disguised translation of a spurious history that is really a romance designed for weak female minds. Be on the lookout for vamping.

How ironic, then, that Leslie was caught completely off-guard once a new champion of the dissenters emerged, as Defoe did, armed with Blount's sharp device. Ambushed by the anonymous pamphlet and irked by its echoing title, Leslie rushed a reply into print in which he incorrectly guessed the political identity of the author. *Reflections upon a Late Scandalous and Malicious Pamphlet Entitul'd, The Shortest Way with the Dissenters* (1703) remains vague about who the author is because Leslie does not know: "There are various Conjectures, as to the Author and his Party: Some think him a Papist, some a Nonjurant Parson, and others think him a Dissenter."[106] Leslie guesses that the writer is a nonjuring parson because he "insists upon the same Topics that are to be found in the Pamphlets and Sermons, which have been printed against the Dissenters since K. William's Death; only his Title is a little more bald, and his Expressions a little more plain than those that have gone before him; but the Spirit, Notion and Application are the same."[107] Wrong. Defoe's hoax explodes in his hands, and Leslie is targeted in turn for verbal abuse in turn: "This impudent *Reflector* on Mr. *Foe's Short Way* (tho' it seems he had some Intimation that the Author was a *Dissenter* but unacquainted with Mr. *Foe's Irony*) would needs fasten it upon a *Non Jurant* or Papist. How like an Ass now he looks while he is mumbling his own Thistle . . . Himself and his Glass can best determine."[108] Leslie never forgot the injury. Defoe, judging from his *Serious Reflections* of 1720, never forgot his triumph and linked it to the success of *Robinson Crusoe*.

"Quaker" Defoe

Calling Blount an accomplice stretches the point, of course, because he was dead by 1693. Who was Defoe's living accomplice? It has long been known that the distinguished Quaker William Penn (1644–1718) visited Defoe in prison, not once but several times, and commissioned his son on Defoe's behalf, first to help him avoid the pillory, then, failing that, to free him from jail.[109] Defoe himself wrote in *An Appeal to Honour and Justice* (1715), "while I lay friendless and distress'd in the Prison of *Newgate,* my Family ruin'd, and my self, without Hope of Deliverance, a Message was brought me from a Person of Honour, who, till that time, I had never had the least Acquaintance with, or Knowledge of, other than by Fame, or by sight, as we know Men of Quality by seeing them on publick Occasions.... [T]he Message was by word of Mouth thus: *Pray ask that Gentleman, what I can do for him?*"[110] Because the individual who eventually freed Defoe from prison was Robert Harley, with Queen Anne's approval, biographers have downplayed William Penn's role in the episode.[111] They have taken at face value Defoe's repeated assertions, delivered in legalistic terms, that he "had never had the least Acquaintance with, or Knowledge of" Penn prior to publishing *The Shortest Way with the Dissenters.* Defoe does not name Penn, and when he proceeds to supply his answer to the question "*ask that Gentleman, what I can do for him?*" the language elevates, invoking the parable of the blind man whom Jesus restored to sight:

> But in return to this kind and generous Message, I immediately took my Pen and Ink, and writ the Story of the blind Man in the Gospel, who follow'd our Saviour, and to whom our Blessed Lord put the Question, *What wilt thou that I should do unto thee?* Who, as if he had made it strange that such a Question should be ask'd, or as if he had said, *Lord, doest thou see that I am blind, and yet ask me what thou shalt do for me?* My Answer is plain in my Misery, *Lord, that I may receive my Sight.*[112]

Knowing that Penn had been labeled the Antichrist by the likes of Leslie, Defoe likens him to Christ and implies by his rewriting of the parable, that he would follow his leader to the very edge of doom. Years later, Defoe was still grateful to Penn for his help at this critical juncture: "Altho' I lay four Months in Newgate Prison after this, and heard no more of it, yet from this time, as I learn'd afterwards, this noble Person made it his Business to have my Case represented to her Majesty, and Methods taken for my Deliverance."[113] What could the old Quaker do for Defoe? Return him to the light; get him out of Newgate Prison. But another question remains: why did Penn interest himself so personally in Defoe's case? Backscheider and other biographers emphasize the fact that Penn himself had spent time in prison for his publications and had connections in the courts of both James II and William, so it was natural for him to protect a prominent Whig caught in the jaws of the law. That Penn interested himself personally is abundantly clear from Defoe's famous letter to Penn from Newgate Prison, dated July 12, 1703. Moore calls it one of the warmest letters Defoe ever wrote. It is also a curious document. After reminding Penn (did he need to be reminded if it was true?) that the two men were complete strangers to each other—"Tho' a Long Apology Suites Neither your Own Temper, Nor my Condition, yet I Can Not but Let you Kno' with all the Thankfullness I am Capable The Sence I have of your Extraordinary Kindness: . . . Concerning your Self For me So Much a Stranger to you"—Defoe goes on to mention an offer on the table that he reveal accomplices in exchange for release from jail. The miracle Jesus would perform in restoring the blind beggar to light required only that the beggar betray Jesus and name him as an accomplice. Defoe rejects the offer:

> Sir The Proposall you are pleas'd to hint By your Son from My Ld Nottingham, of discovering Partys is the same which his Lordship has often Put upon me before.
> Sir In Some Letters which I have Sent his Lordship I have Answer'd him with the Same Assurance I did to the Privy Council, Viz That in the Manner which they Propos'd it I really had No Person to Discover: That if my Life were Concern'd in it I would Not Save it at the Price of Impeaching Innocent Men. No More would I Accuse my Friends for the Freedome of Private Conversation.
> It has been my Character Sir among those who Kno' me, That I Scorn to Lye, and by Gods Grace Ile preserve it while I live. I take the Freedome to give you the Trouble of repeating it, Onely to affirm to you with the More Confidence the Protestation I make. I Sollemnly Affirm that Other than what Passes in Conversation . . . I have no Accomplices, No Sett of Men (as my Lord Call'd Them) with whom I used to Concert Matters, of this Nature, To whom I us'd to show, or Reciev hints from them in Ordr to these Matters, and Therefore to Put it upon Condition of Such a Nature is to Offer me Nothing Attall.[114]

These are heroic lines; however, they serve a purpose other than self-congratulation. They also inform Penn that Defoe would rather die than betray his "Friends." Whether or not Defoe is punning on the common term for the Quakers, he appears to acknowledge and deny that in planning *The Shortest Way*, he had "Private Conversation" with certain individuals he chooses not to name. Defoe will not say, even twelve years later, whether he was protecting his accomplices. All he will say is, "Nor Will it ever be any Part of my Character that I reveal what should be concealed."[115]

No one has ever suggested that William Penn might have been one of the accomplices Defoe was protecting; biographers take Defoe at his word when he denies knowing Penn personally before his duress.[116] Yet there is a ready explanation for Penn's involvement with Defoe at this crucial moment, and once again Defoe's nemesis provides it. The Quaker editor of *The Friend* who reprinted Defoe's letter puts the problem this way: "What William Penn's service to Defoe had been, we leave to be determined by some Friend who may 'edit the letter.'"[117] Here is my suggestion. The question is just the reverse: not what Penn did for Defoe—that we know; he tried to save him from public shaming and prison—but instead what Defoe may have done at Penn's behest, and after "Private Conversation," such that it became necessary to deny all knowledge of Penn once he was taken. How else should we understand the cryptic lines in Defoe's *A Hymn to the Pillory*, again punning on the word for the Quakers:

> Tell them that this is his Reward,
> And worse is yet for him prepar'd,
> Because his Foolish Vertue was so nice
> As not to sell his Friends, according to his Friends Advice.[118]

Penn's effort to help Defoe makes sense in light of Defoe's disastrous effort to help Penn. They join in mutual detestation of and by Charles Leslie.

If the pillory leads us to Leslie, then it also brings in Penn and the Quakers and, with them, another question that has perplexed scholars of Defoe: why after 1703 did he frequently impersonate Quaker authors and depict Quaker characters? Transported to the colonies at the end of *Moll Flanders* (1722), Moll and her *Lancashire* Husband encounter "a very honest Quaker," who advises them to settle where he lives, "and where we should be Accommodated . . . and he invited us with so much kindness and simple Honesty that we agreed to go, and the Quaker himself went with us."[119] Captain Singleton, in the novel of his name, has a dear friend named William Walters, also conspicuously a Quaker. In *A Tour through the Whole Island of Great Britain*, Defoe refers to "the great William Penn."[120] Defoe's last major work of prose fiction, *The Fortunate Mistress* (or *Roxana*, 1724), introduces at its conclusion Roxana's Quaker friend, never named except by repeated Homeric epitaphs of honesty, courage, and wisdom. Delve into Defoe's Quaker writings and it becomes clear what is going on: the battle with Leslie continues. Defoe does not cede speculative ground to the supposed rationalist. But he also refuses to be drawn into the open. He takes cover behind Penn and the Quakers, cloaking his speculative attack on Leslie's theology in a defense of the Society of Friends.

Defoe's nemesis also happened to be the principal antagonist of William Penn and the Quaker movement. "The tussle between Leslie and his Quaker adversaries," observes David Manning, "was no puny pamphlet battle; it was a theologically charged polemical war."[121] Beginning with the work that made him famous—*The Snake in the Grass* (1696)—through two decades of vitriolic combat, the churchman took Penn and the Quakers to task.[122] "*And this was the reason,*" he announces in *The Snake,*

> *that I thought it highly useful to lay open their* Horrid Deceit, *for this purpose chiefly, That I might, by this bring our* Present Quakers *under that* Happy Necessity, *as I thought, of Disowning the* Mad Enthusiasm *of these their Adored* Guides; *and thereby persuade them to return to the* Sobriety *of* Religion; *in* Odium *to which, as a* Carnal *and* Spiritless Dispensation, *they had been Betrayed by these* Pharisaical Pretenders, *to quit the Communion of a* Regularly Constituted, *and* Apostolical Church—*But* (Alas!) *the issue has quite deceived my Expectations; for our* Present **Obstinate** Quakers . . . *pretend themselves to the same* **Extraordinary** Commission, *of* Immediate Divine Revelation; *and, thereby a* Right *to affix* God's Seal, **Thus saith the Lord,** *to whatever their* Rage, *their* Malice, *or their* Folly *shall suggest.*
> If they think these too hard words, they shall have harder yet.[123]

The yet harder words appeared in 1702, just before the publication of Defoe's *The Shortest Way with the Dissenters,* when Leslie published *A Reply to a Book Entitul'd Anguis Flagellatus; or, A Switch for the Snake.* Leslie's *Reply* mentions Penn by name sixty times, subjecting the eminent Quaker to the same hate speech Leslie had bestowed on the deist Charles Blount. Leslie targets these individuals because they stand for groups or movements—the deists and the Quakers. And Leslie wants to equate them, not without doctrinal justification. Leslie saw the two groups as complicit in a plot to overthrow church and crown, and this charge of collusion between deists and Quakers cannot be ignored or attributed to mere spite. Leslie gave forceful expression to a view that had been around for half a century. Quakerism was blasphemy, a virtual deism all the more dangerous because it had achieved a measure of institutional respectability. There were no Socinian or deist churches, but there were Unitarian congregations and Quaker meetings, espousing a theology that zealots such as Leslie viewed as fundamentally un-Christian because insufficiently Trinitarian. For this reason, Leslie argued that the Quakers "are plainly and in Terms, Excepted out of the present Act of Toleration."[124] He accuses Penn of having the blood of thousands of misled people on his hands. Then he adds this stab at the old man's vitals: "Their great Penn is now run *Dry*, which never before *Rested*, till it had *Quickly* given an *Answer* to whatever Touch'd in the Least upon him."[125] Did the aged Penn turn to the impetuous Daniel Defoe as the writer on his side best able to give Leslie what he deserved? Did Defoe, in other words, pick up Blount's weapon to fight Penn's war?

That is exactly what Defoe's enemies thought he was doing and how they made sense of his Quaker writings. I take the title of this book from one of those critics, Francis Bugg (1640–1727), whose *A Quaker Catechism* (1706) carries the subtitle "the Shortest Way with Daniel De-Foe."[126] Bugg uses the phrase "shortest way" not only to renew the old pun about hanging, but also to advise readers that if they wish to track this notoriously elusive author, they should divest him of his Quaker garb to reveal the religious radical beneath. Bugg published a couple of tracts warning the public of Defoe's Quaker shift.[127] *The Quaker's Infallibility Shaken All to Pieces* (1711) begins, "I hope to give them . . . such an impression in their Sides, as shall be visibly seen by all that shall read me with an impartial Eye. . . . And in this Discovery I am upon, no Man shall discourage me, no, not their *Defoe*, nor the *Socinians, Deists,* or any Luke-warm *Laodicean.*"[128] Bugg's lumping Defoe with Socinians, deists, and those without strong theological convictions might seem like indiscriminate mudslinging, since Defoe was a known opponent of the other suspects on that list. Yet Bugg has a specific charge in mind, justified in his view by Defoe's recourse to Quaker impersonations. To identify this charge, consider Leslie's theological equation of Quakers and deists (and all other dissenters) on doctrinal grounds:

> With the *Deists*, in this Cause, are join'd the *Quakers*, and other *Dissenters*, who throw off the *Succession* of our *Priesthood* (by which only it can be demonstrated), together with the *Sacraments* and *publick Festivals*. And if the Devil could have prevailed to have these

dropt, the *Christian* Religion would lose the most *undeniable* and *demonstrative* Proof for the Truth of the *Matters of Fact* of our *Saviour,* upon which the Truth of his *Doctrine* does depend. Therefore we may see the *Artifice and Malice* of the *Devil* in all these Attempts: And let those wretched *Instruments,* whom he *ignorantly* (and some by a misguided *Zeal*) has deluded, thus to undermine *Christianity,* now at last look back, and see the *Snare* in which they have been taken! For if they had prevailed, or ever should, *Christianity* dies with them; at least, it will be rendered *precarious,* as a Thing of which no *certain* Proof can be given. Therefore let those of them who have any Zeal for the Truth, bless God that they have not prevailed; and quickly leave them; and let others be aware of them.[129]

Leslie locates a conspiracy made up of avowed heretics, seemingly moderate dissenters, and more radical sects such as the Unitarians and Quakers.[130] In his mind, this cabal is both religious and political. "The *Deists, Wh—gs, C—mon*-wealths-*men &c.* are altogether against the Church; and upon the same Principle," he repeats in 1707.[131] As the passage suggests, the principle uniting these groups was both religious and political. This cabal fails to accept Leslie's high Anglican interpretation of the Trinity and the sacred rights of the established priesthood and consequently endorses a Revolutionary Settlement that deposed the legitimate King James II and replaced him with the illegitimate William of Orange. These religious and political errors intersect: heretics are traitors to the theocratic state. Of all the groups Leslie hated—and Leslie was an equal-opportunity hater, an anticosmopolitan before there were self-styled cosmopolitans to hate—he singles out the Quakers for special opprobrium. He was not alone: "Many non-Quakers took such exception to the theological precepts of Quakerism, particularly its Christology *vis-à-vis* the doctrine of the Trinity, that they became anti-Quakers who openly challenged the validity of Quakerism and labeled it inherently wicked. . . . Quakerism was perceived by many anti-Quakers as blasphemous primarily because they believed it to be an example of enthusiastic antitrinitarianism commensurate with the Thomistic conception of blasphemy as aggravated unbelief."[132]

Leslie became the leader of this anti-Quaker pack.[133] He thought he could sink the movement by demonstrating its essential similarities to deism. He explains in the preface to *Five Discourses by the Author of The Snake in the Grass* (1700) that his "Letter concerning the Socinian Trinity" is "as proper for the Quaker, as the Socinian Controversy, for they are all one upon this point," the point being the doctrine of the Trinity and the supposed sufficiency of reason and conscience in questions of faith.¹³⁴ Leslie saw little difference between the position of the deists, vis-à-vis sacraments, rituals, and ecclesiastical authority, and that of the Quakers. Blount "tells you what he would be at," he warns. "That is, to throw off all outward Ordinances, Sacrifices, Sacraments, &c. and resolve all to Inward Repentence, which is the very notion of the *Quakers,* whither his great wit has carried him."¹³⁵ The Quakers, he asserts, are as answerable as the Socinians "for the many Absurdities and Blasphemies of this their absurd notion of the Trinity."

What was the Quaker's absurd notion of the Trinity, as Leslie understood it? In *The Sandy Foundation Shaken* (1668), William Penn provides an answer:

> If God, as the Scriptures testifie, hath never been declar'd or believ'd, but as the Holy ONE, then will it follow, that God is not an Holy THREE, nor doth subsist in THREE distinct and separate Holy ONES; but the before-cited Scriptures undeniably prove that ONE is God, and God only is that Holy ONE; therefore he can't be divided into, or subsist in an Holy THREE, or THREE distinct and separate Holy ONES . . . So that either the Testimonies of the aforementioned Scriptures are to be believ'd concerning God, that he is entirely and compleatly, not abstractly and distinctly, the Holy ONE, or else their Authority to be denied by those Trinitarians; and on the contrary, if they pretend to credit their Holy Testimonies, they must necessarily conclude their kind of Trinity a Fiction.¹³⁶

This is an extreme anti-Trinitarianism that later Quakers will do their best to moderate. For Leslie it amounted to sheer blasphemy and justified calling Quakers deists. But theological hotheads such as Leslie and Bugg were not the only ones who equated deists and Quakers. The philosophical David Hume held that "the *Quakers* are, perhaps, the only regular Body of *Deists* in the Universe, except the *Literati* or Disciples of *Confucius* in China," an interesting observation considering that Defoe's next experiment in long prose fiction takes him to China, viewed as a deist utopia, and from there to the moon, where Trinitarianism is something novel.¹³⁷ Other writers of the age equated Quakerism and deism, yielding titles such as the reformed Quaker George Keith's *The Deism of William Penn and His Brethren Destructive to the Christian Religion,* published in London in 1699.¹³⁸ Swift himself associates Quakers, deists, and Socinians.¹³⁹ Richard Smallbroke (1672–1749), the bishop of Lichfield and Coventry, asserts that the "Heads of the Quakers . . . *allegorized* away the *Letter* of the New Testament, by opposing, or at least preferring, a *spiritual* or *inward Christ* to a *literal,* Historical, and Outward *Jesus.* . . . I am far, however, from condemning the *Quakers* as *Deists;* since many of that Sect have been, and no doubt now are, well-meaning, tho' ignorant Persons, that have been imposed on by their Leaders: but I cannot acquit the Founders and Heads of that sect from having been *Deists* in an *Allegorical* Disguise. And for this Assertion I refer the Reader to the several Authorities recorded by the Author of *The Snake in the Grass.*"[140]

A deist in allegorical disguise is a good description of the way Defoe appeared to his enemies. Defoe himself wrote in *The Review,* "I have nothing to do with the Principles of the Quakers; I leave that to the learned Mr. B[ugg] . . . I am not, I say, entering on the Principles of the *Quakers,* it can not be thought I shall go about to defend what I do not profess; but this I may say . . . that be the *Quakers* case right or wrong . . . they have generally speaking, stuck closer to their profess'd Principles, than most, if not than any Sort of People among us."[141] The delicious doublespeak of "it can not be thought I shall go about to defend what I do not profess," coming from an author who does just that with great alacrity, sometimes at his peril, alerts us to an impersonation that may be more than one among many.[142] After stating twice that he will have nothing to do with Quaker principles, the narrator proceeds to celebrate the Quakers for having remained truer to their principles (i.e., not practicing Occasional Conformity) than "any Sort of People among us" (i.e., dissenters). Writing from behind a Quaker mask, Defoe accessed the arguments a cautious but theologically astute deist might have made in response to Leslie. Defoe did learn caution from the pillory, so he searched for ways to defeat his enemy without exposing his chin. His impersonation of the Quaker is one of several disguises; cosmopolitan and Orientalist fictions follow, and *Robinson Crusoe* becomes the most complete disguise of all. All were met in their day by charges of implicit or explicit deism.

As with nearly everything else about Defoe, scholars disagree about the significance of his Quaker personas—that is, when they attend to them at all.[143] In "Daniel Defoe and the Quakers," Ezra Kempton Maxfield assembles relevant documents but cannot escape his overriding hostility toward Defoe for so misrepresenting Quakerism. "One must be blind indeed to read any friendliness whatsoever into any of Defoe's after 1708," he writes. "By no stretch of the imagination can we justify any theory of partisanship toward the Friends in these mysterious pamphlets known as Defoe's 'Quaker Letters.'"[144] If so, then Moore must be blind, because he reads the same material and concludes that, for "an author of the age of Queen Anne, Defoe was unusually sympathetic toward the Quakers."[145]

Both critics may be right. Defoe was clearly sympathetic to the Quakers. In the first *Review* essay devoted to them, he asserts the political and religious legitimacy of the Quaker movement:

> I call the Dissenters, those four sorts of differing People called *Presbyterians, Independents, Baptists,* and *Quakers:* I call these all Protestant, and Christian Dissenters; for I am not so narrow in my Charity, what ever some People may suggest, as not to think the *Quakers* Christians, and many of them better Christians too, than those that pretend to condemn them . . . Of these, I verily believe I speak within Compass, one half would come into the Church of *England,* and Encorporate with her; would the Convocation of the Clergy, now assembled so far consider the Wounds of the Church, and the Easiness of Healing them, as to submit but their Indifferent things to a new Regulation.[146]

The provisions of the Clarendon Code (1662–64) targeted the Quakers specifically, and the 1689 Act of Toleration continued to treat Quakers and Unitarians as beyond the pale of permissible Protestant dissent.[147] So Defoe clearly takes the Quakers' side. With regard to the pressing question of Occasional Conformity, he stands closer to the Quakers, who were unwilling as a matter of principle to swear any religious oath, than he did to dissenters who were willing to compromise occasionally for practical ends. In this passage, Defoe does not say whether the Quakers are among the one-half who would "come into the Church of *England,* and Encorporate with her." He lets the reader assume they would. Rather, he presents such an easy, self-evident proposal for healing old wounds that only the High Church's obstinacy or paranoia could explain its resistance, not fear of doctrines inimical to Anglican and Trinitarian orthodoxy, such as those espoused by deists and Quakers. "Another Objection [to the union of High Church and dissenters] is a Topping One indeed," Defoe writes, "and that is this, you would have us let down a Fence to the Church to let the Bears and Wolves of the Forest in; this is a Plot to pull down the Church."[148] Bears and wolves make odd appearances in Defoe, and we should keep track of them, but for now it is important to see the way he uses the Quaker persona to turn the screws on Leslie. He outfitted another Quaker persona to attack Henry Sacheverell in *A Sharp Rebuke from One of the People Call'd Quakers to Henry Sacheverell, the High-Priest of Andrew's Holbourn* (1715), writing, "It shall be hereafter that when one man shall curse another, he shall say, the Lord make thee as Sacheverell whom the People of the Lord abhor'd."¹⁴⁹ The same Quaker pretext sets the stage for attacks on James Butler, Benjamin Hoadley, and Thomas Bradbury. "Thou hast been busie in the Antichristian ungodly Work of Strife," Defoe's Quaker tells Bradbury. "Thou hast fallen upon the Innocent with Words of Bitterness, engendering malice and Envy, whereby thou hast been the Occasion of much Evil-doing, and hast brought forth Wrath among thy Brethren."¹⁵⁰

Maxfield justifiably complains that this rebuking language misrepresents the Quakers' preferred discourse. He cites the Quakers' repudiation of Defoe's tract against Bradbury: "We the People called Quakers do hereby Advertise all concerned, That we had no Hand in the said Pamphlet, and do utterly disown it, believing it to have been a Contrivance of some Adversary of Ours, whereby to vent his own Invectives against the Government in our Name, and to expose us to the Displeasure thereof, and the Censure of Sober People."¹⁵¹ The Quakers of Defoe's day thought it was un–Quaker-like to use the form of a Quaker sermon to berate known public figures. They may have had other reasons for their sensitivity, however. Manning describes "a fatal paradox in Quaker theology: individual proclamations by first and second-generation Quakers, which were retrospectively deemed incompatible with the public face of Quakerism as a form of Nonconformist Protestantism, could not be denounced because such repudiation would have argued Quakerism out of existence."¹⁵² In other words, new Quakers were doing their best to distance themselves from the more radical theology of their founders. The last thing they needed was a friend like Defoe.

Although quite ill by his own account—disputed, of course, in the biographies—Defoe could not let the Quakers' disowning go unanswered.¹⁵³ He dashed off another Quaker tract, this one aimed at Sacheverell, and appended this notice at the end:

> Whereas there was a publick Notice given in a Paper, commonly call'd the London-Gazette, the 5th Day, and in another Paper call'd the Daily-Courant, the 7th Day of the present Month (by several Ministering Friends, and others, who have become Back-sliders and Time servers) That a Book, entitled A Friendly Epistle, by way of Reproof, from one of the People call'd Quakers was written by an Adversary, and with an evil Intent against the King, Princes, and Rulers of the Land. . . . This is to inform the People, that the said book was written by a Friend in Unity with the People call'd Quakers; and that he is now mov'd to reprove them also in Publick for their Back-slidings.¹⁵⁴

Defoe mocks backsliding Quakers of his day who fail to live up to the more radical principles of their founders. It is unsurprising, then, that the Quakers disavowed Defoe.¹⁵⁵ Unable to attack Leslie directly as a deist, much less as a Jew, but determined to uproot his adversary in the most fundamental way possible, Defoe gave voice to Quaker ideas that rattled Leslie and the religious establishment.

While there is some question about the authorship of *A Defence of the People Call'd Quakers* (1720), its articulation of Quaker theology fits the pattern described here.¹⁵⁶ The opening echoes the opening of the deists' manifesto, the English *Religio Laici* (ca. 1645–48) of Lord Herbert of Cherbury, as smuggled into print by Blount in 1683. The 1720 Quaker tract says: "The several Controversies that are at present about the Fundamental Points of the Christian Religion, and the Heat and Malice with which those Controversies are carry'd on, have induc'd many of every Persuasion to make a further and more exact Enquiry into the Doctrine and Tenets *impos'd* upon them to Believe, and to compare 'em with those deliver'd by our Saviour and his Apostles, and *taught* in the primitive ages of *Christianity*."¹⁵⁷ This is how Herbert and Blount's *Religio Laici* begins:

> There is not any Meditation hath given me greater trouble, than when I think, That a Doctrine so necessary, as the Knowledge of God, with the true Way to serve and worship him, together with the Means to attain everlasting Salvation should be so variously deliver'd and taught in divers Ages and Countries; as also urged in such perplext and difficult terms . . . and after all this, yet to find it presented to me under such terrible Menaces and Execrations, as if among the many Churches in the World, I did not adhere to the right, (which each claimed to be theirs) I could not justly hope for salvation; but, on the contrary, expect eternal Torture, without any prospect of Relief.¹⁵⁸

The Quaker's pacifism masks a deist's freethinking. All the writer does here is defend the Quakers. Yet the terms of his defense come just short of repeating the case the deists had built against Leslie's brand of state religion.

A Defence of the People Call'd Quakers flags several key points, and each can be read as a speculative rebuke of Leslie's theology: "*First,* That They only who are Mov'd thereunto by the Spirit, or particularly Illuminated and Inspired, were Ordain'd to be Preachers of the Gospel of Christ; and that the Christian Religion consists in a Manifestation of his Light in our Minds, without any Rites, or Ceremonies, or Forms of Worship whatever."¹⁵⁹ The author was likely aware that Quakers have their rites and rituals, but he praises the most antinomian aspects of the movement, ignoring accusations of enthusiasm, to confront Leslie on fundamentals. In fundamental terms, dissenters and the High Church differed on the question of what was meant by the phrase "things indifferent." If a union between High and Low Church were possible, it would be through an agreement on the High Church's part to consider some of its Thirty-Nine Articles indifferent enough to drop, thus permitting dissenters to swear their oath of allegiance in good faith, a topic to which Defoe returns on many occasions.[160] The safe Defoe limits the number of indifferent things and advocates reconciliation of High and Low Church on that basis. Judging from this defense of the Quakers, however, "things indifferent" covers just about everything. According to the stipulation as to who does and does not qualify to enter the priesthood, even a woman or a man deserted on an island might qualify if "Mov'd thereunto by the Spirit." To call this view the antithesis of Leslie's defense of ecclesiastical authority is not accurate. It stops short of outright deism, but not by much.[161]

Once again, we find a first-person narrator expressing a position Defoe may or may not have shared. The ensuing defense of the Quakers expands the territory of "things indifferent," yielding either an intensely spiritualized Christianity or no Christianity at all, depending on your point of view:

> *Secondly,* that neither Baptism, or the Supper of the Lord, in the sense they are now receiv'd among Christians, namely as Outward and Visible Signs of an Inward Spiritual Grace, were instituted either by our Savior or his Apostles, or are in the least necessary to Salvation.
>
> And *Thirdly,* That the Religion of the People call'd QUAKERS, is the very same that was Establish'd by Christ, and Practis'd by the most Primitive Christians.[162]

Attacking a male-dominated theology, the narrator embraces the spiritual equality of men and women: "Women are as well under the Inspiration as Men; that they were fellow-labourers in the Gospel with the Apostles."[163] Does this view help explain Defoe's sympathetic depiction of female characters—Will Atkins's pious pagan wife, Moll Flanders, Roxana—which differs so completely from the representation of female characters in Richardson and Fielding? Scholars have never come up with a good explanation for why Defoe ends his last novel, *The Fortunate Mistress (Roxana)* as he did, with the *deus ex machina* of a Quaker friend, who saves Roxana from her irate daughter.

The evidence suggests that Defoe was beholden to Penn and the Quakers for more than legal help in his time of trouble. They camouflaged him in his war with Leslie and inspired him to overcome his enemy *as a writer*. For it is as a writer that I believe Defoe would have understood certain Quaker injunctions about religious symbolism. *A Defence of the People Call'd Quakers* casts the Quaker position in typically extreme terms: "All External Forms of Worship were needless: And notwithstanding *Moses* was oblig'd by such Ceremonials to Awe the *Jews* into a Rev'rence of God, who were incapable of entertaining any higher Notions of Him than what they could receive from their Senses; to *Christians,* who by this heavenly Talent have Him ever manifested to them, it is all Superstition and Vanity."[164] Jesus came to "abolish the Superstitions and Ceremonies of the *Jews,* and to establish a Religion Mental, and with no Ceremonies at all." For a writer, this abolishing raises a problem of representation. What kind of writing would be adequate to "a Religion Mental," which eschewed overt religious symbolism? The Quakers' enemies answered this question themselves—angrily. Each Quaker writer "states things according to his own Conceit, Learning, or Advantage," states Thomas Comber (1645–1699). "And withal they have rare Arts of Equivocation under Colour of Figurative Expressions, and curious salves to bring one another off from the brink of Blasphemy."[165] In a work wrongly attributed to Defoe titled *Defoe's Answer to the Quakers Catechism; or, A Dark Lanthorn for a Friend of the Light* (1706), we hear another answer to this question. Impersonating Defoe to drive a wedge between him and the Quakers, the narrator holds that "a Quaker is a Cynick in Religion," who "hath no more Christianity in him than a Turk. . . . From Socinus he steals arguments against the blessed *Trinity,* and learns to disown all Government from *John* of *Leyden*. . . . [The Quaker's Life] is only a real Lye, his Doctrine contrary to all sober Religion."[166] These are Leslie-like charges against the Quakers, which Defoe tried to refute with his Quaker tracts. The narrative continues in this vein until it peters out with, "I am grown quite weary of drawing his [the Quaker's] Character and cannot but wish him with all his Tribe fairly Embarqu'd for *terra Incognita,* of the late found *Isle of Pines* under Conduct of *Penn* their high Admiral."[167]

Why does this opponent of the Quakers suggest that they all be shipped off under Penn's leadership to the imaginary island made famous in Henry Neville's *The Isle of Pines* (1664)? Readers at the time, Defoe included, would have known this "instant bestseller on the European market" for its reputation not only as a work that engaged the debate about deism and natural religion, but also as "a display of pornographic primitivism."[168] It is the story of a young man and four women shipwrecked on an uninhabited island and the man's rather remarkable populating of the island with 1,789 of his own brood and their descendants over a sixty-year period. There is precious little talk of theology here—the story focuses on manly procreation. On his deathbed, the *Ur*-Father, George Pines, informs his children "of the Manners of *Europe*, and charges them to remember the Christian Religion, after the manner of them that spake the same Language, and to admit no other, if hereafter any should come and find them out."[169] He reminds them not to do what he did of necessity—indulge in a polygamous and incestuous free-for-all.[170] And he charges them to read the Bible once a month "at a general meeting." What makes the Quaker Penn the admiral of such a venture? His theology suggests a primitivism that assumes all will go well in a natural state—without churches and priests and oaths and religious wars. Well, says *The Isle of Pines*, here is your utopia.

The Quakers had a better literary model for their beliefs, however. As we will see at the end of chapter 3, they took special interest in the *Hayy Ibn Yaqzān* by Ibn Tufayl. This Arabic work from the sixth-century CE, which was given new currency in Latin and English translations at the end of the seventeenth century, offered a more positive illustration of Quaker ideas of the inner light and natural virtue. A feral child raised by animals who exercises his native genius—that is, the ability to draw inferential connections and think in a rational, scientific way—evolves his own concepts of religion, in many ways similar to the religious precepts of Islam and Christianity—except, of course, that Yaqzān discovers these truths without the help of revelation. The fictional depiction of natural religion carried obvious advantages to Quakers oppressed by the strictures of the theocratic state and devoted to the idea of a natural light within.

This chapter began with a puzzle and a clue. The puzzle is how Defoe transformed himself from a hosier and brick merchant into the author of *Robinson Crusoe*. The clue is an overlooked passage in which Robinson Crusoe hints at a personal nemesis to equal Cervantes's Duke *de Medina Sidonia*. This clue led to a reexamination of the affair of the pilloried author, and with it, a new look at a troublesome text, Defoe's *The Shortest Way with the Dissenters*. I made the case that in writing this incendiary hoax, Defoe also perfected a narrative device that he would use for the rest of his career. Where scholars have assigned Defoe's principal motive to an attempt to influence parliamentary debate over an Occasional Conformity bill, reopening the question of Defoe's accomplices leads the investigation in a different direction. Defoe's proximity to Blount and his intimacy with the most famous Quaker of his age suggest a context that predates and transcends party politics circa 1701–3. That context is the deist controversy and anti-Quaker polemics of the late seventeenth and early eighteenth century.

An objection will occur to scholars knowledgeable about Defoe. He was no deist. He tells us so himself. Whatever his enemies may have said about him—and were they not motivated to besmirch his character?—Defoe testifies umpteen times to his fundamental orthodoxy within the context of mainstream Protestant dissent. He was a moderate, Trinitarian dissenter. He therefore could not have sympathized with the anti-Trinitarian deists or the radical strain of Quakerism that announces its doubts about the Trinity without apology or backsliding. Even if he adopted their rhetoric, he never promoted their beliefs, or lack thereof. Any suggestion to the contrary, it will be urged, ignores a preponderance of evidence confirming the picture of Defoe that generations of biographers, critics, and editors have handed down. This Defoe is a Presbyterian by family who trained to enter the dissenting clergy, believed faithfully and fervently in the Protestant cause, desired reconciliation with the High Church, and wrote fiercely against deists and freethinkers. His masterpiece, *Robinson Crusoe,* cannot be understood outside the Calvinist tradition of Protestant spiritual autobiography.[171] If G. A. Starr is correct in attributing to Defoe the 1730 *Christianity Not as Old as the Creation,* then Defoe's last literary act was a point-by-point refutation of the deism expressed in Matthew Tindal's *Christianity as Old as the Creation.*[172] "Defoe was capable of flirting with many new ideas," comments Geoffrey Sill, in agreement with Starr's thesis, "but not with Deism."[173] After acknowledging that Defoe's religious views are difficult to fix, Sutherland fixes them just the same by quoting one of Defoe's most fervent statements of religious orthodoxy: "I own and acknowledge the Church of *England* to be a Protestant Reform'd Church, pure in Doctrine, and Orthodox in Profession. However I may differ from her in Church-Government and Ceremonies, which, GOD be prais'd, are points but Circumstantial—and not altogether Essential, or Doctrinal—as *England* is establish'd, I am fully satisfy'd the Civil Administration should be in the Church of *England,* and firmly believe it is Best for Us [the dissenters], most our Interest, and most conducing to the publick Peace, that it should be so."[174] These are not the expressions of a deist or deist sympathizer. Writing for the majority, K. R. P Clark concludes, "Defoe was a spokesman for theologically orthodox Dissent, specifically Presbyterianism. He was neither a republican nor a Deist: his aim was to discredit not the institution of monarchy itself, but the theory of divine right and those who employed it in defense of James II."[175] Novak adds his authority to this view: Defoe was a "staunch supporter of unity among the Dissenters, as well as an equally staunch upholder of the Trinity."[176] While admitting that "it is impossible to reach any close intimacy with him or to read his heart," Furbank and Owens nevertheless intimate that Defoe was "a stickler for religious orthodoxy, [who] regarded Toland as a dangerous heretic and Socinian."[177]

Against such scholarly consensus, it is almost sacrilegious to suggest that Defoe had secret and not-so-secret sympathies with deists and anti-Trinitarian Quakers. So let me be clear: Defoe was no deist. He only wrote like one and was taken for one by his enemies. Likewise, Defoe was no confirmed Quaker; he only pretended to be one to keep readers from concluding that he was something worse. Defoe's writings contain many disparaging comments about deists and freethinkers. In the late work *The Political History of the Devil* (1726), Defoe describes Satan's seduction of Eve: "But to come back to the Method of Satan's tempting her, *viz.* by Whispering to her in her sleep; 'twas a cunning Trick, that's the Truth of it, and by that means he certainly set her Head a madding after *Deism,* and to be made a Goddess."[178] This does not sound like a proponent of deism, even if Defoe's enemies believed the effect of his fictions on impressionable readers was just that of Satan on Eve. There is no denying that Defoe was the author of numerous homiletic works whose purpose was to inculcate the fundamentals of Protestant Christianity. Often taking the form of catechisms, these pedagogical dialogues were written more in fear than in support of public deism.[179]

Another objection may occur at this point. Perhaps I have overstated the antagonism between Defoe and Leslie, "this Man of Gall," as Defoe called him.[180] Defoe had many enemies, Henry Sacheverell and Daniel Finch, the second Earl of Nottingham, among them.[181] Why not view Leslie as just one rival among many, not worthy of the mythic moniker of nemesis? Furbank and Owens acknowledge Leslie's influence on Defoe's most important poem, *Jure Divino:* "In writing *Jure Divino* Defoe had been helped, rather than hindered, by his long-running controversy with Charles Leslie. . . . Defoe by now recognized Leslie as an important adversary."[182] If Leslie proved an inspiration for Defoe's verse satire, might he not have played a similar role for his experiments in prose fiction? Leslie was the living embodiment of positions Defoe sought to demolish. Swift assigned each figure a position of symbolic importance at opposite ends of the nation's theological divide. In *The Protestant Jesuite Unmask'd,* Defoe, or an author closely resembling Defoe, calls Leslie "a Seditious Turbulent *Pamphleteer,*" "a Scribbling State-Casuist," and "a common Poacher upon *Crown-Lands*" whose pen is "like a Scavenger's Broom" and who "plainly says, the Gallows is the best and *Shortest Way with Dissenters.*"[183] Leslie posed a philosophical, theological, and popular threat. He was the leader of the forces Defoe opposed. No other star shone so bright in Defoe's constellation of enemies—certainly not the bombastic Sacheverell, whom Defoe paints as an intellectual lightweight. In *The Secret History of the White Staff* (1714), Defoe reflects on the accidental advantage Parliament gave Sacheverell by treating him so leniently in 1710: "We can have no room to doubt, but they were led into this Snare by the Accident of that worthless Man's [Sacheverell's] Sermon, who was not capable himself to do it with any such Design, or considerable enough to be employed by others that were."[184] As for Nottingham, Defoe takes care of him in *An Appeal to Honour and Justice,* settling old scores through the deathbed relation of a private conversation he had with Queen Anne, in which she apologized for Nottingham's treatment of him during the *Shortest Way* episode: "At first, her Majesty declar'd, That she left all that Matter [Defoe's interrogation and punishment] to a certain Person, and did not think he would have used me in such a Manner. Perhaps these words may seem imaginary to some."[185]

Defoe felt and inspired unusually deep antipathies, to be sure, but he tells us himself, "I will endeavor to single one out from the Herd," and that leader of the pack was Charles Leslie.[186] With him it was open warfare carried on by any means necessary, and Leslie felt the same passion for Defoe. He writes of Defoe's *A Challenge of Peace Address'd to the Whole Nation* (1703), "This *Challenge,* (an odd word) *of Peace,* is indeed a *Declaration* of *War,* to all us of the *High-Church,* and to the *Constitution* of the *Church* of *England.*"[187] In Defoe's case, if not in Leslie's, this hatred spurred literary invention. Defoe's *The Dissenter's Answer to the High Church Challenge* (1704) replies directly to Leslie's *The Wolf Strip'd of His Shepherd's Cloathing* (1704), yet another attempt to expose the heretical Defoe lurking beneath the pretend Quaker. The pamphlet admits the difficulty of answering an author as violent and scurrilous as Leslie without sounding violent and scurrilous: "From this Principle, the Author of a late Pamphlet, with a Title as long as a Book, and call'd *The Wolf Stript,* must not expect a Return of Dirt for Dirt. . . . In like manner, he that will deal with this Author in his own Way, must foul his Mouth with so much Bear-Garden Language, such rude, unmannerly, and unscholar-like Behavior, that he must be tainted with the ungrateful Savour of his Enemy's Malignancy."[188] Defoe gave as good as he got, no doubt, but these lines also reveal a writer seeking better, more elegant ways to disembowel his enemy.

For his part, Leslie took pride in being the public's antidote to Defoe's venom. He fantasized in print that the tables had turned, and whereas Defoe fooled him in 1703, he more than mastered Defoe over the next few years. One of his fictional characters in *The Rehearsal* congratulates the Leslie stand-in that "[Defoe's] *Review* says, he'll have nothing more to do with you, *Master.* He says you *Banter* him to Death, and *Expose* him without Mercy, that People *Laugh* at him, and Ask him when he will justify his *Experiment?* When will he explain his *Dry* and *Wet Martyrdom?* What new *Abuses* he has to cast on the Memory of K. *William,* by way of *Vindication?* You stop his Mouth, and leave him nothing to say. You lay *Traps* for him, and he *Swallows* the *Bait,* tho' the *Hook* be almost Bare!"[189] Leslie took the opportunity of the Tory takeover of 1710 to call publicly for renewed corporal punishment against Defoe. He wrote a "Congratulatory Letter" to the Tory William Lege "Upon his late PROMOTION" to Secretary of State, published under the flamboyant title *Now or Never.* Now is the time, Leslie urged, now or never, to finish Defoe off for once and for all: "Here your Lordship may see Impudence in the Abstract, and riding in Triumph. What bold Names he calls the Doctrine of our Blessed Lord, *the Beast,* and how basely he slurs at Hereditary Right—This Insolence ought to be corrected. And then he says, Depend on't, the Nation begins to see. Yes Mr. *Defoe,* 'tis true indeed, the Nation begins to see. . . . And now I shall leave such Insects to be squeezed by Authority; I would not have him punished Allegorically (a Word he is mightily pleased with) but *in propria Persona,* as he justly deserves."[190]

Fortunately for Defoe, Leslie overplayed his hand. The government ordered his arrest for publishing *The Good Old Cause; or, Lying in Truth* in 1710. Rather than stand trial, Leslie fled England, accepting the post of chief Protestant minister to the exiled Stuart court at St. Germain. The discovery of a letter from him to agents of the Pretender reporting that Scotland was ripe for invasion and providing strategic advice ensured that he would live out his days in exile, following the Stuarts to Italy after the failed invasion of 1715. He was allowed to return to his native Ireland shortly before his death in 1722 and oversaw the publication of the two-volume *Theological Works of the Reverend Mr. Charles Leslie* (1721), a work reprinted as late as 1832 at Oxford. By the end of the nineteenth century, however, Leslie's star had fallen so far that his admiring biographer of 1885 felt compelled to begin with a chapter titled, "Reasons of Oblivion." In all the reasons he gives—and, indeed, in the entire biography—he seldom mentions Defoe by name, even though he discusses works by Leslie, such as *The Wolf Stript of Its Shepherd's Cloathing,* that target Defoe directly. Yet Defoe will have his revenge, and the deist Blount and the Quaker Penn will have theirs through Defoe.

2 Defoe's Lunar Voyage
The Consolidator, 1705

> He has more cunning than a Fox, for when he has done his Mischief, he will not come near the Place again till 'tis forgot; he has more Doublings and Windings than a Hare, to extricate himself out of a Snare, or to draw others into one. In short, *Mr. Church,* he's an original Jugler, a mere *Proteus,* a Saint in his Expressions, and a Devil in his Designs.
>
> —Joseph Browne, *State Tracts*

A Literary Slough of Despond

I take Robinson Crusoe at his word when he intimates at the start of *Serious Reflections* that Defoe, like Cervantes, wrote with an adversary in mind and that, in some way, his novel could be described as an act of literary revenge. As we follow the trail leading from this first clue, bit players in previous accounts become major operators, including the deist Charles Blount, the zealot Charles Leslie, and the Quaker William Penn. The first provided the weapon for the crime that landed Defoe in the pillory; the second was Defoe's principal target; and the third may have conspired with Defoe before the attack and certainly tried to spare him the pillory and free him from jail. Still, a pamphlet-length disguised satire is one thing, and a multivolume novel is quite another. *The Shortest Way*'s mode of ironic first-person impersonation stays with Defoe for the rest of his life and plays an essential role in *Robinson Crusoe,* but this one artistic trick cannot exhaust what Defoe meant when he referred to "having the Emblem explained by the Original." The narrative breakthrough was an aftereffect of other purposes. If these purposes were decisive, where should we look to find Defoe continuing to pursue them, discovering other forms of literary subterfuge in the process?

Asking the question this way points us to works Defoe wrote between 1702 and 1719, but here another problem arises. It is not that Defoe left too few clues; he left too many. In her life of Defoe, Paula Backscheider condenses the difficulty into the chapter title, "Six Hundred Thousand Words."[1] The title suggests Defoe's remarkable productivity. It admits a certain resignation, as well, a feeling familiar to biographers and literary historians who follow Defoe from early to late. Even after efforts to deattribute works have cut the Defoe canon in half, a literary slough of despond remains as one tries to account for the reports, communiqués, poems, letters, essays, satires, journalism, proposals, and miscellaneous narratives that issued from his impetuous pen during the decades before *Robinson Crusoe*. A short way through this morass to the masterpiece has been hard to locate. Arthur Wellesley Secord's observation remains as true today as when he made it in 1963: "The career of Daniel Defoe is, for a number of reasons, difficult to trace. Problems concerning his life, his character, and his writings have hitherto baffled every effort to solve them."[2]

Yet the evidence presented in the previous chapter points to a possible solution. Set aside what Defoe may or may not have believed in his personal theology. Consider what his enemies said about him and what he did as an artist. Those who hated Defoe tried to strip him of his Quaker personas and thought of them as a form of deism in allegorical disguise. They knew that, once flushed from one covert, he would take on other colors that were just as convincing: "When he has done his Mischief, he will not come near the Place again till 'tis forgot; he has more Doublings and Windings than a Hare, to extricate himself out of a Snare, or to draw others into one." The campaign against Leslie continues; the dangers of that campaign continue, as well. The question becomes, What other forms of literary deism did Defoe adopt?

Of the many works of prose fiction Defoe wrote after his incarceration and before *Robinson Crusoe*, two stand out, bookending the time span in question. They are Defoe's first long prose fiction, *The Consolidator; or, Memoirs of Sundry Transactions from the World in the Moon* (1705), published a little more than a year after Defoe's release from Newgate Prison, and *A Continuation of Letters Written by a Turkish Spy at Paris* (1718), published eight months before *Robinson Crusoe* took the world by storm. The former is a lunar voyage modeled on seventeenth-century translations and imitations of the satires of Lucian, the second-century Syrian Greek skeptic known not only for his hostility to Christianity, but also for his atheism, homosexuality, and cosmopolitanism.

The latter is a continuation of a publishing sensation, the first Oriental spy novel in the West, with roots in a broader European Enlightenment linked explicitly to deism. In other words, Defoe's experiments in prose fiction before *Robinson Crusoe* follow models of cosmopolitan and Orientalist fiction known to be hospitable to deism. Why is this fact not better known? Apart from Defoe's reputation as a religious moderate opposed to deism and freethinking, these works have dropped out of sight because they failed. Readers in Defoe's day rejected them, calling for no new edition beyond the first year of publication.[3] Readers have been happy to ignore them ever since. Even scholars find them unbearable. Search the biographies and criticism for mention of them. Search the received theories of the rise or origin of the novel, even those that star Defoe. They are virtually absent. It is a truth almost universally acknowledged that *Robinson Crusoe* was Defoe's first novel, even though he previously published two long works of prose fiction that his contemporaries considered novels.

These cosmopolitan fictions qualify as apprenticeship works for the eventual masterpiece and are unavoidable if our goal remains to understand Defoe's development from popular polemical satirist into the author of *Robinson Crusoe*. However, it is worth underscoring the subjunctive mood of "if our goal remains to understand Defoe's development," for this goal may appear not only naïve, but false. It bespeaks a teleological bias, as if Defoe's purpose in all of his activities were to write the first English novel. One knows the endpoint one wishes to reach and stacks the historical deck accordingly, ignoring the vast number of subliterary, journalistic, political, and otherwise occasional texts that make up the man. Ashley Marshall takes this position to its extreme. "The teleological approach to fiction now seems entirely natural, and a number of critics have attempted to find the germs of *Robinson Crusoe* and other novels in Defoe's earlier writings," she writes. She calls this approach a "dangerously a priori method"—dangerous because it falsifies the truth of history.[4] It also suggests access to Defoe's inner psychology, as does any effort to speculate about a writer's "craft" or "aesthetic." Such access Marshall denies on principle. "In the realm of [Defoe's] inner psychology, what we know for certain is that we do not know much of anything for certain."[5] Marshall's conclusion is that all Defoes are fabricated, except, perhaps, her own. And the worst fabrications are the literary ones that seek and find in him the architect of the modern novel. She describes John Robert Moore's portrait of Defoe as "the father of the novel and on his way to being seen as a master" as a "whitewash."[6] "The now-dominant assumption that Defoe was centrally concerned with literary craft is not grounded in anything provable.... [T]he fiction represents no more than a brief passage in a long and varied career. . . . [W]e have seized on a set of shakily attributed potboilers and named him the father of the English novel."[7] While denying any access to Defoe's psychology, Marshall "can imagine Defoe being baffled by the preferences and predilections of modern scholars: of all he tried to do and all he accomplished."[8] He would be baffled because the literary aspirations we assign to him were not motivating factors. Instead, he thought of himself as a journalist, a businessman, a propagandist, a hack. "Whatever the legitimacy and advantages of the literary view," writes Marshall, "the historians' Defoe would probably be more recognizable to Defoe himself than our version. . . . I suspect he saw himself more or less as he was seen in the decades after his death, as a talented and (at least briefly) important journalist and pamphleteer," a remarkable assertion given the previous denial of insight into Defoe's psychology.[9]

Our first clue refutes these conclusions. In 1720, Defoe compared *Robinson Crusoe* to *Don Quixote*. Defoe's first readers, even those who hated him, described him as a modern Homer for his command of dramatic narrative. Defoe had high literary aspirations in poetry and in prose, fueled in part by an abiding hatred for one man and all he represented. A narrative of Defoe's development becomes possible by tracing his attempts to exact vengeance and retribution. Add ambition and learning to hostility and we would expect to find longer and more complex prose experiments. Attacking this enemy, this hater of Quakers, Unitarians, Jews, Muslims and all things cosmopolitan, Defoe sought out forms that continued the fight on fundamental grounds while offering cover. He therefore embraced genres of prose fiction we now call cosmopolitan, utopian, and exotic. It was common knowledge—and a common fear—that these cosmopolitan fictions fed a growing appetite for popular deism.

Failure before Success

Failure never gets enough credit. Unfinished work, sketchy work, inferior work is easily forgotten. We focus on enduring art and look away from the victims of time's indifference. Yet before *Sense and Sensibility* there was *Lady Susan*. Before *Middlemarch* there was *Scenes from Clerical Life*. Before *Uncle Vanya* there was *The Wood Demon*. Does anyone read—let alone perform—the plays of Henry James? A preoccupation with success skews our understanding of both the artist's development and cultural history.[10] In his study of German tragic drama, Walter Benjamin takes a different approach: "The production of lesser writers, whose works frequently contain the most eccentric features, will be valued no less than those of the great writer."[11] "Lesser" and "eccentric" are not negative judgments here. They refer to an incapacity to combine and reconcile textual elements the writer nevertheless finds it necessary to join. Eccentricities reveal purpose in an unguarded way, bridging biography, politics, and aesthetics. Why not extend Benjamin's insight when lesser writer and great writer are the same person? Defoe moved slowly to *Robinson Crusoe*, through trial and error, experiencing more failure than success along the way. His experiments contain "eccentric features," odd combinations of genres and motives that reveal an artist thinking about his craft—flailing, yes, but learning from his mistakes. Not a conscious artist, critics write; he had a lucky hit with *Robinson Crusoe*, guided by nothing we would call a theory or conception of the genre he is credited with inventing; he was a journalist whose aesthetic found him, not he it. These old tales need rethinking. Defoe's failures schooled him for success. They reveal an aesthetic of the modern novel in embryo—a mixture of motives and expressions whose eventual polish in later works conceals rough origins.

As the title page of the "second edition" of *The Consolidator* indicates (see fig. 2), you do not have to travel far before arriving at (1) an asserted continuity with *The Shortest Way with the Dissenters;* and (2) Defoe's overt polemic against Leslie and the High Church—"*Men of Zeal,* or *Booted Apostles,*" as Defoe's traveler calls them. "Ecclesiastical *Bone-setters,*" he adds for good measure.[12] Defoe or his publisher, or possibly both, used the title page to advertise one of Defoe's most polemical texts:

> Lately Published, the *Experiment,* or *the shortest way with the Dissenters exemplified.* Being an account of the inhumane and barbarous Treatment of Mr. *Abraham Gill,* a Dissenting Minister in the Isle of *Ely;* of his being sent for a Soldier by Mr. *Ferne* an Ecclesiastical Justice of the Peace, and other Conspirators, to the Eternal Honour of the Temper and Moderation of High Church Principles.
>
> *N.B.* The Matter of Fact is attested by several Affidavits of Men of Credit and Reputation in those Parts.

Dedicated to Queen Anne (a dedication that struck one reader as treasonous), Defoe's *Experiment* merely points out that the shortest way he recommended in fiction (violence against dissenters) had been carried out in fact by the church's mistreatment of one Abraham Gill. Who was this Gill, and why did Defoe go to such lengths to defend him? Sutherland devotes several pages of his biography to Gill and concludes that it hardly matters whether he was

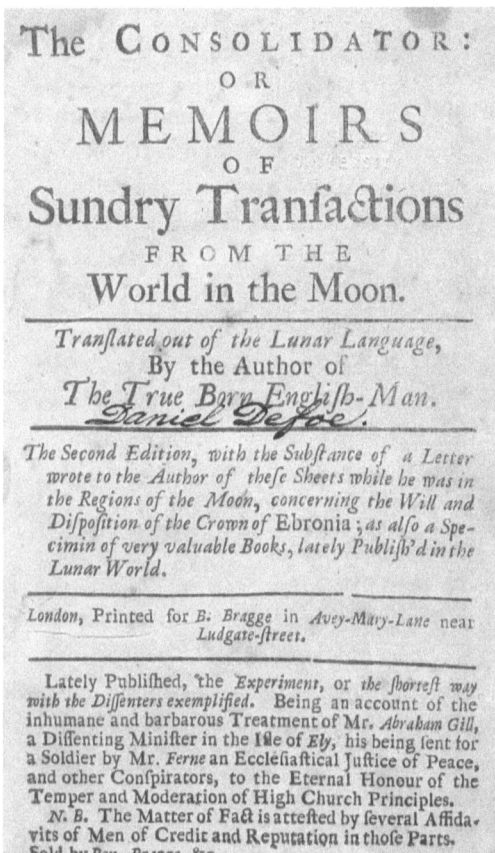

Figure 2. Title page. From Defoe, *The Consolidator*. (Courtesy of Harvard University, Houghton Library)

or was not ordained by the Anglican Church before becoming a dissenting minister; whether he did or did not have one too many wives; was or was not a charismatic troublemaker drawing parishioners away from neighboring clergy.[13] What matters is Defoe's use of the dissenting martyr as a figure for himself. Defoe wrote *The Consolidator* in the shadow of the pillory, if not within the walls of Newgate Prison. The book is 360 pages long and appeared about sixteen months after his release on or around November 8, 1703, after five months on the run and more than five months rotting in Newgate Prison. Defoe could not wait past the title page to attack his enemies and proceeded to republish the crime that had been committed against him and Gill by the theocratic state. Defoe's narrator meets a philosopher on the moon, who listens to the whole sordid affair and then dutifully writes it all down and made a Book of it, and call'd it, *News from the World in the Moon*; and all the Town is like to see *my Minutes* under the same Title; nay, and I have been told, he published some such bold Truths there, from the Allegorical Relations he had of me from our World: That he was call'd before the Publick Authority, who could not bear the just Reflections of his *damn'd Satyrical Way of Writing*; and there they punish the Poor Man, put him in Prison, ruin'd his Family; and not only Fin'd him *ultra tenementum*, but expos'd him in the *high Places of their Capital City*, for the Mob to laugh at him for a Fool: this is a Punishment not unlike *our Pillory*, and was appointed for *mean Criminals*, Fellows that Cheat and Couzen People, Forge Writings, Forswear themselves, and the like; and the People, that it was expected would have treated this Man very ill, on the contrary *Pitied him*, wisht those that set him there placed in his room, and exprest their Affections, by *loud Shouts* and Acclamations, when he was taken down.[14]

Defoe is angry, and it shows. He is angry at those who imprisoned him. He is angry at those who mocked him and those who should have defended him but did not. He is angry at those who impose their theological and political will on him.[15] Throughout *The Consolidator* he pinions named and code-named adversaries, Leslie prominent among them.[16] The lunar allegory permits Defoe to avoid naming his nemesis. Instead we get moon machinations:

> Another Party concern'd in *this Plot* was an old *cast-out Solunarian Priest*, who, tho' professing himself a *Solunarian*, was turn'd out for adhering to the *Abrograzian King*, a mighty Stickler for the Doctrin of *absolute Subjection*.
> This Man draws *the most monstrous Picture of a Crolian* that could be invented, he put him in a *Wolf's Skin* with long *Asses Ears*, and hung him all over full of *Associations, Massacres, Persecutions, Rebellions*, and *Blood*. Here the People began to *stare* again, and a Crolian coud not go along the Street but they were always looking for the *long Ears*, the *Wolf's Claws* and the like.[17]

While Leslie is not the only target of Defoe's *Consolidator*—the editor's notes to the Pickering Master's edition identify about a dozen hated foes—Defoe's special animus for him is evident in these wolf-obsessed lines. Keep this wolf in mind because he will reappear in 1719 in especially dramatic fashion.

In Defoe's hands, the lunar voyage becomes a bare pretext for obvious political satire. Leaving nothing to chance, Defoe even provides the code by which the allegorical bits should be read:

> And since the allegorick Relation may bear great Similitude with our European Affairs on this side of *the Moon:* I shall for the ease of Expression, and the better Understanding of the Reader, frequently call them by the same Names our unhappy Parties are call'd by in *England,* as *Solunnarian Churchmen,* and *Crolian Dissenters,* at the same time desiring my Reader to observe, that he is *always to remember* who it is we are talking of, and that he is *by no means* to understand me of any Person, Party, People, Nation, or Place on this side the Moon, any Expression, Circumstance, Similitude, or Appearance *to the contrary in any wise notwithstanding.*[18]

"Much too long," concludes Paul Dottin, "and too poorly written to take the place in literature that *Gulliver's Travels* takes; yet it did very evidently inspire that immortal work by Jonathan Swift."[19] Maximillian Novak, introducing one of the only contemporary responses to the text, the aptly titled *Moon-Calf,* observes that "*The Consolidator* caused some stir when it was published on 25 March 1705, but probably nothing comparable to what Defoe expected . . . the real reason [it failed] was probably that . . . Defoe's political allegory, which fills a large part of the work, was obscure and labored."[20] Obscure and labored it was. Novak likens it to chaos. "The work is by no means a disaster, but if E.M. Forster could consider that 'Muddle' lay at the heart of *Tristram Shandy,* chaos may be said to dominate the *Consolidator.*"[21] The work is such a mess that critics have not known what to call it and have barely attempted to recover its literary ancestors.[22] Although its recent editors excavate some evidence of positive reception, as in one anonymous gift of £100 from the Duchess of Marlborough, they grant that the work was a commercial and artistic flop. Paul Alkon confesses that his effort to study *The Consolidator* amounted to a masochistic act: "To read *The Consolidator* is an excruciating experience that I can only recommend to other masochistic reviewers, to case hardened historians concerned with political contexts, to any would-be biographers of Defoe who want to see if they are made of the right stuff for such a project, and to students of his fiction who want to see for themselves how bad the master could be at his worst."[23]

Why bother, then? Just as we sought Defoe's rival in the previous chapter, so here we heed what Defoe's enemies say about him. To them it was obvious that a direct line existed from *The Shortest Way with the Dissenters* to *The Consolidator* and that Defoe should be punished for both. "And this is plainer Language than that of the *Gallunarian Pensioner, The Man in the Moon*," wrote a Tom Tell-Truth of Defoe in 1705, "In whose dark Speech, the Mounting Engine, on which he was exalted to that *Lunar* World, is call'd a Consolidator, which in honest plain *English* is a *Pillory*. And he promises to take a Second Flight to the *dark side* of the *Moon*, as soon as another *Consolidator* can be got ready for him; he means the *other Exalting Engine*, which *A True-Born Englishman* calls the *Gallows;* and so Good Night to him: let him take his *Swing* ('Tis the shortest Way to the *Moon*,) upon that *other Consolidator.*"²⁴ This antagonist thought Defoe should be executed for *The Consolidator*, even as he had been pilloried and bankrupted for *The Shortest Way with the Dissenters*. Tom Tell-Truth was not alone. Another of Defoe's inveterate enemies, the Tory agitator William Pittis, connected *The Shortest Way* to *The Consolidator* by way of a verse satire Defoe published in 1705 titled *The Dyet of Poland*. Pittis was eager to expose not only Defoe's politics but also his use of allegory to drive satire: *"He has forgot his Tryal at the* Old-Baily *for writing* The Shortest Way with the Dissenters, *or he would never insist upon an Author's Liberty to chuse what Metaphors He thinks fit; for, though He did not pay so dearly for his Beloved* Ironies *as he deserv'd, yet the Sentence then pass'd on Him by the* Bench *might have had such an Effect upon his Temper, as not to make him* uneasie, *but when he was breaking through the Bonds, he was engag'd in to the Government, in being tyed up to his Good Behaviour."*²⁵ The surety of good behavior should have kept Defoe from writing *The Dyet of Poland* and *The Consolidator*, because these works trade on the same dangerous "Metaphors" as *The Shortest Way*. "Metaphor" here is not so much a figure of speech as a practice of literary deceit through devious appropriation of allegorical structures. It suggests a transition from irony as a figure of speech to irony as a sustained narrative invention, situated in a genre or a combination of genres that fostered the same poise or balance between alternatives at the structural level. For the modern novel to emerge, irony in figure, irony in narrative, and irony in literary structure had to cohere in a writer of unusual dexterity, capable of sustaining paradox without seeming to. Defoe was that writer.

His early readers abhorred this quality that later readers adore. To them Defoe might cast his diabolical thoughts in the voice of a churchman, a Quaker, a Pole, a Chinese philosopher, or the man in the moon, but it was all the same ploy, for which he should pay the ultimate price:

> If neither *China, Poland,* nor Inhabitants of the Moon will protect Folks from being Hang'd, &c. *Your Humble Servant Mr.* Daniel Foe!

you might as well have given us your Name at Large, for every one knows who wrote the Consolidator; *and as to your* Meaning, *they must be Men of profound Stupidity indeed, that cannot find it out by your Gaping, you are so intelligible your self, amongst your want of understanding.... He, that has offer'd up a* Hymn *to the Pillory, and made it clap its wooden Wings for Joy, at the Reception of its New Tenant, would not be much lamented if the Three Leg'd Tree, a Mile and a half out of Town, should pay Him the same Compliment, since it is not the Reader's want of Charity, but his own, that renders him Criminal.*²⁶

Leslie, Pittis, and their colleagues could not get over Defoe's success in transforming a public shaming into a personal and literary triumph. Now they have a better solution: instead of the pillory, try the "Three-Leg'd Tree"—or, as it was also called, the Tyburn Tree, where public executions took place between 1196 and 1783 and women were hanged as witches. We tend to minimize such threats, but the prospect of execution for religious heresy was no laughing matter. Pittis blasts Defoe's "ingenious Confession" in the preface to *The Dyet of Poland*. He does not like Defoe telling his readers how they should and should not read his text. It introduces too many layers of irony and concealment. Defoe writes, "As *Poland* lyes almost in the same Latitude with *England*, so the Character the Poet has here given of the *Poles*, seems so exactly to match what some ill-nature'd People have said of some in *England*, that he easily foresees this Censorious Age will be apt to mis-judge him, as if he had some Oblique Meaning, and that this was a Satyr levell'd at some People nearer Home than the Castle of *Warsaw*."²⁷ To Pittis, the "Censorious Age" will not misjudge Defoe when it accuses him of using the far-off place—this time, Poland—as a thin cover for blatant political satire. One of these censorious readers, Joseph Browne, justifiably complains about *The Consolidator*, "He is so easy to trace thro' all the *Meanders*, turns and shifts he pursues to pass undiscover'd in his Black designs of representing to your World, what a powerful Politick Generous People, the Sect we call *Crolians* are in ours."²⁸ And he is—easy to trace. The work fails to sustain our interest because the political allegory is at once too specific and not specific enough, tied to exact correspondences in politics but not specific enough about the fictional details that would keep alive the representation of characters engaged in dialogues, whether here or on the moon.

Defoe appears to have been aware of this shortcoming of the form—its easy use as a mode of obvious satire. In *The Dyet of Poland* he pretends to rail against interpreters who read his text exactly as it deserves to be read. He calls allegorical interpreters *"Innuendo-Men"* and insists that "no Conjectures of theirs ought to pre-judge his Meaning, in which he demands to be left to himself, and expects to be understood in the following Poem as he *Speaks,* not as every prejudic'd Man may imagine he *meant.*"[29] Unpeeling the layers of irony at work in these lines poses difficulties. Defoe wants the reader of his verse satire to reject the claim of "some ill-natured People" that his Poles stand allegorically for specific individuals "nearer Home." His story should be read on its own terms, not as type or allegory for anything else. Yet in the very next breath he reverses himself: "But suppose there are not places [in Warsaw] call'd directly by those [English] Names. If there are places apply'd to the same Uses, what has anybody to do with the question of Allegories? A poor Author must never Write at all, if he is not at liberty to choose his *Metaphors,* and all the rest of the necessary Figures of Speech to help out his Expression."[30] Now we have a distinction between allegory and metaphor. All writers need their metaphors, Defoe innocently asserts, so do not accuse me of doing exactly what I am doing: making metaphor into types and types into allegorical figures. Defoe is aware of the advantages of allegory as a means of exorcising his hatred for his political and religious enemies, but his comments in *The Dyet of Poland* reveal some ambivalence about the form.

We find this same ambivalence expressed in *The Consolidator.* After relying heavily on the same technique of allegorical satire, Defoe's narrator enters to deny the relevance of allegorical satire to an interpretation of the text: "If any Man shall now wickedly suggest, that this Relation has any retrospect to the Affairs of *England,* the Author declares them malitious Misconstruers of his honest Relation of Matters from this remote Country. . . . If there is any Analogy or Similitude between the Transactions of either World, he cannot account for that, 'tis application makes the Ass."[31] Defoe knew such "malitious Misconstruers" were reading the text as it richly deserved to be read. The ass, in this case, was the author who could not resist lacerating his enemies with overt applications based on obvious analogies and similitudes. Defoe ends up encouraging an interpretation he resists; he deploys allegorical satire, while gesturing toward an alternative.

Defoe's complex relation to allegory affected his poetry as well as his prose and can be traced in part to his political situation as a staunch supporter of William III and the Revolutionary Settlement.[32] The political debate had to do fundamentally with succession. From the Tory and Jacobite perspective, true royal succession led from Charles II to his brother James II to his son James III. In 1688, a disastrous break with true succession occurred, severing legitimate religious and political authority in a second royal coup d'état in forty years: the first, the beheading of Charles I in 1649; and the second, the deposing of James II, who was forced to flee to France when Parliament offered the crown to William of Orange. Writers at the time played out this political debate also in the realm of literary form. They assumed there to be a correspondence between the Royalist position defended by John Dryden in the 1680s and the mode of allegorical satire he perfected in *Absalom and Achitophel* (1681), which harmonized form and content, deploying an ingenious biblical allegory to support James's claim to succession and to crush the Whig upstarts Monmouth and Shaftesbury. The genre itself appears to have been coded Tory. Whig attempts to appropriate political allegory therefore faced a rhetorical problem. Andrew McKendry notes that, since "William's claim to rule was so unconventional, biblical models were at once indispensable and impractical; scripture continued to provide an essential framework for conceptualizing contemporary politics, but its established affiliations with the ideology of divine right made it an unwieldy subtext."[33]

While McKendry focuses exclusively on Defoe's poetry, *The Consolidator* reveals a similar ambivalence in prose. Defoe is resistant to the structure of his own narrative. He has a complex relation to allegory and to forms of satire built upon it. This is a good example of what Benjamin meant by an "eccentricity" of the text. Aware of the hermeneutic limitations of a mode of reading that relies on one-to-one substitutions—for the Poles, read the English; for the lunar Crolians, read the dissenters; and so on—Defoe nevertheless deployed these allegorical structures with alacrity in verse and prose. *The Consolidator*'s allegory defeats its realism, and the claims of realism expose the ploys of allegory. In *The Consolidator*, the suturing together of allegory and history, lunar fable and scientific realism is rough and exposed. This eccentricity of the text leads Geoffrey Sill to declare it "a virtually unique work in the Defoe canon, bearing little resemblance either to his other satires or to his later novels."[34] Yet even while denying the work's resemblance to later novels, Sill admits that resemblance: "If *The Consolidator* succeeds, it does so not through its satiric wit or its comic effects . . . but by disturbing and disrupting our sense of what is usual and ordinary. It is the narrative of a traveller to a strange land that mirrors and reverses his own, one in which the real meaning of his history is finally made apparent. It is in *The Consolidator* that Defoe first confronts us with a fantastic story told by a narrator who asks that we accept his remarkable tale as truth."[35] In other words, *The Consolidator* is a direct precursor of *Robinson Crusoe*, except that it is unreadable, full of ambivalence, full of artless hostility—so great a failure that critics have overlooked its importance in the development of the novel and novelist.

The Artistic Battle between Defoe and Swift

Just as Charles Leslie's *A Short and Easie Method with the Deists* (1698) precipitated Defoe's *The Shortest Way with the Dissenters*, so Jonathan Swift's *A Tale of a Tub* (1704) and its nasty appendage, *A Discourse Concerning the Mechanical Operation of the Spirit*, were among the provocations that spurred Defoe to write *The Consolidator*.[36] The lasting success of Swift's incitement, coupled with the failure of Defoe's reply, has obscured a literary parting of ways that occurred at just this time between two geniuses of prose fiction. We know, in retrospect, that Swift and Defoe were heading in different directions, one to become the finest writer of prose satire in English, and the other to shape the modern novel. Yet in 1704–1705, the two writers were mining the same satiric lode. A political and literary confrontation occurred between them that proved decisive for the history of the novel.

Now if you ask Swift, none of this happened. In a famous remark, he pretended not to remember the name of the fellow who was pilloried. It is a quip that has entered scholarly lore, trucked out from time to time to recall Defoe's low origins and negligibility in the eyes of a true literary genius.[37] The actual quotation is more interesting than its echo, however. The context is a suggestion raised in certain papers (i.e., Defoe's) that the Test Act be dropped as a qualification for public office. The mere idea induces a fit of verbal apoplexy, during which the image of Defoe rises strongly in Swift's mind:

> I know it may be reckoned a weakness to say any thing of such Trifles as are below a serious Man's notice, much less would I disparage the understanding of any Party, to think they would choose the Vilest and most Ignorant among Mankind to employ them for Asserters of a Cause. I shall only say, that the Scandalous Liberty those Wretches take, would hardly be allowed, if it were not mingled with Opinions, that *some Men* would be glad to Advance. Besides, how insipid soever those Papers are, they seem to be levelled to the Understandings of a great Number, they are grown a necessary part in Coffee-house Furniture, and some time or other happen to be Read by Customers of all Ranks, for Curiosity or Amusement; because they lie always in the Way. One of these Authors (the Fellow that was Pillor'd, I have forgot his Name) is indeed so grave, sententious, dogmatical a Rogue, that there is no enduring him; the *Observator* is much the brisker of the two; and, I think, farther gone of late in Lyes and Impudence than his *Presbyterian* Brother.[38]

A later edition adds this note from John Boyle, fifth Earl of Orrery (1707–62): "The fellow that was pilloried, was *Daniel Defoe,* whose name *Swift* well knew and remembered, but the circumstance of the pillory was to be introduced, and the manner of introducing it shews great art and the nicest touches of satire, and carries all the marks of ridicule, indignation, and contempt."[39] It does, indeed, but beyond those nice touches of satire, Swift's comment reveals what he and Leslie feared and wanted to erase: Defoe's popularity. His essays had "grown a necessary Part in Coffee-house Furniture." They lie always in the way because of how they are written, reproduced, and distributed. They lie in the way also because they are pitched to an increasingly secular reader, whose interests align with the weakening of ecclesiastical authority in the state. Swift accuses Defoe of being a hired gun for "some Men" to smuggle their heresies into circulation by vile and dangerous means.

Less well known than Swift's conscious amnesia toward Defoe is what Defoe wrote four years earlier about Swift in *The Consolidator:*

I had heard of a *World in the Moon* among some of our Learned Philosophers, and *Moor,* as I have been told, had a *Moon* in his Head; but none of the fine Pretenders, no not Bishop *Wilkins,* ever found Mechanick Engines, whose Motion was sufficient to attempt the Passage. A late happy Author indeed, among his Mechanick Operations of the Spirit, had found out an Enthusiasm, which if he could have pursued to its proper Extream, without doubt might *either in the Body or out of the Body,* have Landed him somewhere hereabout; but that he form'd his System wholly upon the mistaken Notion of *Wind,* which Learned Hypothesis being directly contrary to the Nature of things in this Climate, where the *Elasticity* of the Air is quite different, and where the *pressure of the Atmosphere* has for want of Vapour no Force, all his Notion dissolv'd in its Native Vapour call'd *Wind,* and flew upward in blew Strakes of a livid Flame call'd *Blasphemy,* which burnt up all the Wit and Fancy of the Author, and left a strange *stench* behind it, that has this unhappy quality in it, that every Body that Reads the Book, *smells the Author,* tho he be never so far off; nay, tho' he took Shipping to *Dublin,* to secure his Friends from the least danger of a Conjecture.[40]

Defoe invokes the dual tradition to which *The Consolidator* belongs: that of lunar and utopian voyages. He refers to Bishop John Wilkins (1614–1672), author of *The Discovery of a World in the Moone,* published in London in 1638 and reissued twice in 1684. This work, like many lunar voyages of the seventeenth century, imitates Lucian's *Vera Historia [A True History]*, published in the second century CE. The word moor refers to Lucian's humanist translator and imitator, Sir Thomas More (1478-1535), author of *Utopia*, published in Latin in 1516 and in English in 1639, with new editions in 1684 and 1685.[41] Having gestured to these humanist and cosmopolitan precursors, Defoe next takes on Swift. To grasp the hostility of Defoe's attack, it helps to recall the provocation. *A Tale of a Tub*, especially sections 8 and 9, told the history of post-Reformation theology through an allegory of three brothers and their father's will, which left them each a coat and some instructions. The allegory rendered innovations on religion ridiculous, and most ridiculous of all was that of the Protestant dissenter, whose coat fared by far the worst through additions and subtractions to the point of shredding. Defoe might have been as much alarmed by Swift's dexterity in allegorical satire as angered by the derogatory portrait of his people. But the insult became insufferable with *A Discourse Concerning the Mechanical Operation of the Spirit*.

Defoe is being polite when he writes that Swift's system is founded on wind. True, the metaphor controls section 8 of *A Tale of a Tub*, the attack on brother Jack, standing for Calvin, which begins, "The Learned *AEolists*, maintain the Original Cause of all Things to be *Wind*."[42] Wind serves Swift as both mock-metaphysical concept ("the same Breath which had kindled, and blew *up* the Flame of Nature, should one Day blow it *out*") and bodily pun ("the Wise *AEolists* confirm the gift of BELCHING to be the noblest Act of a Rational Creature").[43] But wind gives way to something stickier in the *Mechanical Operation of the Spirit*. Swift likens Puritans, Presbyterians, Quakers, Anabaptists, and all dissenters to masturbators who mistake their own gratification for something spiritual: "This Description will hold good in general; but, I am only to understand it, as applied to *Religion;* wherein there are three general Ways of ejaculating the Soul, or transporting it beyond the Sphere of Matter."[44] In increasingly vivid versions of the same, Swift repeats the metaphor of spirit as ejaculation. Dissenting preachers are come artists in his mind. "A master Work-man shall *blow his Nose so powerfully,* as to pierce the Hearts of his People, who are disposed to receive the *Excrements* of his Brain with the same Reverence, as the true *Issue* of it."[45] Swift provides the brief allegory of "a *Banbury Saint*," who, "while he was far engaged among the Tabernacles of the *Wicked,* he felt the Outward Man put into odd Commotions, and strangely prick'd forward by the Inward." This is what he did: "However it came about, the *Saint* felt his *Vessel* full *extended* in every Part (a very natural Effect of strong *Inspiration;*), and the Place and Time falling out so unluckily, that he could not have the Convenience of Evacuating upwards, by Repetition, Prayer, or Lecture; he was forced to open an inferior Vent. In short, he wrestled with the Flesh so long, that he at length subdued it, coming off with honourable Wounds, all *before*."⁴⁶

When Defoe writes of Swift, "All his Notion dissolv'd in its Native Vapour call'd *Wind,* and flew upward in blew Strakes of a livid Flame call'd *Blasphemy,* which burnt up all the Wit and Fancy of the Author," he may have in mind the redundancy with which Swift strokes this metaphor of spirit as ejaculation. He is a one-trick pony, Defoe suggests. Witness his trotting out Darius's stallion as yet another example of how to make spirit come on command: "The *Persian Beast* acquired his Faculty, by *covering a Mare* the Day before."⁴⁷ The joke would not be complete without its misogynistic application: "A very eminent Member of the Faculty, assured me, that when the *Quakers* first appeared, he seldom was without some Female Patients among them for the *furor Uterinus.* Persons of a visionary Devotion, either Men or Women, are in their Complexion, of all others, the most amorous: For, *Zeal* is frequently kindled from the same Spark with other Fires, and from inflaming Brotherly Love, will proceed to raise That of a Gallant."⁴⁸ Defoe's defense of the Quakers specifies that women and men are fundamentally equal in spirit. Here Swift uses a snarky reference to the Quakers to suggest that the privatization of spirit produces nymphomania in women. The obsessive return to this point provokes Defoe's criticism. There is something myopic and strangely inward-turning in Swift's use of satire.

Defoe decides to oppose Swift's substance and outdo his style. In the realm of ideas, Defoe wants to show that spirit moves in ways other than mechanical and scatalogical. He opposes the satirist's reduction of private conscience to erotic euphemism. Imagine, in this light, how Defoe might have viewed the sardonic passage that concludes the *Mechanical Operation of the Spirit:* "For, Human Life is a continual Navigation, and if we expect our Vessels to pass with Safety thro the Waves and Tempests of the fluctuating World, it is necessary to make a good Provision of the *Flesh,* as Sea-men lay in store of *Beef* for a long Voyage."⁴⁹ Swift is being sarcastic, miming views attributed to notables in his brief history of fanaticism, "those which started up in Germany a little after the reformation of Luther."⁵⁰ Defoe may have heard a challenge and an opportunity: why not the seaman son of a German immigrant who makes provision, of the flesh and otherwise, for a life of hardship, portrayed in the most immediate and sympathetic terms, "the beautiful representation of a life of unexampled misfortunes," without a hint that this representation served as constant rebuttal to Leslie and Swift?

Defoe also took aim at Swift's style. The charge that "every Body that Reads the Book, *smells the Author,* tho he be never so far off; nay, tho' he took Shipping to *Dublin*" touches the way Swift writes satire. We have in Swift and most Tory satire instances of what Northrop Frye calls "high norm satire," where the final truth the writer wishes to impart is not hard to detect.[51] Swift was vulnerable on this score. He did not hesitate to introduce passages such as the following:

> BUT, because I am resolved, by all means, to avoid giving Offence to any Party whatever; I will leave off discoursing so closely to the *Letter* as I have hitherto done, and go on for the future by way of Allegory, though in such a manner, that the judicious Reader, may without much straining, make his Applications as often as he shall think fit. Therefore, if you please, from hence forward, instead of the Term, *Ass,* we shall make use of, *Gifted,* or, *enlightened Teacher;* And the Word, *Rider,* we will exchange for that of *Fanatick Auditory,* or any other Denomination of the like Import.[52]

Whether in play or in earnest, Swift states the code of his allegory, possibly because doing so provides another witty means of name-calling. Oh, was calling the dissenter an ass too obscure? Then substitute fanatical orator. Defoe equates the obviousness of this satire with the smell of the author. There is an implied contrast between the hoax that got Defoe in trouble, whose author's odor went largely undetected at first, and Swift's rank performance. Whatever allegorical use the tale of the brothers and their coats may serve, whatever ingenious variations on the theme of masturbation his mechanical operations provide, they can all be boiled down to a "System," and, for the sake of art, it is the wrong one: "He form'd his System wholly upon the mistaken Notion of *Wind,* which learned hypothesis being directly contrary to the Nature of things in this Climate." The phrase "in this Climate" repeats Defoe's earlier suggestion that Swift's imagination might "have Landed him somewhere hereabout." These phrases suggest Defoe's tactile awareness of a prose place that is different from Swift's.[53] The place where Defoe tries to reside would render imperial satire fatuous. There "the *Elasticity* of the Air is quite different, and . . . the *pressure of the Atmosphere* has for want of Vapour no Force." The phrase "want of Vapour" is wonderfully ambiguous. It means what the context suggests: lack of an Earth's atmosphere surrounding a different planet or moon. But "vapour" also means vapid polemics: fuming about nothing. Swift's polemic overrules his art, Defoe suggests, and for that reason his texts always stink of him. No wonder Swift pretended to forget Defoe.

Alas, Defoe was not yet ready or able to turn the same criticism on himself. Invective overrules art so often in *The Consolidator* that Defoe appears not to have realized, or to have realized but not cared, that his critique of Swift applied equally to him. Amid the wreckage we find a writer at cross-purposes. Defoe wants to beat Swift at his own game, allegorical satire, and he wants to write a different kind of satire that is no less devastating but, like *The Shortest Way with the Dissenters,* works on the reader in a different way. The aesthetic criteria for this other kind of satire were by no means clear. The failure of *The Consolidator* signals this struggle within Defoe to transform himself from one kind of satirist, apparently derivative of Swift, into another, not yet named or defined. Defoe took his time making this adjustment. Satire was lifeblood to him, practically second nature; yet when he asked himself what it was about *The Shortest Way with the Dissenters* that captured the popular imagination, the answer may have been an irony requiring the death or invisibility of the author.

Prospero-like, in self-elegy, Defoe abjures his rough satire in 1704. Again, we enter the shadow of the pillory:

> *Had the scribbling World been pleas'd to leave me where they found me, I had left them and Newgate both together; and as I am metaphorically Dead, had been effectually so, as to Satyrs and Pamphlets.* . . .
>
> *For shame, Gentlemen, let him alone, why the Man's Dead: 'tis a Cowardly trick to beat a Man when he is down, but to fight a Dead Man is the Devil.*
>
> *And with submission, Gentlemen, the Allegory is just: for if being tied under Sureties and Penalties not to write, at least, not to write what some people may not like, be not equivalent to being Dead, as to the Pen, I know not what is.*[54]

The elegy is ambiguous, however. Yes, the conditions of Defoe's surety must have kept him from writing "what some people may not like." But did they keep him from writing full-bore satire? Not judging from *The Consolidator,* in which Defoe attacks named enemies, retells English political history from a stridently Whig perspective, defends on the very title page a man the Anglican Church claimed had forged his ordination papers, and calls

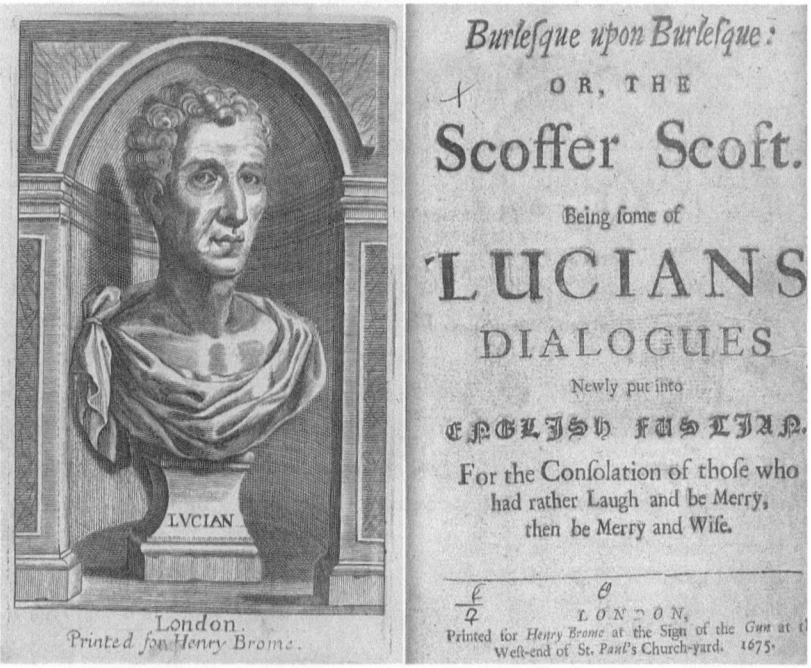

Figure 3. Title page and frontispiece. From Charles Cotton, *Burlesque upon Burlesque; or, The Scoffer Scoft, Being Some of Lucian's Dialogues Put into English Fustian*, 1675. (Courtesy of Yale University, Beinecke Library)

on dissenters to boycott non-dissenting businesses and remove their funds from the financial system in the hope of its collapse.[55] More likely, this death sentence is aspirational. To write past Swift required the transformation of allegorical satire, both because Swift was manifestly better at that game and because Defoe's politics and theology called for a different relation to textual authority. He could not defeat dogmatism with more dogmatism. He needed instead a way of writing that undercut dogma from within, through its very structure. For that, he turned to Lucian and the cosmopolitan tradition (see fig. 3).

The Lucian Revival, 1620–1720

Because scholars have overlooked Defoe's long prose fictions before *Robinson Crusoe*, they have not had to answer an obvious question: why do we find a writer many think of as the prototypical formal realist writing utopian and

Orientalist fictions during the two decades before *Crusoe?* In each case—the moon voyage and the spy novel—Defoe was continuing traditions of classical and humanist writing that predate the Protestant Reformation, Locke, and the rising middle class. In each case, the more we find out about what these traditions meant to readers in Defoe's day, and why they were being revived, the fuller our understanding of the origin of the modern novel becomes. Defoe's failures constitute missing chapters in the history of the English novel.

Biographers, critics, and editors downplay Defoe's relation to Lucian.[56] Yet Lucian had become popular during Defoe's formative years (see fig. 4). New and reissued English translations appeared in 1663 (Francis Hickes's edition was originally published in 1634) and 1684 (by Ferrand Spence).[57] Dryden's four-volume *The Works of Lucian, Translated from the Greek, by Several Eminent Hands* was two decades in the making and appeared posthumously in

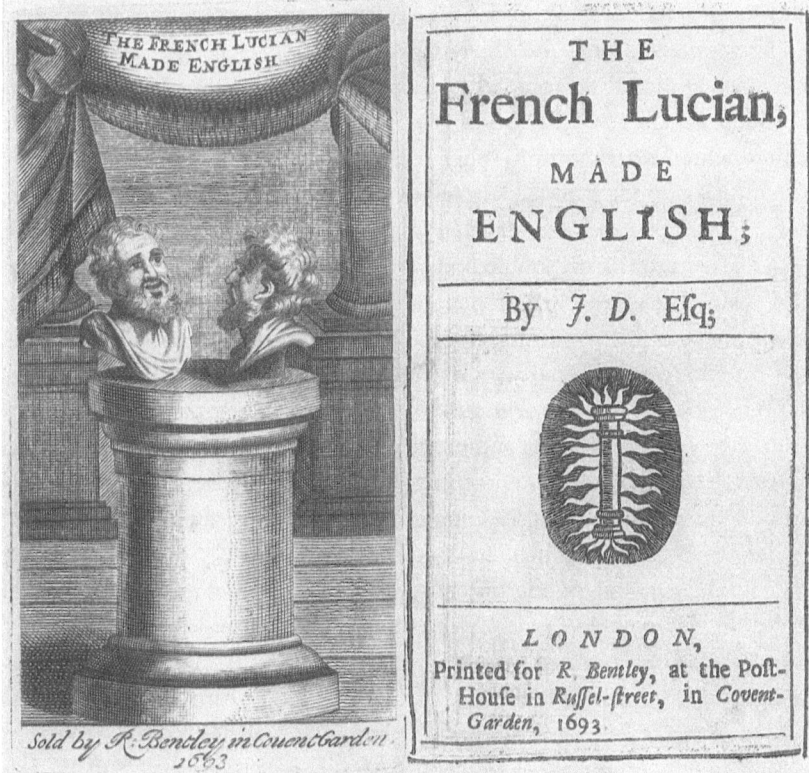

Figure 4. Title page and frontispiece. From J. D. Esq., *The French Lucian Made English*, 1693. (Courtesy of Yale University, Beinecke Library)

1710–11. (Dryden died in 1700.) Between 1680 and 1730, Lucianic imitations proliferated, especially in French, and belonged to an established tradition of *Libertinisme érudit*, a literary movement with close ties to deism.[58] In the year she published *Oroonoko, or the Royal Slave* (1688), Aphra Behn translated Fontenelle's popular imitation of Lucian, *Les entretiens sur la pluralité des mondes* (1686), as *A Discovery of New Worlds*. This is the book that Eliza Haywood's heroine reads when she is accosted by her would-be lover in the second volume of *Love in Excess: or the Fatal Inquiry, a Novel* (1719–20). Perhaps the best-known work of cosmopolitan fiction of the late seventeenth and early eighteenth century, Fontenelle's Lucianic imitation combines romance and science, space travel and satire; it shows women speaking almost as equals with men. Behn complained in her introduction that Fontenelle did not go far enough to depict men and women as equals; however, she was responding to a potential built into the Lucianic model. Its cosmopolitanism created a context for radical inclusiveness and respect for other cultures, religions, genders, classes, and species. As Margaret C. Jacob observes in the introduction to *Strangers Nowhere in the World: The Rise of Cosmopolitanism in Early Modern Europe*, the early cosmopolite "approached those distinctly different from themselves hospitably, with a willingness to get to know them, even like them."[59] The cosmopolitan writer, in turn, sought out forms that simultaneously concealed the position, since it raised suspicions of heresy to represent the gendered, racial, or religious other as equal, and communicated it by literary means. It is in this context that we should understand the early modern revival of interest in Lucian. The emerging cosmopolitan reader enjoyed his profane treatment of all the gods, his fracturing of the usual adventure story through narrative self-consciousness and mockery of the very flight metaphors that helped his supposed betters get off the ground. When Behn as translator takes the unusual step of criticizing the author whose book she is trying to popularize in English (Fontenelle), she points to a potential she and others see in the model to launch a critique of a male-dominated theocratic politics from the safety of polite conversations on the plurality of worlds.

Lucian's relevance to libertine and republican purposes represents only half the story, however. As David Cressy and others have shown, something of a political and religious battle occurred in the seventeenth and early eighteenth century over the meaning and use of Lucianic satire. All sides got in on the act. Anglican bishops and scientific freethinkers, French libertines and English dissenters, contributed to a century-long Lucianic Revival.[60] Defoe was a latecomer to this fight, but he would have known what it meant to enter the fray. In particular, he would have been aware of Lucian's bad reputation in matters theological. The seventeenth-century translators and imitators of Lucian struggle to reclaim a heterodox author for Christian readers. Their efforts help us understand what made Lucian attractive, and dangerous—and why, in turn, Defoe, although he imitates the mode, would not acknowledge the man. Lucian and his adjective, Lucianic, were bywords for heretical thought and profane conduct. In *The Institution of the Christian Religion* (1561) John Calvin defends a Christian doctrine "which the wicked Lucianical men do pleasantly taunt with their scoffes because of the spiritual darknesse wherewith thei be taken."[61] In *Newes from Ninive to Englande brought by the Prophet Jonah*, Johannes Brenz (1499–1570) refers to Lucian as "the scoffer" and adds that there is "a defection apostacie in the which thorough hatred of faith or religion, Atheistes or godlesse men of méere ungodliness and contempt of God with their wicked ringleaders Lucian and Julian the *Apostate* fall away from the sounde and catholique faith."[62] "Ah, wretched *Lucian*, justly named *Atheos*, thou blasphemer and whelpe of Arrius," writes Richard Harvey in *A Theological Discourse of the Lamb of God*, likening Lucian to a known precursor of the Socinians and deists.[63] A "whelpe of Arrius" suggests the ease with which opponents of one heresy could link it to earlier apostasies. Deism is the whelp of Socinianism; Socinianism is the whelp of Arianism; and so on.

Fortunately, Lucian wrote in an elegant, easy-to-translate style of Greek. He became useful in the schools as a prose model. In *The Scholemaster; or, Plaine and Perfite Way of Teaching Children* (1570), Roger Ascham (1515–68) observes that "concerning a schole *Epitome,* he that wold have an example of it, let him read Lucian Περὶ Κάλλους which is the verie *Epitome of Isocrates* oration *de laudibus Helenae.*"[64] So he was the epitome of evil but also the epitome of elegant Greek style for purposes of translation exercises. He was, moreover, a writer of wit and profane good humor. The "Epistle Dedicatory" to Dryden's *Lucian* states that "Lucian has been the Darling Pleasure of Men of Sense in every Nation; and the Favourite of some Princes; and protected by the Patronage of Great Men in every Country, where he has been made to speak the Language of the Place."[65] Lucian's secular appeal collided with Christian concerns about his baneful ideas and influence. The seventeenth-century translators and editors, Dryden included, tie themselves in knots trying to justify their publications by Christianizing a Greek skeptic.

Lucian's seventeenth-century editors and translators did their best to discount his bad reputation. "That he was a most impious blasphemer of our Saviour Christ, and of his sacred doctrine I will not deny," wrote Francis Hickes in 1634, "but that his whole works so much admired and approved of by the most learned in all ages, both for wit and language should be therefore utterly banisht from the world, and condemned to a perpetuall obscurity . . . seems unto me most unjust, and partiall censure."⁶⁶ So what if he blasphemed? He wrote great stuff! And beyond that, he was a philosophical voyager—he traveled with an open mind and keen wit. Travel changed him, made him tolerant of other people, suspicious of his own biases—it made him a cosmopolitan author. Such is Hickes's defense of Lucian:

> about the 40th. Year of his age [he] betook himself to Philosophy; When having by great industry and study, acquainted himself with the several tenents and doctrines almost of every sect, and finding that they not only crost and contradicted each other in the very grounds and principles of all Arts and Sciences, and chiefly in matters of Religion, and in their conceits and opinions of the Gods; but also that their lives and practices were nothing at all agreeable to their rules and precepts: he grew at length into such an utter dislike of them . . . that he bent his style almost wholly against them, and became a sharp and earnest opposer of the titular and mock-Philosophers of that age, laying open to the world in his writings, by way of Dialogue, after a most pleasant and Comical manner, their avarice, intemperance, ambition, and hypocrisie; and so far deriding the senseless superstition, and feigned deities of the heathen, that he thereby got the sirname of *Atheos,* or *Blasphemus,* and was commonly reputed a mocker and derider both of Gods and men.⁶⁷

Note the transition from philosophy to literature. Lucian started writing fiction because of something his travels and philosophy taught him. This made his fictions philosophical and his philosophy fictional. The problem was that the philosophy, to the extent that it could be identified, undercut any national creed bent on political domination—or, perhaps, any creed at all. In his essay "On Atheism," Francis Bacon writes that "the Contemplative Atheist is rare: a Diagoras, a Bion, a Lucian perhaps, and some others."⁶⁸ Lucian was viewed as a contemplative atheist because his literary structures enacted a corrosive skepticism. Historians label Lucian's skepticism "Pyrrhonian," and with good reason. Lucian lived at a time that the ideas of the ancient Greek skeptic Pyrrho (360–270 BCE) gained new currency, thanks to the transformation of Greek lecture notes into the *Pyrrhôneioi Hypotypôseis* (Outlines of Pyrrhonism), by Lucian's near-contemporary Sextus Empiricus (second century CE). Among other indications of extreme skepticism, Pyrrho advanced a critique of the sign function itself. He likened it to a rational induction from part to whole.

Since it is impossible to account for every part, or consider every possible iteration of the sign, closure of meaning becomes a fiction imposed on infinite possibility. David Hume, Karl Popper, and Jacques Derrida are all beholden to this skeptical critique of induction, which was well known in Defoe's day through the translation and dissemination of Sextus Empiricus via Thomas Stanley's *The History of Philosophy*.[69] The pretensions of philosophical system building and theological edifices alike come tumbling down once even the single word cannot signal that for which it was intended. Lucian reads as if he has internalized Pyrrhonian skepticism to the point where philosophy melts into fiction—fiction that must necessarily remain unstable, undercutting its own authority.

In his "Life of Lucian" prefacing the four-volume *Works*, Dryden grapples with Lucian's ill repute. He wants to adapt him for Christian ends but must acknowledge the cosmopolitanism of his model. Lucian, Dryden writes, "travell'd through almost all the known Countries of that Age, to improve his Knowledge in Men, Manners and Arts." His philosophical outlook reflects this cultural openness:

> I think him either one of the *Elective* School, or else a *Sceptic:* I mean, that he either form'd a Body of Philosophy for his own use, out of the Opinions, and Dogma's of several Heathen Philosophers, disagreeing amongst themselves; or that he doubted of everything; weigh'd all Opinions, and adher'd to none of them; only us'd them, as they serv'd his occasion for the present Dialogue; and perhaps rejected them in the next. And indeed, this last opinion is the more probable of the two, if we consider the Genius of the Man, whose Image we may clearly see in the Glass, which he holds before us of his Writings, which reflects him to our sight.[70]

While praising Lucian, Dryden also feels compelled to repeat the ad hominem charges against him. He reminds the reader that there are two stories about Lucian's death: one that he died in bed of gout, unrepentant; the other that he was mauled to death by dogs on his way home from a banquet.[71] Dryden explains why the second story caught on: "If it be true, that he was once a Christian, and afterwards became a Renegade to our Belief, perhaps some Zealots may have invented this Tale of his Death, as a just and signal Punishment for his Apostacy . . . *So early began the want of Charity, the presumption of meddling with God's Government, and the Spirit of Calumny amongst the primitive Believers.*"[72] If only this defense were sincere or long-lasting. Dryden is reluctant to praise or defend Lucian. He can be seen repeating the uncertain story that Lucian *ever* became a Christian only in order to remind readers of Lucian's "Apostacy" from Christ. That way, he could not be accused of ignoring the topic. Dryden also repeats the old charge of Lucian's reported homosexuality. "He is more accused of his Love of Boys, than of Women. Not that we have any particular Story to convince us of this detestable passion in him."[73] There may be no particular Story, but that does not stop Dryden from expressing his detestation of the passion.

In his effort to reclaim Lucian for Christian readers, Dryden makes an interesting and decisive move. He subtly redefines Lucian's mode of satire as akin to Roman models: "For the most part, he [Lucian] rather laughs like *Horace,* than bites like *Juvenal.* Indeed his Genius was of kin to both; but more nearly related to the former. Some Diseases are curable by Lenitives; to others Corrosives are necessary."[74] The author of the "Epistle Dedicatory" saw this as the core of Dryden's exoneration of Lucien: "*The Accusation of Atheism which some have brought against him* [Lucian]*, Mr Dryden has confuted; and it seems obvious, that his exposing the ridiculous Notions of the Divinities of the Heathens, was not unserviceable in opening the Eyes of those Times, and making way for the more easie Reception of the* Christian Truths *of the Gospel.*"[75] Lucian may be rehabilitated as a Christian moralist whose bark is not as bad as Juvenal's bite simply by excising the most Pyrrhonian and Menippean aspects of his satire.[76] Dryden redeems Lucian by classifying his kind of satire as essentially the same as that of Horace and Juvenal, easily adapted to pious ends.

According to Mikhail Bakhtin, this move falsifies Lucian and the history of satire. Bakhtin describes two distinct origins of the genre:

1) A specific, small-scale lyrico-epic genre that formed and developed on Roman soil (Naevius, Ennius, Lucilius, Horace, Persius, Juvenal) and was resurrected in modern times by the neoclassicists (the satires of Mathurin Régnier, Boileau, Kantemir et al.).
2) Another, less well-defined, mixed (mainly prose), purely dialogical genre that appeared in the Hellenistic epoch in the form of the philosophical diatribe (Bion [of Borysthenes], Teles [of Megala]) was reformed and standardized by the Cynic Menippus (third century BCE), and was named in his honor "Menippean satire." We find later exemplars of it in Greek in the work of Lucian (second century BCE), while in Latin there have survived fragments of satires by

Varro (Saturae Menippeae), Seneca's satire Apocolocyntosis ("Pumpkinization"), and, finally, the satirical novel of Petronius (Satyricon). This form of satire was a direct precursor of the main variety of the European novel, represented on ancient soil by Petronius's Satyricon and, in part, by Apuleius's Golden Ass, while in modern times [it is represented by] the novels of Rabelais (Gargantua and Pantagruel) and Cervantes (Don Quixote).⁷⁷

Bakhtin draws a sharp contrast between Roman and Menippean models. His definition gives four times the space to the latter, bestowing on it the highest accolade of his project: a "purely dialogical genre." What made Lucian "purely dialogical"? Not only the fact that Lucian wrote dialogues. The scholars A. Georgiadou and D. H. J. Larmour describe the Lucian effect this way: "Celsus [the second-century anti-Christian Greek skeptic] and Lucian work on the same principle: the former concocts a fictional setting to launch his attacks on the falsehood of Christianity, the latter exposes the mendacity of his predecessors in the art of story-telling by drawing directly from them. [Lucian's] V[era] H[istoria] thus points to its own fictionality and, at the same time, through intertextual references, points to the fictionality of the writings of those poets, historians and philosophers whom Lucian is ridiculing." The result of this skeptical, meta-discursive, intertextual mode of writing is "a work with a sustained blending of two levels of meaning."⁷⁸ The operative word is "sustained." Whereas allegorical satire serving political ends also blends two levels of meaning, its purpose is not to sustain a balance between them. There must be an application. For X read Y, and only Y. In Lucian, the text actually hinders any such translation from one level of significance to another—and this is the strategy Defoe uses—at least sometimes, when he is not deploying the same lunar genre in just the opposite way: as aggressive political satire.

Dryden's attitude toward Lucian tells us something about Defoe's need for caution. In a notorious instance of literary ingratitude, Dryden thanked Charles Blount, who contributed six translations totaling about 160 pages to volume 1 of Dryden's *The Works of Lucian,* by reminding the world of the deist's suicide: "The Wit of Mr. *Blount,* and his other Performances, need no Recommendation from me, they have made too much Noise in the World, to need a Herald."⁷⁹ Readers at the time would have heard the vicious pun, for noise applied equally to the commotion Blount's publications caused and to the noise the gun made that blew out his brains in 1693.

Defoe's treatment of Dryden in *The Consolidator* suggests literary revenge. Selecting one of the many lunar inventions in the narrative—this time, some special glasses—Defoe's traveler sees into the hidden causes of things. Attention turns to the causes of bad poetry, and from there to Dryden, who, if only he had worn the same glasses "might have told his Fate, that having his extraordinary Genius slung and pitcht upon a Swivle, it would certainly turn round as fast as the Times, and instruct him how to write Elegies to O[liver]. C[romwell]. and King C[harles]. the Second, with all the Coherence Imaginable; how to write *Religio Laici*, and the *Hind* and *Panther*, and yet be the same Man, every Day to change his Principle, change his Religion, change his Coat, change his Master, and yet never change his Nature."[80] Defoe's Dryden is nothing but a turncoat Vicar of Bray, a mercenary whose art is all expedience. The charge applies to Dryden's attitude toward Lucian, as well. He loves him; he loves him not. Yet even Defoe could not risk loving Lucian openly. He emulated him instead.

Defoe's Feathery Craft

In her work on the seventeenth-century lunar voyage tradition, Marjorie Hope Nicolson identified "two sections of Lucian's *True History* [that] are of particular importance, so far as the later cosmic voyage is concerned—his means of reaching the moon, and his first observation of that supposed 'planet'."[81] Belaboring the means or mode of conveyance, Lucian simultaneously ridiculed the epic poet's appeal to the muse, the religious writer's appeal to revelation or myth, and the philosopher's appeal to transcendence. Belaboring the first meeting with an alien race, or culture, or species, Lucian undercut the assumed superiority of author or narrator. The native speaks back.

Sure enough, these same aspects of the lunar voyage tradition preoccupy *The Consolidator*. Defoe's mode of conveyance is a feathery craft, with literary antecedents in Lucian's *True History* and *Icaromenippus*, Godwin's *The Man in the Moone* (1638), and Cyrano de Bergerac's *A Comical History of the World in the Moon* (1659). Illustrations of these spacecraft appear prominently in Godwin, Wilkins, and Cyrano; however, to my knowledge, no one has ever rendered Defoe's contraption. This may tell us something about Defoe's approach. His Consolidator is so elaborate, so particularized, so tagged with allegorical correspondences, and so improbable in its propulsive technology—feathers *and* fire—that the thing was never meant to fly. It is a Rube Goldberg machine jigged up on petty disputes rather than an airy vessel bound for the skies.

Defoe combines the propulsive strategies of previous lunar voyagers. Godwin's speedy messenger, Domingo Gonsales, trains geese to carry him aloft; whereas Cyrano's narrator at first relies on liquid propulsion: "I had fastned about me a many small vials filled with Dew; upon which the Sun darting most violent Beams, the heat whereof attracting as it doth the grossest Clouds, drew me insensibly above the middle Region."[82] The dewful approach lasts only one attempt, as the narrator loses control: "I began to break some of the glasses, till I found that my weight had mastered the attraction; so that I began to descend towards the Earth."[83] In the next attempt, Cyrano adds feathers—not that *in reality* or as a matter of *probability,* or *realism,* it mattered a great deal whether dew or feathers bore the author-hero upward. Defoe's Chinese-designed craft runs on combustible fuel *and* feathers, an innovation that Nicolson showers with praise.[84] The classic Lucianic story dealing with feathered conveyance was *Icaromenippus,* available in the Hickes translation alongside *A True History.* Menippus, seeking to fly to the moon and beyond, cuts off an eagle's wing and attaches it to his right arm (he does not say how) and a vulture's wing and attaches it to his left arm—twice we are told the vulture's wing goes on the sinister side. With these wings in place, the narrator ascends to the moon without much trouble. There he meets a man in the moon who convinces him that he would fly much faster and see much further if he lost the vulture's wing and soared like an eagle. Therefore, Menippus chops off the vulture's wing, and without any indication that he found another eagle on the moon to donate a second wing, Menippus soars beyond the moon to greater heights. Defoe was clearly aware of these absurd precedents. So we must read his feathery craft as more than local commentary on the tacking controversy.

We learn a lot about Defoe's craft. There are elaborate descriptions of its means of propulsion; where its 513 feathers come from and what they represent (513 being the number of members of the House of Commons); how it flies; when it once crashed (through the failure of its royal pilot); and further details that border on the obsessive. The tallest and stiffest feather may or may not be Charles Leslie, but Defoe clearly has one unnamed target in mind as he assembles his dark pantheon of churchmen: "There is one extraordinary Feather which, as there is an odd one in the number, is placed in the Center, and is the Handle; or rather Rudder to the whole Machine: This Feather is every way larger than its Fellows, 'tis almost as long and broad again; but above all, its Quill or Head is much larger, and it has *as it were* several small bushing Feathers round the bottom of it, which all make but one presiding or superintendent Feather, to guide, regulate, and pilot the whole Body."[85] This tallest and stiffest of the feathers must write a lot to have a quill for a head.

These blatant attacks on enemies go on too long, and Defoe, like Swift, adds the code by which the political allegory should be read. Of the worst of the feathers we learn, "These *Negative Feathers* are never for going up, but when there is Occasion for it; and from hence these fluttering fermented Feathers were called by the Antients *High-flying Feathers,* and the blustering things seem'd proud of the Name."[86] Defoe's flying machine cannot plausibly bear the weight it is asked to lift, and so it crashes, Icarus-like. The failure appears built into the form. Defoe comments on this quirk. His narrator sincerely promises that if he were to detail the bird that supplied the feathers for the Consolidator, as realism might demand, the "History would be so Romantick, it would spoil the Credit of these more Authentick Relations which are yet behind."[87] The statement appears to reverse our usual understanding of realism: the more real the description, the more tied to controversies that animate invective, the more romantic the relation would appear. Only by maintaining the mask of fiction can the truth be told, only through allegory, realism. Defoe was drawn to paradox—the literary representation of parallel doxologies that fail to cohere. He seems to have made a religion of it as a writer. The seventeenth-century imitators of Lucian revel in paradox, as well. The Lucianic dialogue imported formal tensions between science and fiction, history and allegory, realism and fable. Defoe does the same. In a defensive moment near the end of *The Consolidator,* his narrator turns to the reader and makes a special vow of truth: "But if any one shall scruple the Matter of Fact as I have here related it, I freely give him leave to do as I did, and go up to the Moon for a Demonstration; and if upon his return he does not give ample Testimony to the Case in every part of it, as here related, I am content to pass for the Contriver of it myself, and be punish'd as the Law shall say I deserve."[88] Defoe invites the reader to an impossibility and stakes the truth of his fiction and personal security on it. He appears to have discovered in Lucian and his imitators a way to expand the *Shortest Way* mode onto a larger canvas. The space voyages of Godwin and Cyrano are likewise long first-person narratives in which the reader can but should not equate author and narrator. These narratives are paradoxical, like their mixtures of realism and fantasy.[89] That was their appeal to Defoe. He sought a way beyond Swift, beyond easy allegorical satire, by means of the ludic possibilities of an imaginary voyage.

We see this ludic effect in the other feature of Lucianic satire which interests Nicolson: a focus on the moment of encounter between alien cultures. Of the first meeting with the moon-philosopher, Defoe's traveler explains:

It is not worth while to tell you this Man's *Lunar Name,* or whether he had a Name, or no; 'tis plain, 'twas *a Man in the Moon;* but all the Conference I had with him was very strange: At my first coming to him, he askt me if I came from the *World in the Moon.* I told him, *no:* At which he began to be angry, told me *I Ly'd,* he knew whence I came as well as I did; for he saw me all the way. I told him, I came *to the World in the Moon,* and began to be as surly as he. It was a long time before we could agree about it, he would have it, that I came down from *the Moon;* and I, that I came *up to the Moon.*⁹⁰

This brief parable could come straight out of Kafka. Mere prepositional phrases—down from, up to—sustain the reader in a pleasing indeterminacy. Along with the pleasure, however, we see how quickly good feelings can turn bad. One man calls the other a liar, and the other becomes "as surly as he." Defoe stops the action at just the point where the man in the moon should pass into a mere satiric foil for views the author wants either to endorse or criticize. This is often the role other worlds and other cultures play in English and European fantasy. The Chinese will be idealized at the expense of contemporaries; the Chinese will be mocked, at the expense of contemporaries who idealize the Chinese. Ditto for extraterrestrial beings. The Lucianic model offers an alternative to this imperial use of otherness. Defoe's traveler and the man in the moon come to a perfect understanding. They call in a telescope to prove that Earth and moon are planets of each other: "we came to this Conclusion, and there the Old Man and I agreed, That they were *both Moons* and *both Worlds,* this *a Moon* to that, and that *a Moon* to this, like the Sun between two Looking-Glasses, and shone upon one another by Reflection, according to the oblique or direct Position of each other."⁹¹ The sun between two looking glasses belongs equally to each, as it would to a third, fourth, and fifth set of glasses, just as a God distributed to all peoples belongs equally to all peoples, however different their revelations may be. The friends do not need to agree whose Earth is whose moon. Cultural and cosmic relativism triumphs, as the two become steadfast friends: "Never was there such a Couple of People met; he was the *Man in the Moon* to me, I *the Man in the Moon* to him."⁹²

Defoe unobtrusively fictionalizes aspects of deism in literary form. The ventriloquism of a deist outlook comes unaccompanied by commitment to that outlook. The initial meeting between Defoe's narrator and the lunar philosopher thus marks two interpretations of the same genre—one in which the meeting with the man in the moon triggers a crisis of perspective, and another in which that meeting serves obvious satiric ends and produces no crisis of perspective whatsoever. If the man in the moon served as the Poles do in *The Dyet of Poland*, there would be no issue: the foreign stands as a figure for the familiar, much as a type stands for the thing it typifies. The Lucianic model in its unredeemed form provided an alternative to this colonial use of otherness. It raises the philosophical question: if life exists on other planets, by what right do we automatically consider ourselves superior?

Cyrano de Bergerac's *A Comical History of the States and Empires of the Moon* (1687) begins with the same question. The narrator exclaims to a group of friends, "I believe that the Moon is a World like ours, to which this of ours serves likewise for a Moon." Then he adds, "This was received with the general Laughter of the Company." The "general Laughter of the Company" is telling. Cyrano reflects: "this thought, which because of its boldness suited my Humor, being confirmed by Contradiction, sunk so deep into my mind, that during the rest of the way, I was big with Definitions of the Moon."[93] Their laughter is not ludic; it is nervous and uncomprehending—dismissive of the very possibility of life on other planets. What sunk so deep in the narrator's mind, however, is a paradox "confirmed by Contradiction": that if other life forms exist, we have no right to assume superiority over them. The text asks the reader to engage in a thought experiment, supported by science, whose expanding telescopic perspective makes the possibility of life on other planets increasingly likely. One result of this thought experiment is to equalize faith systems on planet Earth. I emphasize the fruitful tension between two interpretations of the same genre because it helps explain why lunar voyages also functioned as modes of deism in allegorical disguise. Conventionally, the moon figures as a type for life on Earth, setting up predictable allegories. But the moon also functions as a figure for indeterminacy; it eclipses dogmatic correspondences, leaving the other as the other, with equal respect. Just as the deists, as philosophers and philologists, engaged in a process of inferential reason, first to equalize faith systems as legitimate expressions of the human need to believe in something greater, and then to derive from their differences a few common denominators, so the deists, as writers, used the space voyage modeled on Lucian as a disguise to effect the same imaginative leveling of theological differences. For this reason, Cyrano's text could be published at first only posthumously and in heavily redacted form and belongs to a suppressed tradition of erudite libertinism.[94]

The markers of the lunar voyage that Nicolson isolates—the impossible craft and the first meeting of alien cultures—double as deist provocations. They introduce problems of theology, politics, and ethics without seeming to. They are philosophical in their fictionality and necessarily fictional as cover for their subversive philosophy. Other such provocations in Defoe's amorphous *Consolidator* are not hard to find. Before traveling to the moon, the narrator leaps to China and discovers in a library there a volume called *"Natural Right prov'd Superior to Temporal Power;* wherein the old Author proves, the *Chinese* Emperors were Originally made so, by Nature's directing the People, to place the Power of Government in the most worthy Person they could find; and the Author giving a most exact History of 2000 Emperors, brings them into about 35 or 36 Periods of Lines when the Race ended; and when a Collective Assembly of the Nobles, Cities, and People, Nominated a new Family to the Government."[95] Defoe's Chinese originally framed a democratic meritocracy based on consensus of the people. The system declined over time into family monarchy. This claim was intended not to be fact-checked but, instead, to be taken as a plausible alternative to the aristocratic-imperial-ecclesiastical story that makes divine right seem natural. In case the reader missed the republican slant, Defoe continues:

> This being an heretical Book in *European* Politicks, and our Learned Authors having long since exploded this Doctrine, and prov'd that Kings and Emperors came down from Heaven with Crowns on their Heads, and all their Subjects were born with Saddles on their Backs; I thought fit to leave it where I found it, least our excellent Tracts of Sir Robert *Filmer,* Dr. *Hammond, L . . . y, S . . . l* and Others, who have so learnedly treated of the more useful Doctrine of Passive Obedience, Divine Right, &c. should be blasphem'd by the Mob, grow into Contempt of the People; and they should take upon them to question their Superiors for the Blood of *Algernon Sidney,* and *Argyle.*[96]

These lines place responsibility for the death of the republican martyrs Algernon Sidney and Archibald Campbell at the door of Filmer, Hammond, Leslie, and Sacheverell.[97] Coupled with the memorial to a dissenting martyr on the title page, these indications of radical religious and political sympathies explain why Pittis thought the Three-Leg'd Tree was Defoe's fit reward.

Elsewhere, Defoe's lunar voyager discovers an odd contraption that sees into the truth of religion. The narrator tries it on, but once he sees what it shows, he doubts the wisdom of bringing the device back to England: "I had like to have rais'd the Mob upon me for looking *upright* with this Glass; for this, they said, was prying into the Mysteries of the Great *Eye* of the World; That we ought to enquire no farther than he has inform'd us, and *to believe* what he had left us *more Obscure:* Upon this, I laid down the Glasses, and concluded, that we had *Moses* and the *Prophets,* and should be never the likelier to be taught by *One come from the* Moon."[98] One of the remarkable features of the deist theology, to the extent one can be said to exist at all, is the absence of Jesus Christ or any notion of mediation from the list of five common notions (*Notitiae Communes*) of a universal ethical monotheism.[99] In this passage, lunar theology suggests just such a religion without mediation. When the narrator lays down the glasses so as not to see what might upset the mob, he proceeds to say the thing likely to upset Charles Leslie, Jonathan Swift, and every orthodox religious thinker who by this time had learned the literary dog whistles of a looming deist threat. China functions in much the same way. It is not so much the butt of Anglocentric satire as the access point for an alternative perspective that must come from outside the Anglocentric framework. The conclusion that Defoe "delivers a sharp satire on Chinese learning and culture" misses the deistical role China plays in the text.[100] Defoe's traveler glorifies China as a culture far in advance of Western civilization both because the Chinese had the foresight to build 100,000 arks in preparation for Noah's flood—"every Vessel rid out the Deluge just at the Town's end; so that when the Waters abated, the People had nothing to do, but to open the Doors made in the Ship-sides, and come out, repair their Houses . . . and so put themselves in *Statu Quo*"—and because the Chinese, in their desire for knowledge, had attacked the moon in ancient times:

> those Presumptuous Animals fired Red-hot Bullets right up into Heaven, and made a Breach sufficient to encourage them to a General Storm; but being Repulsed with great Slaughter, they gave over the Siege for that time. This memorable part of History shall be a faithful Abridgement of *Ibra chizra-le-peglizar, Historiographer-Royal* to the Emperor of China, who wrote *Anno Mundi* 114, his Volumes extant, in the Publick Library at *Tonquin,* Printed in Leaves of Vitrify'd Diamond, by an Admirable Dexterity, struck all at an oblique Motion, the Engine remaining intire, and still fit for use, in the Chamber of the Emperor's Rarities.[101]

Although repelled in this attempt to take the moon by force, the effort created a "breach" in the atmosphere that permitted lunar wisdom to descend to humanity through China, and allowed the narrator to ascend in his Chinese-designed spaceship through the breach to the moon.

How do we weigh Defoe's decision to write in genres linked to deism against the mean things he says about deists in his texts? The previous answer has been that we take his pronouncements against the deists as decisive and ignore his fascination with deist *devices*. In fact, the text offers devices against those devices. The narrator produces a lunar Engine, or Cogitator as "a more effectual Cure to our *Deism, Atheism, Scepticism,* and all other *Scisms,* than ever the *Italian's* Engine, for curing the Gout by cutting off the Toe."[102] That is, he has invented a cure for irreligion, without resorting to violence. And what is that cure? Defoe is too wise to say. He only lets a moon-philosopher "bid me send all our *Scepticks, Soul-Sleepers,* our *Cowards, Bakers, Kings* and *Bakewells,* up to him into the *Moon,* if they wanted Demonstrations; where by the help of their Engines, they would make it plain to them, that the *Great Eye* being one vast Intellect, Infinite and Eternal *all* Inferior Life *is a Degree of* himself, *and as exactly represents him as one little Flame the whole Mass of Fire;* That it is therefore incapable of Dissolution, being like its Original in Duration."[103] Here and elsewhere, Defoe's traveler sounds as if he has been reading Lord Herbert of Cherbury and Spinoza. On the moon he discovers that "Degrees and Capacities are fitted by Nature, according to Organick Efficacy; and the Reason and Nature of Things are found in themselves."[104] The lunar philosophy of religion appears to separate physics from metaphysics, ethics from theology, politics from faith. So did the deists. The reference to the one "Great Eye" may or may not evoke deistical movements of religious universalism. In any case, the genre builds in the disclaimer that these deist-sounding ideas are only forms of lunacy.

Understandably, Defoe's enemies sensed danger. They were as eager to destroy his spaceship as they were to expose the deistical wolf in Quaker's clothing. A document that Maximillian Novak discovered and reproduced in the Augustan Reprints describes Defoe's motives and tactics. How in the world, Joseph Browne wants to know, had Defoe "stept up from a *Hosier* to a Poet"?[105] Reading *The Consolidator,* he thinks he knows, so he retells Defoe's story with slight adjustments: "A few days ago one of our Brute-Tenders, which is the same as the *Robin Hogs* in your World, was watching the Herd, and observ'd something that was Naked and Bare drop out of the Clouds into the Moon; this Apparition, for so he took it to be, astonish'd the *Hog-herd,* because we have nothing in our Regions but what is sufficiently Cloath'd and Cover'd, Nature abhorring Nudity in the *Moon.*"[106] From a distance, the object looks like a worm; on closer inspection they discover "a helpless Creature extended on the Plain, gaping, stretching, and yawning, as one just awak'd from Sleep."

They try to communicate with it as deists do, in "the Universal Language of the Moon, which we take to be the Voice of Nature," but "finding the thing illiterate and not able to answer, they took it for a Mute Animal, and so by the joint assent of the whole Collective Body of that Province Pronounced this thing . . . a *Moon-Calf.*" The Moon-Calf must undergo the same series of interrogations and punishments Defoe suffered in 1703. He is "strictly examin'd as to his Life and Conversation, in which he confest he had always a great ambition to set his Country men together by the Ears, and every now and then throw them a Bone to pick when they were quiet. . . . He confess'd he never forgave any Body that injur'd or provok'd him once, for which Reason he so often remember'd *somebody* with the Constable at *How,* and the *Crolian* Priest in Cambridgeshire."¹⁰⁷ Defoe was known to fixate on specific people and to hold a grudge. Spiteful motives must have fueled his spaceship: "Thus I fancy he reach'd our Climate, not by the help of his Feather'd Engine, as he wou'd have you believe, but I rather think he floated hither in a Bowl of Punch when the Center of Gravitation was removed from his Corporeity."¹⁰⁸ Amid all this hostility, Defoe's enemies make observations that ring true. "His Philosophy, Politicks, and History are so much of a piece," complains Browne, "that nothing but his own Brains can bear an *Equipoise* to them all."¹⁰⁹ Defoe might have taken this as a compliment. True, only Defoe's brain could make philosophy, politics, and history of a piece, and the means of doing so was a well-hidden aesthetic principle of equipoise, learned from ancient skepticism, practiced by Lucian, and revived in the seventeenth and early eighteenth centuries as a mode of disguised, or literary, deism.

It is clear from the preceding that Lucian solved several problems for Defoe. If the pattern we detected in chapter 1 holds true, then it should not be surprising that Defoe sought refuge in a known form of literary or cosmopolitan deism. David Cressy provides a full account of why writers of many persuasions—from Puritan to Catholic, humanist to scientific and deistical—launched lunar voyages in the seventeenth and early eighteenth centuries. He confirms that during the seventeenth century, the lunar voyage was a known sanctuary for radical writers seeking rhetorical cover. "The matter of lunar soteriology remained a 'difficult question,'" remarks Cressy, with a historian's reserve, before providing chapter and verse on scholarship in early modern literary subterfuge.¹¹⁰ He observes that Wilkins wrote with tremendous reticence and evasion; Godwin delayed publication of his moon shot until after his death; and Cyrano de Bergerac's *L'autre monde* could appear only posthumously and heavily redacted by a friend. These were precedents of which Defoe was likely aware. Simon Tyssot de Patot (1653–1738), another author of fantastic adventure contemporary with Defoe, was accused of Spinozism upon publication of his *Lettres choisies* in 1726. *The Travels and Adventures of James Massey* (in English, 1733) includes a frankly deistical account of religion, via conversation with a skeptical man in the moon, who declares at one point, "I am weary to hear you talk so much . . . of the Power of God. I plainly perceive that you practice the very same thing in your Religion, that we observe in our Mysteries of Nature; when we are at a Loss to give a Reason of a Thing, we say that 'tis the Effect of some latent Power."[111]

A Lunar Theory of the Novel?

Defoe is sometimes said to lack a theory of the genre he is credited with inventing.[112] We have the preface to *Moll Flanders,* that playful apology for the religious realism of the prostitute's memoir, but apparently nothing like the sustained reflection on the new prose fiction set forth in Henry Fielding's preface to *Joseph Andrews* or the combined effect of the preface and postscript to Richardson's *Clarissa.* Read Defoe's *Consolidator* and *Continuation of Letters Written by a Turkish Spy at Paris* in search of such reflections on form and the scattered outline of a cosmopolitan theory of the novel begins to take shape. Relevant here is another feature of the Menippean model that Defoe imitated freely: if the narrator rendered his own mode of conveyance ridiculous, traditional plots met the same fate. Plots of ascent, of pilgrimage or progress, of Providence, of the hero's arrival at some divine destination became ragged when Lucian and his successors got hold of them. In place of teleological plots, works in this Menippean tradition were episodic and discontinuous, picaresque and otherwise random. They offered readers cabinets of curiosities, or, in Defoe's phrase a "curious Chamber of Rarities," full of odd imaginary inventions that stop the narrative dead in its tracks for the sake of detailed description.[113] Defoe's title evokes the first of these, the painfully particularized flying machine. But there are a great many others. Here, too, Defoe and Swift part company. Whereas in part 3 of *Gulliver's Travels* Swift also falls into the Menippean mode, his "engines," such as the invention that squeezes light out of cucumbers or reverses excrement back into food, mock science and weave smoothly into his narrative. Defoe's inventions interrupt the narrative and betray a modern's fascination with scientific projects, and the free thinking behind them.[114]

Defoe's contraptions show special interest in cognition, in picturing the mind at work.[115] They reveal the actions of consciousness in moments of concentration, remembering, forgetting, and converting thought into language:

> There you have that part of the Head turn'd in-side outward, in which Nature has placed the Materials of reflecting; and like a *Glass Bee-hive,* represents to you all several Cells in which are lodg'd things past, even back to Infancy and Conception. There you have the Repository, with all its Cells, Classically, Annually, Numerically, and Alphabetically Dispos'd. There you may see how, when the perplext Animal, on the loss of a Thought or Word, *scratches his Pole:* Every Attack of his Invading Fingers knocks at Nature's Door, allarms all the Register-keepers; and away they run, unlock all the Classes, search diligently for what he calls for, and immediately deliver it up to the Brain; if it cannot be found, they intreat *a little Patience,* till they step into the *Revolvary,* where they run over little Catalogues of the minutest Passages of Life, and so in time never fail to hand on the thing; if not just when he calls for it, yet at some other time.[116]

This remarkable description of the brain searching for something momentarily forgotten reveals a plastic understanding of the brain's search mechanism, its capacity to shift and adapt itself to problems posed. Fueling these shifts, a constant amid change, are systems of classification, or genres. The genres behave like cognitive categories themselves, artificial yet necessary: "Classically, Annually, Numerically, and Alphabetically Dispos'd." When solving problems, the moon being scans the available categories, looking for a form that fits. Failing in the first attempt, he enters yet another machine: "They step into the *Revolvary,* where they run over little Catalogues of the minutest Passages of Life, and so in time never fail to hand on the thing; if not just when he calls for it, yet at some other time."

As the cognitive contraptions multiply, Defoe's lunar voyager describes brain function in more and more minute terms: "like a Prince, in his Seat, in the middle of *his Palace the Brain,* issuing out his incessant Orders to innumerable Troops of *Nerves, Sinews, Muscles, Tendons, Veins, Arteries, Fibres, Capilarij,* and *useful Officers,* call'd *Organici,* who faithfully execute all Parts of *Sensation, Locomotion, Concoction,* &c. and in the Hundred Thousandth part of *a Moment,* return with particular Messages for *Information,* and demand New *Instructions....* All this is as plain to be seen in these Engines."[117] Following this path, Defoe arrives at the paradox that, without language, the mind cannot know the brain's own operation—its processes are too many, too small, and too quick to name without the help of metaphor. This paradox of empiricism drives "another sort of Machine, which I never obtained a sight of, till the last Voyage I made to this Lunar Orb, and these are called *Elevators:* The Mechanick Operations of these are wonderful, and helpt by Fire."[118]

It is difficult to escape the impression that we are entering the artist's smithy, where Defoe teaches himself the as yet uninvented art of novel writing. He fictionalizes his progress, stepping into the "Elevator," which carries him to yet another cranial cross-section, which is "wholly applied to the Head, and works by Injection," revealing the intimate relation of thought to language:

> This indeed is an admirable Engine, 'tis compos'd of *an Hundred Thousand* rational Consequences, *Five times the number* of Conjectures, Supposes, Probabilities, besides an innumerable Company of fluttering Suggestions, and Injections, which hover round the Imagination, and are all taken in as fast as they can be Concocted and Digested there: These are form'd into Ideas, and some of those so well put together, so exactly shap'd, so well drest and set out by the Additional Fire of Fancy, that it is no uncommon thing for the Person to be intirely deceived by himself, not knowing *the brat of his own Begetting,* nor be able to distinguish between Reality and Representation.[119]

In books 1 and 2 of *An Essay Concerning Human Understanding* (1690), already in its seventh edition by 1716, John Locke describes the empirical process by which we come to have ideas. In book 3, on language, he explains how "*Man* therefore had by Nature his Organs so fashioned, as to be *fit to frame articulate Sounds,* which we call Words. But this was not enough to produce Language; for Parrots, and several other Birds, will be taught to make articulate sounds distinct enough."[120] Leaving aside the decision to make a parrot Crusoe's only articulate companion before the arrival of Friday, Defoe's lunar epistemology appears to reverse Locke's logic. Language for Locke expresses preexisting ideas in the mind: "The Comfort and Advantage of Society, not being to be had without Communication of Thoughts, it was necessary, that Man should find out some External sensible Signs, whereby those invisible *Ideas,* which his Thoughts are made up of, might be made known to others. . . . Thus we may conceive how *Words,* which were by Nature so well adapted to that purpose, come to be made Use of by Men, as the *Signs of* their *Ideas.* "[121] Defoe's lunar machine reverses this progression. The speed and complexity of cognitive processing are so great that the mind cannot know its own operations before affixing language to them. The point holds not only for false ideas, but for all of them—all, in a strikingly modern phrase, are brats of the mind's own begetting, thus erasing the distinction between reality and representation. Commenting on this passage, Michael Seidel astutely observes that this machine "does what his later works do as a matter of course, allow characters to screw into themselves . . . the mind—its consciousness, its unconsciousness, its subconsciousness, and its predispositons and biases—produces both reality and representation. . . . There is a kind of quixotic sense that mental territory is the new world for writers with the energy to pay attention to the way individual minds supplement action."[122] Here again, amid the wreckage of the failed work, we find elements that critics link piecemeal to this or that aspect of Defoe's great achievement, for the feature Seidel isolates, of characters screwing into themselves while remaining intensely interesting, blurring the boundary between reality and representation, goes to the heart of what makes the first part of *Robinson Crusoe* great.

Consider another well-known problem in *Robinson Crusoe:* the small matter of journal keeping. The difficulty is that the whole novel sounds like journal keeping in the first person, even though Crusoe runs out of ink early on and does not invent a solution. The prose has a quality of automatic writing, no sooner thought than written, an immediacy even down to errors of grammar and sequence. Yet the prose also has the quality of reflection, of being written in retrospect after the story has taken place. Was this accidental? It seems a naïve effect, artless, found but not sought. Did Defoe think about this effect and consciously strive to achieve it? On the moon, Defoe's traveler discovers a "Noble Invention"

> being an Engine I would recommend to all People to whom *'tis necessary to have a good Memory;* and which I design, if possible, to obtain a Draft of, that it may be Erected in our Royal Societies Laboratory: It has the wonderfullest Operations in the World: One part of it furnishes a Man of Business . . . to write his Letters with one Hand, and Copy them with the other. . . . Another part of it furnishes him with such an Expeditious way of Writing, or Transcribing, that a Man cannot speak so fast, but he that hears shall have it down in Writing before 'tis spoken.[123]

Three hundred years before audio recording, let alone voice recognition software, Defoe imagines a capacity for immediate expression of thought in printed and replicated texts. Crusoe speaks and writes as if he is in possession of such a machine. In the Lucianic tradition, this idea is not even original; Defoe would have found similar machines in Godwin's *The Man in the Moone* and Cyrano's *L'autre monde*.[124]

One final Menippean contraption is worth our notice. As we have seen, *The Shortest Way with the Dissenters* required a sustained irony that left the true author's position initially undetectable. What did it take to write this way? In *The Consolidator*, Defoe's narrator enters a "*Devil's* Ware-house" that contains a "*Memory's Garden* where all of the Devil's incentives grow." Among these incentives, he finds "the wonderful Art of *Wilful Forgetfulness*," which he calls "a thing, indeed, I never could find any Person completely Master of . . . for that it is impossible for any Man to oblige himself to forget a thing, since he that can remember to forget, and at the same time forget to remember, has an Art above the Devil."[125] It is an "Art above the Devil," perhaps, but also an art suspiciously like that of the writer who could make his enemies believe he was one of them in *The Shortest Way with the Dissenters*, and like that of the lunar voyager who could enter into the alien's perspective.

About two years before Defoe published his *Consolidator*, which is to say, in the midst of his legal woes, an obscure Protestant schoolteacher named David Russen, who made his small fame with a scurrilous attack on the Anabaptists, published an appreciation of Cyrano de Bergerac's *A Comical History of the States and Empires of the Moon*.[126] Like the Christian apologists for Lucian already considered, Russen composed *Iter Lunare; or, A Voyage to the Moon* (1703) with the purpose of converting a cosmopolitan voyage to Christian purposes. He argues that the lunar voyage, by virtue of its very improbabilities and paradoxes, prepares the reader to receive the most auspicious truths of religion, and does so in a pleasing way. Russen draws evidence of the possibility of space travel and extraterrestrial life from classical and modern sources. Even if the story of a dialogue with the man in the moon strains credulity, it serves a larger purpose:

> Indeed, there are in it [Cyrano's *L'autre monde*] many things which among us are altogether unusual, improbable, or perhaps, above the Power of Nature, as far as Nature is understood by us, or above what our Capacities can explicate from those Principles we have generally received. . . . Our Author has placed them in the Moon, as the Customs of that Country, where they may pass for Probable, on as good Grounds, as many wise Men conjecture that the Moon is an Earth, and like ours, Inhabited. On this Conjecture it is, that the whole Treatise is grounded.[127]

The theoretical possibility of life on another planet, which "many wise Men" (i.e., astronomers) endorse, justifies Russen in calling an improbable moon voyage probable. Science proves the miraculous; rational Christianity does no more or less. The genre therefore fosters an acceptable Protestant amalgam of realism and the supernatural. According to Russen, the purpose of this mixture is not, as some feared, to present plausible alternatives to Western culture and religion by equalizing all competing faith systems here on Earth. The instrument is not deistical. Instead, the work combines and reconciles religious sublimity with empirical reality. That is why Russen objects to the English translator's decision to render Cyrano's title as *A Comical History*:

> But the Title that the Translator gives it seems to be too full of Levity, and unbecoming the Gravity which a Treatise of so serious Matter doth require. For though it is interlaced with much Matter of Mirth, Wit and Invention, of things either doubtful, or meerly feigned, and so in some sense may be ranked with Sir *Thomas Moor's Utopia,* Don *Quixot's Romantick* Whymseys, or *Poor Robin's Description of Lubbardland;* yet is it throughout carried on with that strength of Argument, force of Reason, and solidity of Judgment in the Demonstration of things probable, that it may not be unbecoming the Gravity of *Cato,* the Seriousness of *Seneca,* or the Strictness of the most rigid *Peripatetick* or Cartesian; and instead of *Comical,* may deserve the Epithete of the *most rational History of the Government of the Moon.*[128]

The lunar voyage combines pleasing fiction with Stoic philosophy to yield a mode of Christian teaching. Russen acknowledges the influence of More, Cervantes, and whoever was behind the yearly anthologies of Poor Robin, predecessor of Benjamin Franklin's *Poor Richard's Almanac,* whose messengers delivered yearly almanacs of parodies and faux prognostications to the delight of the reading public for about a hundred years, from 1660 to 1770.[129] For Russen, these "comical" authors explain a minor part of the genre's appeal, for the work deals with serious matters of theology and government, and deals with them in the right way. He does not indicate how the work manages to be both comical and serious at the same time, though it is clear he desires such a work and thinks he finds this amalgam in Cyrano's moon voyage. Even the improbable probabilities of a realist-fantasy play to the text's advantage as a mode of religious instruction: "That White is Black, and Black White; That One may be and not be at the same time; That there may be a Mountain without a Valley; That Nothing is Something . . . are Paradoxes which startle Sense, and above our Comprehension. Indeed, to us they are so, who have not Understandings fitted to the Conceptions of such things."[130] Far from unsettling received ideas, the moon voyage reinforces Christian teaching by helping the reader overcome a rational perspective that leaves no room for divinity. Paradox redeemed. The potential relativism of a narrative showing that "White is Black, and Black White" therefore gives way to a mode of religious instruction, proving a "Divine Being, to whom all things are possible." In this context, Russen seizes on the opening sequence of *L'autre monde*, in which the narrator returns to his study after his friends laugh at his idea of life on the moon and other planets: "I went into my Study, where I found upon the table, a Book opened without my help, written by *Cardan;* which though I had no design to read, yet as it were forcibly, I cast my eyes upon a story of that Philosopher, who relates, that studying one night by Candle, he saw two great old men come through the doors, though bolted; who after many Questions he propounded to them, answered finally, that they were Inhabitants of the Moon, and then vanished."[131] For the schoolteacher, this anecdote holds spiritual significance. He ignores the humanist text and author to which Cyrano alludes because text and author import the radical origins of the lunar voyage. "*Cardan*" stands for Girolamo Cardano (1501–76), the Italian Renaissance astronomer, physicist, logician, and metaphysician, whose controversial tracts eventually led to his arrest on October 6, 1570, and forced abdication of all previous views, with agreement never to teach or publish again.[132] Russen focuses instead on the encounter itself, which confirms the efficacy of invisible spirits: "And certain it is an observing person may take notice of some extraordinary Passages in the Course of his Life, of which he can give no rational account, but must with our ingenious Traveller to the Moon, place them on the score of Preternatural Causes, and explicate them by the officious Services of those kind Agents which invisibly assist and inform us."[133] Such efforts by Christian authors to rehabilitate Lucian and his imitators suggests the effectiveness of the Lucianic mode as a means of concealment. The same text could be read as a humanist's critique of cultural chauvinism and as a justification for that chauvinism. The same premise—the plurality of worlds—could be read as a confirmation of Universal Christianity and as a threat to that universality. The same genre might provide a platform for easy allegorical satire or a basis for the second kind of satire that Bakhtin identifies with the emerging novel. Unfortunately, Defoe's own text turns on the swivel of these possibilities. A vehicle of predictable, redundant, and excessively topical satire, *The Consolidator* also expresses a freethinking, even deistical, outlook on occasion. Overshadowed by unflattering comparison with Swift's *A Tale of a Tub*, Defoe's fantastic space voyage contains a conception, without the execution, of a new mode of satire, no longer Swiftean but, instead, Lucianic and modern, counter-allegorical because built on paradox, not transcendence.

The evidence presented in this chapter indicates that about sixteen months after Defoe emerged from Newgate Prison, he published a lunar voyage of about 360 pages that his enemies linked to the offense that put him in prison, *The Shortest Way with the Dissenters*. Defoe's contribution to the lunar voyage tradition occurs toward the end of a century-long publishing vogue that included new and reissued English translations of Lucian, as well as imitative and pedagogical works—many first appearing in French—modeled on the Syrian Greek satirist. Because it is difficult to imagine Defoe involving himself in a literary enterprise without knowing its historical and political significance, reconstructing the discourse surrounding the Lucianic Revival supplies a missing context for Defoe's discovery of the form we now call the novel. In this chapter, I have paid special attention to the Christian apologists for Lucian and his seventeenth-century imitators. Their attempts to exonerate Lucian from specific charges help us reconstruct those charges: Lucian was homosexual, he wrote mockingly of Christianity, he was likely an atheist, and his fictions were devious and seemingly destructive of all myth and dogma. Some heavy apologetic lifting was necessary to convert this heretical author to Christian purposes. A lunar theory of the novel views these efforts to exonerate Lucian and his imitators as reacting against the very qualities that made Lucian an attractive model for cosmopolitan authors seeking to disguise their freethinking views of religion in popular fiction. According to this account, we should not expect to find an unambiguous early modern defense of literary cosmopolitanism. A manifesto such as Anthony Kwame Appiah's *Cosmopolitanism: Ethics in a World of Strangers* (2006) was impossible at the time because the position dovetailed with an anthropological, ultimately relativist view of religious differences associated with the deist movement and outlawed in most national contexts. Instead of explicit defense or explanation, Defoe stages a fight with Jonathan Swift over the art of satire. He introduces deist scenarios such as the first meeting with the moon-philosopher that were familiar to readers of previous lunar voyages. He inserts into his capacious satire set pieces of metacognitive description, picturing the writer's mind in the act of invention. Although *The Consolidator* would never be a popular favorite, it helped pave the way for future success.

If this move to cosmopolitan fiction were a one-off in Defoe's case, it might be easy to ignore. However, eight months before *Robinson Crusoe*, Defoe published another long cosmopolitan fiction, and there is some evidence that he was working on it years before 1718. Another commercial, aesthetic, and historical failure, *A Continuation of Letters Written by a Turkish Spy at Paris* continues Defoe's vendetta against Charles Leslie and introduces thematic and stylistic elements that contribute directly to the success of *Robinson Crusoe*.

3 Cosmopolitan Defoe
A Continuation of Letters Written by a Turkish Spy at Paris, 1718

> But now I hope in a successful *prore*,[1]
> The Fates have fix'd me on sweet *England*'s Shore;
> And by these various wandrings true I found,
> Earth is our common Mother, every ground
> May be ones Country, for by Birth each Man
> Is in this world a *Cosmopolitan*,
> A free-born Burgess, and receives thereby
> His Denization from Nativity.
> —James Howell, *Epistolae Ho-Elianae*

> A *True-Born Englishman*'s a Contradiction,
> In Speech an Irony, in Fact a Fiction
> A Banter made to be a Test of Fools,
> Which those that use it justly ridicules.
> A Metaphor invented to express
> A man *a-kin* to all the Universe.
> —Daniel Defoe, *The True-Born Englishman*

Defoe's Spy Novel

Eight months before Defoe published part 1 of *Robinson Crusoe*, he brought out the anonymous *A Continuation of Letters Written by a Turkish Spy at Paris*.[2] If Defoe meant to capitalize on the success of the equally anonymous *Letters Writ by a Turkish Spy*, he failed. No second edition followed; remainders were being advertised the following year in the back pages of the third edition of *Robinson Crusoe*. Defoe's contemporaries did not devour his *Turkish Spy*, and subsequent generations have forgotten it. With rare exception, biographers, critics, and literary historians pass it over, as well, and view *Robinson Crusoe* as Defoe's first novel, even though readers at the time referred to *Letters Writ by a Turkish Spy* as a novel. "And to speak freely," writes one irate reader at the end of the seventeenth century in response to another publication, "when . . . there appeared to me every where the foot-steps of a conceited Home-breeding, and every Leaf almost stuft up with the Praise of This, and the Diminution and Undervaluing of other Countries, confirmed with far fetch'd Arguments, devised on purpose rather to amuse and ensnare, than impartially to instruct the Reader: I did conclude, that our unknown Author's intention was to give us a Novel, such as the *Turkish Spy*, or the like (wherein of late years some have taken a priviledge to intermingle Truth with their own Inventions, accommodating the whole more to their own Fancies, or else to the Humors of such as they seek to please, than to the sacred Laws of History)."[3] It would appear that Defoe published *a* novel shortly before he published *the* novel. An art historian might travel the world to inspect a newly discovered sketch for the *Mona Lisa;* yet here we have a long prose fiction appearing eight months before *Robinson Crusoe* that even scholars ignore. Glossing over Defoe's early experiments, we reduce him to a political schemer and journalistic hack who discovered the formula for novel writing late in life and by chance. Quite a different picture emerges when attending to the cosmopolitan Defoe.

The work earned its obscurity for many of the reasons that Defoe's lunar voyage crashed and burned. If, as Maximillian Novak observes, *The Consolidator* was an accidental muddle, *A Continuation of Letters Written by a Turkish Spy* is a purposeful mess. Not only does the work fail to interest because of its relentless topical satire, but its very form, a public miscellany made up of private letters, is meant to be fractured and messy. The discordant parts fail to cohere when read according to the standards of coherence that Defoe's next experiment, *Robinson Crusoe,* helped create. One witty critic likens this to a case of fratricide.[4] Indeed, Defoe's masterpiece is surrounded by the wreckage of false starts, tedious experiments, failed texts. The book we call *Robinson Crusoe* is really part 1 of a trilogy whose second two parts have been amputated and forgotten by all but scholars. If the failures now seem unreadable, that does not mean they are unimportant. Defoe's *Letters Written by a Turkish Spy* reveals an author applying the *Shortest Way* mode of first-person narrative to a longer and more ambitious fiction and exploring many of the themes that will preoccupy *Robinson Crusoe*. The hero, Mahmut, is a cosmopolitan castaway, marooned not on an island but in Paris, yet no less isolated and surrounded by danger. The work itself, as we will see, continues the pattern we detected in *The Shortest Way with the Dissenters* and Defoe's Quaker writings: of mortal combat with Charles Leslie and the High Church by means of another form of deism in literary disguise.

Fortunately, one scholar has opened the way to integrating Defoe's earlier prose fiction with his major novels. In *Enlightenment Orientalism,* Srinivas Aravamudan constructs a literary history in opposition to Edward Said's argument that every Western representation of the East must be an act of cultural imperialism. Aravamudan locates works by Western writers committed on principle to a fair—or, he would say, *ethnographic*—depiction of the other. Among these works are Defoe's lunar voyage and his cosmopolitan spy novel modeled on Giovanni Paulo Marana's *Letters Writ by a Turkish Spy.* These works "follow the itinerary of European knowledge regarding the East influenced by the utopian aspirations of Enlightenment more than the materialism of political interest. . . . [A] transcultural cosmopolitan, and Enlightenment-inflected Orientalism existed at least as an alternative strain before 'Saidian' Orientalism came about."[5] With this insight, Aravamudan restores fantastic, Oriental, and otherwise cosmopolitan works such as Defoe's *A Continuation of Letters Written by a Turkish Spy* to the history and theory of the English novel. He retrieves what the realism hypothesis of Ian Watt and the dialectical method of Michael McKeon leave aside: the penetration of Occident by Orient, the welcoming of Oriental influence by Western writers whose purposes square with a sympathetic and reasonably well-informed representation of Eastern and Near Eastern times, places, and characters.

What caused Enlightenment Orientalism to flourish in the West, if not an imperialist motive? Although Aravamudan does not answer this question directly, he adduces evidence, pointing to the spread of public deism as a key factor. Aravamudan writes of Simon Tyssot de Patot's *Voyages et avantures de Jaques Massé* (1710) that here we find "a Chinese prisoner who had once been a Catholic but now teaches that all men are equal and abjures Christianity in favor of an explicitly stated universalism. We learn that the critique of Christian theology intersected with Islamophilia."[6] Which Western writers were responsible for this critique of Christianity that dovetailed so well with a reasonably accurate and sympathetic representation of the Eastern other? The case of Tyssot de Patot might have suggested an answer, since he was accused of Spinozism at age seventy-two and fired from his university post in Holland upon publication of his *Lettres choisies* (1727). Whatever the accuracy of the label to Spinoza's actual thought, "Spinozism" became a code word for deism. The early deists—Herbert, Spinoza, Blount, Toland, and Vico especially—undertook an anthropological and philological study of world religions to dislodge church influence. They sought to subvert theocracy by means of a critical and philological study of religious rhetoric. This is the opening gambit of Herbert and Blount's *Religio Laici* (ca. 1645, 1683). The deists claim to be so upset by the specter of religious violence, and threats against them personally, that they commit to figuring out a cure for this evil. Applying science to the problem, they theorize the need for an accurate study of world religions in all times, places, and languages. The purpose of this survey is to derive a list of the fewest possible notions all religions have in common as an antidote to warfare over specific, or special, revelations. Such a study would occupy several lifetimes, the deists admit; therefore, they take up a representative sample and arrive at five *Notitiae Communes* (Common Notions). The list itself was important and controversial; the method of deriving the list was possibly even more important and controversial. It treated all expressions of religion as objective data in an empirical process of inferential reason. While this reduction of faith systems to the abstraction that became "religion" might signal a lack of respect for the truth claims of any single religious order, it also implied a lack of judgment against any and open curiosity about its nature.[7] The deist project therefore implied a stance of equanimity toward religious and cultural differences. The "critique of Christian theology intersected with Islamophilia" not because religious skeptics were converting en masse to Islam, but because their principles made denigration of other religions hypocritical. No doubt there were deist hypocrites such as Shaftesbury and Voltaire, as there are dabblers of every persuasion.[8] There were also deists who followed their ideas where they led, and some of the most far-sighted and necessarily cautious of them wrote Oriental and utopian fiction. Aravamudan links Enlightenment Orientalism to those he calls the "proto-Spinozists" (i.e., the deists), whose "comparative erudition," "burgeoning interest in human universality," and "universalist and cosmopolitan aspirations" fed a more sympathetic study and representation of the East.[9]

A genuine interest in Eastern times, places, and peoples was in keeping with the entire tendency of a pan-European deism. As critical philology, deism challenged the conceptual and linguistic structures of state religion; as positive theology, deism derived a short list of Common Notions by treating different faiths as theoretically equal expressions of the human need to believe in something greater. As outlawed challenge to Christianity, deism assumed literary disguises, lunar and Oriental fictions among them. Again, these deist authors did not wake up one day to the greater truth of Islam; a prior set of philosophical convictions led them to single out denigrated religions and assert their legitimacy. They conducted detailed philological studies of other cultures and religions and thereby promoted toleration of political and religious differences. Aravamudan describes this strategy as it relates to Defoe's spy novel: "Defoe employs a deliberate nonrealism to narrate the *West* into a parallel ethnographic time . . . even as the East is depicted as rational and universal in its vision."[10] The genres of Enlightenment Orientalism fall within this deist project.

Because this cultural context has played a marginal role in the received theories and histories of the novel, it has been necessary for scholars such as Aravamudan to make a case for its relevance, just as it is necessary in the case of Defoe to account for his decision to write ambitious works of prose fiction in extrarealist genres associated with literary deism. Granted, Defoe might have used these cosmopolitan genres for anti-cosmopolitan and anti-deistical purposes, turning the forms back against their makers. This will be the assertion of those who deny that Defoe had any sympathy for deism. The mere adoption of controversial forms does not prove agreement with the authors who previously deployed those genres, or the controversial ideas contained in them. Although genres acquire cultural reputations, they never code essentially for a set ideology. Genres are sites of contested authority.[11] The contemporaries who accused Defoe, a known opponent of deism, of spreading deism through his fiction were aware of these cosmopolitan contexts, as well. Leslie and ideologues like him feared that someone would come along with the intellectual acumen and rhetorical chops to take deism out of speculative, pulpit, and pamphlet debate into public currency. There were no deist churches, although Quaker, Unitarian, and Masonic gathering places came close. Instead, Defoe's enemies feared that his fictional works would provide sanction and sanctuary. Judging by Defoe's gravitation to cosmopolitan genres, their fears were justified. Watch his failures, in other words, for the motives behind his success. Instead of viewing *Robinson Crusoe* as a departure from these previous cosmopolitan forays, view it as more of the same, better executed, and much better concealed.

Just as it was necessary before taking up *The Consolidator* to fill in some of the missing history of the Lucianic Revival, so here, before considering Defoe's *A Continuation of Letters Written by a Turkish Spy*, it is necessary to detail the little-known history of the work he continued.

The Secret History of the *Turkish Spy*

It would take a spy equipped with time travel and some truth serum to disclose just who was responsible for the work Defoe continued. Despite the century-long, transatlantic fame of the English *Letters Writ by a Turkish Spy* and the French *L'espion du Grand-Seigneur* (later, *L'espion dans les cours des princes chrétiens*, and later still, *L'espion turc*), authorship of both the English and the French *Turkish Spy* remains shrouded in mystery.[12] The generally accepted facts pertain to a work written by a Genoese exile to Paris named Giovanni Paulo Marana (1642–93). He appears to have fled Genoa after being arrested for a false denunciation in 1670 and arrested again on suspicion of collusion with the French envoy.[13] Resettled in Paris, he composed either the first 102 letters of an epistolary spy novel—the first of its kind—or those letters plus a great many more, which were lost, discovered, and published anonymously by English and French "translators" over the next decade: "On 19 November 1683, Marana was permitted by authority of the King to have printed in Italian and in French the first part of *L'esploratore turco e le di lui relazioni segrete alla Porta ottomana* (1684) 'da lui tradotto dall'Arabo.'. . . Immediately, a French edition, identical in title and contents, appeared in Amsterdam."[14] However, the expected continuations from Marana himself did not follow. In 1690, in his preface to *Les événements les plus considérables du règne de Louis le Grand*, Marana offered an oblique explanation: "I have received complaints from all sides, that according to my promise, I did not give the public the continuation of my Turkish Spy. . . . The difficulties that I have encountered—either because of the slowness of those who do me the honor of translating the relations of Mahmut the Arab, or because of the ordinary delays of the revisers of books, or, finally, because of certain secret obstacles—are the reason why for three years, about a dozen small volumes that are complete in my language, are not yet [available] in yours."[15] Marana chooses not to reveal the "secret obstacles" that kept him from publishing the additional volumes, which he claims already to have written. The evidence suggests that the Catholic Church and its Inquisition put a stop to his fiction.[16] Soon after publication of the first 102 letters, Marana received a letter from his protector, French Ambassador François Pidou de Saint-Olon, who reproached him for taking "une occasion peu nécessaire de parler irrespectuesement des mystères de notre religion" (an unnecessary opportunity to speak disrespectfully of the mysteries of our religion).[17] Although the original "three small volumes" included fawning praise of Louis XIII and escaped being placed on the Inquisition's Index of Forbidden Books (*Index Librorum Prohibitorum*), subsequent volumes, many published in Holland, were banned for reasons that will soon be clear.

Poor Marana! Instigator of a century-long publishing craze, he could not cash in on his brilliant first issue and left the field open for enterprising publishers to shelter under his name and story—with its promise of more volumes, its vanished author (some suspected a mental breakdown and retreat back to Italy), and its assignment of blame for perceived heresies to the sad Genoese and his singular protagonist, the brilliant Muslim spy named Mahmut. "There is . . . strong evidence," writes William H. McBurney, "that an Italian manuscript of all letters was completed by 1686 and that *The Turkish Spy*, as it now exists, was entirely [Marana's] work."[18] Yet he adds, "Definite proof of this still hinges upon the missing French or Italian manuscript from which the last seven volumes of letters were translated into English."[19] McBurney combed the major research libraries of the world in search of this manuscript, without success. To the father of Tennyson's A. H. H., the historian Henry Hallam, it was obvious that no such French or Italian originals existed. Marana, he wrote, "is entitled to the praise of the invention, and to the first volume; but that the rest were written by one or more Englishmen, as well as originally published in this country."[20] This would mean that five-sixths of the "original" *Turkish Spy* was written by English authors between 1687, when an English translation of 101 of Marana's original 102 letters appeared, and 1694, when the unknown English editor(s) drew the line on further additions by calling the final installment "Volume the Last," and by appearing to kill off Mahmut in the last of the 644 letters. In addition to external evidence (the French *L'espion turc* is largely a translation of the eight-volume English set), Hallam bases his claim of English authorship on "internal evidence . . . partly founded on a skeptical, or at least wandering tone in religion, characteristic of the reign of William III, but not so much of the continental writers."[21] The evidence before Hallam might have permitted a more confident conclusion: a 1690s English origin makes sense because the work is preoccupied with the deist controversy erupting in England at that time.

On the French side, the situation is no clearer:

> The authorship of the *Espion turc* is, in reality, an intricate problem and even today there is no certain proof as to who wrote most of the letters in the complete series. . . . Documents exist which prove that Gian-Paulo Marana, an Italian political refugee residing in Paris, is the author of the first 102 letters (that is, the contents of the three small volumes published in Paris, 1684–1686). Sixty-three other letters have been identified pretty surely as from the pen of the English

author Daniel Defoe. These were published first (and only once) in English as the *Continuation of Letters Written by a Turkish Spy at Paris* (London, 1718), a separate volume from the regular English set, but included in the 1742 and subsequent editions in French as part of the regular series.[22]

Notice the offhand comment that in 1742 the still expanding *L'espion turc* absorbed Defoe's *Continuation*. In fact, the French text appeared in London eleven years after Defoe's death as a separate volume, its letters preserved in nearly their exact order, as volume seven of the fifteenth edition of *L'espion turc*.[23]

Defoe was familiar with these details of the spy novel's origins, although it is impossible to say just when his interest in the spy novel began. The second volume of *The Family Instructor*, first published in 1718, justifies publication of a sequel in light of the success of the *Turkish Spy*: "*I am not ignorant, that as Times and the Humour of the People go, it is a bold Adventure to write a second Volume of anything*; nor is the Success of a First Part any Rule to expect Success to a Second. . . . [A]nd if the *Turkish Spy*, and such other Books, from the known Variety of them, have pleased and diverted the World, even to the Seventh or Eighth Volume: If this Subject is less pleasing, and fails of running the same Length with those looser Works, it must be because People have less Pleasure in Things that are instructing, than in Things merely humouring and diverting."[24] The didactic tone of this statement belies the fact that in 1718 Defoe published just such a "looser," "meerly humouring and diverting work." Moving backward in time from 1718, we know that he published another Turkish spy story in 1717 under the title "The Conduct of Christians Made the Sport of Infidels in a Letter from a Turkish Merchant at Amsterdam to the Grand Mufti at Constantinople." If Defoe was testing the waters for a Montesquieu-like spin-off from Marana, with new characters and setting, the idea did not fly. Apart from topical response to the Bangorian controversy, this incursion into Marana-land went nowhere.[25] Moving further back, we hear of Defoe's interest in the original *Letters Writ by a Turkish Spy* from a memorandum to Robert Harley in 1704, which "mentioned with approval a book in eight volumes published in London about 7 or 8 years ago called *Letters Writ by a Turkish Spy*."[26] Is it possible Defoe was recommending a work he had a hand in writing? In *Curiosities of Literature* (1798), Isaac D'Israeli (1766–1848), the father of the eventual prime minister, summarized the tradition of guesswork surrounding authorship of the eight-volume *Letters Writ by a Turkish Spy*:

> Whatever may be the defects of the *Turkish Spy,* the author has shewn one uncommon merit, by having opened a new species of composition, which has been pursued by writers with inferior success, if we except the charming *Persian Letters* of Montesquieu. *The Turkish Spy,* is a book which has delighted us in our childhood, and to which we still recur with pleasure. But its ingenious author is unknown to three parts of his admirers.
>
> In Mr. Boswell's *Life of Johnson* is this dialogue concerning the writer of the *Turkish Spy.* "B. Pray, Sir is the *Turkish Spy* a genuine book? J. No, Sir. Mrs. Manley in her life, says, that *her Father wrote the two first volumes;* and in another book, *Dunton's Life and Errours,* we find that the rest was *written* by *one Sault,* at two guineas a sheet, under the directions of Mr. Midgeley." . . .
>
> I do not know on what authority Mrs. Manley advances that her father was the author; but this lady was never nice in detailing facts. Dunton indeed gives some information in a very loose manner. He tells us, p. 242, that it is probable, by reasons which he insinuates, that *one Bradshaw,* a hackney author, was the writer of the *Turkish Spy.* This man, probably was engaged by Dr. Midgeley to translate the volumes as they appeared, at the rate of 40*s* per sheet. On the whole, all this proves at least how little the author was known while the volumes were publishing, and that he is as little known at present.[27]

The editors of the Pickering Masters edition identify the probable author with no greater certainty, briefly noting that the English translation was attributed to William Bradshaw.[28] In light of this confusion about the authorship of five-sixths of the original eight-volume set, and given that Defoe was already a mature man in his late twenties and early thirties when these volumes appeared, it is surprising that scholars have shown little interest in a statement Defoe added to the preface of his *Continuation,* since it appears to take credit for some of the original letters, which, for unstated reasons, the previous editor withheld from *Letters Writ by a Turkish Spy,* to be included now in *Letters Written by a Turkish Spy:*

> If our Correspondent at *Vienna,* to whom *Mahmut* committed his Papers, and to whom they were faithfully delivered by his Successor, does not deceive us, we may expect a yet greater Variety, towards the Conclusion of his Residence, than has yet seen the Light, and perhaps some Remains of things omitted in the Time of former Publication,

which, as they come to Hand, shall be communicated with the greatest Exactness, whether they may exactly correspond with the Chronology of former Publications or no; and tho' there may seem a little Confusion in such a Retrospect, yet I doubt not the Beauty of the Subject shall make full Amends for any Disorder in the Dates.[29]

Defoe dances around a claim of authorship of some of the letters in the original eight-volume set, a dance he continues with the unfortunate title, *A Continuation*. As a sales pitch, his hint that he had a hand in the original *Turkish Spy* may be spurious, and no scholar has ever taken the suggestion seriously. Nevertheless, it is impossible to rule out the possibility that those "Remains of things omitted" from the original volumes came easily to the editor's hand *because he wrote them*. Defoe conspicuously flags some of these letters that may not "correspond with the Chronology of former Publications" in book 3, just before the second letter 12: "Note *This Letter should have been printed in page 157, Book* II, [and] *Letter* XII *in the same Book, should have been placed here.*" Was this note meant to be taken seriously? Was it a way to lay claim to part of the original, justifying the unfortunate title? Or was it part of the joke built into the miscellaneous genre of prose fiction to which Cervantes and Laurence Sterne also contribute, in which alerting readers to missing and misplaced chapters and pages they might skip or compose themselves was part of the fun?

Defoe's editors, French and English, have taken these directions seriously. In the seventh volume of the French *L'espion turc,* published in London in 1742, letters 1–64 are numbered consecutively and not only follow the order of Defoe's *Continuation* but also follow out his directions for correcting continuity in the miscellany. In the Pickering Masters edition, the editor, David Blewett, follows Defoe's directions to the extent of redating and repositioning letters Defoe did not even mention. "Three letters have been moved in the Pickering and Chatto edition from their places in the first edition," he writes. "A note in Book III before the second of two letters numbered XII . . . points out that 'This Letter should have been printed in page 157, Book II, and Letter XII in the same book should have been printed here.'" But when the editor tries to follow these directions, problems arise: "Letter XII in Book II, however, does not begin on page 157. Letter X does, and the question arises as to which letter in Book II—the one that begins on page 157 or Letter XII (which begins on page 167)—is intended."[30] Blewett solves the problem this way: "In fact both Letters X and XII deal with events of the Nine Years' War, which are datable to May and August 1692 respectively. Book III deals with events that took place in 1692. Both letters have therefore been transferred to Book III, redated 1692, and renumbered XIII and XIV. (The last two letters of Book III become XV and XVI.)"[31] Were these editors correct to correct the original? What if Defoe's main reason for adding his note about misplaced letters was to add verisimilitude and seeming chronological precision to what is finally a loose miscellany, all the while alerting the reader to a "Beauty of the Subject [that] shall make full Amends for any Disorder in the Dates"? And what if, in addition, these directions are actually meant to signal authorship of some of the original *Letters Writ by a Turkish Spy*? In that case, both editors have fallen prey to Defoe's deceit. I ask these editorial questions because they suggest that Defoe may have started writing ambitious prose fictions early—in his thirties with *Turkish Spy*, and in his forties with *The Consolidator*. That would make the masterpiece of his fifties less of a shock. Granted, Defoe has never been suspected of being one of the "translators" of Marana's original 102 letters into the 644 letters of the eight-volume set. But what are we to make of the ease with which Defoe's sixty-four-letter *Continuation* was absorbed into the French *L'espion turc* in 1742? Previous editions of the French *Turkish Spy* are translations of the English *Letters Writ by a Turkish Spy*. Defoe's *Continuation* fit so well in style, theme, and narrative progression that it could be inserted entire, without damage to the existing volumes. In addition, as I point out later, echoes of the editor who closes the eighth volume in 1694 can be heard in Defoe's preface to the *Continuation* in 1718. This may only mean that Defoe was a good mimic of the previous text but was not mimicking himself. What we can conclude is that Defoe's participation in the development of the English spy novel, like his participation in the Lucianic Revival, reveals his familiarity with the genre's checkered past.

Orientalism and Literary Deism

What drew Defoe to the Turkish spy novel? The mercenary motive of capitalizing on someone else's best seller provides insufficient explanation. This work, I believe, fits the pattern we have observed in previous chapters: Defoe's mortal battle with Charles Leslie led him to deploy rhetorical weapons of known deist association. *The Shortest Way with the Dissenters,* modeled on an ingenious pamphlet by the deist Charles Blount; the Quaker writings, permitting expressions of more radical religious nonconformity than Defoe himself is known to have espoused; the lunar voyage, modeled on Lucian and his seventeenth-century libertine successors—these efforts stand out amid a great many other writings in prose and poetry as creative solutions to the problem of uprooting Leslie and his cohort. William Pittis connected *The Shortest Way with the Dissenters* to *The Consolidator,* and I would extend Pittis's short way with Defoe to include *A Continuation of Letters Written by a Turkish Spy.* It is unnecessary to argue that Defoe was a deist in any doctrinal sense, to observe that all of these texts, the *Continuation* included, were known deist vehicles in Defoe's day. They present us with a pattern of rhetorical behavior, if not of personal conviction.

Hallam refers to the *Turkish Spy*'s "wandering tone in religion, characteristic of the reign of William III." More specifically, there are direct ties between the spy novel and the deist controversy gaining steam in England during the 1690s. This is a matter of historical record, not interpretative surmise. Consider first of all the angry response of early readers who attack the original *Letters Writ by a Turkish Spy* as heretical. *Eugenia; or, An Elegy upon the Death of the Honourable Madam,* by Matthew Morgan (1652–1703), imagines a moment when true religion will triumph and false will meet its fate in the flames:

> But now the scatter'd Atomes shall Unite,
> Which were dispers'd in Shipwrack or a Fight:
> All wicked Authors now must Prostrate lie,
> And dread those heavenly Powers they did defie,
> Old *Hobbs, Occhinus,* and the *Turkish-Spy;*
> Now they shall be condemn'd unto a Flame,
> As here their Writings did deserve the same;
> That Scribler with a stalking-Horse doth advance,
> And his sly *Atheism* lurks behind *Romance;*
> That *Masquerading,* ill-dissembled Man,
> Before the *Scriptures* puts the *Alcoran;*
> And doth prefer that Grand Impostor's Dove,
> To that bless'd Spirit of Immortal Love,
> Who with Good motions in our Minds doth move;
> Young Rake-Hells with these Principles are imbu'd,
> Who from their Cradles Swear, are early Lewd;
> At a cheap rate their Consciences do sell,
> Are very forward Candidates for Hell.[32]

The poet groups the *Turkish Spy* with works of the atheistical Hobbes and Bernardino Ochino (1487–1564), whose publications outraged Catholics and Reformed Protestants alike, and who was accused of authoring the notorious deist hoax *Traité des trois imposteurs.*[33] The author sees through the romance to its designs on impressionable readers, soon-to-be "Young Rake-Hells," titillated by popular fiction. Mahmut, through the charm of his character, will lead them to share, or at least entertain his perspective, which is that of a deist vis-à-vis religion in the West, though a true believer when it comes to Islam. *A Brief Vindication of the Fundamental Articles of the Christian Faith*, by John Edwards (1637–1716), also warns against Marana's *Turkish Spy*. Edwards attacks a rival author who "under the pretence of declaring against *Systems of Divinity* (which is his Common Subject) strikes at all the Received and Celebrated Doctrines of the Christian Church, and represents them as indifferent and precarious. . . . [The] *Turkish Spye* doth not express *his mind more fully*. Thus he disposes his Readers to be of no Church, of no Religion. Or at least he would perswade them that one way of Religion is as good as an other: which is the prevailing doctrine of these days,"—a neat expression of the prevailing doctrine of cosmopolitan deism.[34]

Notice that the *Turkish Spy*'s critics are not responding reflexively to this or that passage in Marana. They read with a mission, alert to hidden arguments connecting the seemingly disconnected letters. The *Turkish Spy*'s critics also read character differently. They understood character as more of a function than a person. Take the spy. The character as spy excited the readers' interest because of its singularity, its odd suspension amid cultures, nations, and religions—its cosmopolitanism. His perspective is simultaneously knowing and unknowing, controlled and imperiled. And his personality wins the readers' sympathy, even if his antipathy for the West is visceral. Clever and confused, heroic and quixotic, the narrator as spying protagonist provided subversive authors with multiple layers of deniability when it came to statements they made on touchy topics. Moreover, the spy novel engages the reader in a spirit of inquiry. Looking for the thread that unites disparate letters into a coherent narrative, or the identity that unites a scattered character, readers constructed a subtext, thrilling or appalling, depending on their theology.

The expectation that readers would peruse the spy novel in search of a hidden thread connecting random letters motivates Montesquieu's famous boast that a *chaîne secrète* connects the 161 letters of his *Lettres persanes* (1721; *The Persian Letters* 1722). The nature of this secret chain has long puzzled scholars, and Montesquieu's own explanation raises more questions than it answers. I quote from a mid-eighteenth century English translation of *The Persian Letters*:

> There is nothing in the PERSIAN LETTERS that has given readers so general a satisfaction, as to find in them a sort of romance, without having expected it. It is easy to discern in them the beginning, the

progress, and the conclusion of it: the several different persons introduced, are connected together by a sort of chain. . . . To conclude, in common romances digressions can never be admitted, except when they themselves constitute another romance. Reasoning cannot be intermixed with story, because the personages not being brought together to reason, that would be repugnant to the design and nature of the work. But in the form of letters, wherein personages are introduced at random, and the subjects treated of do not depend on any design, or plan, already formed, the author has the advantage of being able to blend philosophy, politics and morality with romance, and to connect the whole by a secret, and, as it were, undiscoverable chain.[35]

The word "chain" appears twice, with two different meanings. In the first instance, "chain" means the beginning, middle, and end of a story involving characters. For "chain" we might substitute the plot of romance, which draws the reader in and explains the work's success: "There is another reason why these romances, generally speaking, succeed, and that is, because the persons introduced give themselves an account of what happens to them, which causes the passions to be felt more sensibly than any narrative made by another could do. This is likewise one of the causes of the success of some admirable works which have appeared since the PERSIAN LETTERS."[36] When Montesquieu next uses the word "chain," it means something less obvious. It appears to be the conceptual bond that holds together an otherwise scattershot collection of letters: "wherein personages are introduced at random, and the subjects treated of do not depend on any design, or plan, already formed." The miscellany of letters gives the author newfound freedom: "the advantage of being able to blend philosophy, politics and morality with romance, and to connect the whole by a secret, and, as it were, undiscoverable chain."[37] In the first instance, romance provides the principle of cohesion, but here, whatever the secret chain may be, it unites philosophy, politics, ethics, *and* literature. For Montesquieu, as for Defoe, there were good reasons for keeping the secret secret. Both authors embrace genres of Enlightenment Orientalism because of their capacity to stage a critique of theocracy by literary means. In playful near-apology, Montesquieu writes:

> There are in them [the *Persian Letters*] some strokes, which many have looked upon as too bold. But these are requested to take the nature of the work into consideration. The Persians, who were to

play so considerable a part in it, were all on a sudden transplanted to Europe, that is, removed to another world, as it were. At a certain time therefore it was necessary to represent them as full of ignorance and prejudices. The author's chief design was to display the formation and progress of their ideas. Their first thoughts could not but have a dash of singularity in them: it was apprehended there was nothing to be done but to give them that sort of singularity which is not incompatible with understanding. It was only to represent their situation of mind at seeing any thing that appeared extraordinary to them. The author, far from having a design to strike at any principle of our religion, thought himself even free from the imputation of indiscretion. These strokes appear always connected with a manifestation of surprise, or astonishment, and not with the idea of inquiry, much less with that of criticism. In speaking of our religion, these Persians should not appear better informed than when they talk of our manners and customs. And if they sometimes seem to look upon the tenets of our religion as singular, the singularity they discover in them fully shews their ignorance of their connexion with other truths thereof. The author justifies himself in this manner, as well on account of his attachment to these important truths, as through respect for the human species, which he certainly could not have had an intention to wound in the tenderest part. The reader is therefore requested not to cease one moment to consider those strokes as the effects of surprise in persons who ought to be surprised, or as the paradoxes of men who spoke of what they did not understand. He is likewise requested to consider that the whole beauty of the invention consisted in the constant contrast between the real state of things and the singular, or whimsical manner in which they were contemplated.[38]

The entire passage reveals an exquisite command of irony. Montesquieu advises the reader not to draw the conclusion that the text invites—that the cosmopolitan perspective of *The Persian Letters* reduces religion to a question of national manners and customs. The attitude of "inquiry" or "criticism" that the author disavows is exactly the effect the spy novel creates by virtue of its literary structure. About this structure, Montesquieu is disarmingly candid: "The whole beauty of the invention consisted in the constant contrast between the real state of things and the singular." Emphasis falls on the constant contrast as much as on the oppositional poles: real and singular. Indeed, by the time

Montesquieu's irony is done with these terms, they have traded places. The singular becomes the most real, and the real looks strange. The passage coyly pins the blame for any perceived "stroke" against religion on a special kind of character. Montesquieu calls it the singular character, and we should take note of this category because all of Defoe's important fictional characters are singular in much the same way and for much the same reason.

Singularity was doubled-edged at the time Montesquieu and Defoe wrote. In English, most historical uses emphasize "the fact or quality of differing or dissenting from others or what is generally accepted, especially in thought or religion."[39] This is the meaning Richard Baxter has in mind when he asks Dr. Stillingfleet, "Is our Consent with the Universal Church, or your Singularity from it, liker to Schism and Separation?"[40] Singularity as dissent does not carry favorable connotations. It suggests a character flaw: "The World is So Overgrown with Singularities in Behavior and Method of Living," complains Isaac Bickerstaff in *The Tatler*, "that I have no sooner laid before Mankind the Absurdity of one Species of Men, but there starts up to my view some new Sect of Impertinents, that had escaped Notice."[41] Richardson's Sir Charles Grandison holds that "Singularity is usually the indication of something wrong in judgment."[42] But singularity conveys the opposite meaning at the same point in time. The Presbyterian minister John Flavel (1630–91), whose *Navigation Spiritualized* (1682) was well known in Defoe's day, uses the word "singular" to refer to Christ: "He is described by the singularity of his mediation, as one Mediator."[43] The singular is now the essential and true. In the arts and sciences, we still speak of a singular achievement, preserving the meaning this word held in the sixteenth century: "Dylygently to attayne in al artys and crafte gret syngularyte."[44] The astute early feminist Mary Astell plays on both senses of the word in her admonition to women, *A Serious Proposal to the Ladies* (1697): "And pray what is't that hinders you? The Singularity of the Matter? Are you afraid of being out of the ordinary way and therefore admir'd and gaz'd at? . . . Singularity is indeed to be avoided except in matters of importance, in such a case why shou'd not we assert our Liberty, and not suffer every Trifler to impose a Yoke of Impertinent Customs on us?"[45] The wonderful reversal—singularity should be avoided except in matters of importance—protests a culture in which convention regulates aspiration, especially for women. To break the convention, Astell dignifies the category of the singular. A female scholar might seem singular in the first sense, but she is also singular in the second, a prototype for the future.

Montesquieu (and his translator) can be seen twisting the meaning of the word, now this way, now that, to suit his purposes. His Persians are completely idiosyncratic, and their heretical statements should be discounted on that basis: "And if they sometimes seem to look upon the tenets of our religion as singular, the singularity they discover in them fully shews their ignorance of their connexion with other truths thereof." Is this a sincere conviction on the author's part or a bone tossed to pious and censorious readers? The use of free indirect discourse in the first person rivals Defoe's. The author appears quite sincere in labeling the Persians' difference a sign of their ignorance. At the same time, the text suggests the opposite understanding of singularity. Representative of a sophisticated cosmopolitan outlook, suspended not innocently but strategically between cultures, the Persians offer the cosmopolitan author a screen against direct responsibility for statements detrimental to church and state.[46]

Writing in dangerous times, the translator(s) and editor(s) of the *Turkish Spy* added layer upon layer of editorial commentary to conceal a deism that readers nevertheless detected. Because the original volumes appeared serially between 1678 and 1694, the editor(s) were able to use successive prefaces to respond to the early reception, much of it hostile yet fascinated. The text wraps itself in an elaborate story of transmission, beginning with the fiction of Mahmut himself, the supposed author of the letters, making a hasty escape from his apartment in Paris, presumably after being exposed as a spy for the grand seignior in Turkey. He leaves behind a satchel of letters, which the editor, also a character in the fiction, discovers when he takes up residence in the same apartment. He explains, "I here offer you a Book written by a *Turk* whose Matter is as instructive and delightful, as the Manner of finding it, was strange and surprising. I doubt not, but you would know where 'twas written; and perhaps, whether the Author be living; and whether you might expect a *Romance,* or a *real History.*"[47] We are next introduced to a "Man of Letters," presumably Marana, who left Italy in 1682 and settled in Paris. "Scarce had he been Two Months in *Paris,* when, by changing his Lodging, he discovered, by meer Chance, in a Corner of his Chamber, a great heap of Papers; which seemed more spoil'd by Dust than Time."[48] He is about to discard them when his eye falls on an inscription in Latin: *"Ubi amatur, non laboratur; [aut] si Laboratur, labor amatur."* These lines from Saint Augustine surprise the Italian; he translates them as, "Where Love is, there is no Labour; and if there is Labour, the Labour is loved." Intrigued, he decides to edit the letters. Seeking information from the landlord about the author, he is told that the previous tenant was "a Stranger, who said he was a Native of *Moldavia,* Habited like an *Ecclesiastick,* greatly Studious, of small Stature, of a very course Countenance, but of surprising Goodness of Life."[49] We learn other details about Mahmut, among them that "he had always a Lamp Day and Night burning in his Chamber" and that "this Strangers greatest Friend, and whom he saw often, was a Man which most People took for a *Saint*, some for a *Jew*, and others suspected to be a Turk."⁵⁰ This friend returns in Defoe's *Continuation*, as we will see, even though the landlord in the original volume "thinks he died miserably; it being suspected, that he had been thrown into the River."

The fictional frames multiply. Although Marana himself promised additional volumes and claimed they were ready for the press in 1684, they did not materialize. The editor of the English *Letters Writ by a Turkish Spy* therefore concocts a story of international intrigue to explain the discovery and translation of additional letters. "*Three years have now elaps'd, since the* First Volume *of* Letters, *written by a Spy at* Paris, *was publish'd in* English. *And, it was expected, that a* Second *should have come out long before this. The favourable Reception which that found amongst all Sorts of Readers, would have encouraged a speedy* Translation *of the Rest, had there been extant any* French Edition, *of more than the* First Part."⁵¹ The editor of *Letters Writ by a Turkish Spy* explains that after "strictest Enquiry" the French and Italian originals could not be discovered, so that "*it was a Work despaired of, to recover any more of this* Arabian's Memoirs." The editor appoints an agent, Mr. Saltmarsh, first name, Daniel, who goes to Italy in search of the long-lost continuation of the *Turkish Spy*. Is the name Daniel Saltmarsh a clue as to the original author, or one of the original authors, of *Letters Writ by a Turkish Spy?* The bookseller John Dunton (1659–1733) employed a mathematician named Richard Sault and credits this Sault with being the author of the English *Turkish Spy*. Novak repeats this possibility in his biography of Defoe, writing, "John Dunton maintained that his brother-in-law, Richard Sault, wrote [the 542 letters of volumes 2–8] in a matter of days. Certainly, there was not much of a trick to it."⁵² This attribution, like everything else about *Turkish Spy*, is disputed. There was another Saltmarsh who might have provided the anonymous translator(s) with a *nom de guerre:* John Saltmarsh (ca. 1612–47), whom William Penn described as "forerunning Friends appearance" and Douglas Gwyn calls "the most impressive figure from the radical scene of the 1640s."⁵³ Did the unknown translator of Marana attribute the discovery of the manuscript to a new religious radical, not John but Daniel? This Daniel Saltmarsh travels to Italy in search of the missing volumes of Marana, and it turns out that the Florentines, were "busie in Printing, and so successful in Selling the continued Translation of these Arabian Epistles." Daniel, "an English Gentleman," discovers the lost volumes in the home of "that Eminent and Learned *Physician, Julio de* Medicis, of the *House* of Florence," whose immense library "of no less than

Six Thousand choice *Treatises*" yields the much sought continuation of Marana's *Turkish Spy:* "I chanced to open the *Italian Translation* of the *Turkish Spy,* which was so celebrated all over *Europe,* and which I had read both in *French* and *English* . . . I found it to agree exactly with those Translations I had seen: which made me ask this *Gentleman,* Whether there were no more *Volumes* of it printed. He presently shewed me *Six* more, and told me, the *Eighth* was in the Press."[54] Daniel's host generously gives him these Italian volumes, which he carries "through *Germany* into *Holland,* where I kept them as a Secret Treasure; being desirous, if possible, that the *Six Volumes* which are not yet *Translated* out of *Italian,* might first speak my Native Tongue, that so we may not always be obliged to the *French* for the most acceptable Products of the Press." Saltmarsh offers the manuscript to the editor, asking that he locate a single translator. "I will willingly venture a Share of the Cost, but I would have no more than a Third Person concern'd in it. . . . We have the Opportunity of obliging the Nation, with a Work so long expected, and so much desired by all that have seen the *First Volume.*"[55]

The apologetic prefaces suggest that early readers detected the same secret chain we saw in Montesquieu—they complained of the work's deism. By the eighth and final volume, the editor drops all pretense. The volume begins:

> TO THE READER . . . There remains nothing now, but to answer a few Objections, which may be made against the Contents of some *Letters* in all these *Volumes,* and particularly in the Two Last. . . . Some People . . . find Fault with our *Arabian,* for the seeming Lewdness of his Sentiments, and the profane Expressions of *God* and his *Works;* saying, That he writes more like a *Disciple* of *Carneades* and *Epicurus,* than of *Mahomet.* . . . They add, That in some of his *Letters* he seems to Banter all *Religion;* whilst in others, he appears like a *Hypocrite,* extravagantly Devout and Zealous, even to the Height of *Enthusiasm* and *Divine* Madness.[56]

Where you might expect a cautious editor to reject the criticism and certify the text in Christian terms, this one does neither:

> In Answer to this; 'Tis desir'd, That these Gentlemen will please to consider, that our *Author,* tho' a profess'd *Mahometan,* yet is a Man endu'd with Sense and Reason, which he had much improv'd by Reading and *Histories,* by the Studies of *Natural, Moral,* and

Political Things, and by his own Experimental Observations in the World. That therefore, when he seems to descant with an unwarrantable Libertinism, profanely Glancing with a *Religious* Kind of wantonness on *Divine* Matters; it ought not to be taken so much for his own proper diect Thoughts, as the result of other Mens Errors, and the Epidemical *Mistakes* and *Superstitions which have infected the World*. . . . In a Word, he appears, in all his Letters, a *Deist* rather than an *Atheist;* as some would represent him. And it is well enough known, to those who Travel in *Turkey,* and Converse with Men of Sense there, that there are Abundance of *Deists* among the *Mahometans,* as well as among us *Christians:* And our *Arabian* demonstrates, that he is one of these.[57]

Of course Mahmut is a deist, the editor explains. He is a learned cosmopolitan. It would violate the editor's charge to alter Mahmut's discourse one iota. Blame the genre you are reading and your own fascination with Mahmut's singular character, not the author or editor.

These bold maneuvers help explain why the *Turkish Spy* became both a publishing sensation and a religious scandal by the end of the seventeenth century. The mere mention of the title evoked anger toward an emerging public deism. "Let me be free with you," John Edwards warns his Socinian antagonist in *The Socinian Creed,* "and tell you that it is the sense of your Friends that, if your Pen runs for the future in this strain, you will write rather like a *Turkish Spy* than a *Christian Preacher.* I beseech you therefore, Sir, by all that is good and sacred, and by that Repute which you have heretofore gain'd among the Religious and Pious, that you would not dissemble with your self, and choak your inward Perswasions, and abuse your self and the world too."[58]

Defoe preferred spy to preacher. He seized on the previous editor's deistical defense of the spy novel and expanded it into a justification that applies to many of his later fictions:

> It was objected, I know, to the former Volumes of this Work, that the *Turk* was brought in too much debasing the Christian Religion, extolling *Mahomet,* and speaking disrespectfully of Jesus Christ, calling him the *Nazaren,* and the Son of *Mary,* and it is certain the Continuation must fall into the same Method; but either *Mahmut* must be a *Turk* or no *Turk,* either he must speak his own Language or other Peoples Language, and how must we represent Words spoken by

him in the first Person of invincible *Mahmut* the *Arabian,* if we must not give his own Language; and how can this Work be a Translation, if we must not translate the very Stile of the Original?[59]

Echoing the previous editor, Defoe acknowledges the heterodox content of his *Continuation* but pleads the translator's freedom to offer the reading public Mahmut's own words with as much fidelity as possible. His vocation as mere editor of a translated text requires accurate transmission, even if what is transmitted strikes some censorious readers as heretical. Although our author is lying through his teeth—although he is not translating anything originally written in Arabic or Italian—he does clear space for the cosmopolitan novel. So what if Mahmut follows the deist John Toland in calling all Christians "Nazarenes," followers of a human sage from Nazareth?[60] What if Mahmut passes harsh judgment on the rites and rituals not only of Catholicism but of all Christianity? The translator, like the editor, shall not censor or alter the original, unless the original really does cross the line into outright atheism, as some of Mahmut's letters apparently do. Defoe teasingly offers "this caution to the Reader, that when he reads those [irreligious] Parts, he is desired to take them as the Words of the *Arabian,* not the Words of the Translator. . . . If any thing may be said to be left out of the Original, it can only be such Places where *Mahmut* may have taken more Liberties than might be proper for the Repetition of Christian Readers." He continues,

> It is true, the Translator has some Letters on these Subjects which he has not thought fit to make publick, because of the nice Palates of a censorious Age, who will take all Advantages to insult the Publication of such a Stile, while yet they concern not themselves to hear the Deity of our blessed Lord insulted every Day in publick, by those who call themselves Believers, and even the Being of a God denied by a much worse Infidelity than that of a *Mahometan.*
> It is an Observation not unworthy the Remark of our *Arabian* . . . that the practical Atheism, so rife in the World in this Age, is a Sin engrossed among Christians; that the *Mahometans* know nothing of it.[61]

The role of translator relieves the anonymous author from responsibility for what his angry Arab says about the West. Defoe will adopt the same pose in the preface to *Moll Flanders* (1721/22) and in the preface to *The Fortunate Mistress* (1724), also known as *Roxana.* It is interesting in this context that Roxana's identity remains concealed until late in the narrative, when she foolishly performs a Turkish dance she learned in Paris. Was Defoe alluding to the mask he adopted earlier in his career, learning to dance (i.e., write novels) by imitating the Turkish Spy at Paris?

Defoe's defense of the translator's freedom does not stop there. In terms again suggestive of his later defenses of his novels, Defoe explains why translating Mahmut's Arabic into English provides the writer with an impossible yet irresistible challenge:

> If it were possible to give the Reader (in the Translation) the same Ideas he would conceive, were he to read the Original; could I translate, or indeed could our Language express the Story with the same Vivacity, the same Spirit, and the same Energy of Words as the old exquisitely qualified *Arabian* delivered it, how much superior would it be to what it now appears; with what Pleasure, with what Raptures and Extasies must it be received?
>
> But 'tis not to be done: I may translate the Words, and I have some Hopes the Reader will suggest that I have done my Duty; but to render the sublime Flights of the incomparable *Mahmut*, his bright Ideas, his surprising Turns of Wit, and Flights of Fancy; I say to render these exactly in our Language, is as difficult as 'tis for a Painter to represent the Passions, or a Carver to make his Figures speak.[62]

The reference to other arts suggests Defoe's awareness of the conditions of his own inchoate art. This art values the expressions of a singular character—a Muslim man of letters with inclinations toward mysticism. Even in prose his effusions contain a sublimity that the translator can only hope to approximate. A perfect translation of Mahmut's original Arabic being impossible, the translator adopts "the best Rule in all Tongues, (*viz*) to make the Language plain, artless, and honest, suitable to the Story, and in a Stile easie and free, with as few exotick Phrases and obsolete Words as possible, that the meanest Reader may meet with no Difficulty in the Reading, and may have no Obstruction to his searching the History of things by their being obscurely represented."[63] Notice that Defoe's defense of realism takes place in the context of the desire to represent the sublime. Realism itself, historical veracity, accuracy of representation in a Lockean sense, is an afterthought. Defoe echoes and embellishes ideas found in the original volume of Marana's *Turkish Spy:* "And if the Translation be not Eloquent as the *Arabick*, do not accuse the Author, seeing it is not possible to reach the Force and Beauty of the Original."[64] The goal is not realism at first. The goal appears to be making the sublime seem natural in prose, thus lowering the sublime to human scale. After all, the editor, or translator, or whoever he is, is lying. In seven of eight volumes, eight of nine if you count Defoe's, there is no original Marana that he translates. All the sublimity he imagines in the original is there in the translation, and only there. Here we find Defoe defining the sought-after form as a combination of the sublime and history writing, allegory and realism. It is a combination he will perfect in the first part of *Robinson Crusoe.*

Does there exist a secret chain uniting the disparate letters of Defoe's *Continuation?* In addition to a fabricated story of transmission and pseudo-apologies for freethinking, Defoe's *Continuation* introduces deist scenarios buffered from detection by the surrounding fiction. Defoe gives us one of these in the sudden interest Mahmut takes in Quietism and its founder, Miguel de Molinos (1628–96). Letter 4 in book 4 of Defoe's *Continuation* and its 1742 translation as letter 57 of volume 7 of *L'espion turc* enter into a long discussion of the Quietist movement. The letter begins, "Ces Nazeréens sont les plus adonnez à la fiction & aux inventions humaines qu'aucun Peuple que jaye jamais connu";[65]

> These *Nazarens* are the most addicted to Fiction and Forgery of any People I ever met with; it is a received Custom among them, that whenever they have to do with any Sect or Opinion of People, differing from their own, the first thing they go about is, to represent them as monstrous and unnatural, either in Person or in Principle, or perhaps in both; dressing them up in ridiculous Shapes, and imposing a Thousand Stories about them upon the Credulity and Ignorance of the Vulgar, that they may entertain immoveable Prejudices and Aversions against the Persons and Principles they profess.
>
> It would amaze thee, illustrious Prince of Wisdom, to hear what absurd romantick Tales, what imaginary Histories, and what innumerable forged Stories, they tell of our sublime Prophet *Mahomet.*[66]

Mahmut uses the word Nazarens to refer to all of Christian Europe and England. He lodges Edward Said's later complaint against Western cultural imperialism—a bunch of forged stories, fake histories, and sentimental tales—masking violent appropriation. "What fabulous Miracles they muster up to be pretended by him [Mahomet]; how he used Sorcery and Witchcraft, and feigned the Inspiration of the Spirit of God by the help of a Pidgeon; how his

Tomb, in which is his Coffin, hangs suspended in the Air between Heaven and Earth; and what strange Inspirations and Agitations he was represented by to his Followers; all which the true Musselmans disown, and take no Notice of."[67] Defoe puts this complaint in the mouth of a Muslim man of letters, a spy on the West. "It would not be as surprising," observes Beyazit H. Akman, "if we were reading these lines in a work written by a real Turkish spy. However, it is Defoe himself who seems well aware of orientalist depictions of the East and is consciously writing against these conceptions. Casting aside national and xenophobic tendencies and distancing himself from related political interests (the essence of many previous and contemporary travelogues about the Middle East), Defoe seems able to observe events in a more objective and disinterested manner, an unusual characteristic in the popularized canon of the era."[68] An unusual characteristic, perhaps, but also a characteristic that unites *Robinson Crusoe*, *Moll Flanders*, and *Roxana*.

Apropos of nothing, the same letter transitions to a detailed explanation of the Quietist movement and what happened to Molinos in France. "There is another Example of their Injustice in the Story of Father *Molinos*, a Dervice of great Fame among them, and who they call the Quietist; because he placed the sum of Religion in the secret Contemplations of the great One God, and declared against the Pageantry of Worship with which the *Nazarens* abound."[69] Explaining how Molinos ran afoul of the Inquisition, leading to his death in prison, Defoe again exorcises his own ghosts: "This Book he wrote [*The Spiritual Guide*] argues very strenuously against *Pennances, Mortifications, Visions, Extasies, vocal Prayers*, the Abuses of Confession, and the Insipidness of Catholick Sermons and Books; and, in a Word, against all their ecclesiastick Frippery, by which they carry on the Cheat of their Religion at *Rome* among the People, and from whence they spread the Fraud over the World."[70] These protests are deniable in multiple ways: as pertinent only to the French Catholic scene; as delivered by an irate Arab; and as tending toward a completely internalized, spiritualized Christianity void of institutional or doctrinal form.[71] Yet Defoe counts on some of his readers to discover the analogue to England. Quietism was to French Catholicism what Quakerism was to the English Protestant Reformation, and both were linked to deism. There existed "a natural affinity between Quietism and the deistic movement."[72] Both grant women a prominent place in a spiritualized theism unmoored from specific tradition and ritual. Both were violently opposed by church authorities in England and on the Continent. Both, indeed, were given derogatory names and rose above these brandings. The enemies of the Society of Friends devised the word "Quaker" in mockery.[73] After Molinos circulated a Prayer of Quietude, his enemies labeled his movement "Quietism," and the name stuck. Just as Charles Leslie feared and attacked Unitarians and Quakers as virtual deists, so Defoe champions the contrary position under cover of a literary Orientalism that sees Jews, Quakers, Anabaptists, Huguenots, and Quietists as natural allies.[74] And just as Leslie and Sacheverell fomented violence against the dissenters, so the Turkish spy reports violence perpetrated against Molinos, whose final catastrophe went this way:

> In a word, if ever the Popes and popish Tribe were like to turn Hugonots, now was the Time; but the Jesuits, who were too cunning not to see the Danger, and to ward off the Blow, finding the new Doctrine of *Molinos* get Ground, and that all People forsook the *Confessionals,* thought it Time to lay about them; and therefore taking the Alarm, in behalf of Religion, they first branded *Molinos* for a Heretick, and accused him for denying the Trinity, so they call their Doctrine of the three Persons or as we call it, of three Gods, maliciously inferring that his Maxims tended to the destroying of the Humanity of their Prophet Jesus. . . . These Accusations, and some others, made such a Noise, that the Inquisition took Cognizance of 'em; but the Office for that Time found nothing blame-worthy in *Molinos,* or in his Doctrine. . . . This put the Jesuits almost out of their Wits; so that they caused a Report to be whisper'd about, that the Bishop being a *Spaniard,* he might as well be of the Race of the *Jews;* but this did not hinder the Number of the *Quietists* from increasing every Day. . . . However . . . the Cardinal *de Estrees* . . . betrayed him, and from his greatest Friend, became his Accuser and Enemy, and left not till he got him into the Prisons of the Inquisition, where he ended his Days.[75]

Why this excursion into Molinos and the Quietists? Was it only to defend the French Huguenots and attack Catholicism? Defoe once again conceals a direct attack on Leslie and the Anglican establishment through a defense of Molinos and the Quietists. It is a replay of the strategy he employed in his Quaker writings (see chapter 1). This helps to explain why Defoe embraced the *Turkish Spy,* despite its reputation as a vehicle of literary deism. Nor does Defoe's Mahmut take a back seat to the original hero when it comes to mocking religious hypocrisy. Mahmut calls the Christians he observes "the greatest Hypocrites in the World; Religion is made a mere Guise of Deceit, and the outside they put on to appear Devout."[76] He notes the warfare among Christians from a detached perspective and wonders what could possibly justify such carnage: "The Animosity among these *Nazareens* is so great, and they pursue one another with such implacable Fury, that it looks as if they were firmly resolv'd never to have peace with one another any more; but were to root those they quarrel with from the face of the Earth."[77] From his outsider's perspective, all that is good about Christianity relates to the original example of Jesus Christ, but Mahmut cannot see any connection between the "original institution" and the rites and rituals he observes in Paris: "These *Nazareens* are the most detestable of all pretenders to Religion in the World; for at the same time that they call themselves the Disciples of their Prophet *Jesus,* they have brought into their forms of Worship, so many Innovations, and Traditional Corruptions, which himself never directed, that their Religion has now very little of the first Institution in it. . . . [They] have corrupted their Religion to that degree, that it is now one of the greatest pieces of confusion and Buffoonry on Earth."[78]

As these rhetorical extremes suggest, one way Defoe could mask the implicit deism of his model was to sacrifice the authority of his hero. Defoe takes a page from his *Shortest Way* playbook: he exaggerates his protagonist's hostility and degrades his character in the process. In Defoe's hands, Mahmut becomes a Charles Leslie of the East, hostile to all faith systems except his own, crude in his frequent anti-Semitism, dictatorial in his advice to younger relatives. Like the Lucianic voyage, whose upward engine was meant to sputter, heroes in the cosmopolitan tradition often devolve rather than evolve, alienating the reader more and more as the narrative progresses. Defoe gives us a pure instance of this damaged character in *The Shortest Way with the Dissenters,* where he offers a too attractive glimpse into the mind-set of a learned, articulate fanatic. But notice how the pattern persists: as a character, the Robinson Crusoe of *Farther Adventures* is an embarrassment compared with the Crusoe of *The Life and Strange Surprizing Adventures.* He degenerates into a clichéd colonialist, religious fanatic, and racist responsible for the death of his best friend, Friday. By the same token, only a credulous and charitable reading of *Moll Flanders* would find that the titular character improves over time, her last-minute confession and reprieve being a *deus ex machina* if ever there was one. Readers of *Roxana* watch her character corrode to the point of seeming to acquiesce in her maid's silencing of her own daughter. This is a pattern of characterization in Defoe's fictions that scholars have not explained, but the explanation can be found in the cosmopolitan fictions he wrote before *Robinson Crusoe.*

Why spy? Arthur Weitzman's conclusion about the *Turkish Spy* series in general holds for Defoe's participation in it:

Mahmut's defence of his own religious beliefs is a knife that cuts two ways. On the one hand, it boldly rips the fabric of Christian self-righteousness by having a foreigner hold up a mirror to its hypocrisy and inconsistencies; while on the other hand, it subtly cuts the inner lining of all dogmatic and absolute opinions. In doing so, Marana and his successors in this genre attempted to destroy the whole cloth of dogmatic religion and preconceived beliefs and substitute skepticism and relativism in their place. . . . [I]t may be said to be in the central tradition of the eighteenth-century deists and *philosophes*, who also believed that they were bringing enlightenment to Europe by their direct attacks on Christian orthodoxy.[79]

The fictional spy novel provided cover for a subversive cosmopolitan deism. Just as Defoe borrowed a deist's narrative device, adopted Quaker personas, and launched a lunar voyage, so the same set of motives led him to continue an epistolary spy novel—all forms carrying known deist associations by the time Defoe chose them. Yet the absence of deism from our received histories of the novel, coupled with Defoe's strident denunciations of deists and libertine freethinkers, makes these easy to overlook. We accept the harsh criticism Defoe levels at known deists as his final word on the matter and ignore his proximity to the literary practices of these same deists. We minimize statements of an impending deist threat, assigning them to alarmist zealots who seek to foment a crisis where none exists. Indiscriminate mudslinging comes to mind whenever we hear charges of deism leveled. Yet it is best to heed these dire warnings, which are frequent and detailed. "There seems to be a conspiracy in much of the *English* Nation," writes Joseph Jacob in 1703, "to fabricate a *Christian Religion* if they can without a *Christ*: Not only are *Deists* prodigiously multiply'd, who are infinitely *worse than Mahometans;* and *Socinians,* which are a sort of baptiz'd *Mahometans,* do no less as a *Curse* increase and multiply, but also, if you search the *Sermons* and *Writings* of the *Clergy,* you shall often find *Nomen Christi non est ibi.*"[80] Observations like this recur throughout the period. "Is it not more than Time," asks Benjamin Atkinson in 1730, "for Christians, especially Protestants, to lay aside their lesser Differences, and join together against Deism, which is breaking in upon us like a Flood?"[81] We do not need to agree with an author who claims that fully a third of the population of London were deists by 1752 to see that there was plenty of cause for alarm:

'Tis too visible that a spirit of infidelity, under various disguises, has gone abroad into the world, attacking the foundations of *Christianity* with a rude effrontery, and in all appearance with too great success, for I have reason to believe, that a third part, if not more, of all this great metropolis, above the common level, are infected either with deism, arianism, or the impieties of *Socinus;* and as for the mob, they are so sunk in sensuality, and so totally lost in vice and ignorance, that they are as void of understanding, have as imperfect notions of the great ends of their being, and have as little concern about an eternal Hereafter, as the beasts that perish.[82]

Defoe, a highly astute cultural observer, was well aware of this context when he chose to imitate cosmopolitan genres with a reputation for feeding popular deism. Why he made this decision is a matter of speculation. No one argues that Defoe was sincerely a deist. This would make him a liar a hundred times over in his pious declarations and homiletic works. Why, then, did he risk association with the deists by virtue of the way he wrote? Perhaps the explanation is political: all we observe here is predictable Tory and High Church name-calling. Defoe was no true deist; his Puritan, republican, Williamite, and then Hanoverian-Whig ideology exposed him to such accusations by Tories and High Church zealots who saw every threat to the Anglican establishment as part of a deist conspiracy. It is possible, in other words, to write the deist question off as a side issue and assign motivation purely to party ideology. Another excuse might be that Defoe was perfectly aware of the bad reputation of the genres he imitated before *Robinson Crusoe* but sought to turn these forms back against their proponents. However, that is not what he did when he appropriated Blount's *King William and Queen Mary Conquerors* and turned it against Leslie and the High Church. That is also not what he did, according to his enemies, when he launched his feathery craft in imitation of Lucian and his humanist successors. In *A Continuation of Letters Written by a Turkish Spy at Paris,* the same pattern persists.

Aesthetic Problems in the *Turkish Spy*

Defoe's spy novel failed for several reasons. First of all, another artist, Montesquieu, transformed Marana's premise into an original fiction, the *Lettres persanes*, a work immediately translated into English and enduringly popular ever since. Defoe's *Continuation* is weak by comparison. In addition, Defoe's model, the English *Letters Writ by a Turkish Spy,* remained popular through the end of the eighteenth century. An enterprising publisher claims a 26th edition in 1770—surely an exaggeration, but indicative of the lifespan of the first Turkish letters, in contrast to Defoe's one edition wonder. Bad timing and better art by others plagued Defoe, but internal problems also doomed his experiment. We have already seen one of them. The main character is an inconsistent assembly, who only occasionally attracts the reader's sympathy. The title page reveals another problem (see fig. 5). Repeating the formula of the original, Defoe's *Continuation* promises an impartial account, court intrigues, state secrets, and a political chronicle spanning the revolutionary years 1687–93 (the original eight-volume *Turkish Spy* covered the years 1637–82). The frontispiece, with its image of a world-weary Mahmut seated at his writing desk, also promises the history of a Turkish spy named Mahmut, who lived incognito for forty-five years, impersonating a Moravian priest in the Paris of Louis XIII and Louis XIV. It was an ambitious chronicle, to be sure, and one conveyed entirely by letters, each adopting a style appropriate to its correspondent—whether military, ecclesiastic, political, or personal. As a whole, the collection is diffuse, uneven, scattershot in topic, and loose in chronology. The work is so amorphous that scholars cannot decide what to call it. They refer to the *Turkish Spy* variously as a "philosophic voyage," a "chronicle," an "extended soap opera," a "serial docu-drama," "travel diaries," and a "spy novel," the first of its kind.[83] This heterogeneous quality presented challenges to the continuer. In effect, Defoe tried to bring narrative coherence to a miscellany of letters. His solutions, although unsuccessful in the final analysis, provide insight into the formation of the novel during the first decades of the eighteenth century.

The first problem was the resuscitation of Mahmut himself, along with his close friend, the Jewish Nathan, both left for dead by the previous editor. In the last letter of *Letters Writ by a Turkish Spy,* Mahmut writes to his friend Dgnet Oglou:

> To tell thee in short, *Nathan Ben Saddi,* the *Sultan's* Agent *Incognito* at *Vienna,* a *Jew* by Descent and Religion, is, I fear, privately murder'd by some Order from the *Divan.* But, for what Reasons I know not, unless it were in Complyance with the Old Maxims of the *Sublime Port,* which seldom suffer any *Slave* to go to his *Sepulchre* in Peace, who has serv'd the *Grand Signior* many Years in any eminent Station. He has been miss'd at *Vienna* these Eight Weeks, and within a Day or two after his First Absence, the Body of a Dead Man was found floating on the *Danube,* but so disfigur'd with Wounds, as it could not possibly be known who he was; which gives me the greater Suspicion that it was he. And if so, I may expect to be serv'd so my self in a little Time. For my Turn is next.[84]

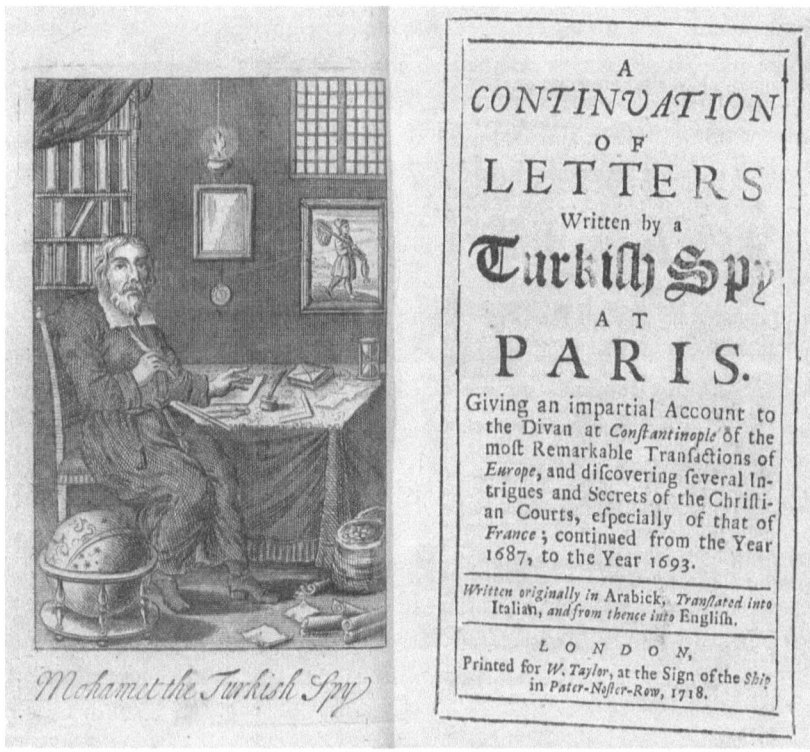

Figure 5. Title page and frontispiece, Mahmut at his desk. From Defoe, *A Continuation of Letters Written by a Turkish Spy at Paris*, 1718 (Courtesy of Harvard University, Houghton Library)

For unstated reasons, Mahmut assumes his fate and that of the Jew are connected and begs his friend, "If thou hast any Love or Friendship for me, be watchful on my Behalf: Attend the Whispers of the Court, and observe the Language of those who discourse with their Fingers Ends."[85]

Here the *Letters Writ* ends and Defoe's *Letters Written* begins. In the iconic image that accompanied the previous editions, Mahmut was old. Defoe made him even older: "It is true, our *Arabian* grows ancient, and we find him casting his Thoughts upon the Pleasures of their *Mahometan* Futurity; but as Christians should, when they grow nearer a future State, have their minds ting'd with the Glories they expect; so we find his Understanding so far from a Decay by his Years, that he speaks of religious things with so much the more Relish and Taste, as if he realiz'd on Earth the Heaven he expected."[86] Mahmut's old age presents yet a third layer of otherness—he is a spy, he is Muslim, and he is ancient. While the Mahmut of the original eight volumes asks repeatedly to be relieved of his post, Defoe's Mahmut has grown desperate, begging to return to his homeland, after "having been forty and eight Years, as one buried alive, among Infidels, and Strangers . . . that I may not die among Dogs, and be blended in Earth with Infidels, and Enemies of *Mahomet*."[87] Mahmut's imminent end accelerates and unites the thinly spun plot of the miscellany: no more love fantasies; no more elaborate efforts not to be seen naked in the public bath (suggesting circumcision)—just a desperate desire to return home and exasperation at all the hypocrisy he sees around him.

News that Mahmut will be relieved of his post as spy for the grand seignior inspires raptures, soon extinguished. I quote the first-person narrative in full because it exhibits the pace, energy, conviction, and odd hovering between realism and allegory that characterizes the prose rhythms of *Robinson Crusoe*. At the climax of Defoe's spy novel, the hero suffers a terrible reversal:

> Judge you, my Friend, how surprizing all these good Tidings were to a Soul ready almost to fly out of its Prison at the first Account of it, and who had lived eleven Moons in the most perfect State of Satisfaction that it was possible for me to represent to my self in the World. . . .
>
> Nay, as if Fate intended to sport with my Misfortunes, and I was still to be made more miserable than any Man was before me, I was still lifted up higher, to add to the Weight of my Fall, and to dash me utterly to pieces by the Force of it. In a Word, my Deliverer arriv'd, and I receiv'd a Letter from him, dated at *Marseilles*, where he landed, assuring me that he lost no Time to come forward, and promised himself a singular Pleasure in dismissing me, and setting me at full Liberty for my Return.
>
> Is it possible all this could be an *Ignis fatuus*, to ensnare my Mind, and plunge me in the deepest Despair; was there anything now but the single Hazard of Mortality between me and my Deliverance? who would not have looked upon himself as a Freeman, and have begun to truss up his Baggage to depart?
>
> But see the Product of surprizing Decrees, the next Letter I received was from *Chalons*, where my dear Friend was taken sick, and sent an Express, a faithful Messenger, to desire me to come to him thither, for that he was dangerously ill.
>
> It was with a Surprize of Grief, that I received this Account, and immediately I posted to *Chalons;* but it was with an inexpressible

Sorrow, that when I came to him he had but just Life left in him enough to know me, and being not able to speak, expired in my Arms.

Thus all my Comforts are blasted at once, and the hopes I had entertained of being set free from the disconsolate Circumstances I am in, are entirely cut off.[88]

The exile's condition intensifies the miscellany and lends it moments of spiritual grandeur. A harmonizing of realism and the sublime occurs. As in *Robinson Crusoe*, the words seem to be simultaneously spoken in the present and thought in the future looking back. Anguish prompts religious questioning, an outpouring that captures the narrator's theological struggle with words and phrases poised between religious and secular meanings. Deliverance means both Mahmut's return to Turkey and his spiritual homecoming. "Surprizing Decrees" expresses either Mahmut's Job-like persistence in his faith or a mocking reference to blind chance. "All my Comforts" echoes Old and New Testament sources but also sounds a note of despair and resignation, an angry protest against divine caprice.[89] This style of elevated everydayness is infrequent in Defoe's lunar voyage and everywhere present in *Robinson Crusoe*. We hear it again in the preparations Mahmut makes for his friend's burial. Duty will not permit Mahmut to accompany the body back to Mecca, so he does the following:

It was with great Secrecy that I caused his Body to be washed with clean Water, and having hired a Carriage, which they call here a Hearse, I embalmed the Corps, and caused it to be put into a Coffin of Lead, and went away with it as travelling for *Paris*.

When I came upon the Road to a Place where the Ways parted, sloaping one towards the Right, and one towards the Left, I discharged the Hearse and its Attendance, having told them, that another Hearse was to meet me there, and so setting the Coffin upon the Ground, they went their Way. Here, with a just Solemnity of Tears, I buried my deceased Friend, laying the Coffin on one Side with his Face towards the sacred Repository at *Mecca*, that he may wake again with his Eyes directly against the golden Gate at the Entrance into Paradise.

And now I am a disconsolate Mourner indeed.[90]

In contrast to religious writing that refers to and depends on the miraculous, here we have a narrative premised on faith but moored in human psychology and directly perceived reality. The language hovers between the allegorical mode—where words such as "Road" and "Place," "Right" and "Left," and phrases such as "the Ways parted" shimmer with a second meaning—and the realist mode, where the same words and phrases refer to a particular time and place and an individuated character caught up in trying circumstances. Mahmut's confession of mixed motives is human and personal. He is sad about the death of his friend but also heartbroken that the death delays his return to Turkey. "Condole with me, my Friend *Hassan*," he writes, "and deliver the Letter here inclosed to the *Reis Effendi*, that I may obtain another Successor, and may not die here among *Mahomet's* Enemies, and my Dust be blended with that of Infidels, Enemies to *Mahomet*, Blasphemers and Idolaters."[91]

What is the literary source of this humble sublimity of expression? As I mentioned, Defoe did more than revive Mahmut. He also brought his Jewish friend Nathan back from the dead on the chance that the body left floating in the Danube at the end *Letters Writ* was not in fact his. Nathan returns to provide Mahmut with a valuable gift: the secret for surviving a life of perpetual geographic and spiritual exile:

> It is the Sum of humane Misery to have no Body to communicate our Joys and Griefs with: the Heart is not able to contain its own Excesses, but they will break out; and if we have not a Friend to unburthen the Soul to, it will discover its Burthen in every Line of the Countenance.
>
> Old *Nathan* the *Jew* furnish'd me with an Equivalence for this Violence of the Mind, which was a kind of a Charm, repeating a certain Number of Words in (a Corruption of) the *Syriac* Tongue, and then to tell my whole Story with my Face towards the Sun, as if I were talking to a particular Friend.[92]

It is possible to hear, as others have, anticipations of *Robinson Crusoe* in this passage. Novak builds an article on the phrase "the Sum of Human Misery," arguing that Mahmut's predicament doubles Crusoe's so that here we find the thematic seed for the story of the twenty-eight-year castaway.[93] I am more interested in the author's reference to "a Charm" and what it means for a Jewish character left for dead in the previous installment to supply it. Charms are formal. They usually contain ritual language repeated verbatim, as this one does. Charms also charm—they please and seduce and divert. Mahmut may not even understand the "certain Number of Words in (a Corruption of) the *Syriac* Tongue" Nathan advises him to repeat. Nevertheless, the words have a salutary effect. They offer an equivalency, meaning, in this context, a substitute for rage and depression. This might be interpreted in a therapeutic sense: just tell your story as if to a friend, and you will discover a substitute satisfaction for the pain of exile. I suspect a different meaning of equivalency, however, again more in keeping with the overarching deist context of cosmopolitan fiction. Thomas Stanley's *The History of Philosophy* (1701) treats "Equivalence" as one of "The Phrases of the Skeptics" and explains what equivalency means and how it works: "This Phrase, *Not more this than that,* declareth likewise our affection, by which we are brought by reason of the equivalence of contrary things, to *aporia.*"[94] In Sextus Empiricus, "Equivalence" is one of the commonplaces of philosophical skepticism understood not in the sense of marking a fixed correspondence between two things but, rather, in the sense of holding contradictory ideas in suspension—a dialogue without dialectics. This understanding of "Equivalence" casts the Jew's advice in a different light. It recommends a philosophical outlook, not an emotional outpouring.

The oddity of an Arab crediting a Jew with such saving wisdom invites a search for other philo-Semitic moments in this cosmopolitan text. Easy to miss because surrounded by an abundance of anti-Semitic rhetoric, Mahmut devotes an extended discussion to the style of the Book of Job. I quote some of this passage here and return to it in chapter 4 when accounting for the genres of *Robinson Crusoe:* "I cannot, Sage Register of humane Knowledge, pass over here the Confession of the *Jews,* and the Testimony they give of the Truth I assert, (*viz.*) that the Wisdom and Knowledge, as well divine as humane, which was entrusted from Heaven with Mankind in those *post diluvian* Ages, as they are called, was committed immediately, and in a more than ordinary Portion, to the *Arabians,* above all the Nations of the World."[95] Mahmut singles out the Book of Job as so well written, so divinely construed, that it must be of Arabic, not Jewish, origin.[96] The anti-Semitic mask permits Mahmut to voice remarkable praise for the *style* of the Book of Job. The language, not the content or allegorical application, is his concern:

> This, I say, the *Jews* acknowledge, in publishing to the World, among the Books which they call Sacred; the Book or Story of *Job* the patient: This Book is not only graced with being written in the most sublime Stile that the *Hebrew* Language was ever written in, and by which it appears that the ancient *Hebrew* was preserved in its highest Purity and Dignity of Expression; but it gives undoubted Testimony to this great Principle, (*viz.*) that God revealed himself from Heaven to the *Arabians,* for by the Confession of all the Geographers in the

World, *Job* and his three Friends were *Arabians:* I say, that God revealed himself from Heaven to the *Arabians*, in the like and perhaps every Way as glorious a Manner, as he did afterwards to the other Posterity of *Abraham*, the *Israelites*.⁹⁷

Through Mahmut, Defoe expresses an aesthetic appreciation for the way Job is written: "No Example like it can ever be produced, thro' the whole History of Time among the *Jews*, even by their own Confession."⁹⁸ The proviso that Job is too good to be of Jewish origin reflects Mahmut's character as a casual anti-Semite. He reminds a Jewish correspondent that when Jamaica was inundated after a massive earthquake, "I am assured that the Jews, for there are a great many Families of the Nation in that Island, I say, the *Jews* in the Extremity of the Terror they were in, upon Occasion of this Earthquake, called upon Jesus the Son of Mary to save them. I have no room to question the Truth of this Fact; because diverse *Jews* here have not only heard of it, but do approve and justifie the Relation."⁹⁹ Mahmut advises another Jewish correspondent, "Be wise then, and cease to adhere to the Oracles of *Moses*, and the Talmudic Systems of thy misguided Rabbies, seeing their Oracles have succeeded by the appointment of God, every one exceeding the other in Purity and Excellence."¹⁰⁰ Sentiments like these crop up throughout the narrative. So one might ask, why does Defoe conspicuously revive Nathan, the Jew, long enough to give Mahmut the charm needed to survive as a narrator of his own woes? And why does Mahmut grudgingly admire the style of Jewish biblical narrative? Perhaps Defoe does not care about consistency in this rambling work. Or perhaps his language seems to him merely descriptive, an instinctive verbal violence akin to Trollope's anti-Semitic language. Or perhaps, Defoe means to disguise the implicit cosmopolitan deism of the text, and with it an implicit philo-Semitism and Islamophilia, by undercutting Mahmut's character.

The cosmopolitan freedom of the letter miscellany allows Defoe room to experiment with voice and narrative and speculation about writing itself. In this sense, the Turkish letters serve as a kind of sketchbook for Defoe's later work. His speculative sketches recur as integrated motifs in Crusoe's journal keeping and cross-notching. And yet, when critics discuss Defoe's *Turkish Spy* at all, they extract from it an anti-deist position. They draw selectively from passages in which Defoe and the original editor are at pains to show Mahmut as no friend of Western freethinking. They stress Mahmut's passive obedience to the grand seignior and his unquestioning faith. Katherine Clark describes the work's "frequent and lengthy attacks on Catholic, Socinian, Deist, and atheist views and practices—religious themes which indicate an even stronger connection to a central message in *Robinson Crusoe,* namely, the triumph of salvation and redemption over natural religion: a theme found in the first volume and defended more explicitly through the doctrine of the Trinity in the two *Crusoe* sequels."[101] Like the "Equivalence" that Nathan recommends as an antidote to exile, Mahmut himself resides in contradiction. He is a mouthpiece for deist commonplaces, except when his bifurcated character cautiously undoes these exposures. He is an odd assemblage of philosophe and mystic, deist and fanatic. We are supposed to care when Mahmut confesses, "I'll tell thee from Experience, that 'tis the most unhappy Part of Life to be without a Friend to unbosome the Secrets of the Soul to. Joy and Grief are in themselves Passions too strong for humane Nature to restrain."[102] Are we also supposed to care when Mahmut chastises his own nephew for abandoning his studies in divinity in terms that recall the verbal lashings of Crusoe's father? "Weak Man," Mahmut scolds, "what art thou doing? Knowest thou that Peace is the Glory of Life, and that a Scene of serene Cogitation, just Action, and the Study of Wisdom, is not only the most suited to the Happiness of an exalted Soul in the Station of Life, but is an Emblem of Paradise; and guides the Soul to the shining Gate of Bliss, where thy Father's Fathers, to a hundred Generations, should have received thee with Musick and Dances; and where all the happy Generations of thy Ancestors, would have rejoyced over thee? Now I esteem thee as lost."[103]

Degrading the mouthpiece of deism was one way to disguise deism. Mahmut becomes a zealot for his cause, and therefore a hypocrite in turn—alert to the errors of all religions save his own. He transforms before our eyes from a trenchant observer of Western hypocrisy into a growling enthusiast who interprets military losses as divine retribution for the Turkish authority's not taking a stronger hand against licentiousness. "I swear to thee by the hoary Scalp of thy Father *Aleb,* and thy Grandfather *Raleb,* belov'd by *Mahomet,* and Favourites of Men . . . if thou punish not severely the guilty Offenders, the Christians, who have already driven thee out of *Peloponesus,* for the Sins of the Mussulmans, shall drive thee also out of *Macedonia;* and thou shalt no longer preside over the Isles of the Arches."[104] Mahmut must take a fall, just as Crusoe does in *Farther Adventures.* Music in church aggravates him. The firing of canons and any form of religious spectacle sets his pen ablaze. Like Crusoe, he imagines himself as a Jonah figure: "One would think the old *Arabian* Prophet *Jonah* had been here [in Paris] on the same Errand that he was sent to *Nineveh.*"[105] A narrator who attacks Catholic infallibility now praises Mirza, "thou Lamp of Truth, and Light of Believers, whose Oracle the Faithful believe with Fear. In thy most pure Explanations of our holy Law, are no doubtful Reserves, among thy

Obedient Hearers, no Schisms or Separations, but all listen with Attention to the Law of thy Lips, speaking Words of Heavenly Solace, and guiding to the Mystical Fields, which surround the Gates of Paradise. Sublime *Mirza!*"[106]

Add to these gyrations Mahmut's use as mere proxy for Defoe's blatant political satire. Letter 3 turns, as the letters often do, to politics. After some diminishment of the Pretender, living under French protection, the narrator pretends astonishment that "the King of *France,* or of the *Francks,* in whose Country I reside, who thou knowest is taken with us for the greatest King among the Nations of the *Messiah;* should at the same time that he profess'd so sincere a Friendship for the *English* King, suffer that so mean and so weak a Person as the Prince of *Orange,* and who had no assistance but that of the *Dutch* to Support him, should invade and attack his Friend and Allie the King of *England.*"[107] Here again we find Defoe failing because he cannot restrain the sheer hostility he feels for his enemies. Authorial anger overwhelms the reader's natural curiosity about Mahmut and his fate in Paris. The events of 1688 and their aftermath must be relitigated not once, but several times. Defoe becomes boring, and it is again clear why his *Continuation* gained little traction with the reading public. Defoe uses and abuses his own hero so that Mahmut becomes inconsistent with himself. Defoe never solves a problem in his source material for which a previous editor was already apologizing in 1694: "it is thought necessary to prefix something more by way of General *Preface,* not so much regarding the Translation, as the seeming Original Abruptness and Obscurity of our *Arabian* Author Himself in some Places, with his frequent Change of Subjects, his Digressions and Startings from Matters of Fact, the then present Wars, Transactions, and Intrigues of *Christian* Courts, States, and Kingdoms (for which he was chiefly sent to *Paris*) and his Immethodical falling upon Philosophical, Divine, and Moral Contemplations, and even to Ancient, Obsolete Histories, which some think were altogether Foreign to his Business."[108] The character of Mahmut offers a rather thin pretext for all manner of business foreign and domestic; he seems more collage than character, now a swarthy Turk enamored of a married Helen of Troy, now a philosopher and divine. The best the editor can say is "give him [Mahmut] leave sometimes to lay aside the Cares and Busie Toils of Life. And wonder not, if he seems in some of his Letters, very Melancholy; in others, of a contrary Humour, chearful and frolicksom: For these Unevennesses of Temper happen to every Man."[109] Given these inconsistencies in style and substance, it is no wonder that Defoe's *Turkish Spy* floundered. Yet as a formal and thematic precursor to *Robinson Crusoe,* the text is inescapable.

The *Hayy Ibn Yaqzān of Ibn Tufayl* and *Robinson Crusoe*

Having established Defoe's interest in one mode of Eastern fiction—the spy novel—it is worth asking whether his interest in Orientalist models extended to other notable texts. Scholars have explored the possible relevance of "The Seven Voyages of Sinbad the Sailor" in *The Arabian Nights Entertainment*. Surely, Defoe was aware of this popular fiction, which was entering a fifth edition in 1718. Perhaps the idea of a protagonist whose very narrative kept death at bay, an object of despotic love and violence, contributed to the conception of *Moll Flanders* and *Roxana;* however, the patterns we see emerging in Defoe's confrontation with Leslie and the High Church make the other famous work of Enlightenment Orientalism far more relevant. This work travels under the heading of "the Hayy," and was known in Defoe's time by several Latin and English titles. The translation to which Defoe would have had easy access is *The Improvement of Human Reason, exhibited in the Hai Ebn Yokdhan: Written in the Arabick above 500 Years Ago, by Abu Jaafar Ebn Tophail* (1708, 1711).[110] Given the thematic parallels between the Hayy's story of an infant washed up on a deserted island and raised by animals and *Robinson Crusoe*'s story of a grown man washed up on a deserted island and raised by nature and his own ingenuity, scholars have sought, but never found, definitive proof that Defoe read this work and wove it into the fabric of *Robinson Crusoe*. Aravamudan identifies thematic connections between the Hayy and *Robinson Crusoe* but concludes tentatively: "From such passages we might infer that if *Crusoe* was influenced by the *Hayy,* it could be partly in the manner of a foil to berate, rather than solely as a model to emulate."[111] Novak suggests borrowings but also disapproval: "Parallels to the life of Crusoe are remarkable. Yokdhan is completely isolated for more than twenty years, dresses in animal skins, and indulges in religious speculations. He even has a 'Vision of the Angelic World' in the manner of Defoe's hero; so that one is led to speculate as to whether or not Defoe knew al-Tufail's work. Yet, so far from being the 'idea' of *Robinson Crusoe,* as one writer has suggested, it is almost the complete reverse."[112] Novak thinks *Robinson Crusoe* is almost the complete reverse of the Hayy because the Arabic story of an infant discovering ethics on his own, without texts or churches, meshes with a deistical take on religion, and Novak does not think *Robinson Crusoe* partakes of a similar literary deism. By contrast, Samar Attar's list of parallels between the Hayy and *Robinson Crusoe* reveals how both works import deist ideas through imaginative fiction:

Ibn Tufayl's and Defoe's works share several characteristic features. Both are about man's ability to survive in a natural state, free of society, history and tradition. Both support the empirical method of science and emphasize the power of human reason. The two works affirm the possibility of man's attaining the true knowledge of God and things necessary to salvation without the help of established religious institutions or formal instruction. Human reason, both works stress, may, by observation and experience, arrive at knowledge of natural things, and from there progress to supernatural and divine matters. Both question traditional doctrines and values, suggest innovations in religious and educational concepts and advocate, to different degrees, religious tolerance, non-violence, and peaceful coexistence among people who adhere to various sects.[113]

These are characteristics of literary deism. Parallels between *Robinson Crusoe* and the Hayy make perfect sense once we restore the deist context to Defoe's literary biography and to the history of the early modern novel.

Why, then, have scholars had such a hard time tracing the direct influence of the Hayy on Defoe's novel? The clues we have followed so far provide a ready answer. By the opening of the eighteenth century, the Hayy had been exposed as an instrument of literary deism and a favorite text of the Quakers. As much as Defoe favored the creation of a fictional experiment in social deprivation, he could not afford to associate himself with a work whose title page announced the sufficiency of human reason, exclusive of revelation: "In which is demonstrated by what Methods one may, by the meer **Light of Nature,** attain the Knowledg of things **Natural** and **Supernatural;** more particularly the Knowledg of GOD, and the Affairs of another Life."[114] Ockley's 1708 translation begins with a message from "The Bookseller to the Reader" advertising what must have been the most enticing aspects of the text:

> *The Design of the Author (who was a Mahometan Philosopher) is to shew how Humane Reason may, by Observation and Experience, arrive at the Knowledge of Natural Things, and from thence to Supernatural; particularly the Knowledge of God and a Future State. And in order to this, he supposes a Person brought up by himself, where he was altogether destitute of any Instruction, but what he could get by his own Observation.*
>
> *He lays the Scene in some Fortunate Island, situate under the Equinoctial; where he supposes this Philosopher, either to have been*

bred... *without either a Father or Mother; or else expos'd in his Infancy, and providentially suckled by a Roe. Not that our Author believ'd any such matter, but only having design'd to contrive a convenient place for his Philosopher, so as to leave him to Reason to himself, and make his Observations without any Guide.*[115]

The Hayy's exoticism concealed an especially pure instance of the deist thought experiment: what *are* human beings by their nature, and in nature? Is natural religion not only possible but proved by the behavior of test cases such as that of a child raised by animals? The Hayy's semi-realistic, semi-conceptual fiction suggests this conclusion: human beings are naturally capable of reason; the inferences they draw first about natural things provide the foundation for social, ethical, and divine knowledge. Edward Pococke's Latin translation of the Arabic original as *Philosophus Autodidactus* (1671) puts the argument in a fictional nutshell. We have a story of the uncertain generation of a child, born either to a princess and set adrift Moses-like or auto-generated from the equatorial ooze—either way stranded on an island and raised by a roe, or goat, or gazelle, who suckled him and kept him warm and safe. The text depicts the child's gradual yet ineluctable growth into rationality and faith conjoined. The fiction similarly unites stark realism, philosophical inquiry, and fable, a good example being the pathetic scene when little Yaqzān, distraught over the death of his "mother," cuts open her chest cavity to restore her to life. He fails, but scientific curiosity takes hold.

The Quakers immediately recognized parallels between the Hayy and their own theology. George Keith, while he was still a Quaker, published an English translation of Pococke's *Philosophus Autodidactus* as *An Account of the Oriental Philosophy* (1674).[116] Robert Barclay's early Quaker work, *Apology for the True Christian Divinity* (1678), points to the Hayy as confirming the Quaker's argument about the primacy of an inward gift, grace, and light: "Yea, there is a book translated out of Arabic, which gives an account of one Hai Eben Yokdan, who, without converse of man, living in an island alone, attained to such profound knowledge of God, as to have immediate converse with him, and to affirm, 'That the best and most certain knowledge of God, is not that which is attained by premises premised, and conclusions deduced, but that which is enjoyed by conjunction of the mind of man with the supreme intellect.'"[117] Here was the Quaker position supported and protected by fiction—deism in allegorical, or counter-allegorical disguise. The problem was, the disguise had slipped. While Ockley's 1708 edition boasts its natural religion on the title page, an Appendix adds this disclaimer: "There are a great many

Errors both in his *Philosophy* and *Divinity:* And it was impossible it should be otherwise, the one being altogether *Aristotelian,* the other *Mahometan*. I shall . . . confine my self chiefly to the Examination of this Fundamental Error of my Author, *viz. That God has given such a Power of Faculty to Man, whereby he may, without any external Means, attain to the Knowledge of all things necessary to Salvation, and even to the Beatifick Vision it self, whilst in this State.*"[118] If Defoe did read some version of the Hayy and find inspiration in its deist thought experiment, there was nothing to be gained by acknowledging the influence of a work known for its deist and Quaker associations.

Here, then, are two modes of Enlightenment Orientalism, one of which we are sure Defoe knew because he imitated it—the novel of the Turkish spy—and the other of which Defoe most likely knew because its stark experiment in minimalism parallels Crusoe's twenty-eight years as a castaway. We also know that readers at the time viewed these two works—the *Hayy Ibn Yaqzân,* and *Letters Writ by a Turkish Spy*—in tandem.

In 1701 an anonymous author published a revealing dialogue between the fictional Mahmut and Androgeo Ben-Jockdon, the protagonist of the Hayy. The narrator dreams a prodigious monster, which he compares to Hobbes's Leviathan. The monster stamps its foot, then disappears,

> but in his room there appeared a vast and most populous City. And here among the Crowd was Little *Mahmut,* the *Turkish Spy,* that had been lost at *Paris,* and never heard of these many Years; and he was got very close talking with an odd kind of Man, that was unlike to all the rest, and was of no Country, and of no Parents, that were known to him; thinking himself to have been Born immediately out of the Earth, therefore he was call'd *Androgeus;* who having been found in *Arabia,* was thence Translated into *Spain,* and there made the Companion of the *Spanish Critick;* as he was now of this Disguis'd *Turk.*[119]

The author writes for an audience that is familiar with two modes of Eastern-inflected cosmopolitan fiction—the *Autodidactus* of Ibn Tufayl and the *Turkish Spy* of Marana. The characters remark on each other's fate, embedded in different expressions of the same cosmopolitan impulse. "*Prithee dear* Androgeo, *where are we now?*" asks Mahmut, as well he might of the superior intellect, the self-taught philosopher and theologian. Androgeo does not know, either: "Why! Truly I am altogether at a loss: I am as much surpriz'd as I was in that Hour, when the Earthquake first clave asunder the Mountain, where I lay Buried Alive, and gave me a view of the Heavens, and Sea, and Earth, and a Thousand Varieties in each of them; or as when I first beheld another Man like to my self, who had thought before, that I was the only Man in the World."[120] Mahmut and Androgeo are confused to find themselves together in someone else's dream. What, then, do they discuss? They discuss the forms, or genres, they find themselves in. *"If you are at a loss,"* says Mahmut to Androgeo, *"I must needs say, I am little better at present; however, I am resolved to serve my Master, and it shall be hard, but that I will find my self, as well as I have done hitherto."* Mahmut's admission resonates on political and literary levels: Mahmut stays in place and never questions the authority that requires outlandish sacrifice of him. He serves his grand seignior most faithfully. The form of which he is a part—the spy novel—may also serve a master, when it becomes a vehicle of easy satire. Androgeo has this critique of the *Turkish Spy* in mind when he answers, "I have no Masters to serve: You may serve yours as you see good. And the Observations I make are for my self, not for another: Since there is none that I care to Please or Displease; being the Slave of (none as you are) and having been Born Free."[121] The basis for Androgeo's confidence is the different kind of story of which he is a part. It partakes of the utopian and scientific side of humanism, stretching from Plato through More to Bacon and into the early modern obsession with philosophical utopias and experiments in deprivation reducing the human organism to its most basic level to reveal the nature of human nature. Androgeo got his knowledge the honest way, he believes—auto-didactically, without help from society or its texts. Yet this isolated purity of enlightened intellect also breeds scorn for others. Mahmut exposes this weakness, simultaneously alluding to the title of Defoe's first great satire, published the same year: *"Why! Then I perceive you can be no other than a* True Born Englishman, *or a* Free Born Englishman; *who will be sure to think meanly, and to speak meanly too, of all the World beside himself."*[122] Mahmut attacks Yaqzān for his arrogant self-sufficiency, likening him to the xenophobic true-born Englishman of Defoe's poem. Nevertheless, Mahmut comes off worse. The genre of the *Turkish Spy* lends itself so easily to political use that it lacks the potential universalism of the Hayy, as the protagonist of the Hayy tells Mahmut directly. After Mahmut sings the praises of "the Glory of his Sovereign Master . . . the Standard of our Prophet to be set up among the Western and Northern Infidels, with their Cross under our Victorious Crescent," Androgeo replies, "Surely you Rave to talk at such an extravagant Rate." Mahmut admits, "I did not know when and how to rave, as well as when and how to be sober, I could never be fit for this Important Service, which the most August Port, has been pleas'd to entrust me with."[123] Then he tries to strike a Faustian bargain with Androgeo:

> Mah. I would reveal my whole Heart to you, and would tell you many notable and secret Transactions, which you may be quite (or almost) a Stranger to; if at least you will promise me to be Assistant to some great Design, which may be no less for your own Advancement, than it is for the Interest of my Master.
> Andr. Let me know what the Design is, and then you shall know my Answer, But *Mahmut* must not forget who I am; and that I shall never contribute to *Enslave* my Self or Another.... But prithee once in thy Life be Open-hearted and Free; and thou shalt see that I shall deal, with as much Openness and Frankness as thou can'st desire. Tell me what great Thing is it thou hast in thy Head?
> Mah. Didst never hear of the Art of Governing by Parties?
> Andr. Yes I have: But tell me, what's that to your present Business?
> Mah. It is a great deal.
> Andr. Is it so, old Foxcraft? Here I defie you: For I am of no Party at all, 'tis impossible for you to Govern me.
> Mah. And I say 'tis impossible for you to be of no Party: And therefore this sort of Governing, will not fail to reach you, as well as all the World beside.[124]

The dialogue breaks off at just this point; yet it neatly summarizes a culture in which the Hayy and Marana's *Turkish Spy* were counterparts. Defoe may have been engaged in a similar internal debate as he scanned the literary horizon for models for his new art of prose fiction. Under conditions of extreme religious and political anger, when every publication of whatever kind was sure to be read through the prism of party politics and ideology, which forms held out hope of an alternative? The question assumes that Defoe sought an alternative, that more than propaganda drove him. The same set of motives that led Defoe to defend the Quakers, that fueled his moon voyage and lodged him with a Turkish spy, also made the Hayy attractive as a model of prose fiction. Of course, direct parallels are difficult to prove—and Defoe had every reason to feign ignorance of such an overtly philosophical text. In some ways a blueprint for the autodidactic structure of Crusoe's survival story, the Hayy was nevertheless too extreme, too obviously a deist thought experiment carried out by fictional means. Having been exposed in his Quaker guise and tied to the deists on the strength of his lunar voyage and Turkish spy, Defoe sought a thicker shield. He therefore moderates the revealing, experimental quality of the Hayy. We still have an experiment in isolation, but in *Robinson Crusoe* it is that of a socialized man with remarkable amnesia toward his past, who is stranded solitary on an island and forced to re-create security and faith not quite from scratch, but close enough.[125] A spiritual quest along recognizable Protestant lines replaces the Hayy's naked plot, following human growth from helpless infant to ethical adult by means of a powerful capacity to gather empirical evidence, make causal connections, and reach accurate conclusions.

Once again, there is no need to argue that Defoe was sincerely a deist to acknowledge the fact that he sometimes wrote like one. This chapter reveals further motives for his doing so. Branded a deist by Charles Leslie and the Anglican establishment, Defoe not only fought back against his critics but left them behind as he explored new genres. He pursued an apprenticeship in long forms of prose fiction that provided opportunities for expanding what I have called the *Shortest Way* mode of ironic first-person narration. In the process, he moved gradually from fictions still closely tied to satire to prose genres that had no precise name. He attempted to unify the miscellany of the *Turkish Spy* and in the process experimented with elements of plot, character, theme, and literary form that contributed to his masterpiece.

4 Defoe's Deist Masterpiece
The Life and Strange Surprizing Adventures of Robinson Crusoe and *The Farther Adventures of Robinson Crusoe*, 1719

> But I desire not to be the Promoter of unanswerable Doubts in Matters of Religion; much less would I promote Cavils at the Foundations of Religion, either as to its Profession or its Practice, and therefore I only name Things.
> —Daniel Defoe, *Serious Reflections*

Robinson Crusoe's First Critics

In 1724, a charismatic Anglican minister named John Checkley (1680–1753) was tried in Boston for publishing excerpts from Charles Leslie's *A Short and Easie Method with the Deists* coupled with his own *A Discourse Concerning Episcopacy*.[1] Here is our history in a nutshell: Defoe got in trouble in London in 1702–1703 for opposing Leslie's *Short and Easie* with his *The Shortest Way with the Dissenters*. Twenty years later, across the Atlantic, Checkley ended up in court for publishing Leslie's *Short and Easie* as an antidote to *Robinson Crusoe*. In the version of his speech in self-defense later published in London, Checkley fingered Defoe as the ringleader of the deists—their very oracle:

> The *God of Order* did not create a Number of People all at once, *without Order and Government,* and then leave them to scramble for Property and Dominion, as some Deistical Republicans would have us believe contrary to the express Words of Scripture.

And to shew that I do not abuse them, tho' I could bring a Multitude of Quotations from their own Writings . . . I shall only produce three Lines from their *Veteran Mercenary,* their Oracle, *Daniel de Foe,* who certainly knew his own Scheme.

To be as free as Nature first made Man,
E'er the base Laws of Servitude began,
When wild in Woods the noble Savage ran.

This is their wild Notion of an independent State of Nature.[2]

These are serious charges, even if Checkley misattributes the lines of poetry to Defoe, when they actually come from Almanzor, the hero of Dryden's *The Conquest of Granada* (1672). Checkley repeats these lines because they remind him of the tropes of literary deism he detects in *Robinson Crusoe,* who, once shipwrecked, becomes "as free as Nature first made Man" and discovers in his friend, the virtuous cannibal Friday, a goodness founded in "an independent State of Nature"—exactly the position deists took when they advanced the virtuous pagan as incisive criticism of state religion.

Checkley's accusation that Defoe is the deists' oracle sidesteps accuracy by not invoking shared concepts or principles—but, of course, Defoe is too smart and too cautious for that. When he wants to sound the deist, he imitates a Quaker minister or a lunar philosopher or an angry Arab. Never does he provide the equivalent of a deist manifesto, although parts of *Serious Reflections* come close, as we shall see. Defoe is not a deist like Charles Blount, who redacts deist principles and promulgates them through the first English anthology of naturalist and radical writings, the *Oracles of Reason* (1693). Defoe is a menace because his fiction serves as conduit for an outlawed speculative deism past the church's supervision—past responsible philosophy and accepted theology—into the hearts and minds of common readers by means of enchanting prose fiction.

Defoe does not deceive Checkley, any more than he did Francis Atterbury (1663–1732), dean of Westminster and bishop of Rochester, who, like Leslie, was detected in treasonous collaboration with the deposed Stuart court. These men—Atterbury, Leslie, and Gildon—all prominent public intellectuals—view Defoe as a political and theological threat. Atterbury writes,

He seems to have a worse Design, than he dares own . . . , for if we trace him throughout all his Pamphlet, we shall find him no other than a Leveller, and consequently an implacable Enemy to any thing above himself, which is the most dangerous of Enthusiastick Delusions, or rather a desperate Contrivance of the Needy to bring all things into Common, or under that Colour, to thrust themselves into the Estates they have no Title to. In short, such Advocates are more to be fear'd than profess'd Enemies, as filling the Heads of the People with Wild and extravagant Notions.[3]

While one could be a leveler without being a deist and a deist without being a leveler, Defoe's enemies accuse him of both. They are motivated, no doubt, by spite and party politics, and Defoe's friendlier critics and biographers find little justification for these charges. Nevertheless, their outrage also has a textual basis.

In future generations, *Robinson Crusoe* becomes a classic children's story, the kind of tale Louisa May Alcott praises in 1875 as a sentimental favorite—one of "the dear old stories that all children love so well."[4] However the book's first critics read it as a subversive deistical work. They did not find Crusoe's adventures charming. Indeed, they considered the book a charm in the medieval sense: an object of alluring magic, a talisman of special properties communicating strange effects. Describing Defoe's hold on the reading public in 1710, Leslie wrote these strangely prophetic words:

> There's a Secret; that the World will know in a little time; 'tis a Charm or somewhat worse; That Men should be stanch Doctors, and ill B——s; No Nearer, says the Mariner, lest we run the Vessel on Shelves and Quick-sands; for the Time won't bear that Church-Men should speak plain Sense; tho' *Reviews and Observators* may . . . and that without Punishment. . . . Give me leave, my Lord, to quote one Passage of the Pilloried Scribbler. "But after all, their Eyes will be open'd, and I may freely tell you, all the Peoples Eyes do already begin to be open'd, they begin to see Jacobitism riding upon them a Gallop, bestriding the Beast call'd *Non-Resistance* . . ." Here your Lordship may see Impudence in the Abstract, and riding in Triumph. What bold Names he calls the Doctrine of our Blessed Lord, *the Beast,* and how basely he slurs at Hereditary Right—This Insolence ought to be corrected. And then he says, Depend on't, the Nation begins to see. Yes Mr. *Defoe,* 'tis true indeed, the Nation begins to see; . . . And now I shall leave such Insects to be squeezed by Authority; I would not

have him punished Allegorically (a Word he is mightily pleased with) but *in propria Persona,* as he justly deserves.[5]

In sputtering rage Leslie calls for state violence against Defoe's body. What menace does Defoe pose? What is it beyond his politics and lax theology that so unnerves Leslie and Gildon? Defoe has a charm in store, "or something worse." Leslie's charm conjures Prospero's rough magic—a force difficult to subdue except by force, a power a good man should abjure, break, bury, drown. The secret quality of the charm is its effect on readers, for they never suspect themselves of being seduced until it is too late. Leslie fears a narcotic-like quality in Defoe's writing that awakens the imagination even as it lulls certain defenses to sleep. Indeed, Defoe slips a cognitive description of this charm into *Robinson Crusoe* when Crusoe says, "There are some secret moving Springs in the Affections, which when they are set a going by some Object in View; or be it some Object, though not in View, yet render'd present to the Mind by the Power of Imagination, that Motion carries out the Soul by its Impetuosity to such violent eager Embracings of the Object, that the Absence of it is insupportable."[6] This is your brain on fiction. The prose artist charms the reader with a figuration of the real. Leslie admires and fears Defoe's artistry, which may help explain why his attack on Defoe in 1710 sounds like an eerie forecast of a book published nine years later. The "something worse" behind Defoe's charm Leslie will not state directly. He reveals it only in code: "that Men should be stanch Doctors." Swift used a variant of "stanch" in *Gulliver's Travels,* also in a maritime context: "Our Ship was staunch, and our Crew all in good Health."[7] "Stanch" and "staunch" are alternative spellings of the same idea: airtight, self-sufficient. While this might mean as little as a Low Church Protestant appeal to conscience, Leslie's alarm suggests he has a more dangerous foe in mind, a deist who renounces assistance from all revealed religion.[8] Leslie's use of the word "doctor" similarly connotes an innocent meaning—a doctor was someone trained in theology, a learned divine—and a more caustic sense: a doctor for Leslie is what Crusoe becomes to Friday, someone foolishly self-sufficient as regards theology, like a surgeon who operates on himself. Leslie likens Defoe's theology to a ship smashing into shoals and quicksands. Nine years before *Robinson Crusoe,* he suspects that Defoe will release a charm on readers, convincing them to take spiritual guidance into their own hands, as Robinson Crusoe does on his island. Stop this threat to ecclesiastical authority now, before it is too late, Leslie warns. Punish Defoe "not Allegorically, but *in propria Persona.*"

By 1711, Leslie had fled to the Stuart court at St. Germain rather than stand trial for treason. Now it is up to his disciple, Charles Gildon, to sink Defoe. Gildon takes up the charge with the zeal of a reformed apostate. He is that "malicious but foolish Writer" Defoe reflects on at the start of *Serious Reflections*. As a younger man, Gildon was the compatriot of the ill-famed Blount, the radical deist who supplied Defoe with his weapon against Leslie and the High Church. Gildon helped Blount publish *Oracles of Reason* in 1693 and brought out the posthumous *Miscellaneous Works of Charles Blount, Esq.*, in 1695.[9] After Blount's supposed suicide, Gildon might have continued the deist's work. Quite the opposite occurred.[10] Was it his friend's sudden and suspicious demise that led Gildon to his change of heart? As we have seen, there are conflicting accounts of Blount's suicide. "It is strange," notes Macaulay, "that the circumstances of Blount's death should be so uncertain. That he died of a wound inflicted by his own hand, and that he languished long, are undisputed facts. The common story was that he shot himself; and Narcissus Luttrell, at the time, made an entry to this effect in his Diary. On the other hand, Pope, who had the very best opportunities of obtaining accurate information, asserts that Blount, 'being in love with a near kinswoman of his, and rejected, gave himself a stab in the arm, as pretending to kill himself, of the consequence of which he really died.'"[11] So Blount died a suicide either by a stab wound to the arm or a bullet to the brain. Macaulay adds, "Gildon's rhapsody about the death of his friend [prefacing *The Miscellaneous Works of Charles Blount, Esq.*] will suit either story equally." In other words, Gildon, who probably knew the truth of Blount's death, said nothing. Perhaps he, too, feared for his life.

We have already observed the violence of Leslie's attack on Blount and his fury that "his blasphemous Works (many of which were well nigh lost) . . . are of late carefully collected and reprinted, to the scandal of a Christian country."[12] Gildon was the very culprit who did the collecting and reprinting of Blount. Leslie's statement was an all but direct threat. After reading Leslie's *Short and Easie*, Gildon recanted, issuing his own misleadingly titled *The Deist's Manual* (1705), which is, more accurately, a manual on how not to be a deist. The preface disavows Gildon's earlier defense of Blount's suicide "to remove an Opinion, I have formerly too much contributed to, by my defence of a Friend's Death, for whom I had a particular Value, not Imagining, it wou'd have been of that ill Consequence, which I am afraid it was."[13] The ill consequence was appearing to endorse not just suicide, but also Blount's amalgamation of Herbert, Spinoza, Hobbes, and Milton into an English deism exerting popular appeal. *A Deist's Manual* republishes the letter Gildon received from Leslie certifying his recovery from deism and issuing his marching orders. God "has given you the True Spirit of Repentence," writes Leslie, "to bring forth the fruits whereof; that is, to make what Satisfaction you can for the Injuries you have done to Religion, by answering what was publish'd formerly by your self against it."[14] Satisfaction connotes violent revenge, as in a duel. Leslie was telling Gildon to seek satisfaction from himself through public recantation and to hunt down like offenders—orders Gildon followed to the letter.[15] Gildon's repentence did not impress Pope, who mocked him in *The Dunciad Variorum* (1729): "*Charles Gildon,* a writer of criticisms and libels of the last age: He published Blount's blasphemous books aganst the Divinity of Christ, the Oracles of reason &c. He signalized himself as a Critic, having written some very bad plays."[16]

Gildon had one other quality that put him in a good position to criticize Defoe. He was what we now might call—at the risk of anachronism—a failed novelist. Even though classically trained, even though conversant in the history of literature in several languages, Gildon failed where Defoe succeeded. He was therefore in a good position to recognize Defoe's genius.[17] Despite himself, he pinpoints the key feature of his rival's success—*Robinson Crusoe's* immense translatability:

> *The Fabulous* Proteus *of the Ancient Mythologist was but a very faint Type of our Hero, whose Changes are much more numerous, and he far more difficult to be constrain'd to his own Shape. If his Works should happen to live to the next Age, there would in all probability be a greater Strife among the several Parties, whose he really was, than among the seven* Graecian Cities, *to which of them* Homer *belong'd: The* Dissenters *first would claim him as theirs, the* Whigs *in general as their, the* Tories *as theirs, the* Non-jurors *as theirs, the* Papists *as theirs, the* Atheists *as theirs, and so on to what Sub-divisions there may be among us.*[18]

How prescient the angry can be. *Robinson Crusoe* did live into the next age, and the one after that, and seems likely to live on. The reason *Robinson Crusoe* lives, according to Gildon, is that the novel means so many different things and is therefore claimed by many different causes. There has arisen "a general Strife among the contending Parties," whether the question is the genre, or the context, or the motive, or the meaning of this inscrutable text. If you are an anticolonialist, here you will find an enemy or a friend. If you believe that Jesus Christ died for humanity and that true religion is impossible without his intercession on our behalf, here you will find confirmation—or, as Gildon and Checkley warned, just the reverse. If you are looking for a modern myth of political economy, here you will find it, and also that myth subverted. And it is just this labile quality that Defoe's enemies find so dangerous—so charming and disarming.

Praise, even damning with faint praise, was not Gildon's purpose, however. After explaining why *Robinson Crusoe* is so popular, Gildon ridicules the grammatical errors and solecisms on every page: "All but the very *Canaille* are satisfied . . . of the Worthlessness" of the performance. The claim of realism excites his mirth. "Your Book is nothing but a Romance," he tells Defoe, and to prove it he asks questions such as, How did Xury learn English so fast? And how could Crusoe have stripped naked to swim to the wreck and then start shoving biscuits into his pants pockets?[19] Ultimately, however, Gildon's concern is not with realism or the lack thereof. The fundamental charge is heresy.

It is strange to read this condemnation, because we have come to assume that *Robinson Crusoe* is a book about spiritual growth, and the reformation of the soul. As one of Defoe's best biographers puts it,

> The pattern of salvation as presented in the lives of several characters in *The Family Instructor* is repeated in Crusoe, Friday, and Atkins's wife. Crusoe's repentance and ultimate salvation is assured at the moment he says, "I look'd back upon my past Life with such Horrour, and my Sins appear'd so dreadful, that my Soul sought nothing of God, but Deliverance from the Load of Guilt that bore down all my Comfort." He moves then haltingly and with some setbacks, through the process made familiar in *The Family Instructor*. The fact that Friday asks questions that Crusoe cannot answer in no way detracts from Defoe's point. When Friday asks why God does not "kill the Devil now," Crusoe has no answer, but, by analogy to himself, Friday concludes that God may be giving even Satan a chance for repentance and pardon. Defoe takes the opportunity to comment on the natural, universal aspect of Friday's questions and on the necessity for revelation.[20]

Paula Backscheider builds on the line of argument Martin J. Greif advanced in 1966, which was expanded into book-length treatments by G. A. Starr and J. Paul Hunter. "Far more than the account of a practical man's adjustment to life on a deserted island," Greif argues, Defoe's novel "is the record of a notable spiritual pilgrimage across the sea of life, from a lawless course of living to true Christian repentance: a symbolic voyage from sin and folly to the gift of God's grace attained through sincere belief in Jesus Christ."[21] *Robinson Crusoe* is a modernized *Pilgrim's Progress;* the novel works along the lines of an elaborate fictional catechism.

This confident identification of *Robinson Crusoe*'s religious meaning is not limited to traditional criticism. The Marxist-Hegelian approach taken by Michael McKeon yields the same result:

> What is crucial about Robinson Crusoe's achievement of social success is not the degree of his elevation but his capacity to justify each station to which he attains as the way of nature and the will of God. . . . [*Robinson Crusoe*] represents the hard-won lesson that the metaphysical realm of the Spirit may be accommodated and rendered accessible as the psychological realm of Mind. It is Defoe's remarkable achievement not simply to have provided this psychological access to spiritual crisis but to have specified it, with the mediating guidance of Puritan casuistry and soteriology, to the concrete dimension of material and social ambition. . . . For these reasons he is the great exemplar not only of the Weber thesis but of progressive ideology.[22]

These analyses echo an advertisement in the *Morning Chronicle and London Advertiser* for Wednesday August 17, 1785, that describes *Robinson Crusoe* as "a System of Religion and Morality." The point seems so obvious that interpretations begin with the assumption that Providence rules the narrative and recognizable conversions take place. Defoe's enemies, however, were not taken in by this show. Gildon rages against Defoe's assurance that "*the just Application of every Incident, the Religious and Useful Inferences drawn from every Part, are so many Testimonies to the good Design of making it Publick, and must Legitimate all the Part that may be called Invention or Parable in the Story*":

> But when it is plain that there are no true, useful, or just Inferences drawn from any of the Incidents; when Religion has so little to do in any Part of these Inferences, when it is evident that what you call Religion, is only to mislead the Minds of Men to reject the dictates of Reason, and embrace in its Room a meer superstitious Fear of I know not what *Instinct* from unbodied Spirits; when you impiously prophane the very Name of Providence, by allotting to it either

contradictory Offices, or an unjust Partiality: I think we may justly say, that the Design of the Publication of this Book was not sufficient to justify and make Truth of what you allow to be Fiction and Fable."[23]

The attack is thorough. Although *Robinson Crusoe* masquerades as a pious work, it counters wholesome religious ends. In the novel, the very notion of Providence becomes so twisted in actual use that one suspects satire more than sermon. The structure of the work, with its conspicuous display of inferences and applications to be drawn from the story, provides only the empty shell of trusted allegory, now filled with devious content: "I am far from being an Enemy to the Writers of Fables, since I know very well that this Manner of Writing is not only very Ancient, but very useful, I might say sacred, since it has been made use of by the inspir'd Writers themselves; but then to render any Fable worthy of being received into the Number of those which are truly valuable, it must naturally produce in its Event some useful Moral, either express'd or understood; but this of *Robinson Crusoe,* you plainly inculcate, is design'd against a publick Good."[24] Some scholars attribute Gildon's animus to personal jealousy and even syphilitic insanity, but these are trenchant criticisms. Instead of becoming an early novelist as he wished, Gildon inadvertently became an early critic of the novel. What he hates about *Robinson Crusoe* are exactly the qualities that help make the work a modern novel. Like the combatants who attacked *The Shortest Way,* Gildon hopes to alert eighteenth-century readers to the dangers of this subliminally deistical text. He exposes passages that have convinced generations of readers that Crusoe undergoes a sincere repentance and conversion; that Friday, through Crusoe's catechism, abandons paganism for Christianity, as does Will Atkins's wife, the unnamed virtuous pagan of part 2. Gildon will not fall for pious gestures toward an overarching Providence guiding the modern pilgrim's progress. But neither will Gildon name the false religion that *Robinson Crusoe* inculcates, lest he resurrect his own freethinking past. Instead, he hurls insults, appropriating Defoe's own characters, Friday and Crusoe, to attack their author for making them such religious imbeciles. In exasperation, D—l [Daniel, but also Devil] pleads, "Why, ye airy Fantoms, are you not my Creatures? Mayn't I make of you what I please?" to which Crusoe replies, "Why, yes, you may make of us what you please; but when you raise Beings contradictory to common Sense, and destructive of Religion and Morality; they will rise up against you *in Foro Conscientiae;* that *Latin* I learned in my *Free-School* and *House Education.*"[25] Gildon's Crusoe complains of being the author's tool to advance heresy. He holds his creator in contempt "for the making me such a Whimsical Dog," a man who loses all trace of religion after three weeks at sea (thus giving sailors everywhere a bad name, as *Tristram Shandy* did clockmakers), who even when he rediscovers faith next loses it "upon every Whimsy, you make me extravagantly Zealous, and as extravagantly Remiss," Gildon's Crusoe complains.[26] The dispute turns ugly when Gildon's Friday and Crusoe force-feed Defoe the first two volumes of *Robinson Crusoe* and toss him in a blanket, Sancho-like, until he excretes his book over everything.

Gildon does not accept any of the religious material scholars take at face value. Of Crusoe's frequent moral reflections, he writes that they "seem brought in only to increase the Bulk of your Book; they are seldom Just or truly Religious; but they have this terrible Circumstance, that they demonstrate that the Author has not the Fear of God before his Eyes. *Ludere cum Sacris* is what he has not at all scrupl'd."[27] Taking aim at Crusoe's "Sortes Virgilianae of the Bible"— a *sortes* fueled by a dose of green tobacco steeped in rum—Gildon writes: "The Impiety of this Part of the Book, in making the Truths of the Bible of a Piece with the fictitious Story of *Robinson Crusoe*, is so shocking that I dare not dwell on it; but must say, that they make me think that this Book ought to be printed with *Vaninus*, the *Freethinker*, and some other Atheistical Tracts, which are condemned and held in Abhorrence by all good Christians."[28] Placing *Robinson Crusoe* on the same shelf as works by Lucilio Vanini (1585–1619), Gildon consigns the novel to a subversive tradition of naturalist and occult philosophy inimical to any established church. Mentioning Vanini also recalls the circumstances of his death, which Leslie and Gildon would love to visit on Defoe. Chased out of four nations; jailed in the Tower of London for forty-nine days after seeking asylum in England; arrested in Toulouse, France; and charged with heresy on the strength of his *De admirandis naturae reginae deaeque mortalium arcanis* (1615), a work that argues the likelihood of human evolution from primates, Vanini was sentenced to death by burning. The account of the Magistrate Gramont relates that, "before putting fire to the stake, Vanini was ordered to put forth his sacrilegious tongue for the knife. He refused; it was necessary to employ pincers to draw it forth, and when the executioner's instrument seized and cut it off never was heard a more horrible cry. One might have thought that he heard the bellowing of an ox which was being slaughtered."[29] Having pilloried Defoe, Leslie and Gildon wish they could finish the job and silence the reprobate forever. They want to add Defoe's name to the long list of Arians, Socinians, and deists who have met their just reward.[30]

As an interpreter of *Robinson Crusoe*, Gildon has few successors.[31] Critics point out problematic scenes, such as the conversion of Friday, and themes, such as cannibalism, but they do not argue that the entire book is constructed to perplex interpretation and forestall the conclusions it appears to endorse, especially with regard to religion. On the contrary, the main line of Defoe scholarship dismisses Gildon's charge as baseless. "This is entirely false," writes Paul Dottin. "De Foe, a staunch Dissenter, always waged an implacable war against Jacobite Priests (Nonjurors), Roman Catholicism, and Atheists, whom he called Mendevils."[32] The vehemence of this denial, which is entirely characteristic of the general attitude toward Gildon, keeps us from reading *Robinson Crusoe* as Gildon read it: as a work that weaves together highly charged scenarios that both evoke and conceal a deist outlook. Crusoe's disobedience to his father; the Jonah-like catastrophes at sea; Crusoe's feverish, tobacco-induced religious dream; the virtuous cannibal; the invention of society and government from scratch; all that talk about Providence and premonitions—these are the poisoned pills Gildon discovers in an all-too-charming narrative. Reader beware. *Ludere cum Sacris* is the charge, and it is Gildon's duty to expose the ruse:

> But when I found that you were not content with the many Absurdities of your Tale, but seem'd to discover a Design, which proves you as bad an *Englishman* as a Christian, I could not but take Notice in this publick Manner of what you had written; especially when I perceiv'd that you threaten'd us with more of the same Nature, if this met with the Success which you hop'd for, and which the Town has been pleas'd to give it. If by this I can prevent another Accession of Impieties and Superstition to those which the Work under our Consideration has furnish'd us with, I shall not think my Labour lost.[33]

Perhaps Gildon was a special case—a reformed deist desperate to please his mentor. He sounds an alarm few heard then or have heard since. But there was another reader of *Robinson Crusoe* in 1720 whose view scholars have never considered. She has been overlooked because she is a character in a seldom read part of Defoe's fiction. Ever the trickster, Defoe introduces an "antient Gentlewoman" into *Serious Reflections*. This Gentlewoman is smart, and a deist. She seems to conclude, as Gildon does, that *Robinson Crusoe* implies a deistical outlook on religion—but for her, that is a good thing.

Any reader of *Serious Reflections during the Life and Surprising Adventures of Robinson Crusoe* (and there aren't many) will agree that Defoe does not trouble himself often to refer back to events in the first two volumes. One possible reason is that he had not written them yet. Parts of *Serious Reflections* appear to have been written in the 1690s.³⁴ The word "during" in the title stands out here. The third part of the trilogy is likely a collage of essays and observations Defoe generated in the process of writing *Robinson Crusoe*. It served as an intellectual testing ground and escape valve for the masterpiece: "I took my Pen and Ink to disburden my Thoughts, when the Subject crowded in fast upon me; so I have here communicated some of my Observations for the Benefit of those that come after me."³⁵ Yet one section that was surely written after parts 1 and 2, which Defoe took some trouble weaving into the fiction, is Crusoe's encounter with the "antient Gentlewoman": "About the Time that I was upon these Enquiries, being at a Friend's House, and talking much of my long Travels, *as you know Travellers are apt to do;* I observ'd an antient Gentlewoman in the Company listen'd with a great deal of Attention, and as I thought, with some Pleasure, to what I was saying: And after I had done, Pray, Sir, *says she,* turning her Speech to me, give me Leave to ask you a Question or two? *With all my Heart, Madam, said I;* so we began the following short Dialogue."³⁶ Defoe's Gentlewoman is a bold thinker. She wants Crusoe to admit that his story is really all about religion, and she applies Socratic persistence to Crusoe's efforts to misunderstand, forget, or willfully avoid her questions. It is an exchange much like the wonderful scene in *Robinson Crusoe* in which Crusoe pretends not to hear Friday's unanswerable question about why God does not kill the Devil. The Gentlewoman wants to draw a different lesson from Crusoe's story. She presses her point relentlessly. "Is there not one common End and Design in the Nature of Men," she asks, "which seems to run thro' all their Actions, and to be form'd by Nature, as the main End of Life, and by Consequence is made the chief Business of Living?" Crusoe evades, but the old Gentlewoman, also Defoe's creation, we must remind ourselves, will not be put off: "Pray, don't distinguish me out of my Question, we may talk of what is the true End of Life, as we understood it here in a Christian Country another time; But take my Question as I offer it, what is mankind generally a-doing as their main Business?"³⁷

In this exchange, Defoe presents a philosophical dialogue on *Robinson Crusoe* and the nature of religion between a Christian colonialist (Crusoe) and a deist (antient Gentlewoman), and the Christian colonialist is no match for the deist. The Gentlewoman overpowers Crusoe with the same question deists were posing as they trained their new tools of philology and anthropology on diverse faith systems to produce what David Hume would call a natural history of religion. Defoe's Gentlewoman grasps the anthropological implications of the narrative whose protagonist she interrogates. She hears a different view from the one Crusoe expresses; yet Crusoe's first-person narrative is our only source of information. Defoe's irony is in play. As was the case in *The Shortest Way*, for this double voicing to work, Crusoe must lose authority. Pressed to answer the Gentlewoman's charge that his story is all about religion, Crusoe throws Hobbes at her: "The main Business that Mankind seems to be doing is to eat and drink, that's their Enjoyment, and to get Food to eat is their Employment, including a little, their eating and devouring one another."[38] The Gentlewoman replies, "That's a Description of them as Brutes," to which Crusoe answers, "They are worse than the Brutes; for the Brutes destroy not their own Kind, but all prey upon a different Species.... But Man for baser Ends, such as Avarice, Envy, Revenge, and the like; devours his own Species, nay his own Flesh and Blood." Defoe does not allow Crusoe the last cynical word. The Gentlewoman replies, "All this I believe is true; but this does not reach my Question yet.... But pray, sir, is not Religion the principal Business of Mankind in all the Parts of the World; for I think you granted it when you nam'd Idolatry, which they, no doubt, call Religion?"[39] The Gentlewoman suggests that the very story Crusoe tells provides no justification for his colonialist and theological biases. Crusoe again evades her challenge, arguing that a "Great Part of the World ... is resolv'd into the lowest Degeneracy of human Nature. I mean the Savage Life.... I see nothing in the Life of some whole Nations of People ... in which the Life of a Lion or an Elephant in the Desarts of Arabia, is not equal." The old Gentlewoman will have none of this: "You avoid my Question too Laboriously, Sir, I have nothing to do either with the Ignorance or Hypocrisy of the People, whether they are blindly devout, or knavishly and designedly devout, is not the Case; but whether Religion is not apparently the main Business of the World, the principal apparent End of Life, and the Employment of Mankind?"[40] Finally, Crusoe wakes up. "What do you call Religion?" he asks. Her answer provides the deist commonplaces in brief: "'By Religion, I mean, the Worshipping and Paying Homage to some supreme Being, some God, *known or unknown,* is not to the Case, so it be but to something counted supreme.... [M]y Opinion is, that paying a divine Worship, Acts of Homage and Adoration, and particularly, that of Praying to the Supreme Being, which they acknowledge, is deriv'd to Mankind from the Light of Nature with the Notion of Belief itself.'"[41] The old Gentlewoman's understanding of religion is that of a confident deist. Note her indifference toward specific revelations—some God, any God, known or unknown, satisfies her. The pronoun "they" in this passage ("the Supreme Being, which they acknowledge, is derived to Mankind from the Light of Nature") has no clear antecedent. For readers at the time, however, the sources of her natural religion would have been clear: a group that included Lord Herbert of Cherbury,

Spinoza, Toland, Blount, Matthew Tindal, the third Earl of Shaftesbury, William Wollaston, and Anthony Collins, among others.

Reading *Robinson Crusoe,* Defoe's Gentlewoman perceives a deistical take on religion that contrasts with Crusoe's role as colonizing Christian seizing an island and its native inhabitant as by divine right. Remarkably, she holds Friday up against Crusoe the same way critics today hold Friday up against Defoe, insisting that protagonist and author have done a great wrong to Friday and others like him: "Why! did not your Man *Friday* and the *Savage* Woman you tell us of, talk of their old Idol they call'd *Benamuckee?* And what did they do?" To which Crusoe can only respond, "It is very true they did."[42] Here is an author accusing himself through a fictional character of not pursuing cosmopolitanism to its logical conclusion—by representing the other in the other's own terms, offering, in this case, a fuller account of the benefits of Benamuckeeism, or natural religion, as reported by happy and virtuous pagans: "And did not *Friday* tell you they went up to the Hills and said *O* to him? Pray, what was the Meaning of saying *O* to him: but *O* do not hurt us; for thou art Omnipotent, and canst kill us; *O* heal our Distempers; for thou art Infinite, and can'st do all things: *O* give us what we want, for thou art Bountiful: *O* spare us, for thou art Merciful: And so of all the other Conceptions of a God?"[43] The wise Gentlewoman challenges Crusoe's fair dealing when it comes to representing and judging other people's faiths. Her cosmopolitan impulse collides with the chauvinism of a Protestant Englishman who has no compunction about trading slaves or striking bargains with a Catholic missionary if it will maintain order in his colony.[44] Defoe was too much the artist to work out this contradiction in plain sight. Instead, he invented a character who would embody the contradiction, a Janus-faced figure, both type and countertype, Christian hero and secular voyager, and embedded this character in a capacious, layered, and playfully self-referential multivolume narrative.[45] The Gentlewoman probes the source of this original and surprising approach to prose fiction as far as Defoe will let her:

> *R.C.* Well, Madam, I grant all this, pray what do you infer from it? What is the Reason of your Question?
> *Old Gent.* O sir, I have many Inferences to draw from it for my own Observation; I do not set up to instruct you.[46]

After exposing a deist strain in Defoe's writing, the Gentlewoman concludes with the words Defoe's religious readers fear most: "I do not set up to instruct you." A dialogue that does not instruct, a novel that does not preach, a narrative that allows the reader to draw inferences—this is subversive and slippery work. Defoe's enemies identify it as such, and his Gentlewoman seems to concur with their assessment. She is Defoe's creation, his critic, and his coded confession. Guilty as charged. Without instruction, Crusoe must think for himself and make his own way, just as he did on his island. "I thought this serious old Lady would have entertain'd a farther Discourse with me on so fruitful a Subject, but she declined it, and left me to my own Meditation, which indeed she had rais'd up to an unusual Pitch; and the first thing that occurr'd to me, was to put me upon inquiring after that nice thing, I ought to call Religion in the World."[47] If the woman's question and inference are so fruitful, why not allow the dialogue to play out? What exactly is the "subject" that raises Crusoe's meditation "up to an unusual pitch"? Caution prevented "further Explication" in the case of Defoe's nemesis; caution here prevents Defoe from allowing the old Gentlewoman to state what she infers—that unbeknownst to its own hero, *Robinson Crusoe* conveys deist ideas by literary means, not directly but indirectly, not as argument but through the charm of its narrative. In a case like this, we do not expect to find a preponderance of evidence supporting the claim of deist influence; we expect, subtle and deniable hints of subversive intent, such as the dialogue with the antient Gentlewoman buried in *Serious Reflections*. Defoe's enemies detected these hints. Defoe's biographers and editors by and large do not, or note them only to deny their significance.

And so we return to the question with which this book began: how did the brick merchant become a novelist? Defoe hints that a surpassing hatred for one individual motivated him, serving in some complex way as the catalyst of *Robinson Crusoe*. We have followed that clue to Defoe's signal work. It remains to interpret the novel itself.

Two Jonahs and the Genres of *Robinson Crusoe*

On first setting out, it is customary for interpreters of *Robinson Crusoe* to discuss the opening in which Crusoe rejects his father's stern advice to stay in England and start a career, maintaining and improving his middle-class status through hard work and piety. Crusoe himself calls the decision his "Original Sin," words that have inspired many Christian and allegorical readings.[48] "Defoe's eighteenth-century prodigal, a seaman representing the sinner's miserable condition once deprived of divine grace by original and actual transgression," writes Martin Greif, "is primarily an account of a spiritual experience, an allegorical story of conversion employing metaphoric symbols readily recognizable to an audience familiar with a similar set of symbols found repeatedly in the sermons, tracts, and other religious writings of both Anglican and dissenting divines."[49] There is little reason to dispute this reading, since Defoe wove it so deeply into the text. But rejection of the father's command alludes to a different biblical story equally pertinent to the genres of *Robinson Crusoe*. That is the Jewish story of the prophet Jonah, who disobeyed God's command that he warn the people of Nineveh of impending doom; was punished for his decision; and then, when he agreed to do God's bidding, suffered exactly the public shaming he predicted when God changed his mind and spared Nineveh.

Why Jonah? There are two answers to this question, a doubleness Defoe may have found useful. First, Christian readers found in Jonah a familiar allegorical and nautical framework. The Baptist preacher and prolific author Benjamin Keach (1640–1704) teaches in his *Gospel Mysteries Unveil'd* (1701) that our "blessed *Jonah* was thrown into the Sea of God's Wrath, to lay that dreadful Storm our Sins had raised."[50] Jonah anticipates Christ. Jonah, in a sense, is Christ's antithesis—waiting to be reversed and therefore redeemed. "We have now found the Man," writes the Cambridge Platonist Benjamin Whichcote (1609-1683), "of whom it is spoken in the Gospel, that his *Eye was evil because God's was good.*"[51] He continues, "That which makes the Wonder the greater; Jonah *whom we find in this* Distemper, is of all the Prophets the *Type of Christ*. Our Savior instanceth in him, *There shall no Sign be given, but the Sign of the Prophet* Jonah."[52] The transformation of Jonah into a typological sign could not be clearer, and it would have been impossible to evoke the story without calling to mind not only this view of Jonah, but this *way of reading*. "Now the Lord *Jesus Christ* has made that Storm a Calm & the waves to be still," explained Increase Mather (1639–1723). "Jonah was an Eminent *Type* of Christ in this respect, he was willing to be thrown into the Sea, that so the storm might cease."[53]

For most of the brief biblical fable, Jonah is not willing to do anything at God's behest or for the glory of his faith. The "Distemper" to which Whichcote refers is Jonah's boldness in talking back to God, refusing his task, accepting it only after being threatened and then complaining when God spares Nineveh. Of this Jonah, Whichcote writes: "I am sure in this Temper and Disposition of his, he is no Type of Christ."[54] So is he a type or not? Clearly, the biblical prophet poses a problem for Whichcote, and I suspect Defoe was aware of this problem in the figure of Jonah. As type or anti-type, Jonah remains recognizably Christian. But as counter-type, a character who resists neat allegory, Jonah is something else altogether. Whichcote accuses Jonah of "great Refractoriness and Disobedience. . . . We shall find him *stupid* and *senseless,* and more blockish than the Idolatrous Marriners; and of them, they use to say, *None nearer*

Death, none farther from God. Those stupid Persons learned this in the Storm to apply to their Gods."[55] He berates Jonah for fainting in crisis—Robinson Crusoe does the same—and for praying only when death looms. Whichcote even anticipates his readers' confusion: "But you will ask, Wherefore do I blemish the Reputation of a Prophet, of a Type of Christ?"[56]

This conflicted Jonah becomes a perfect analogue for Robinson Crusoe. Defoe could count on pious readers' recognizing the connections among Jonah, Crusoe, and Christ and drawing conclusions entirely wholesome: "It comes as no surprise, therefore, after the prodigal's arrogant boast of safety from all that is without his newly built wall, a boast reminiscent of Jonah's attempt to hide from God, that Robinson Crusoe is assailed by providential earthquakes and storms."[57] Crusoe becomes a type for Jonah, and because Jonah is a type for Christ, Crusoe syllogistically becomes a type for Christ. Hence, Crusoe "knows himself a son of the Heavenly Father, is knit in mystical union with the glorified Christ, and is strengthened and confirmed by the gifts of the Holy Spirit."[58] Defoe provides many parallels to support this reading: Crusoe and Jonah receive a command from the Father. Both reject it and go to sea. Both pose a threat to people around them because of their bad decisions. The crew of Jonah's ship throws the prophet overboard, and he is swallowed by a whale. The master of Crusoe's ship curses Crusoe as a "Token of Misery" before Crusoe is swallowed by a deserted island, where he lives under constant threat.

Whichcote's struggle to allegorize Jonah points to another interpretation of the reluctant prophet in Defoe's day, which viewed his flaws as favorable and heard in the narrative not a cautionary tale against shirking one's duties, but instead, a courageous stand against arbitrary religious authority. Late in his principal work, *Characteristicks of Men, Manners, Opinions, and Times* (1711), the third Earl of Shaftesbury, a reluctant deist but a deist just the same, inserts into "Miscellaneous Reflections" an extended "criticism" (meaning here a literary appreciation) of the book of Jonah. "WHATSOEVER of this kind, may be *allegorically* understood, or in the way of PARABLE or FABLE," Shaftesbury writes, "this I am sure of, That the *Accounts, Descriptions, Narrations, Expressions,* and *Phrases* [of Jonah] are in themselves many times exceedingly *pleasant, entertaining, and facetious.*"[59] Shaftesbury directs attention to the literary qualities of the text. Its representations are pleasant, entertaining, and facetious because a second, comic awareness exists within the narrative, an acknowledgment that Jonah has every right to resist God's command. After all, Jonah accurately predicts the result of agreeing to go to Nineveh to warn the inhabitants of impending doom. In a philosophical dialogue, Jonah would be close to bettering God, and that is the quality of the writing that attracts the deist, not God's final, authoritative reminder that Jonah has no right to question God's command, no right to weigh his life in God's own scale. The King James Version (4.9–11) presents the dialogue:

> And God said to Jonah, Doest thou well to be angry for the gourd? And he said, I do well to be angry, even unto death.
>
> Then said the LORD, Thou hast had pity on the gourd, for the which thou hast not laboured, neither madest it grow; which came up in a night, and perished in a night:
>
> And should not I spare Nineveh, that great city, wherein are more than sixscore thousand persons that cannot discern between their right hand and their left hand; and also much cattle?[60]

When deists read these lines, they downplay God's overwhelming assertion of authority, which banks on the obvious fact that Jonah did not create the gourd, the people of Nineveh, or their cattle. They read instead as their teachers the humanists read, against the religious grain, hearing a deep resistance to being ordered about by an overbearing deity. Instead of subservience, they read what Shaftesbury calls a "popular pleasant Intercourse, and Manner of Dialogue between God and *Man*."[61] In Jonah they find a work of profound questioning, coupled with humble details that make the prophet's plight human. They discover, in other words, a comic sublime in the style of the Hebrew Bible.

Shaftesbury praises Jonah as a model for the polite, cosmopolitan style he advocates throughout *Characteristicks*. Although *Characteristicks* is replete with anti-Semitic remarks, the deist in Shaftesbury cannot help praising the actual composition of the Hebrew Bible, which exhibits the same qualities he finds in Jonah: "Besides the many Songs and Hymns dispers'd in Holy Writ, the Book of *Psalms* it-self, *Job, Proverbs, Canticles,* and other intire Volumes of the sacred Collection, which are plainly *Poetry,* and full of humorous Images, and jocular Wit, may sufficiently shew how readily the inspir'd Authors had recourse to HUMOUR and DIVERSION, as a proper Means to promote *Religion,* and strengthen *the establish'd Faith.*"[62] The problem for Shaftesbury was that when he tried to reproduce Jonah's plight in this polite style, it came out sounding like this: "Pettish as this Prophet was, unlike a Man, and resembling rather some refractory boyish *Pupil;* it may be said that GOD, as a kind *Tutor,* was pleas'd to *humour him,* bear with his Anger, and in a lusory manner, expose his childish Frowardness, and shew him *to himself.* . . . [Jonah] fairly plays the

Truant, like an arch *School-Boy;* hoping to hide out of the way. But his *Tutor* had good Eyes, and a long Reach. He overtook him at Sea; where a Storm was ready prepar'd for his Exercise, and a Fish's Belly for his Lodging."[63] Frowardness? The earl's paraphrase is mannered yet risky in style and substance. Shaftesbury secularizes sacred text and belittles Jonah's conflict, transposing the ancient story to his own time and class. God becomes tutor; prophet becomes schoolboy. Omniscience comes down to good eyes. Omnipotence becomes a long reach. Jonah's soul-shattering ordeal becomes an Exercise, connoting schoolwork; the fearful Leviathan his lodging, a word evoking a young man's rooms at college. Shaftesbury's rendition is indeed polite, and arch, and supercilious. It is playful to a fault, a willful lowering of stakes, as Shaftesbury ignores the great theological debate at the heart of the story. Shaftesbury is not only reading but redacting the Bible as literature—and not even as solemn literature but as lighthearted social satire. Aware of his own irreverence, Shaftesbury draws back quickly with a disclaimer: "But fearing lest I might be mis-interpreted, shou'd I offer to set these Passages in their proper Light (which however has been perform'd by undoubted good Christians, and most Learned and Eminent Divines of our own Church) I forbear to go any further into the Examination or Criticism of this sort."[64]

Defoe is not so delicate. He praises Jewish writing in even more extravagant terms, albeit behind the mask of a Muslim. This is what Mahmut, the hero of Defoe's *A Continuation of Letters Written by a Turkish Spy,* says of the Book of Job:

> The whole Tenour of that Book, which they call of *Job,* intimates
> strongly a Supremacy of divine and natural Knowledge, infinite
> Transcendencies of Wisdom shine in every Part of it, all rational and
> supernatural Powers are exerted, in the Significancy of Expression, the
> Pungency of Replies, the Beauty of Stile, the Vivacity of Expression;
> in the arguings of his Friends, and the Sufferings of himself, all
> generous Principles are urged, acted, and improv'd; the most
> passionate Expostulations that can be conceived, break out from the
> mouth of the grave Patriarch, under his strong Pressures, as from a
> Spirit overwhelmed; yet tyed down to the Principles of Humility,
> Resignation, Penitence, and all the graces of a religious Mind; and
> all these appear in a resplendent Manner, even unutterable in any
> Language since that time known in the World: Nay, even unutterable
> in the very same Language, by any other Mouth.[65]

DEFOE'S DEIST MASTERPIECE / 153

Is there higher praise for anyone or anything in all of Defoe's work? The passage suggests an awareness of a humble sublime in prose that Defoe would go on to approximate in the books that made him famous—a philosophical sublime, a playful sublime, built on irony, not transcendence. For Defoe, unlike Shaftesbury, did have the literary genius to modernize biblical narrative. A few days after being saved from the second crisis at sea, Crusoe encounters the friend who had invited him onto his father's ship in the first place. Unfortunately for Crusoe, the reunion takes place in the father's presence:

> My Comrade, who had help'd to harden me before, and who was the Master's Son, was now less forward than I; the first time he spoke to me after we were at *Yarmouth,* which was not till two or three Days, for we were separated in the Town to several Quarters; I say the first time he saw me, it appear'd his Tone was alter'd, and looking very melancholy and shaking his Head, ask'd me how I did, and telling his Father who I was, and how I had come this Voyage only for a Trial, in order to go farther abroad; his Father turning to me with a very grave and concern'd Tone, *Young Man,* says he, *you ought never to go to Sea any more, you ought to take this for a plain and visible Token that you are not to be a Seafaring Man.* Why Sir, said I, will you go to Sea no more? *That is another Case,* said he, *it is my Calling, and therefore my Duty; but as you made this Voyage for a Trial, you see what a Taste Heaven has given you of what you are to expect if you persist; perhaps this is all befallen us on your Account, like* Jonah *in the Ship of Tarshish. Pray,* continues he, *what are you? and on what Account did you go to Sea?* Upon that I told him some of my Story, at the End of which he burst out with a Strange kind of Passion. What had I done, says he, that such an unhappy Wretch should come onto my Ship? I would not set my Foot in the same Ship with thee again for a Thousand Pounds. This indeed was, as I said, an Excursion of his Spirits which were yet agitated by the Sense of his Loss, and was farther than he could have Authority to go.... *And young Man,* said he, *depend upon it, if you do not go back, where-ever you go, you will meet with nothing but Disasters and Disappointments till your Father's Words are fulfilled upon you.*[66]

What do we have here? Philosophical depth and disarming simplicity, a purity of style making everything quite clear, yet somehow, as in a Kafka fable, obscure and funny. The scene is entirely believable within the confines of realism, yet repeats a biblical pattern, as the Master asserts. And then, smuggled in here and there, poignant expressions of double-consciousness, such as Crusoe's comeback that he thought the Master's tirade went "farther than he could have Authority to go." Whose authority are we talking about here? Go where? Was tarring Crusoe as a Jonah figure what the Master had no authority to do? Crusoe is his own man, not some "Token" or type? But that is also exactly what he becomes in the playing out of the fiction, and how he might plausibly be read. The narrative achieves a poise or equilibrium between two possible Jonahs, the type and the individual, and two possible Crusoes, the prodigal and the skeptical adventurer. With Jonah, Defoe signals his choice of a narrative frame, or genre, that is immediately recognizable in two opposing ways: as a spiritual autobiography of the Protestant type, akin to *Pilgrim's Progress,* and as a story that wobbles out of allegorical control into the comic sublime, the Panegyrick on humanity or, simply, the philosophical novel. In Jonah, Defoe located a biblical model that would satisfy his readers' expectation that an important work of prose fiction be edifying and amenable to a Christian—and, indeed, Protestant—outlook. In Jonah he also tapped into a submerged and subversive tradition of counter-allegory. Counter-allegory runs counter because it does not propose a different set of substitutions. The hermeneutic stability of allegory does not persist in counter-allegory; that is what makes it counter, not as a matter of theme or topic, but on the level of sign and signification. Try as they might, signs in *Robinson Crusoe* no longer work as they should in Christian allegory. This goes for the most conspicuous signs in the novel: Crusoe's name and the footprint in the sand.

Our Man Kreutznaer

Just as Jonah exists as anti-type of Christ in Christian iconography and as reluctant human prophet in Jewish scripture, so Robinson Crusoe, judging by successive attempts to analyze and picture him, wears a Janus face. Defoe planned this effect, and the original 1719 Clark and Pine engraving of a heavily armed but downcast Crusoe, standing between ship and enclosure, captures this symbolic ambivalence (see fig. 6). Defoe built conflict into his hero's very naming. He did not choose the name "Robinson Crusoe" because it was an *ordinary* middle-class name, as Ian Watt suggests.[67] An extraordinary concentration of intellectual and geographic history lies behind it, as Defoe himself relates in the famous opening of the novel:

DEFOE'S DEIST MASTERPIECE / 155

I was born in the Year 1632, in the City of *York*, of a good Family, tho' not of that Country, my Father being a Foreigner of *Bremen*, who settled first at *Hull:* He got a good Estate by Merchandise, and leaving off his Trade, lived afterwards at *York*, from whence he had married my Mother, whose Relations were named *Robinson*, a very good Family in that Country, and from whom I was called *Robinson Kreutznaer;* but by the usual Corruption of Words in *England*, we are now called, nay we call our selves, and write our Name *Crusoe*, and so my Companions always call'd me.[68]

The low-hanging fruit is the proximity of *Kreutznaer* to the allegory of a hero who first forgets the Cross (*Kreutz* in German) and then recovers it by growing nearer (*näher* in German, *nader* in Dutch, and "naer" in Defoe's

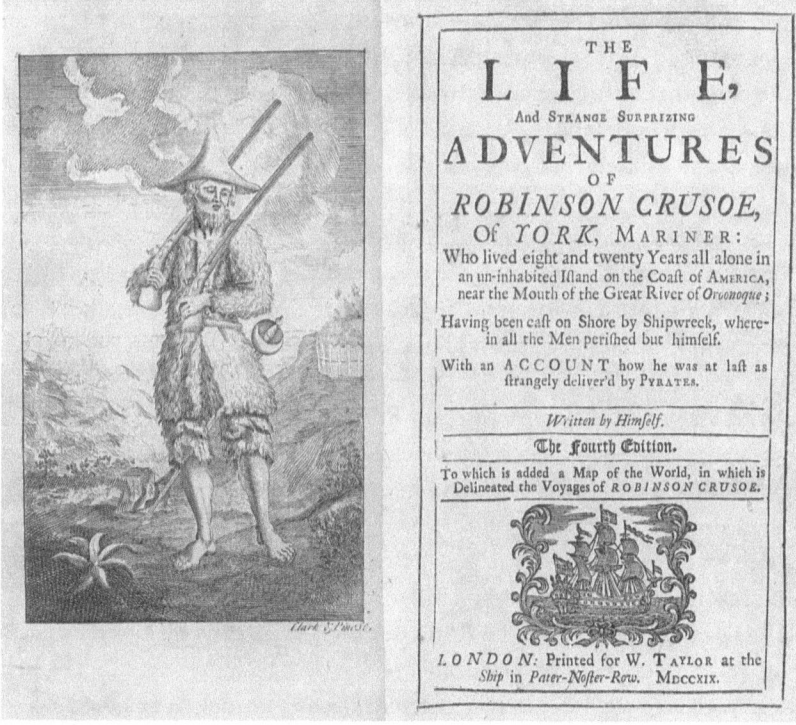

Figure 6. Title page and frontispiece. From Defoe, *The Life and Strange Surprizing Adventures of Robinson Crusoe*, 4th edition, 1719. (Courtesy of Harvard University, Houghton Library)

shortening) to a noticeably Protestant Christianity.[69] It follows "that in Crusoe's name we have an etymological intimation that he is to be regarded as a Christian wayfarer, and that his *Life and Adventures* is to be taken as a spiritual journey."[70] However, a problem develops when scholars take this etymology at face value, for *Kreuz* is one of those primal words whose force is antithetical. *Kreuz* also means a cruiser, or adventurer, and it is worth observing that one of the sources for *Robinson Crusoe* was Woodes Rogers's *A Cruising Voyage round the World* (1712). Derived from the Latin *crux*, a *Kreuz* is also a crucial or controversial point. Derived from common German usage, a *Kreuz* might also be a physical crossing or bridge, so a *Kreutznaer* may be someone whose ancestors lived near a bridge over the river Naher, which flows, yes, not so far from Bremen in the German Palatine. The tension between these two origins of the same name—one allegorical and the other geographical, one typological and the other confusing—led David Marshall to conclude: "Scholars have tried to translate and decipher the German name *Kreutznaer*, and the overdetermined significance of *Kreuz* or cross, which can refer to the cross of a sword, an anchor, or a mast, or, of course, a *crucifix*. . . . The cross that Kreutznaer or Crusoe constructs [on his island] can be seen as a representation of his name. It is a symbolic or even hieroglyphic signature, a kind of literal self portrait."[71]

With regard to "Crusoe" itself, scholars have long speculated that the name may have derived from a classmate of Defoe's at Morton's Academy, Timothy Cruso, though they have not explained why Defoe might have named his hero after such an insignificant figure.[72] A more important foreign transplant may have been relevant to Crusoe's naming: Christian Rosenkreuz (1378?–1484?), the purported founder of the Rosicrucian movement. Did Defoe hear the sounds of Crusoe in Rosicrucian? Defoe's literary enemies, Swift and Pope, had been busy mocking the Rosicrucians, using them as code for their attacks on deists and freethinking dissenters: Roger Lund observes that in "the characterization of the Hack [in *A Tale of a Tub*], who is at once wit, atheist, Rosicrucian, and religious fanatic, Swift incarnates the conflation of modern error which lies at the heart of his satiric strategy."[73] Joining in the mockery of the Rosicrucians, Alexander Pope issued expanding versions of his mock-epic poem "The Rape of the Lock," in which Rosicrucian spirits serve as epic machinery but turn out to be powerless to protect the heroine's virginity—her lock—from violation. *The History of the Life and Adventures of Mr. Duncan Campbell* (1720), usually attributed to Defoe, includes a prefatory poem that attacks Pope for his dependence on the Rosicrucian machinery:

Pope first descended from a *Monkish* Race,
Cheapens the Charms of Art, and daubs her Face;
From *Gabalis,* his Mushroom Fictions rise,
Lop off his *Sylphs*—and his *Belinda* dies;
Th' attending Insects hover in the Air,
No longer, than they're present, is She Fair . . .
But if these truant Body-Guards escape,
In whip the *Gnomes* and strait commit a Rape;
The curling Honours of her Head they seize,
Hairs less in Sight, or any Hairs *they please.*[74]

A note to the word "Gabalis" reveals the author's familiarity with both Pope's poem and the history of the Rosicrucians: "see *The History of the Count de Gabalis,* from whence he has taken the Machinery of his Rape of the Lock." The book referred to is *The Count of Gabalis, Being a Diverting History of the Rosicrucian Doctrine of Spirits viz. Sylphs, Salamanders, Gnomes, and Daemons,* by the Abbé de Villars (Nicolas-Pierre-Henri [1635–73]). Did Defoe counter these easy dismissals of the Rosicrucians by weaving their name into that of his hero? In "A Memoir of His Life and Writings," prefacing *The Works of Daniel De Foe* (1811), William Hazlitt observes, "It ought not to be forgotten that Defoe has some sarcasm in his 'System of Magick,' or the Sylphs and Gnomes, which Pope may have deemed a daring invasion of his 'Rosicrucian Territory.'"[75]

The quasi-mythic, quasi-historical Christian Rosenkreuz bears a strange resemblance to Robinson Crusoe. The movement Rosenkreuz started often refers to him by his initials, C.R, or his sign, R.C., the Rosy Cross, just as Defoe does his hero in *Serious Reflections.* R.C. was a spiritual and geographic voyager. One of the founding documents of the Rosicrucian movement, *The Fame and Confession of the Fraternity of R: C:, Commonly, of the Rosie Cross* (1652), describes its hero this way:

> But that we do not forget our loving Father, Brother *C.R.* he after many painful Travels, and his fruitless true Instructions, returned again into *Germany,* the which he (by reasons of the alterations which were shortly to come, and of the strange and dangerous contentions) heartily loved: There, although he could have bragged with his Art, but specially of the transmutations of Metals; yet did he esteem more Heaven, and the Citizens thereof, Man, than all vain glory and pomp.

Nevertheless he builded a fitting and neat habitation, in which he ruminated his Voyage, and Philosophy, and reduced them together in a true Memorial.[76]

Like Defoe's literary career, the history of the Rosicrucians began, according to Thomas de Quincy, with a literary hoax that produced outsize effects: "To a hoax played off by a young man of extraordinary talents in the beginning of the seventeenth century, but for a more elevated purpose than most hoaxes involve, the reader will find that the whole mysteries of Freemasonry, as now existing all over the civilised world after a lapse of more than two centuries, are here distinctly traced. . . . Freemasonry is no more or less than Rosicrucianism as modified by those who transplanted it to England."[77] Freemasonry is also closely tied to deism.[78] This was the secret enemy Pope sought to trivialize in "The Rape of the Lock" by rendering the Rosicrucians as insubstantial sprites; this may also have been the secret association Defoe wanted to draw between his hero and a suppressed tradition of radical religious thought.

These suspicions increase when we turn to the other conspicuous clue Defoe left as to his hero's geographical origins: Crusoe's father is an immigrant to England from Bremen in the German Palatine. Bremen was not an innocent choice. The scholar Andrea Walkden relates Bremen's significance:

By choosing Bremen as the birthplace of Crusoe's father, Defoe connects Crusoe's family history to the larger outlines of European history and to the controversial foreign policy of George I, Elector of Hanover, in particular. In 1712, Hanover had seized the German duchies of Bremen and Verden from Sweden, and in 1715, less than a year after his coronation, George was urging the British fleet, originally sent to the Baltic to protect merchant shipping, to block Swedish supply lines to their military bases in Germany. This was illegal under the 1701 Act of Settlement, which stipulated that a monarch who held territories independently of the British crown could not use British resources to defend or maintain them. The resulting debate split the ruling Whig party in two, one side lobbying parliament to supply money for George's anti-Swedish policy, the other protesting that British money was being used to support Hanoverian expansion. Bremen and Verden were only formally ceded to Hanover in the summer of 1719, a few months after the publication of *Robinson Crusoe*, and Defoe could reliably have expected his first audience to spot the political allusion.[79]

An event even more pertinent to *Robinson Crusoe* occurred in the summer of 1709, when a massive influx of immigrants from the Palatine arrived on English soil, strongly encouraged by our author, who devoted his journalistic skill to convincing the English public that the arrival of ten to fourteen thousand German refugees was good for the nation and that the immigrants should be resettled in England in small communities. Defoe himself drafted resettlement plans and submitted them to Parliament. The whole campaign blew up in his face, however, when the anti-immigrant Tories of 1710 gained control. They viewed these German Protestants as likely foes and used all means possible to expel them from England.[80] Historians note Defoe's mixed motives for wanting to resettle so many of his fellow Calvinists in England. "In the whole affair of the Palatine immigration," writes O. F. W. Fernsemer, "there was a hidden design of the Whigs against the established Church to increase the number and strength of the dissenters."[81] Fernsemer speculates, therefore, that the reference to Bremen may amount to an extraordinary act of contrition and substitution: I promised you Palatines resettlement in England; you got starvation in camps, deportation, and a perilous passage to America. Here is *Robinson Crusoe*—your own story—as compensation. On one of the lists of immigrants entering New York in 1709–10 Fernsemer locates a Johannes Creutz, whom he proposes as another candidate for our man Kreutznaer.

Amid these etymological and geographic signals it is easy to lose sight of a basic question: if Kreutzaer is translated "by the usual Corruption of Words in *England*" into Crusoe, what, then, is the English geographical equivalent to the German Bremen? Where, to put the point bluntly, does *Robinson Crusoe* originate in England? This geographical question was on Jonathan Swift's mind as he began *Gulliver's Travels* in conscious imitation of the opening of *Robinson Crusoe*. Despite his quip that he could not remember the name of the fellow that was pilloried, Swift seems obsessed with Defoe at the start of *Gulliver's Travels*. An early reader of that work complained that the "Account which the Author is said to give of himself and Family, his Travels, &c. are manifest Forgeries, not one Word of them being in the Original; so that they seem to have been added to the *English* Version by the Author of *Robinson Crusoe*, to inhance the Price, and other Reasons very obvious."[82] Swift slyly weaves Defoe into the narrative when Gulliver informs us on page one that he married into the family of Mrs. Mary Burton, whose father is a "hosier on Newgate Street."[83] The words "hosier" and "Newgate" in close proximity mean to evoke Defoe, but in evoking him this way Swift also makes Defoe Gulliver's father-in-law. Swift had clearly read *Robinson Crusoe* and was aware of the names and geographical coordinates Defoe assigns his hero. After establishing a family connection between Defoe and the Gullivers, Swift next insinuates where this whole mess of secular-spiritual adventurers—these English Bremenites—originates. Cousin Sympson's letter to the reader goes out of its way to assert the writer's intimate friendship with Gulliver and "likewise some Relation between us on the Mother's Side," before explaining: "ALTHOUGH Mr. *Gulliver* was born in *Nottinghamshire*, where his Father dwelt, yet I have heard him say, his Family came from *Oxfordshire;* to confirm which, I have observed in the Church-yard at *Banbury,* in that County, several Tombs and Monuments of the *Gullivers.*"[84] Banbury is the English Bremen. Swift, like Leslie and Gildon, wants to tar *Robinson Crusoe* with radical origins, and Banbury was no innocent resting place, either. In 1600 the good people of Banbury, in their reformist zeal, tore down the town's two great crosses. They were cross-naysayers in earnest.[85] Banbury was Cromwell's operational base during the Civil War, and the first great battle occurred there, with the people of Banbury firmly on the parliamentary side. Anabaptists and Brownists were holding their independent meetings there by 1621, and in 1664 a Friend's Meeting House was established. Tying Gulliver to Banbury recalls Swift's "The Mechanical Operation of the Spirit," with its belittling attack on Protestant dissenters as "Banbury saints" who have the amazing ability to ejaculate at the sound of their own words.[86] These saints were also sometimes labeled Jewish.[87] So many were their detractors that Banbury became synonymous with storytelling and deceit: "The town's reputation for untruth underlies later sayings: the apparently proverbial phrase 'Banbury glosses' was used in 1530 and 1571 to mean twistings of the truth, and may be the origin of the term 'a Banbury story' denoting a tall tale."[88]

Refusing to acknowledge Defoe by name, Swift twits him in fiction. He turns Defoe's play on German names into native terms and situates the English Defoes and Gullivers in Banbury in an offhand remark. He makes Defoe the father-in-law of a character who sails four long voyages without once thinking to pray; who has amnesia for the people of his past before he gains philosophical reasons for hating them; who adapts to his changing environment so well that he goes mad and sheds with horses, revolted by the smell of his own brood. In 1726, Swift retaliates against Defoe's provocation.

The exact symbolism of the names Kreuznaer and Robinson and Crusoe and Bremen may never be known, but one point is clear: Robinson Crusoe and its derivation from the German mean either something deeply religious and allegorical or something simply secular and historical; either the name anticipates the story of a prodigal redeemed, or it anticipates the history of a man chance has cast on an island to make do as best he can. In that sense, *Kreutznaer/*Crusoe is a torn figure, type and countertype. Defoe described his own situation along similar lines in *The Review* of October 22, 1709: "It was my Disaster first to be set a-part for, and then to be set a-part from the Honour of that Sacred Employ."[89] Two prepositions, "for" and "from," capture the ambivalence and the wit of Defoe's predicament. This same ambivalence is woven into the name of his hero. Contradictory, opaque to himself—now a humanist respectful of cultural differences; later a jingoist for colonial and evangelical domination; one minute a calculating secularist playing for advantage, the next a starstruck mystic reporting visions of the angelic world; here a reflective human being with qualms about selling Xury into slavery, there a slave trader willing to risk life and limb to maximize profits moving forward—Crusoe is sage and stooge, Christ figure and schlemiel. He is a "Robin" in the seventeenth-century folk understanding of the name as playful trickster spirit: "'Tis Robin or some Spirit walkes about, / Strike him, quoth he, and it will turne to aire."[90] And he is the son of Robin in the sense children of Defoe's generation would have known: progeny of Robin Hood, an adventurer at odds with church and state.[91]

The Footprint in the Sand

If this analysis holds, it should help solve at least some of the puzzles that have perplexed scholars all these years. One conundrum is surely the remarkable scene in which Crusoe, thinking he is alone on the island, discovers a single footprint in the sand (see fig. 7).[92] Robert Louis Stevenson calls the scene "one of the four supreme moments in imaginative literature."[93] Richard West refers to it as a "terrifying and unforgettable moment . . . a master stroke of imagination which established Defoe as a genius."[94] Scholars have assembled collections of essays and honored their great figures with titles such as *Defoe's Footprints*.[95] Homer O. Brown considers the footprint an emblem for the entire book. After "Robinson Crusoe experiences the incredible shock of seeing the 'naked footprint of a man,' the hidden self-other structure of the book is brought into the open. The footprint is the merest sign of the *near* presence of another human being—yet shouting significance for Robinson is the very fact of its inadequacy of signification. . . . A footprint in the sand—a partial signature whose power lies in its mystery and ambiguity."[96] Yet even with all this attention, I am not sure we have an adequate explanation for either the sign itself or the world's reaction to it.

Here is the famous passage:

Figure 7. Plate no. 58, The footprint in the sand. From François Aimé Louis Dumoulin, *Collection de cent-cinquante gravures . . . des voyages et aventures surprenantes de Robinson Crusoé,* [1810] 1962. (Courtesy of Harvard University, Houghton Library)

It happen'd one Day about Noon going towards my Boat, I was exceedingly surpriz'd with the Print of a Man's naked Foot on the Shore, which was very plain to be seen in the Sand: I stood like one Thunder-struck, or as if I had seen an Apparition; I listen'd, I look'd round me, I could hear nothing, nor see any Thing, I went up to

DEFOE'S DEIST MASTERPIECE / 163

a rising Ground to look farther, I went up the Shore and down the Shore, but it was all one, I could see no other Impression but that one, I went to it again to see if there were any more, and to observe if it might not be my Fancy; but there was no Room for that, for there was exactly the very Print of a Foot, Toes, Heel, and every Part of a Foot; how it came thither, I knew not, nor could in the least imagine.[97]

Attempts to explain the sign of the footprint in the sand have been many, beginning with Crusoe's own. His swirling thoughts move from the primitive (he thinks at first that the footprint belongs to the Devil), to the scientific (he goes back to confirm that "there was exactly the Print of a Foot" not his own). There is only one print, and that adds to the mystery. A one-legged cannibal? The chance effect of water and wind? In his semiological analysis of the sign, Robert Folkenflik compares the footprint to a "Gestalt duck-rabbit" and links it to a larger "semiological crisis" in early modern England.[98] What was this semiotic crisis, and how did Defoe get mixed up in it? Here the analysis loses specificity: "An epistemological crisis is a semiotic crisis is a hermeneutic crisis and the upshot in the world of Crusoe is a series of profoundly ambiguous events."[99] But what is the common denominator of all of these crises, and why is Defoe involved?

As before, Defoe's nemesis provides an answer, but we must follow these antagonists into unfamiliar territory. Something happened to Leslie in the process of revising his *Short and Easie* for a much demanded second edition. The title page of the second edition adds the following indication of a new target:

To which is Added, a *Second Part*
TO THE
JEWS.
Shewing, That these *Four* RULES
do Oblidge them as much, or more than
The DEISTS to the Acknowledgment
Of *Christ*.
With an Answer *to the Most* Material *of
Their* Objections, *and* Prejudices *against*
Christianity.[100]

Between the first and second editions, Leslie appears to have realized that the deists' case for an ethical monotheism not tied to any specific revelation could always call in Judaism for support. True, the Jews had their revelation, but it was different from that of the Christians, making their common denominator a shared ethics, not revelation. Leslie's answer to this leveling maneuver was that the two religions do share a single revelation, only the Jews have not yet learned how to interpret it. Writes Leslie, "I tell this to the *Deists,* lest they think that the *Jews* have some stronger Arguments than they know of; that they are not persuaded by the Miracles of our blessed *Saviour,* and by the fulfilling of the Prophecies in him, that were made concerning the *Messiah.*"[101] They are not persuaded, but you must be if you want to find a way back from deism to Christianity.

Leslie's suspicion that Judaism aided deism, and vice versa, runs counter to the received view, possibly based on the notorious examples of Shaftesbury and Voltaire, that deism was hostile to Judaism. The Haskalah movement of Jewish Enlightenment in Germany and early reform Judaism bear strong deist influence.[102] Scholars who have resisted the view of deism as inherently anti-Semitic have described a pan-European and English philo-Semitism in the work of Spinoza, Blount, Toland, and Wollaston.[103] So Leslie's observation of a league between deists and Jews was astute and much in keeping with the popular tendency to hold Judaism accountable for deism. Deism had a Jewish reputation in part because of its connection to Spinoza, and it mattered little that the Jewish authorities in Amsterdam had excommunicated him in 1656. Blount, the deist who figures so prominently in this history, was the first English translator of Spinoza.[104] In *The Rod, or the Sword* (1702), Robert Fleming warned, "If Reason recoil in the Breasts of some, at the thought of *Atheism* in its *naked Dress;* yet with a little refining, Men can bring their Thoughts to admit of it, under the notion of *Spinosism,* or *Deism,* to the renouncing of the Principles of *Christianity,* and *all revealed Religion.*"[105] John Breuhowse, author of *The Highland Spectator* (1744), observes that "the Opposers of Jesus Christ and his Religion are the *Deists* and the *Jews.*"[106] In *An Appeal to All That Doubt, or Disbelieve the Truth of the Gospel, whether They Be Deists, Arians, Socinians, or Nominal Christians* (1742), William Law observed that "when the old *Jews* left off the *Idols* of the Heathens, they fell into an Idolatry of another kind, which was this, they *idolized* the Rites and Ceremonies of their own true Religion; they placed that *Confidence* in the outward Letter, and expected that Good from their outward Rites, which they should have . . . expected from God above. This is the Idolatry of the rational Deist."[107] Robert Adam's *Religious World Display'd,* published in Edinburgh in 1809 and in Philadelphia in 1818, accounts for the origin of deism this way:

> In most ages of the Church, Deism has attended the triumphs of Christianity, either as a captive, a rebel, or an enemy. Some Pagans,

in the evangelic age, preferred a rational theism to an absurd idolatry, and became proselytes at Jerusalem, without adopting the Jewish ritual. Many of the exiled Jews, on the destruction of their capital, seem to have retained no other peculiarity, than the exclusive tenet of the Divine Unity. Both Pagans and Jews of this cast united in forming a sect, but little known in ecclesiastical history, the *Hypsistarians,* or Caelicolae of the 3d century. These were a sect of Deists, formed by such of the Jews and Gentiles as, deserting the religion of their ancestors, substituted *naturalism* in its place. Three laws of Honorius, in the Theodosian code, were directly formed against them; in one of which, he ranks them with the heathens, as Cromwell did our *English* Deists.[108]

These routine associations between deism and Judaism help explain why Leslie set himself the task of extending his method against deism into an attack on Judaism, as well. The problem appears to have obsessed him. Even his sympathetic late nineteenth-century biographer Robert Joshua Leslie noticed the fixation:

> Leslie does not appear to have been brought into much personal contact with Jews, but the plan he had marked out naturally suggested dealing with them next in order, and the subjects were of a kindred nature. Indeed, he assumes perusal of the method with the Deists before that with the Jews, while in both the same rules are laid down and essentially the same line of argument adopted so far as it can apply. For none can admit the genuineness of the New Testament who deny that of the Old; and on the other hand, though Deists may not be Jews, Jews are Deists.[109]

What stands behind the declaration, "Though Deists may not be Jews, Jews are Deists"? Judging from Leslie's argument, it is a view of language and interpretation. Leslie believed that deists and Jews share a *hermeneutic* failure. Deists have forgotten and Jews never learned how to read the prophecies of the Old Testament as anticipations of the New Testament. Thus, it becomes necessary to teach them the correct way of reading potent religious signs and stories. Leslie therefore engages in a spirited defense of typology and figural interpretation. In *A Short and Easie Method with the Deists,* he writes,

> *We also have a more sure Word of Prophesie,* for the Proof of this *Jesus* being the *Messiah,* that is, *The Prophecies* which had gone before *Him,*

from the Beginning of the World; and *All* Exactly *Fulfill'd* in Him . . . and so *Often*, by *All* the *Prophets*, in several Ages, Fore-Told; How can this be an *Imposition* or a *Forgery?* . . . This is Particularly *Insisted* on, in the *Method* with the *Jews*. And even the *Deists* must Confess, That that Book we call the *Old Testament* was in being, in the hands of the Jews long before our *Saviour* came into the World. . . . Old Prophecies . . . *cou'd not have been Contriv'd to Countenance a New Cheat*. . . . For this therefore I refer the *Deists* to the *Method* with the *Jews*. . . . Yet they [the Jews] cannot yield. Why? Because they think that the *Gospel* is in *Contradiction* to the *Law*.¹¹⁰

Because the older scripture so clearly foretells the New Testament, the evidence that might make against Christian priority—"that Book we call the *Old Testament* was in being, in the hands of the Jews *long before our* Saviour *came into the World*"—becomes, paradoxically, the surest sign that the second came first. This manner of reading needed to be retaught from generation to generation. Leslie assumes that task, and he singles out two groups—deists and Jews—who are obtuse on principle when it comes to this manner of reading texts and the world. Leslie devotes extraordinary energy to helping the deists reclaim this way of reading while damning any Jew who does not get with the program. Despite framing his work as a dialogue, on this point of typology and the typological reading of the Hebrew Bible as the Old Testament, he is willing to sacrifice all pretence of impartiality, as his deist again and again berates Jews and Judaism for not grasping the significance of their own prophecies:

> Deist. By the Account you have given, there is but one *Religion* in the World, nor ever was. For the *Jewish* was but *Christianity* in *Type*, though in time greatly *Corrupted*.¹¹¹
> Deist. What say the *Jews* to this? For I cannot imagine how they can get off of it.¹¹²
> Deist. This is shameful! And plainly to avoid the *Prophecies* against them.¹¹³
> Deist. This Argument is to the *Jews*. And if I were a *Jew* it wou'd move me.¹¹⁴
> Deist. I must have recourse to the *Jews*, in answer to these *Prophecies* of the *Messiah*, which you have brought: For they, owning these *Scriptures* as *Revelations* given them by *God*, must have some Solution or other for them; or else give themselves up as Self-Condemned.¹¹⁵

Having converted the deist at the expense of the Jew and proved the Jew self-condemned, Leslie draws the final typological lesson: "As the *Door* was kept *Open* to *Christ* before He came, by the many and Flagrant *Prophecies* of Him; and by the *Types* Representing Him: so was the *Door* for Ever *Shut* after Him, by those *Prophecies* being all *Fulfill'd* and *Compleated* in Him, and Applicable to none who shou'd come after Him; and by all the *Types* Ceasing, the *Shadows* Vanishing when the *Substance* was come."[116] Leslie considers his argument so airtight that resistance to it must be met with verbal violence. "If the *Revelation* of *Moses* be *true*," he writes, "that of *Christ* must be *true* also. . . . so that I hope you are involved in the happy Necessity, either to renounce *Moses,* or to embrace *Christ*."[117] Conversion becomes a complement: "We do believe and pray for the *Conversion* of the *Jews*. For this end they have been so miraculously preserved, according to the Prophecies so long before it. And when the Time shall come, as they are the most honourable and antient of all the Nations on Earth, so will their *Church* return to be the *Mother* Christian *Church.*"[118]

Leslie's attack on the Jews isolates what we might call a rhetorical figure, but what was actually the linchpin of the Trinitarian Christianity Leslie defended. For Leslie, typology is to representation what the Trinity is to faith, mutually reinforcing components that unite matter and spirit, sign and signified, by means of an overarching yet invisible *translatio*. He took the defense of the Trinity to its philosophical and linguistic extremes and coupled these arguments with expressions of rhetorical violence that dramatize what was at stake. Leslie wants to reassert the primacy of typological interpretation in the face of a threat he feels to this system.

Deist philology also took interest in typology, as Blount's notorious *Great Is Diana of the Ephesians* (1680) makes clear by its very title. This phrase, taken from Acts 19–38 in the New Testament, epitomizes the story of Paul's first mission to Ephesus, which almost caused a riot. Juxtaposed with this suggestion of violence was an austere scholarly study of ancient rites and rituals, none of them Christian. The subtitle explains: "Or the Original of Idolatry together with the Politick Institution of the Gentiles Sacrifices." On the surface *Great Is Diana* appears to be nothing more than a scholarly account of ancient rites and rituals. Its homegrown philology deceived the Royal censor, Roger L'Estrange, and won the book an immediate date with the common hangman. Fifteen years later, Leslie was still fuming over Blount's ruse. In his anger he describes the literary maneuvers of a resourceful deist:

> The Design and whole Import of that Book, is under the name of the Gentile Sacrifices, and Religion, to Blaspheme, and, like a *Mad Dog*, to Curse and Reproach the whole Institution of God, as well under the Law as the Gospel. . . . He Instances almost in every Circumstance of our Saviour's Life, and Death, his Miracles and Proofs of his Divinity, by telling over the Story, in something that he finds or makes like it among the Heathens; and for which he gives all the ill Names can be to the Heathen Worship, as being contradictory to Reason; with a But the Christian Religion is not so——when he has made them the very same, and no more grounds for believing the one than the other; and that so plainly, that none who have but half an Eye can help seeing that the whole is meant to Ridicule and Blaspheme the *Christian* Religion, in this most Malicious and Provoking manner . . . Would God it had never been heard or wrote, that there might have been no necessity of ever mentioning of it.[119]

Once again it is possible to use the intemperate Leslie as an alarmist reporter of what his enemies, including Defoe, were doing. They were twisting religious allegory into a vessel of critique. Playing on the expectation that readers would interpret allegorically, they created false equivalencies—counter-allegories, in other words. Blount's implied parallels between pagan and Christian practices should redound to the advantage of Christianity. Instead, Blount's philology levels Christian and pagan practices and suggests a parallel between the most sadistic of the heathen rituals, those involving human sacrifice, and Christianity. Blount's complication of heresies injects heterodox conclusions into the shell of allegory. It is the "telling over the Story" that angers Leslie: Blount is a kind of philological storyteller, an employer and waster of allegory. To rescue allegory from this devious and dangerous appropriation, Leslie had to restore the fundamental trope of allegory—typology—to its proper use.

Leslie probably thought he was defending Christianity by explaining how typology works. Yet when he made the structure of typology explicit, he also exposed a problem in this sign of signs: "But these *Types* may be overvalu'd, when we rest in them, without looking forward to what they Represent."[120] He acknowledges a precarious balance in the typological system between sign and signified. The material sign, indicative of things real, must stand for itself and give way to a spiritual signification that completes and fulfills it. Dally in the material, delay the move to what it represents, and danger lurks. By the same token, if the sign empties of material significance too quickly and predictably, the opposite danger appears: not materialism but lifeless abstraction. Erich Auerbach places this dilemma within Christian figural representation at the center of his study of realism in the West. He describes an oscillation within the Christian tradition between realism and allegory, an oscillation concentrated in the typological sign itself, which Auerbach calls "Figura."[121] In Auerbach's account, as in the deist philology of Herbert and Blount, Paul holds a privileged position:

> The negative reaction which [the Gospel according to St. Mark] aroused in Jerusalem, both among the Jewish leaders and among the majority of the people, forced the movement to embark on the tremendous venture of missionary work among the Gentiles, which was characteristically done by a member of the Jewish diaspora, the Apostle Paul. With that, an adaptation of the message to the preconceptions of a far wider audience, its detachment from the special preconceptions of the Jewish world, became a necessity and was effected by a method rooted in Jewish tradition but now applied with incomparably greater boldness, the method of revisional interpretation. The Old Testament was played down as popular history and as the code of the Jewish people and assumed the appearance of a series of "figures," that is of prophetic announcements and anticipations of the coming of Jesus and the concomitant events. The total content of the sacred writings was placed in an exegetic context which often removed the thing told very far from its sensory base, in that the reader or listener was forced to turn his attention away from the sensory occurrence and toward its meaning.[122]

The phrasing is cautious and scholarly, but Auerbach's meaning is clear: the rhetorical figure that Christianity counted on to supplant Judaism carried its own risks. Auerbach spells them out in offhand comments scattered throughout *Mimesis*. He is careful to observe that Paul was a Jew, and the method of figural interpretation was "rooted in Jewish tradition." Similarly, he writes that "rigid, narrow, and unproblematic schematization is originally completely alien to the Christian concept of reality." But he immediately adds, "It is true, to be sure, that the rigidifying process is furthered to a considerable degree by the figural interpretation of real events, which, as Christianity became established and spread, grew increasingly influential and which, in its treatment of actual events, dissolved their content of reality, leaving them only their content of meaning.... [F]igural interpretation must inevitably become a simple and rigid scheme."[123] That's a lot of rigidity in one sentence. Although Auerbach offers a careful philological account of the figure of Figura and its implications for Western literature, he also diagnoses a tendency within typology to oscillate between material history and symbolic abstraction, realism and allegory. Auerbach's references to rigidity and the dissolving of reality suggest also the potential violence of figural interpretation once it sets the blueprint for historical destiny. Auerbach does not risk exposure with the controversial phrase "Great is Diana of the Ephesians" (a title both Goethe and Freud adopt), but his philological method derives from the same impulse to view Paul's mission to convert the Gentiles as a crucial moment in the history of the West, when hints of allegory in the Hebrew Bible were mobilized in a systematic way for purposes of mass conversion.

Leslie's concern that "these Types may be overvalu'd, when we rest in them, without looking forward to what they Represent" suggests that the dilemma within typology had become a source of open conflict by 1700. His diagnosis is accurate, after all. Deists and Jews did oppose typology. The deists resisted typology in part because of their campaign against miracles: the big ones of direct exclusive revelation and prophecy and the small figures of speech that called on readers to effect a miraculous transition from earthly sign to transcendent meaning. Deists were anti-Trinitarians not only in thought but also in style. They opposed divine right on the level of argument and through a critique of the tropes associated with it, of which typology was one.[124] They trained their tools of philological analysis on miraculous linguistic signs. For Jews there was another reason to resist typology. Put simply, it appropriated Jewish scripture for Christian ends. It was a figure of their erasure, or forced conversion.

As we have seen, Defoe's *Consolidator* and much of his verse satire relied on just such typological structuring. He published homiletic works that teach the young the principles of typology, same as Charles Leslie.[125] But that is only part of the story. Defoe also opposed Leslie on this most fundamental question of signification, as openly as he could, in and through fiction. The footprint in the sand is an emblem of that resistance. Consider how the footprint, as a sign, works and refuses to work. The footprint gives every indication of typological significance; it also undoes the possibility of typological significance. The footprint invites—indeed, it provokes—a series of contradictory readings, each motivated by a rapid change in Crusoe's mentality. To the fearful Christian, the footprint symbolizes the devil; to the stranded survivor, it is the mark of a cannibalistic enemy. Looking back in *Serious Reflections* on his run-in with the footprint, Crusoe describes his first reaction as a form of hypochondria: "You may be sure, while I had this Fancy [belief in the Devil] in my Head, I was of Course over-run with the Vapours, and had all the Hypochondriack Fancies that ever any melancholy Head could entertain; and what with ruminating on the Print of the Foot upon the Sand, and the Weight of the Devil upon me in my Bed, I made no difficulty to conclude, that the Old Gentleman really visited the Place."[126] Fear generates hypochondria, and hypochondria generates thoughts of the devil. The text presents a behavioral account of religious superstition, a natural history of religion, in fiction. In that sense it subverts Leslie's doctrinaire Trinitarian and typological Christianity by means of the way it is written.

Just as Defoe could not confront Leslie's defense of the Trinity directly and passes as Trinitarian in his beliefs, so he was in no position to subvert Leslie's defense of typology explicitly. We have already seen Defoe's ambivalent attitude toward Jews and Judaism in *A Continuation of Letters from a Turkish Spy*. Defoe need not have had any special relation to Jews or Judaism to understand—as an artist writing at the beginning of the eighteenth century—both the role that signs play in allegory and the role that signs play in more secular, historical forms. He knew why Leslie insisted on the typological system. But Defoe sought to give the historical its due. This set up a competition between the genres of allegory and history to which Defoe alludes on many occasions, especially when justifying the purpose or design of *Robinson Crusoe*. "I *Robinson Crusoe* being at this Time in perfect and sound Mind and Memory, Thanks be to God therefore; do hereby declare . . . that the Story, though Allegorical, is also Historical; and that it is the beautiful Representation of a Life of unexampled Misfortunes."[127] These lines are confusing because we normally think of allegory and history as quite different. Does the statement mean that the biography of a shipwrecked traveler stands for something else—for the sin, atonement, and redemption of a Christian Everyman? In that case, the historical suffers for the sake of the allegorical. Does it mean that the rich historical account of Robinson Crusoe has some vague correspondence with a larger framework of significance that is left undetermined? In that case, the allegorical suffers at the expense of the historical. Yet Defoe sought to combine the allegorical and the historical in the very structure of his prose. His previous experiments in long prose fiction find him attempting to do just that, unsuccessfully. The remarkable effect of the footprint in the sand should be read in this light. It is the sign that permits this mixture, the solution to an aesthetic problem. It stands out for the same reason that other fraught moments in the long narrative stand out: the encounter with the dying goat, the sprouts of barley growing as if by magic outside his door, a plain earthenware pot.

Here, then, is a hermeneutic context that makes sense not only of the footprint in the sand, but also of many similar signs in *Robinson Crusoe*. They are Defoe's silent rebuttal to Leslie's type-driven hermeneutics. These signs create a shimmering effect, not a direct analogue of sign to signified. The prevalence of such shimmering signs unsettles the work's relation to allegory. The footprint is nothing in isolation, but startling—world changing—in context. Defoe prepares the reader for it with a narrative that positions the reader between allegorical and realist expectations. Like the footprint, Jonah is type and countertype, *Kreutznaer* is Christ figure and adventurer, Crusoe is spiritual pilgrim and scoundrel. His story is allegorical; his survival is random. The society he builds on the island is utopian and ideal. The society he builds on the island is a temporary expedient that falls apart when he neglects it. The footprint is a symbol; the footprint is as material as the particles of sand composing it. This one sign stands out among many others that create a similar effect. These are shimmering signs, resisting pure allegory.

A "Coining of Providences"

Starting with Jonah, we were able to identify Defoe's tactics on the level of genre—his creation of a style that combines realism and biblical narrative, humble representations of ordinary life with spiritual grandeur and daring. These are not the only generic elements that matter, but they influence how other elements, such as spiritual autobiography and the colonialist adventure story, factor in.[128] Taking up Crusoe's name and heritage, we noted suspicions of radical republican and deistical origins, which Swift, Gildon, and Defoe's own character, the philosophical Gentlewoman of *Serious Reflections*, confirm. With the footprint in the sand, we identified a feature of the novel found throughout part 1 (it is a measure of its greatness), less so in part 2 (where there is a falling away from this particular excellence), and seldom in part 3 (which makes no real effort to sustain the fiction)—that feature being the shimmering instability of potent signs.

The deist elements of *Robinson Crusoe* remain hidden to many serious readers. Scholars treat with all seriousness the fact of Crusoe's and Friday's conversions and the sincerity with which the text evokes Providence over and over. It is therefore necessary to take up these two ideas—Providence and conversion—because they are so deeply woven into the story. When Crusoe declares he is "delivered," first spiritually and then physically and materially, Providence and plot correspond. As Providence plays out in its upward and teleological direction, it requires conversions from bad to good, fallen to redeemed, and these human plots follow the same path. We have seen in the descriptions of Crusoe as a Christ figure and prodigal son that both Providence and conversion cohere in the general allegory. If, however, *Robinson Crusoe* is allowed its *counter*-allegorical dimensions, then we would not expect Providence to function like a well-oiled machine or conversions to be quite so happy or necessary.

The labile treatment of perhaps the most important theological concept in the book raises the question of just how serious the author himself is about the claims Providence makes on character, story, and the reader. Was Gildon right to accuse Defoe of a "Coining of Providences," transforming Providence from serious theological concept to a matter of human convenience?[129] Context is important here. Crusoe is not the protagonist we have come to expect from later psychological novels. He sits at the juncture of two competing conceptions of character—that of the cosmopolitan tradition and that of the Christian metaphysical tradition. Character in the cosmopolitan tradition is a vessel for diverse thoughts, amblings, adventures, experiments. Character in the Christian metaphysical tradition strives to reach a destination equal to its fullest being, as Petrarch tries to do on his ascent of Mount Ventoux. Cosmopolitan character does not operate under the requirement of self-consistency; the Christian metaphysical character does. Character in the cosmopolitan tradition is a skeptical construct, like the Leslie figure Defoe impersonates in *The Shortest Way.* Crusoe is such a construct. He embodies but does not resolve cultural anxieties. He is rough and ready and frighteningly independent. No wonder he never stays home for long. For this reason, when he entertains an idea such as Providence, Crusoe is more a barometer of the word's tortured history and multiple associations than a firm advocate of any one of the things he means by it.

The word "Providence" is ubiquitous in the three parts of *Robinson Crusoe.* Crusoe's usages are so various that it is surprising critics have been able to choose a single definition and identify it as Defoe's meaning, or even Crusoe's.[130] The first mention occurs in the preface, where the author assures the reading public of the modesty and seriousness of the story, promising that it has a "*religious Application of Events to the Uses to which wise Men always apply them.*" Such applications testify to "*the Wisdom of Providence in all the Variety of our Circumstances, let them happen how they will.*"[131] Although this wisdom is divine, it is legible in earthly signs. For instance, in the opening sequence, the ship master warns Crusoe to read the will of Providence in the warning signs he receives vis-à-vis a seafaring life. This view of Providence deprives the hero of personal freedom, including the freedom to make mistakes. It assumes that a correct reading of the will of Providence is available from the natural signs on hand. Again and again, the story contradicts this hopeful determinism, as Crusoe himself observes: "I was still to be the willful Agent of my own Miseries; and particularly to encrease my Fault and double the Reflections on my self, which in my future Sorrows I should have Leisure to make; all these Miscarriages were procured by my apparent obstinate adhering to my foolish Inclination of wandring abroad, and pursiing that Inclination, in contradiction to the clearest Views of doing my self good in a fair and plain pursuit of those Prospects and those Measures of Life, which Nature and Providence concurred to present me with, and to make my Duty."[132] Despite being invoked as a governing concept that might easily be taken to control the *arche* of the story itself, Providence has no settled meaning in *Robinson Crusoe*. It can be seen devolving into a merely personal, or national, strategy of domination.

Crusoe wavers, speculates, and contradicts himself, often without knowing it. Driven to despair by his isolation, he begins to doubt the very idea of Providence: "I had great Reason to consider it as a Determination of Heaven, that in this desolate Place, and in this desolate Manner I should end my Life; the Tears would run plentifully down my Face when I made these Reflections, and sometimes I would expostulate with myself, Why Providence should thus compleatly ruin its Creatures, and render them so absolutely miserable, so without Help abandon'd, so entirely depress'd, that it could hardly be rational to be thankful for such a Life."[133] A Calvinist might reply that Providence ruins some of its creatures so that others, the elect, may thrive. "Philosophically, the argument is circular," writes Christopher Hill, "but Calvinism did not exist primarily as a philosophical system. It gave courage and confidence to a group of those who believed themselves to be God's elect. It justified them, in this world and the next."[134] That is exactly what we see Providence giving Crusoe: courage and confidence. We pass unobtrusively out of the theological into the therapeutic—the truth or falsity of Providence is no longer the issue. The idea makes him feel better: "I frequently sat down to my Meat with Thankfulness, and admir'd the Hand of God's Providence, which had thus spread my Table in the Wilderness. I learned to look more upon the bright Side of my Conditions, and less upon the dark Side; and to consider what I enjoy'd, rather than what I wanted."[135] As a psychological concept, "Providence" joins a host of other terms Crusoe uses to substantiate a middle region between metaphysics and matter: these are the apprehensions, intuitions, premonitions, wayward hints, secret clues, dreams, and other communications with the spiritual world that arrive in the natural course of life. *A Vision of the Angelick World*, the final section of *Serious Reflections*, reads like a sound check for Crusoe's wavering convictions, his search for a vocabulary bridging natural and divine realms. Gildon makes fun of this whole vocabulary when he has his fictional Defoe lament that he did not obey the "*Secret Hint*" he had not to walk alone the very night he was mugged in "*a great Field betwixt Newington-Green and* Newington *Town, at one a Clock in a Moon-light Morning.*"[136] Other critics take Defoe's apparitions more seriously.[137]

The meaning of Providence shifts as Crusoe's situation changes. When revisiting his island in *Farther Adventures*, Crusoe admires the buildings that have sprung up, which remind him of the structures he assembled thirty years earlier: "This was excellently well contriv'd; nor was it less than what they afterwards found Occasion for; which serv'd to convince me, that as human Prudence has the Authority of Providence to justify it, so it has doubtless the Direction of Providence to set it to Work."[138] Yes, Calvinism seeks to reconcile these contraries—the human and the divine descriptions of Providence cohere in the idea that good work is a sign of election, and election ensures the discovery of the best means of work. While permitting the reader this reassuring coherence, Defoe also develops a character grappling with the very idea of Providence and coming to conclusions based as much on experience as on church doctrine. Crusoe's experience is vivid; church doctrine pales by comparison—and readers can make of this what they will. Defoe will not tip his hand, except that he will not guide the reader, which is the greatest tip-off of all.

Having slipped from God's will to human ingenuity, Providence has not finished its human descent. In one of the battle scenes of *Farther Adventures*, we learn that the Tartars "pour'd their Arrows in upon us so thick, that we were fain to barricade the Side of the Boat up with the Benches, and two or three loose Boards, which to our great Satisfaction we had by mere Accident or Providence in the Boat."[139] Accident or Providence? Are these then the same? The same diminishment occurs when Providence becomes a forceful man's go-to argument for ignoring the wishes of the women in his life. At the start of *Farther Adventures*, Crusoe, ever hankering after fresh adventures, must decide whether to abandon wife and children again at the ripe old age of sixty: "My Wife, who saw my Mind so wholly bent upon it, told me very seriously one Night, That she believ'd there was some secret powerful Impulse of Providence upon me, which had determined me to go thither again."[140] He agrees.

Sadly—or fortunately—Crusoe's wife soon dies, leaving him free to follow his desires, with only one more woman—his friend, the widow—standing in the way: "my Wife being dead, I had no Body concern'd themselves so much for me, as to perswade me one Way or other, except my ancient good Friend the Widow, who earnestly struggled with me to consider my Years, my easy Circumstances . . . and above all, my young Children: But it was all to no Purpose, I had an irresistible Desire to the Voyage; and I told her, I thought there was something so uncommon in the Impressions I had upon my Mind for the Voyage, that it would be a kind of resisting of Providence, if I should attempt to stay at Home; after which, she ceas'd her Expostulations."[141]

By the time Crusoe dubs himself an instrument of Providence—slaughtering twenty or thirty natives in revenge for the killing of Friday (a killing for which he was directly responsible)—it becomes difficult to escape the impression that Providence does not control the narrative. Rather, a self-serving narrative controls Providence, revealing it as a concept easily appropriated for personal and national advantage. A person or nation knowing the will of Providence can become the armed instrument of God's will. This is the logic of fanaticism. Defoe thus degrades his own hero to illustrate the abuses of Providence. By the end, Crusoe has become a ridiculous, Quixote-like figure who tilts at a Muscovite idol in a display of ill-advised religious zeal:

> I confess I was more mov'd at their Stupidity and brutish Worship of a Hobgoblin, than ever I was at any Thing in my Life; to see God's most glorious and best Creature, to whom he had granted so many Advantages, *even by Creation,* above the rest of the Works of his Hands, vested with a reasonable Soul, and that Soul adorn'd with Faculties and Capacities, adapted both to honour his Maker, and be honoured by him, sunk and degenerated to a Degree, so more than stupid, as to prostrate it self to a frightful Nothing, a meer imaginary Object dress'd up by themselves, and made terrible to themselves by their own Contrivance.[142]

What does our rational, honorable narrator do in the face of this insult? He puts his entire party at great risk by slashing the idol with his sword: "But what signify'd all the Astonishment and Reflection of my Thoughts; thus it was, and I saw it before my Eyes, and there was no room to wonder at it, or think it impossible; all my Admiration turn'd to Rage, and I rid up to the Image, or Monster, call it what you will, and with my Sword cut the Bonnet that was on its Head in two in the middle, so that it hung down by one of the Horns."[143]

Nor does this intemperate act slake Crusoe's thirst for idol smashing. "Your Zeal may be good," remarks one of Crusoe's companions, "but what do you propose to yourself by it? Propose, *said I,* to vindicate the Honour of God, which is insulted by this Devil Worship. But how will it vindicate the Honour of God, *said he,* While the People will not be able to know what you mean by it?"[144] Crusoe's solution is to convince other members of his party to invade the Muscovite compound, capture and tie up a number of natives, and force them to watch the destruction of their idol: "We took all our Prisoners, and brought them, having unty'd their Feet, and ungagg'd their Mouths, and made them stand up, and set them just before their monstrous Idol, and then set fire to the whole," an exploit that sparked Dumoulin's attention (see fig. 8).[145]

Little remains of the cosmopolitan Crusoe. He has become a casualty of the author's need to conceal his book's implicit deism, just as Defoe's Gentlewoman infers. The text does not support the conclusion that, "while Defoe is impersonating Robinson Crusoe, he is also impersonating on another level Providence itself."[146] Defoe cannot impersonate Providence itself because he is too busy impersonating Crusoe's confusion about Providence. The novel does not resolve the confusion. Why does Defoe make Providence such a problem in *Robinson Crusoe?* Once again, this move makes sense once we recover the deist context. The view of Defoe as an anti-deist has led to the misapprehension that he was not a keen observer of and surreptitious player in the deist controversy. That context offers a ready explanation for the perplexed uses of Providence found in the novel. The deists were well aware of a problem within the idea of Providence. The movement can be said to have divided between a more radical initial phase, which excluded the idea of Providence from its list of religious essentials, and a more moderate middle phase, which allowed Providence back in.

The deist method of deriving a minimum list of notions of a natural or universal religion might require the inclusion of Providence, since it is a feature of so many religions. Providence is one of those bridging terms that connects divinity and history. It suggests a deity reaching down into human affairs to set the course of events. As personalized as the concept may be in certain uses, it carried potency for the larger ambitions of states armed with religion, and religions armed with states. Providence is an assertion of mastery. Any religion that seeks to justify its advantage in one place and make it permanent everywhere will enjoy a concept like Providence. That it took such firm root in Calvinism is no surprise. An oppressed minority that knows itself elect will reach for Providence as central to its mythic structure. However, deism developed as a peace movement. Its first articulation came from a dashing English

Figure 8. Plate no. 146, Destruction of the Muscovite idol. From François Aimé Louis Dumoulin, *Collection de cent-cinquante gravures... des voyages et aventures surprenantes de Robinson Crusoé*, [1810] 1962. (Courtesy of Harvard University, Houghton Library)

diplomat, poet, man of letters, and musician, Edward, Lord Herbert of Cherbury (1583–1648), who failed to stave off the Thirty Years' War when he served as the ambassador to France between 1619 and 1624.

Friend of Descartes, Gassendi, and Grotius, Edward, Lord Herbert of Cherbury was also a first-order yet largely neglected thinker. He possessed a flamboyant character and did not shy away from intrigues or duels, of which there were too many for a diplomat trying to forestall war. He appears to have insulted a favorite of Louis XIII and suffered the disgrace of an early recall to England. Herbert's diplomatic failure produced a philosophical recompense called *De veritate prout distinguitur a revelation, a verisimili, a possibili, et a falso* (1st ed., Paris, 1624; 2d ed., London, 1633), which was translated into French in 1639 but not translated into English until 1937.¹⁴⁷ In this work, Herbert tried to accomplish with reason what he had failed to do with diplomacy: present a case for religious tolerance and peace. A complex and little-studied epistemology precedes the main event—the list of Common Notions derived from an empirical survey of world religions—but it is entirely relevant. Herbert proposes a different picture of the mind from that of his friend Descartes. In Herbert's model, all knowledge relies on comparison. There is no metaphysical point of absolute certainty, first principle, or *cogito ergo sum*. Instead of a philosophy of identity, Herbert spells out an epistemology of difference, where all knowledge relies on a comparison of at least two things, and there is no pure knowing, no sameness without difference. The dialogic hermeneutics of Bakhtin and Gadamer are distant relatives of this attempt to formulate a non-Cartesian picture of the mind as inherently relational and categorizing—a genre generator of sorts. If in epistemology nothing exists in isolation, and sameness is always the result of a perceived difference, then in ethics a deep philosophical justification exists for toleration of all religious differences and an end to forced conversions.

Given this philosophical commitment to peace, it is understandable that Herbert and Blount would leave Providence off the list of the Common Notions. They were painfully aware how easily the concept could be weaponized in the service of competing religious armies. Here are the five Common Notions as Charles Blount transmitted them to English readers in 1683, under the guise of a complimentary letter to John Dryden:

That there is One onely Supreme God.
That He chiefly is to be Worshipped.
That Vertue, Goodness, and Piety, accompanied with Faith in, and
    Love to God, are the Best ways of Worshipping Him.
That we should repent of our Sins from the Bottom of our Hearts,
    and turn to the Right Way.
That there is a Reward and Punishment after this Life.¹⁴⁸

No sign of Providence here, or of any specific revelation, election, Messiah, or divinely sanctioned government. The stripped-down list, radical in its implications, was soon augmented by a sixth and seventh Common Notion. In 1693, Blount included in his *Oracles of Reason* a work signed "A.W." titled *An Essay on Natural Religion.* This essay reappeared in 1745, appended to *A Summary Account of the Deists Religion.* Perhaps hoping to increase sales, the title page flags the appended essay, calling it "the strongest Arguments against the Necessity and Advantages of a DIVINE REVELATION yet published," and attributes the piece to a surprising source: "To which are annex'd, Some Curious Remarks on the *Immortality* of the SOUL; and an ESSAY by the Celebrated Poet, JOHN DRYDEN, Esq; to prove that NATURAL RELIGION is alone necessary to *Salvation,* in Opposition to all DIVINE REVELATION."[149] While it is doubtful that Dryden was the author of this deist tract, the new version of the Common Notions does become noticeably more moderate because it restores Providence to the list along with the concept of providential government:

> That there is one Infinite Eternal God of all Things.
> That he governs the World by Providence.
> That 'tis our Duty to worship and obey him as our Creator and Governor.
> That our Worship consists in Prayer to him and praise of him.
> That our Obedience consists in the Rules of Right Reason, the Practice whereof is Moral Virtue.
> That we are to expect Rewards and Punishments hereafter, according to our Actions in this Life; which includes the Soul's Immortality, and is proved by our admitting Providence.[150]

The second, third, and sixth items compensate for the omission of Providence from the first list, thereby reuniting religion and politics. This more cautious version of the Common Notions makes its way into Benjamin Franklin's letter to Ezra Stiles of March 9, 1790:

> You desire to know something of my religion. It is the first time I have been questioned upon it. But I cannot take your curiosity amiss, and shall endeavor in a few words to gratify it. Here is my creed. I believe in one God, the creator of the universe. That he governs by his providence. That he ought to be worshipped. That the most acceptable service we render to him is doing good to his other children. That the soul of man is immortal, and will be treated with

justice in another life respecting its conduct in this. These I take to be the fundamental points in all sound religion, and I regard them as you do in whatever sect I meet with them.[151]

I emphasize the deists' ambivalent response to Providence because this same ambivalence permeates *Robinson Crusoe*. Defoe does not impose a Calvinist solution to the problem. Instead, he reveals the various ways that a character may invoke Providence under extreme conditions. A good example of this effect is Crusoe's famous reaction to the sprouted barley, which he initially takes to be a sign of God's providential intervention in his life. Dumoulin recognizes the power of this moment in the text (see fig. 9):[152]

> It is impossible to express the Astonishment and Confusion of my Thoughts on this Occasion; I had hitherto acted upon no religious Foundation at all; indeed I had very few Notions of Religion in my Head, or had entertain'd any Sense of any Thing that had befallen me, otherwise than as a Chance, or, as we lightly say, what pleases God; without so much as enquiring into the End of Providence in these Things, or his Order in governing Events in the World: But after I saw Barley grow there, in a Climate which I knew was not proper for Corn . . . it startled me strangely, and I began to suggest, that God had miraculously caus'd this Grain to grow.[153]

Primitive man grows into scientific man before our eyes as his brain supplies the missing information in the form of a memory of having shaken out a useless bag of chicken feed in *the exact spot*. Stooge only briefly, Crusoe revisits his first interpretation. And what does he do? He remodels the concept of Providence to suit his need: "I ought to have been as thankful for so strange and unforeseen Providence, as if it had been miraculous; for it was really the Work of Providence as to me."[154] The author represents his character willingly embracing a fiction as if it were real because his psychic life depends on it. Yet the scene also could be read as a Christian's sincere attempt to understand the role of Providence in his life. Not to force a decision between these views appears to have been Defoe's goal, and if it was, he achieved it.

A complicated question in the castaway's lonely struggle, Providence also comes into play in Crusoe's interactions with others. One moment the thought of Providence stays Crusoe's murderous hand, as he contemplates how best to punish cannibals for their outrage against humanity, and the

182 / THE SHORTEST WAY WITH DEFOE

Figure 9. Plate no. 29, Crusoe discovers the sprouted barley. From François Aimé Louis Dumoulin, *Collection de cent-cinquante gravures... des voyages et aventures surprenantes de Robinson Crusoé*, [1810] 1962. (Courtesy of Harvard University, Houghton Library)

next moment Providence demands that Crusoe become its instrument in eradicating the evil from the face of the Earth. The concept may have no meaning apart from the human context that gives it meaning. Completely confused by the competing directives of Providence, Crusoe as much as throws up his hands:

From hence I sometimes was led too far to invade the Sovereignty of Providence, and, as it were, arraign the Justice of so arbitrary a Disposition of Things, that should hide that Light [of Christ] from some, and reveal it to others, and yet expect a like Duty from both: But I shut it up, and check'd my Thoughts with this Conclusion, 1st, That we did not know by what Light and Law these should be condemn'd; but that as God was necessarily, and, by the Nature of his Being, infinitely holy and just, so it could not be, but that if these Creatures were all sentenc'd to Absence from himself, it was on Account of sinning against that Light, which, as the Scripture says, was a Law to themselves, and by such Rules as their Consciences would acknowledge to be just, tho' the Foundation was not discover'd to us. And, 2dly, That still as we are all the Clay in the Hand of the Potter, no Vessel could say to him, Why hast thou form'd me thus?[155]

Crusoe's thoughts are magnificently jumbled. He pretends to apologize for invading the "Sovereignty of Providence," but does so just the same. He regrets daring to "arraign the Justice of so arbitrary a Disposition of Things," thereby repeating the charge of cosmic caprice. He suggests an openness to religious differences and rejection of any doctrine that damns the other, then reverts to a standard rendition of the Athanasian Creed, the same position Leslie would have taken against any tolerance for non-Trinitarian Christian and all non-Christian religions: "as God was necessarily, and, by the Nature of his Being, infinitely holy and just, so it could not be, but that if these Creatures were all sentenc'd to Absence from himself, it was on Account of sinning against that Light, which, as the Scripture says, was a Law to themselves, and by such Rules as their Consciences would acknowledge to be just, tho' the Foundation was not discover'd to us."[156] However roundabout the logic, Crusoe still ends up agreeing that there must be some reason that tradition condemns all people who live and die outside faith in a Trinitarian Christianity. The natives' natural religion must be deficient; otherwise, their faith would more closely match that of Christianity, which is then a truer expression of natural religion. Does Defoe believe this? Does Crusoe? The overarching irony forestalls a decision—or, rather, it permits several decisions.

Like the name *Kreutznaer*, our hero contains contradictions. There may be a way to bridge these contrary uses of Providence or rank-order them, but there is also a way not to do so. Leah Orr acknowledges that "Crusoe never solves the second major problem in his religious system, between a generous Providence that allows all to be saved, and a merciless Providence that has predestined most of the world to damnation."¹⁵⁷ The phrasing suggests we should expect Crusoe to solve the problem. As we have already seen, Crusoe is only intermittently philosophical, and sometimes quite obtuse. There is even a question how mechanically adept he is.¹⁵⁸ He is not prepared to reconcile dialectical oppositions endemic to the very idea of Providence; he is equipped only to display them, like a stooge or an unwitting sage. Crusoe appears to be both simultaneously when he states with confidence in *Serious Reflections,* "I distinguish much between using Force to reduce Heathens and Savages to Christianity, and using Force to reduce those that are already Christians, to be of this or that Opinion; I will not say but a War may be very just, and the Cause be righteous, to reduce the Worshippers of the Pagods of *India,* to the Knowledge and Obedience of Christianity, when it would be a horrible Injustice to commence a like War, to reduce even a Popish Nation to be Protestant."¹⁵⁹ Crusoe's experiences teach him intolerance instead of wisdom. To the extent the space among author, narrator, and protagonist is thought to collapse, such passages provide fodder for accusation against Defoe himself. Has Defoe lost control of his irony? Is irony beside the point? Such is Orr's conclusion: "The Crusoe who exclaimed proudly on his island colony that 'I allowed Liberty of Conscience throughout my Dominions' differs radically from the Crusoe who plans Christian world domination. Can Crusoe be Roger Williams and Hernán Cortés all at once? Defoe does not seem to depict Crusoe's inconsistencies ironically or invite us to critique his religious doctrine."¹⁶⁰ This study reaches a different conclusion. Defoe does not intrude with authorial asides or explanations, à la Fielding. Instead he leaves the reader with Crusoe alone on an island. Identifying with Crusoe, we join him in his struggle for food, water, shelter, patience. His dilemmas become our own. We care enormously about him, even though he is confused—indeed, because of his confusion. This is the source of the novel's power, and it is possible only because Defoe allows for religious ambiguity and spiritual conflict. In part 1 of *Robinson Crusoe,* Defoe exchanges theological coherence for psychological conflict, steadfast faith for fluid experience, allegory for inconsistency, type for character.

Suspect Conversions

Readings of *Robinson Crusoe* that take the concept of Providence seriously tend to focus on three notable conversions—of Crusoe alone, of Friday with Crusoe's help, and of Will Atkins's wife with help from Crusoe and the Catholic priest—which appear to confirm the providential structure of the narrative. I leave aside the initial vow of faith Crusoe utters in spontaneous prayer with other members of the crew when his first ship is sinking. This example does epitomize, however, Gildon's complaint against all of *Robinson Crusoe*'s conversions: that they are all so clearly *motivated* by circumstances, and their effects seem to wear off—or, as he angrily puts it, "I am afraid, with all your Sagaciousness, you do not sufficiently distinguish between the Fear of God, and the Fear of Danger to your own dear Carcass."[161] Erasmus had written the paradigmatic version of this complaint against late, desperate prayer in "The Shipwreck," a fictional dialogue in his *Colloquies*.[162] The rudimentary fiction protected the author from conclusions that might be drawn when repentance arrives, as at the end of *Moll Flanders*, only after all hope has been lost. Defoe uses the humanist trope, as well. All of his conversion scenes are richly embellished with realist detail that complicates the moral message considerably.

In the first major conversion, Crusoe has fallen ill with an ague. He is so sick he cannot walk and can barely feed himself. He thinks he is close to death and must try something, anything, to break his fever. It is a dramatic high point of the narrative. "I went, directed by Heaven no doubt; for in this Chest I found a Cure, both for Soul and Body, I open'd the Chest, and found what I look'd for, *viz.* the Tobacco; and as the few Books, I had sav'd, lay there too, I took out one of the Bibles which I mention'd before, and which to this Time I had not found Leisure, or so much as Inclination to look into; I say, I took it out, and brought that and the Tobacco with me to the Table."[163] The conflation of drug and religion is so artfully done that the reader need not see it as more than accidental, or less than providential, that in going to his chest for tobacco Crusoe rediscovers his Bible. The latter, an afterthought at first, soon takes center stage, but first Crusoe tries to self-medicate (see fig. 10):[164]

> What Use to make of the Tobacco, I knew not, as to my Distemper, or whether it was good for it or no; but I try'd several Experiments with it, as if I was resolv'd it should hit one Way or other: I first took a Piece of a Leaf, and chew'd it in my Mouth, which indeed at first almost stupify'd my Brain, the Tobacco being green and strong, and that I had not been much us'd to it; then I took some and steep'd it an Hour or two in some Rum, and resolv'd to take a Dose of it when I lay down; and lastly, I burnt some upon a Pan of Coals, and held my Nose close over the Smoke of it as long as I could bear it, as well for the Heat as almost for Suffocation.[165]

This is a meticulous description of a man driven to the last extreme. And here we arrive at the passage that so offended Gildon and led to the comparison with

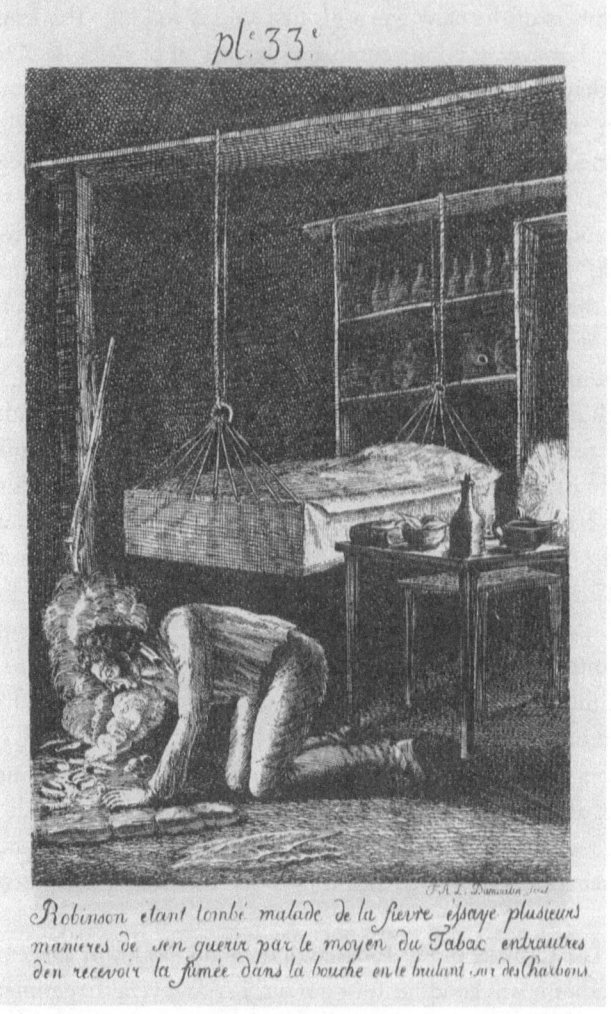

Figure 10. Plate no. 33, Crusoe sick and bent over the tobacco. From François Aimé Louis Dumoulin, *Collection de cent-cinquante gravures... des voyages et aventures surprenantes de Robinson Crusoé*, [1810] 1962. (Courtesy of Harvard University, Houghton Library)

Vanini: "In the Interval of this Operation, I took up the Bible and began to read, but my Head was too much disturb'd with the Tobacco to bear reading, at least that Time; only having open'd the Book casually, the first Words that occurr'd to me were these, *Call on me in the Day of Trouble, and I will deliver, and thou shalt glorify me.*"[166] Here begins Crusoe's spiritual recovery, his conversion to a more constant faith. After taking the potion and falling asleep, Crusoe wakes refreshed, thinking he has slept through the night. Because the narration is retrospective, and Crusoe has been able to compare his marks on the cross—his timekeeping device—with actual dates back home, he discovers he is one day off, which occasions these *Kreutznaerean* remarks on crossing and recrossing:

> I drunk the Rum in which I had steep'd the Tobacco, which was so strong and rank of the Tobacco, that indeed I could scarce get it down; immediately upon this I went to Bed, I found presently it flew up in my Head violently, but I fell into a sound Sleep, and wak'd no more, 'till by the Sun it must necessarily be near three a-Clock in the Afternoon the next Day; nay, to this Hour, I'm partly of the Opinion, that I slept all the next Day and Night, and 'till almost three that Day after; for otherwise I knew not how I should lose a Day out of my Reckoning in the Days of the Week, as it appear'd some Years after I had done; For if I had lost it by crossing and recrossing the Line, I should have lost more than one Day: But I certainly lost a Day in my Account, and never knew which Way.[167]

Smoking, drinking, lost time, and scripture all work together on Crusoe. There are ways to allegorize this, no doubt. Just as Crusoe needed strong tobacco for his body to break the hold of his fever, so he needed the chance passage from the Bible to awaken him from his theological slumber. Crusoe had to pass outside ordinary time into a spiritual frame of mind in which his own suffering gained meaning. That is why he loses track of a day, even though the physical crossing and recrossing of the Line should have canceled each other in the reckoning. The accidental association of personal revelation and mental dissociation need not distract the reader from a greater truth beginning to shine in on Crusoe at this moment: "While I was thus gathering my Strength, my Thoughts run exceedingly upon this Scripture, *I will deliver thee;* and the Impossibility of my Deliverance lay upon my Mind in Bar of my ever expecting it: But as I was discoursing myself with such Thoughts, it occurr'd to my Mind, that I pored so much upon my Deliverance from the main Affliction, that I disregarded the Deliverance I had receiv'd."[168] With this Crusoe knelt down and "gave God Thanks aloud for my Recovery from my Sickness." These sentiments repeat so often that resistance to the conclusion that *Robinson Crusoe* updates *Pilgrim's Progress* in modern, economic terms might seem perverse.

The same could be said for the famous scene that finds Crusoe tending to Friday's spiritual needs, teaching him the falsity of his pagan religion and the outlines of a truer one. Critics typically take the success of Friday's conversion as a foregone conclusion, and with good reason. Crusoe himself later refers to Friday as a Protestant.[169] Yet there is a textual prehistory of this conversion scene, which includes Montaigne's "Of Cannibals" (1580). This essay compares what cannibals do to their conquests after battle to what the Spaniards do to natives in the New World, or what the Inquisition does to presumed heretics at home—a comparison that plays to the disadvantage of cultured Europeans and to the advantage of the cannibals. A hundred years before Hume, Montaigne had reduced metaphysical debates to expressions of habit and custom. Charles Cotton's translation (1st ed., 1685–86; 4th ed., 1711) puts the point this way: "I find that there is nothing barbarous and savage in this Nation [of cannibals], by any thing that I can gather, excepting, That every one gives the Title of Barbarity to every Thing that is not in use in his own Country: As indeed we have no other Level of Truth and Reason, than the Example and Idea of the Opinions and Customs of the Place wherein we live."[170] Such cultural relativism was implicit in the bare mention of the virtuous savage and the topic of natural religion generally. The question of Friday's conversion cannot be separated from this context. Crusoe may try to make Friday better, but Defoe was sure to make him good from the start. This native goodness introduced the deists' question of what made him good. As Defoe's Gentlewoman complains in *Serious Reflections*, Crusoe is not overly curious about this question. His reticence may have to do with the fact that the noble savage was a well-known trope of literary deism. Attacking Matthew Tindal's *The Rights of the Christian Church Asserted* (1706), William Carroll observes that, "notwithstanding all his Arts to conceal himself, and his Design, this Author hath shew'd him to be an *Atheist*, because his Leading *Epicurean*-Principle of the *State of Nature* is perfectly *Atheistical*."[171] So even though Friday behaves in an abject way, placing Crusoe's foot on his head as soon as they meet, his very appearance in the text gave the philosophical novelist an opportunity to enter the deist controversy unobserved.[172]

The account of Friday's conversion is rich on every level. Defoe contrasts two methods of weaning Friday off his bad habits. Breaking Friday of his desire for human flesh requires some careful sequencing on Crusoe's part. Crusoe begins with goat-meat broth, moves then to a little boiled meat, and completes the gustatory retraining "with roasting a Piece of the Kid; this I did by hanging it before the Fire in a String, as I had seen many People do in *England*."[173] The method works. Friday, relishing the roasted animal, vows off human flesh in signs unmistakable to Crusoe: "He took so many Ways to tell me how well he lik'd it, that I could not but understand him; and at last he told me he would never eat Man's Flesh any more, which I was very glad to hear."[174]

In contrast to this gradual instruction, Crusoe's method for converting Friday from his religion is rough and hasty. Crusoe is a better cook than metaphysician or, as he calls himself, "Doctor":

> During the long Time that *Friday* has now been with me, and that he began to speak to me, and understand me, I was not wanting to lay a Foundation of religious Knowledge in his Mind; particularly, I ask'd him one Time, Who made him? The poor Creature did not understand me at all, but thought I had ask'd who was his Father: But I took it by another Handle, and ask'd him who made the Sea, the Ground we walk'd on, and the Hills and Woods; he told me it was one old *Benamuckee,* that lived beyond all: He could describe nothing of this great Person.[175]

Abandoning curiosity about Friday's belief system, Crusoe begins the next paragraph, "From these Things I began to instruct him in the Knowledge of the true God." How one interprets this sequence depends on the genre framing the action. If you agree that *Robinson Crusoe* is a work akin to Protestant spiritual autobiography, the legitimacy of Friday's pagan theology is never a possibility. The words "I began to instruct him" not only follow; they follow necessarily. Read this work as an instance of cosmopolitan fiction of a deist hue and Crusoe's "I began to instruct him" reads as a jarring non sequitur. Defoe's Gentlewoman challenges Crusoe on this very point: Why weren't you more ethnographic and less dogmatic? Why didn't you ask more questions of Friday to find out how he came to have a good character without knowing anything about Christ? The catechism can be read in these two different ways, depending on whether you think Friday's conversion is authentic or staged:

> From these Things I began to instruct him in the Knowledge of the true God. I told him, That the great Maker of all Things liv'd up there, pointing up towards Heaven: That he governs the world by the same Power and Providence by which he had made it: That he was Omnipotent, could do every Thing for us, give every Thing to us, take every Thing from us; and thus, by Degrees, I open'd his Eyes. He listen'd with great Attention, and receiv'd with Pleasure the Notion of *Jesus Christ,* being sent to redeem us, and of the Manner of making

our Prayers to God, and his being able to hear us, even into Heaven. He told me one Day, that if our God could hear us up beyond the Sun, he must needs be a greater God than *Benamuckee*, who liv'd but a little Way off, and yet could not hear, 'till they went up to the great Mountains where he dwelt, to speak to him: I ask'd him if ever he went thither, to speak to him? He said, No, they never went that were young Men; none went thither but the old Men, who he called their *Oowokakee*, that is, as I made him explain to me, their Religious, or Clergy, and that they went to say *O*, (so he call'd saying Prayers) and then came back, and told them what *Benamuckee* said.[176]

The mere mention of a religious priesthood sets Crusoe off. He commences a rant against any settled clergy: "I endeavour'd to clear up this Fraud to my Man *Friday*, and told him, That the Pretence of their old Men going up to the Mountains to say *O* to their God *Benamuckee*, was a Cheat, and their bringing Word from thence what he said, was much more so; that if they met with any Answer, or spoke with any one there, it must be with an evil Spirit: and then I enter'd into a long Discourse with him about the Devil."[177] Intolerant of any faith system that endows a priestly caste with authority over private conscience, Crusoe, without broth or boiled meat, goes straight for the kill, calling the devil the source of Friday's false theology. Crusoe champions the doctrine of Christ as mediator between God and humanity, while he despises the notion of old men interceding between a pagan people and their deity. This confuses the student, and in perhaps the most famous lines of the work, Defoe lets Friday ask a simple but profound question:

> I found it was not so easy to imprint right Notions in his Mind about the Devil, as it was about the Being of a God. Nature assisted all my Arguments to evidence to him even the Necessity of a great first Cause and over-ruling governing Power, a secret directing Providence, and of the Equity and Justice of paying Homage to him that made us, and the like. But there appear'd nothing of all this in the Notion of an evil Spirit, of his Original, his Being, his Nature, and above all, of his Inclination to do Evil, and to draw us in to do so too. And the poor Creature puzzl'd me once in such a Manner, by a Question meerly natural and innocent, that I scarce knew what to say to him. . . . Well says *Friday*, but you say, God is so strong, so great, is he not much strong, much Might as the Devil? Yes, yes, says I, *Friday*. God is stronger than the Devil, God is above the Devil, and therefore

we pray to God to tread him down under our Feet. . . . *But,* says he again, *if God much strong, much Might as the Devil, why God no kill the Devil, so make him no more do wicked.*[178]

Friday may be new to Christianity, but he identifies the problem of theodicy immediately. Surprised and baffled, Crusoe pretends not to hear Friday's question: "I was strangely surpriz'd at his Question, and after all, tho' I was now an old Man, yet I was but a young Doctor, and ill enough qualify'd as a Casuist, or Solver of Difficulties: And, at first, I could not tell what to say, so I pretended not to hear him, and ask'd what he said? But he was too earnest for an Answer to forget his Question, so that he repeated it in the very same broken Words, as above."[179] Here again Defoe introduces markers of two different genres and the traditions behind them. If you are a reader inclined to discover a religious application, then Crusoe's admission that Friday's question stumped him passes as an endearing aside before he recovers himself and delivers a streamlined version of Christian fundamentals. It is not that Friday's question really troubles Crusoe or has any intellectual weight. It is the kind of question that a child might ask. In this case, attention falls not on Crusoe's pretending not to hear Friday but, instead, on the answer he eventually gives, and its truth. The editor of the Pickering Masters edition favors this conclusion, while acknowledging Defoe's use of Friday as representative of natural religion. "The reference here is to what is known as 'natural theology', the knowledge of God that can be obtained by human reason, as opposed to 'revealed theology', the more complete knowledge revealed by God himself in the scriptures. The distinction is explained at length by Defoe in his *Family Instructor* (1715)."[180]

Crusoe's own explanation for his befuddlement—"I was now an old Man, yet I was but a young Doctor, and ill enough qualify'd as a Casuist"—raises the issue of casuistry. As G. A. Starr explains, the word at the time had a bad meaning associated with Catholicism—hair splitting or logic chopping to evade personal responsibility for sin—and a good meaning associated with the Protestant emphasis on the exercise of conscience, guided by an inner light. Starr believes he knows which kind of casuistry Defoe espouses:

> In the course of resolving Friday's doubts, Crusoe becomes adept at the kind of casuistry which had been recommended and exemplified in the writings of a century of English divines. In his hands, as in theirs, casuistry is a heuristic mode: in "laying things open to [Friday], I really informed and instructed myself in many things that either I did not know, or had not fully considered before, but

which occurred naturally to my mind upon my searching into them for the information of this poor savage." In other respects Crusoe may be an "absolute lord and lawgiver," but his responses to Friday's "serious inquiries and questions" are remarkably free from dogmatism; discovery rather than dictation is the order of the day, and Crusoe's probing is casuistical in the best sense.[181]

Notice that there is never a doubt that Crusoe resolves Friday's doubts. Nor is there a doubt that Crusoe himself becomes a better man for ministering to Friday. He discovers important truths in the course of his instruction, making the practice "heuristic." Starr's analysis, influential for the past fifty years, imbues Defoe with a piety and sincerity other readers, including his early critics, find lacking. Is Friday's conversion so charming? Is it really so edifying? That hesitation of Crusoe's, that pretending not to hear Friday's question, and Crusoe's noting that Friday repeated the question "in the very same broken Words, as above," signals a different genre and tradition. According to this reading, casuistry serves as a screen for the issues in play. Whether Catholic or Protestant, casuistry exists within Christianity. Friday's question comes from outside Christianity. This is another of those cosmopolitan moments that infuriated Gildon. Friday stands for the deists' appeal to natural religion. It is not better casuistry that Crusoe lacks but a reply to the deist challenge as exerted by a native who, in his broken English, poses and repeats tough questions. The fiction covers this over. We are allowed to think, encouraged to think, that a typical master-servant relationship exists between these men. Crusoe names and possesses his native discovery, calling him "my Man Friday," not my new companion, my interlocutor, my friend.

Take too seriously either Friday's unanswerable question or Crusoe's found catechism and we lose the balance that has preserved *Robinson Crusoe* from the fate of Defoe's earlier experiments in prose fiction. It is true, however, that to maintain this awareness of an aesthetic balance that was simultaneously political and theological, one must reject Starr's assertion that Crusoe's "responses to Friday's 'serious inquiries and questions' are remarkably free from dogmatism; discovery rather than dictation is the order of the day." How gentle and free from dogmatism does Crusoe sound when he calls Friday's religion a fraud and a cheat, or when he binds the Muscovites with rope and chains and forces them to watch the destruction of their idol? Crusoe relies more on authority and force than on argument and persuasion. Yet it would be an exaggeration to call this a scene of failed conversion. Friday accepts Crusoe's teaching and seems delighted by the doctrine of Christ. A skeptical reader might question Friday's cheerful acceptance. He does not struggle much with Christian theology or remain troubled long about the devil. As a convert, he is easily satisfied. Perhaps the core of Christianity is self-evident, even as taught by an inexperienced teacher. Or perhaps Defoe's irony lurks here as well, setting up Crusoe's rough-and-ready catechism against Friday's primitive religion. A truly pious reader might question the propriety of this scene—a comic riff on serious theological debate and a lighthearted mockery of the soul's progress. Is Friday really saved? Or is he, in his innocence, simply trading one set of superstitions for another?

The conversion of Will Atkins's wife follows the same pattern and borders on absurdity. A French Catholic priest who does not speak or understand English convinces Crusoe that the common-law marriages that have sprung up between European white men and native women on his island must be solemnized in marriage, and that for him to perform the service, the women first must be baptized. Atkins's response to this news is honest and worldly: "*Lord! SIR*, says *Will. Atkins,* How should we teach them Religion? Why we know nothing our selves; and besides, Sir, *said he,* should we go to talk to them of *God,* and *Jesus Christ,* and *Heaven* and *Hell,* 'twould be to make them laugh at us, and ask us, What we believe our selves?"[182] To this practical realism, Crusoe can only respond: "*Will. Atkins, said I to him;* though I am afraid what you say has too much Truth in it, yet can you not tell your Wife that she is in the Wrong? That there is a God, and a Religion better than her own; that her Gods are Idols." Atkins replies, "but with What Face can I say any Thing to my Wife of all this, when she will tell me immediately it cannot be true?"[183] The scene ends with Atkins's wife and Atkins kneeling together in prayer:

> *Wife.* That me would understand, that me fain see; if he teachee all good Thing, forbid all Wicked Thing, he reward all good Thing; punish all wicked Thing, he makee all Thing, he give all Thing, he hear me when I say O to him, as you go do just now; he makee me good, if I wish be good, he spare me, no makee kill me, when I no be good; all this you say he do, yet he be great God; me take, think, believe him be great God; me say O to him with you my Dear.[184]

As virtuous pagans go, Will Atkins's wife is an even purer instance than Friday. She does not eat other people, for one thing, and she appears almost saintly in her intuitive piety and forgiveness of her husband's faults.

Return the book to the deist controversy that gave rise to it, and Friday's question, "Why God no kill the Devil?" as well as Atkins's question, "But with what Face can I say any thing to my Wife of all this?" become deist provocations. The deist wants to know what made Friday and Will Atkins's wife good before they met Christians. Although "natural religion" does not figure prominently in the deists' Common Notions, it is implied by the method that produced a religious universalism. A rational inference from the behavior of people in many times and places might suggest grounds for "goodness" not moored in partial faith systems vying for universal dominion. This would be a religion derived from nature and would refute Hobbes's cynical account of aggressive human instinct. Naturally, such a religion would disavow forced conversions and other imperialistic ventures, at least in theory.

Here, then, is the subtext that Friday's very presence in the novel evokes, despite his abject obedience to Crusoe. He is there to raise questions, not to promote exploitation of dark races. The questions he raises are primarily religious. If Friday's natural religion excludes Protestant ideas that Crusoe thinks essential, if deism excludes special revelations for reasons of peace, by what right does Crusoe conclude that Benamuckeeism is worse for all that? Maybe aspects that Crusoe thinks essential, such as a theory of the devil, make no sense to natural beings for a reason. Friday is there to provoke such deistical questions, even as his willingness to convert to Protestant Christianity and become Crusoe's servant shields the author from detection. Successful conversion masks the dialogue that precedes it.

Admittedly, this reading of Friday's suspect conversion counters generations of Defoe scholars whose shared tendency has been to read Crusoe's attention to Friday's spiritual needs in just the opposite way—as a refutation of the natural religion the virtuous pagan represents:

> For a quarter-century before the publication of *Robinson Crusoe*, since, that is, the lapsing of the Licensing Act in 1694, the religious controversies in England were intensified by deists—men like Charles Blount, John Toland, Matthew Tindal, Anthony Collins, Thomas Woolston—who challenged the ceremonies and mysteries of Christianity, and who stood by reason; reason, they said, shows us how to find, through nature, the goodly but distant Deity. Friday's "natural" religion is Defoe's answer to the deists. For instance, the name Benamuckee clearly means "much good," and represents the good-natured, beneficent god of the deists and, through the influence of Shaftesbury, Defoe's era. . . . Defoe thus uses Friday's

natural religion to criticize deistic assumptions about nature and humans—and also about God.[185]

This commentary at least acknowledges the presence of deistical elements in the text. But the debate between deism and Christianity has been decided before the interpretation arrives. There can be no doubt that Friday's natural religion is insufficient and that Crusoe converts him to a better understanding. As we have seen, this interpretation relies on a prior decision to read the work through the lens of Protestant spiritual autobiography. Defoe left many cues signaling this genre, the signs of successful conversion among them. Brush the velvet back the other way—read Crusoe as Gildon does, as an act of deist literary subterfuge—and the significance of Friday's conversion shifts. Friday's role may well be the opposite of what this critic alleges: not to disprove deism but to introduce it in pleasing form.

Sweet Revenge

This book began with a passage from *Serious Reflections* that attacks Charles Gildon and suggests a nemesis on par with Cervantes's Duke *de Medina Sidonia,* a now obscure individual who drove a literary genius to greatness. After this passage, Robinson Crusoe runs through a catalog of memorable scenes in parts 1 and 2, as if to say, "If you have not read it already, buy this book." Then he lights on the two gratuitous animal killings that end part 1, which have puzzled scholars for three hundred years: "The Story of the Bear in the Tree, and the Fight with the Wolves in the Snow, is likewise Matter of real History; and in a Word, the Adventures of *Robinson Crusoe,* are one whole scheme of a life of eight and twenty Years, spent in the most wandring desolate and afflicting Circumstances that ever Man went through, and in which I have liv'd so long in a Life of Wonders."[186] These slaughters may well be real history, but they are as charged with significance as Crusoe's name and the footprint in the sand. They seem to occur after the true end of *Robinson Crusoe,* which finds Crusoe rescued and delivered back to England. Crusoe travels to Lisbon to recover property amassed in his absence but has a premonition that he should not return to England by sea. Although Crusoe promises, "As I have troubled you with none of my Sea-Journals, so I shall trouble you now with none of my Land-Journal," he provides a detailed description of this additional adventure. Setting out "about the middle of *October,*" the party, which includes Friday, is overtaken by a freak early snow. W. R. Owens explains that "in *Mists Weekly Journal* for 4 January 1718, there had appeared a news item about heavy snow falls in the Pyrenees, which had caused 'ravenous Beasts' to come down from the mountains into the forests of Languedoc: 'a troop of Wolves, with six Bears among them came down into a Village near——and attack'd the Inhabitants in the very Market-Place. . . . In one incident, a group of seven bears attacked and killed two fleeing men. 'A third having more Courage, stood his Ground, and one of the Bears rising upon him, he clept his Piece into his Mouth, and shot him dead upon the Spot.'"[187] Was Defoe such a realist that he inserted news directly from the papers into his narrative, just to support the verisimilitude of his book? Or is there something more going on? Defoe goes out of his way to have Crusoe go out of his way to encounter a ravenous wolf and lumbering bear. Why?

Snowbound beneath the mountain pass in the Pyrenees, Crusoe's party encounters a guide, who materializes out of nowhere. He promises them safe passage, as long as they have firearms sufficient to ward off the ravenous animals. As soon as they begin their ascent, however, Crusoe's party encounters a pack of wolves and a bear: "It was about two Hours before Night, when our Guide being something before us, and not just in Sight, out rushed three monstrous Wolves, and after them a Bear, out of a hollow Way, adjoyning to a thick Wood; two of the Wolves flew upon our Guide, and had he been half a Mile before us, he had been devour'd indeed, before we could have help'd him." Defoe singles out a leader of the pack. Dumoulin likewise singles out this wolfish scene for illustration (see fig. 11):[188]

> One of them fastned upon his Horse, and the other attack'd the Man with that Violence, that he had not Time, or not Presence of Mind enough to draw his Pistol, but hollow'd and cry'd out to us most lustily; my Man *Friday* being next to me, I bid him ride up, and see what was the Matter; as soon as *Friday* came in Sight of the Man, he hollow'd as loud as t'other, *O Master! O Master!* But like a bold Fellow, rode directly up to the poor Man, and with his pistol shot the Wolf that attack'd him into the Head.[189]

What possibly could have brought a wolf to Defoe's mind as he concluded part 1 of *Robinson Crusoe*? Charles Leslie enjoyed changing his enemies into animals. He makes William Penn into a snake; Defoe is his wolf. Leslie's *The Wolf Strip'd of Its Shepherd's Cloathing* is a savage attack on Defoe, stripping him of his Quaker garb and adding charges of treason and symbolic regicide. Answering this pamphlet in 1704, Defoe refers to "the Author or Authors of this Wolfish Book."[190] Leslie's charmingly titled *Salt for the Leach* (1712) carries

DEFOE'S DEIST MASTERPIECE / 197

Figure 11. Plate no. 91, Friday kills the wolf. From François
Aimé Louis Dumoulin, *Collection de cent-cinquante gravures . . .
des voyages et aventures surprenantes de Robinson Crusoé*, [1810]
1962. (Courtesy of Harvard University, Houghton Library)

this inscription on its title page: *"Il Lupo perde il Pelo, ma non il Vitio,"* which
Leslie paraphrases as, *"The Wolf cannot Conceal his Voracity in the Sheep's Cloathing; and the Butcher does but awkwardly act the Shepherd."*[91] Defoe was both
wolf and butcher in Leslie's menagerie of hate. In *The Finishing Stroke* (1711),
he is at it again:

And was not this an *Independent* State? Most Certainly! And extends not only to *Murder,* but to *Theft, Robbery,* or even *Cheating* or *Lying,* or whatever may be Hurtful to Humane Society. Wherein if ever Man is Permitted to be his own *Judge,* and to *Avenge* it in others, according to his own Discretion, there is a Fair *End* to all Human Society, and I should be as much Afraid to meet a *Man* as a *Wolf.* I kill a Man whom I think a *Rogue* and an *Enemy* to Human Society—And another Kills me for my Pains—And another Kills him—And so to the End of the Chapter!¹⁹²

In *The Protestant Jesuite Unmask'd* (1704), Defoe, or someone who sounds a lot like him, prepares an attack on Leslie with this inscription from Matthew 15.7: "*Beware of false Prophets which come to you in Sheeps-cloathing.* With my Service to Mr. *Lesley.*" He then writes, "I will endeavor to single out one [Jacobite] from the Herd." He describes Leslie as "one of the Leaders of [James II's] Partizans, and wages eternal War with all his Enemies." The writer asks whether Leslie "did not deserve to stand in Mr. *De* Foe's place" in the pillory.¹⁹³ Defoe enjoys impersonating his nemesis; he employs his enemy's techniques, as well. It would be absurd to argue that *Robinson Crusoe* is a consistent allegory in which human beings are metamorphosed into animals, or vice versa. The winter of 1718 may have been snowy near where Defoe's fictional characters traipsed, and no one in three hundred years has claimed that Defoe chose to end his most famous work with the symbolic execution of his archenemy, transformed into a wolf. Nevertheless, strong evidence supports this conclusion. And Defoe was not done yet.

With the wolf at least there is a reason for the killing. It attacks Crusoe's guide, as Leslie did Penn, so Friday has to shoot it. The killing of the bear, by contrast, seems entirely gratuitous. The bear does its best to avoid Crusoe's party before Friday taunts it with a rock and lures it up a tree, setting the stage for a final slaughter. Prefacing the memorable confrontation between Friday and the bear, Defoe inserts a suspiciously long parallel between bears and human beings:

> But never was a Fight manag'd so hardily, and in such a surprizing Manner, as that which follow'd between *Friday* and the Bear, which gave us all (though at first we were surpriz'd and afraid for him) the greatest Diversion imaginable: As the Bear is a heavy, clumsey Creature, and does not gallop as the Wolf does, who is swift, and light; so he has two particular Qualities, which generally are the Rule of his Actions; First, As to Men, who are not his proper Prey; I say, not his proper excessive Prey;

because tho' I cannot say what excessive Hunger might do, which was now their Case, the ground being all cover'd with Snow; but as to Men, he does not usually attempt them, unless they first attack him: On the contrary, if you meet him in the Woods, if you don't meddle with him, he won't meddle with you; but then you must take care to be very Civil to him, and give him the Road; for he is a very nice Gentleman, he won't go a Step out of his Way for a Prince; nay, if you are really afraid, your best way is to look another Way, and keep going on; for sometimes if you stop, and stand still, and look steadily at him, he takes it for an Affront; but if you throw or toss any Thing at him, and it hits him, though it were but a bit of a Stick, as big as your Finger, he takes it for an Affront, and sets all his other Business aside to pursue his Revenge; for he will have Satisfaction in Point of Honour; that is his first Quality: The next is, That if he be once affronted, he will never leave you, Night or Day, till he has his Revenge; but follows at a good round rate, till he overtakes you.[194]

This elaborately human description of the bear, which veers dangerously close to announcing the topic of revenge, invites the question, who is your bear, Mr. Defoe? Who is the lumbering counterpart to the scheming wolf? Back in 1703, responding to the fact that *The Shortest Way* had alarmed even his dissenting allies, Defoe wrote, "All the Fault I can find in myself as to these People [the Dissenters] is, that when I had drawn the Picture[,] I did not[,] like the Dutchman, with his Man and Bear write under them, This is the Man, and This is the Bear, lest the People should mistake me."[195] Moore believes that Defoe wrote *The Quaker Sermon; or, A Holding-Forth Concerning Barabbas* (1711), and I see no reason to doubt the attribution.[196] The sermon explicates a verse from John 18:40, which runs, "*Then cried they all again, saying, not this Man but* Barabbas, *now* Barabbas *was a Robber.*"[197] The text is not coy about the modern equivalent for the New Testament Barabbas, or Bar—s, as the name comes to be shortened: "Let us, Friend, bring this matter a little home to our selves; we have a Barabbas of these Days, as *Barabbas was the* Henry S——l of those."[198]

Well might the story of Barabbas have been on Defoe's mind as he concluded *Robinson Crusoe*. Just as in the Gospels, two men were arrested—one a notorious robber, and the other Jesus of Nazareth—and the mob granted clemency to Barabbas, so in 1703 and 1709, two arrests occurred. One was of Defoe for writing *The Shortest Way*, and the other was of Sacheverell for preaching and publishing *The Perils of False Brethren*. In each case, the mob and state favored Barabbas's equivalent, Sacheverell, not Christ's equivalent, Daniel Defoe. Even the charges against the two men were the same: "This *Henry Barabbas* was cast into Prison for *Sedition*, and brought to a solemn Tryal for *Sedition*. . . . [A] Gang of *Seditious fellows* were his Guard. . . . All the Cry in the Streets was, Doctor *Barabbas:* People must be knock'd down that would not joyn in the *Cry* for him, and pluck off their Hats to grace his Procession."[199] The first arrest brought interrogation after accomplices, whom Defoe protected, and a guilty plea in hopes of leniency, despite which Defoe was pilloried, held in Newgate Prison for almost six months, bankrupted, and made to turn scribbling agent for the state. The second trial was a state affair in Parliament attended by Queen Anne and the third Earl of Shaftesbury, who took meticulous notes. Sacheverell's light sentence made him a church hero in the eyes of Tories, Jacobites, and a rapidly mobilized mob, which, on March 1, 1710, ransacked the contents of nineteen dissenters' meeting houses and torched them in the streets in the worst London riots of the first half of the eighteenth century, riots that continued over the next three months throughout England. Sacheverell commenced a hero's progress through the English Midlands, a victory tour that generated huge crowds and a landslide election for the Tories in 1710. If Defoe was angry at Sacheverell in 1702, when the churchman's call for violence against the dissenters helped trigger *The Shortest Way*, imagine how he felt after the riots and Tory takeover of 1710.

Sacheverell could be Defoe's bear, and if he is, Defoe enjoys killing him. Dumoulin also enjoys the encounter, devoting three illustrations to the bear's taunting, baiting, and execution (see figs. 12–14).[200]

Ever dutiful, Friday asks Crusoe's permission to harass the bear. Crusoe is reluctant to grant it at first, ostensibly for fear of Friday's life:

> *O! O! O!* says *Friday*, three times, pointing to him; *O Master! You give me te Leave, me shakee te Hand with him; me make you good laugh.*

> I was surpriz'd to see the Fellow so pleas'd; *You Fool you*, says I, *he will eat you up: Eatee me up! Eatee me up!* says *Friday*, twice over again; *Me eatee him up: Me make you good laugh: You all stay here, me show you good laugh.*[201]

After Friday gets the bear's attention by throwing a rock at its head, he lures it up a large oak tree and onto a long limb that grows thinner. Twice—and the point is emphasized, twice—Friday lures the bear out onto the thinning branch.[202] The entire party stands below as chorus:

> When we came to the Tree, there was *Friday* got out to the small End of a large Limb of the Tree, and the Bear got about half way to him; as

DEFOE'S DEIST MASTERPIECE / 201

Figure 12. Plate no. 92, Friday taunts the bear with a rock. From François Aimé Louis Dumoulin, *Collection de cent-cinquante gravures . . . des voyages et aventures surprenantes de Robinson Crusoé*, [1810] 1962. (Courtesy of Harvard University, Houghton Library)

soon as the Bear got out to that part where the Limb of the Tree was weaker, *Ha*, says he to us, *now you see me teachee the Bear dance;* so he falls a jumping and shaking the Bough, at which the Bear began to totter, but stood still, . . . [and] he calls out to him again, as if he had suppos'd the Bear could speak *English; What you come no further?*[203]

Figure 13. Plate no. 93, Friday and the bear on the limb. From François Aimé Louis Dumoulin, *Collection de cent-cinquante gravures... des voyages et aventures surprenantes de Robinson Crusoé*, [1810] 1962. (Courtesy of Harvard University, Houghton Library)

The bear does come further, venturing onto the thinning branch a second time, at which point Friday "goes out to the smallest end of the Bough, where it would bend with his Weight, and gently lets himself down by it." Pursuing Friday, the bear shimmies back down the trunk of the tree, "and just before he could set his hind Feet upon the Ground, *Friday* stept up

DEFOE'S DEIST MASTERPIECE / 203

Figure 14. Plate no. 94, Friday shoots the bear. From François Aimé Louis Dumoulin, *Collection de cent-cinquante gravures... des voyages et aventures surprenantes de Robinson Crusoé,* [1810] 1962. (Courtesy of Harvard University, Houghton Library)

close to him, clapt the Muzzel of his Piece to his Ear, and shot him dead as a Stone."²⁰⁴

Sweet revenge. And the payback was even sweeter for being undetectable except by Defoe's most hated and hateful foes. Gildon knew something was up with these animal killings. He turns the favor back on Defoe, making his

Crusoe exceedingly eager to blow Defoe's brains out: "Come, *Friday*, make ready, but don't shoot till I give the Word":

> *Fri.* No shoot Master, no shoot; me will show you how we use Scribblers in my Country.
> *Cru.* In your Country *Friday*, why, you have no Scribblers there?
> *Fri.* No Matter that Master, we have as many Scribblers as Bears in my Country; and me will make Laugh, me will make *D—l* dance upon a Tree like *Bruin.* Oh! Me will make much Laugh, and then me will shoot.[205]

In cosmopolitan fiction, Ovidian tales, beast fables, and certain kinds of satire, such as Swift's in the fourth part of *Gulliver's Travels,* the line between species is thin and frequently crossed. We think nothing of Lucian's narrator Lucius becoming an ass under a witch's spell because such transformations often happen in the fantastic genre of Menippean satire. The situation here is vastly different. There is no reason to suspect Defoe has taken a parting shot at his enemies by allegorizing them into beasts. He assigns the dirty work to Friday, who only wants to amuse his master, and the description is so fully realized that this odd conclusion to *Robinson Crusoe* could not possibly be said to play out the execution of Defoe's nemesis and his bombastic second.[206] If the story of *Robinson Crusoe* involves the sublimation of hatred for sympathy, satire for panegyric, in an act of undetectable literary revenge, then here, in these incongruous animal killings, is a fit conclusion indeed—except that these killings conclude part 1 and are followed by two more parts, which few now read or study. Even here, Defoe's failures illuminate his success, providing an important context for his literary achievement and its origins in a suppressed, heavily disguised cosmopolitan and deist tradition. Vestiges of this tradition explain some of the deist scenarios we observed in the famous part 1. But vestiges of that tradition also explain the strange failures of *Farther Adventures.* The very character of Robinson Crusoe degenerates, shifting uncomfortably from the fascinating monitor of survival in *Robinson Crusoe* to an out-of-control zealot and capitalist-colonizer in *Farther Adventures,* a man, moreover, who is directly responsible for the death of his best friend on Earth, a loss treated with shocking brevity.

The sequence leading to Friday's death begins appropriately: "I have now done with the Island."[207] As Crusoe's ship again sets sail, we are told of "meeting nothing remarkable in our Passage but this—." "This" happens to be the series of bad decisions on Crusoe's part that leads to the death of Friday. A man on the mast sights an entire nation of savages in canoes approaching the ship. Crusoe corrects this account, saying there were only 126 vessels approaching—a characteristically concrete detail. Crusoe, acting as captain, decides to lower two longboats full of men into the water, in theory to guard against the natives setting fire to his ship. He regrets this decision immediately: "We called to our Men in the Boats, not to let them come too near them. This very Order brought us to an Engagement with them, without our designing it. . . . [A]bout 50 Arrows came on board us from those Boats; and one of our Men in the Long-Boat was very much wounded."[208] The first order was bad enough. Crusoe's next spells Friday's doom: "About half an Hour afterwards they came all up in a Body a-stern of us, and pretty near us, so near that we could easily discern what they were, tho' we could not tell their Design: and I easily found they were some of my old Friends, the same Sort of Savages that I had been used to engage with."[209] Has not Crusoe traveled a long way from his island? Why should he assume these newly encountered natives are akin to the cannibals who used to visit him from time to time? Seen one savage, seen them all? His stereotyping leads to the crazy idea to send Friday on deck to parlay with the invaders, who have already showered his crew with arrows. Surely Friday speaks their language and knows their customs. Friday does as ordered while Crusoe and his crew cower behind protection. Dumoulin's recreation of the scene fittingly renders Friday almost invisible (see fig. 15).[210]

> Upon this I order'd my Men to keep close, lest they should shoot any more Arrows, and made all our Guns ready; but being so near as to be within hearing, I made *Friday* go out upon the Deck, and call out aloud to them in his Language, to know what they meant, which accordingly he did; whether they understood him or not, that I knew not: But as soon as he had call'd to them, six of them, who were in the foremost or nighest Boat to us, turns their canoes from us; and stooping down, shew'd us their naked Backsides . . . whether it was done in meer Contempt, or as a Signal to the rest; but immediately *Friday* cry'd out they were going to shoot, and unhappily for him poor Fellow; they let fly about 300 of their Arrows, and, to my inexpressible Grief, kill'd poor *Friday*, no other Man being in their Sight. The poor Fellow was shot with no less than three Arrows, and about three more fell very near him; such unlucky Marksmen they were.[211]

Figure 15. Plate no. 129, The death of Friday. From François Aimé Louis Dumoulin, *Collection de cent-cinquante gravures . . . des voyages et aventures surprenantes de Robinson Crusoé*, [1810] 1962. (Courtesy of Harvard University, Houghton Library)

It never enters Crusoe's head to blame himself for his friend's death. The massacre of the Madagascars, which Crusoe was powerless to stop, began after a crew member named Tom Jeffries raped a native girl and was apprehended by her people, killed, and strung up in a tree. Crusoe sees the retribution exacted by his shipmates as excessive and sadistic. When Friday dies, Crusoe becomes enraged. He orders his crew to strafe the natives with lead shot that destroys twenty or thirty in their canoes. He is pleased with himself about this act and reports it in detail, before saying goodbye to Friday: "And now I name the poor Fellow once more, I must take my last Leave of him; poor honest *Friday!* we bury'd him with all the Decency and Solemnity possible, by putting him into a Coffin, and throwing him into the Sea: And I caused them to fire eleven Guns for him, and so ended the Life of the most grateful, faithful, honest, and most affectionate Servant, that ever Man had."[212] Momentary signs of affection—"They had killed my poor *Friday*, who I so entirely lov'd and valu'd, and who indeed so well deserved it"—are followed by expressions of the great inconvenience the loss of Friday's free labor causes Crusoe. "We were now under Sail again, but I was the most disconsolate Creature alive, for want of my Man *Friday*, and would have been very glad to have gone back to the Island, to have taken one of the rest from thence for my Occasion."[213] In life, Friday was a dear companion. In death, he is lost property. On Crusoe's island, Friday is not only a primitive heathen and faithful servant but a fellow human being. Off the island he is a useful tool. The idiosyncratic relationship in *Robinson Crusoe* gives way to a strict master-slave dynamic in *Farther Adventures*. In part 1, Defoe takes his story out of bounds, to an unmapped island. In this uncharted place, Crusoe must make his own society without institutions to guide him, recover his religion without an established church, teach and command Friday without example or correction from others. Certainly, Crusoe brings all his prejudice and privilege to the island, but in isolation they carry him only so far. Experience counters received ideas; solitude begins to work on his mind. Survival requires humility and independence. Readers treasure part 1 for this development. We forget parts 2 and 3 because they revert to type. Crusoe becomes an ordinary adventurer among others. Friday becomes a faceless native, impossible to differentiate from other dark-skinned people. There are good reasons, in other words, that part 1 has become an enduring classic of world literature, while parts 2 and 3 have faded, and those reasons have to do with *The Life and Strange Surprizing Adventures of Robinson Crusoe* being a masterpiece of literary deism.

5 Defoe, Deism, and the Novel
Serious Reflections during the Life and Surprising Adventures of Robinson Crusoe, 1720

This history began with a single quotation from Defoe's *Serious Reflections*—the moment when Robinson Crusoe hints that "the famous History of *Don Quixot* was an emblematic History of, and a just Satyr upon, the Duke *de Medina Sidonia*," but that when a "malicious, but foolish Writer, in the abundance of his Gall, spoke of the *Quixotism* of R. Crusoe, as he called it, he shewed, evidently, that he knew nothing of what he said; and perhaps will be a little startled, when I shall tell him that what he meant for a Satyr, was the greatest of Panegyricks." Then Defoe, or Crusoe, or Defoe speaking through Crusoe adds: "Without letting the Reader into a nearer Explication of the Matter, I proceed to let him know, that the happy Deductions I have employ'd myself to make from all the Circumstances of my Story, will abundantly make him amends for his not having the Emblem explained by the Original." This book pursues the nearer explication of the matter that Defoe wisely withholds. I have followed this first lead, and the result is an account of Defoe and the origin of *Robinson Crusoe* that differs considerably from the accepted views of biographers, literary historians, and editors.

Erich Auerbach and the *Ansatzpunkt*

Now, it is safe to say that those who disagree with my argument will question the decision to single out one enemy above all others and make him the starting point of an entire book. What if this clue does not merit serious discussion, or, even if it does, what if I have misidentified Defoe's prime antagonist? Defoe had many enemies. Why choose Leslie for special attention? Personal pique does not a literary history make. Let me, therefore, clarify the rationale behind this starting point.

In "Philology and '*Weltliteratur*,'" Erich Auerbach reflects on this question of the *Ansatzpunkt*, or point of departure, for historical inquiry. He observes that, when it comes to something as vast as world literature, the sheer abundance of historical information threatens any possible synthesis:

> In order for someone to penetrate and then construct an adequate presentation of the material of *Weltliteratur*, he must command that material—or at least a major part of it—himself. Because, however, of the superabundance of materials, of methods and of points of view, a mastery of that sort has become virtually impossible. We possess literatures ranging over six thousand years, from all parts of the world, in perhaps fifty literary languages. Many cultures known to us today were unknown a hundred years ago; many of the ones already known to us in the past were known only partially. In addition to all of these difficulties, there is the consideration that one cannot concern himself solely with the literature of a given period; one must study the conditions under which this literature developed; one must take into account religion, philosophy, politics, economics, fine arts, and music.[1]

Auerbach encounters the problem of interpretation in the context of any possible philology of *Weltlitatur*, but the point holds even for the analysis of a single author, especially one as prolific and varied as Defoe. The available information exceeds the synthetic embrace of any one person. This empirical excess presents the researcher with a fundamental problem of historiography, which Auerbach puts succinctly: "The phenomena treated by the philologist whose intention is synthesis contain their own objectivity, and this objectivity must not disappear in the synthesis: it is most difficult to achieve this aim."[2]

Attempting to capture the objective integrity of literary sources, even as he synthesizes them, Auerbach relies on the idea of the *Ansatzpunkt*. "But how is the problem of synthesis to be solved?" he asks. "In order to accomplish a major work of synthesis it is imperative to locate a point of departure [*Ansatzpunkt*], a handle, as it were, by which the subject can be seized. The point of departure must be the election of a firmly circumscribed, easily comprehensible set of phenomena whose interpretation is a radiation out from them and which orders and interprets a greater region than they themselves occupy."[3] The choice of *Ansatzpunkt* is both scientific and, he admits, aesthetic. It is scientific because a decision about what comes first must follow a comprehensive view of the field. But the starting point is more than an inductive inference, or thesis. It reflects aesthetic judgment. Like the opening image in a poem, or scene in a story, or clue in a police procedural, its significance only becomes clear over time. "The historical synthesis of which I am speaking," writes Auerbach, "although it has significance only when it is based on a scholarly penetration of the material, is a product of personal intuition and hence can only be expected from an individual. Should it succeed perfectly we would be given a scholarly achievement and a work of art at the same time."[4]

Auerbach contrasts this approach to a theory-first mode of inquiry that tries to solve the hermeneutic dilemma by starting with an abstract concept or scheme and organizing the historical information to prove its relevance. Auerbach considers this theory-driven approach less satisfactory:

> A good point of departure must be exact and objective; abstract categories of one sort or another will not serve. Thus, concepts like "the Baroque" or "the Romantic," "the dramatic," or "the idea of fate," "intensity," or "myth," or "the concept of time" and "perspectivism" are dangerous. . . . For a point of departure should not be a generality imposed on a theme from outside, but ought rather to be an organic part of the theme itself. What is being studied should speak for itself, but that can never happen if the point of departure is neither concrete nor clearly defined.[5]

The clue with which this investigation began is an *Ansatzpunkt* in the same way. Drawn from the historical record—in this case, one of Defoe's own texts, a commentary on *Robinson Crusoe*—it is not chosen at random. Instead, it follows intensive study of Defoe's works, their sources, and the critical traditions that followed from them. The starting point does not function as a typical thesis; its significance unfolds over time as this first clue leads to others, radiating out, as Auerbach suggests, to "a greater region than they themselves occupy." The historical Charles Leslie, a human adversary in Defoe's biography, transforms into something more: he becomes a figure for the deist controversy itself and Defoe's complex part in it.

Francis Bacon reminds us of the mythic significance of the term "nemesis": "*Nemesis* is said to be a Goddess Venerable unto all, but to be fear'd of none but Potentates and Fortune's Favorites. She is thought to be the Daughter of *Oceanus* and Nox. She is pourtraicted with Wings on her Shoulders, and on her Head a Coronet; bearing in her Right Hand a Javelin of Ash, and in her Left a Pitcher with the Similitudes of *Aethiopians* engraven on it; and lastly, she is describ'd sitting on a Hart."⁶ The description conveys an iconography of confusion, which Bacon proceeds to explicate. Nemesis is an object of veneration because all aggrieved parties call on her to exact revenge on their behalf. Nemesis is also an object of fear because all aggrieved parties call on her, and her actions are unpredictable. Revenge seldom arrives soon enough; thus, thoughts of revenge become self-consuming, like a javelin maintaining shape yet reduced to ash. The word "nemesis" also means what it has come to mean in popular parlance, not a mythic goddess but an archenemy. This multivalent quality of the nemesis—as enemy and avenging spirit—captures Defoe's relationship with Leslie. Leslie matters as a man, but he matters even more as a set of ideas, which Defoe decided to confront and uproot.

Now, hatred, one might argue, is not a credible motive for writing a book such as *Robinson Crusoe*. But why not? Scholars have no trouble crediting Dante when he explains at the end of *La Vita Nuova* that love for Beatrice "determined me that I would say nothing further of this most blessed one, until such time as I could discourse more worthily concerning her."⁷ Christian Neoplatonism provides a ready framework for conjoining love and literary invention. Hatred appears to have no such handmaiden. Yet Defoe stops just short of admitting at the start of *Serious Reflections* that hatred for one man, the English Duke *de Medina Sidonia*, motivated his discovery of the form of the novel. Why, then, does *Robinson Crusoe* not read as satire? Approaching Crusoe by way of Defoe's previous attempts at long prose fiction provides an explanation. What Defoe learned from these failed experiments was that revenge and retribution had to be worthy of their cause, not their target. The cause was the set of principles, affiliations, and artistic aims that drove Defoe to innovate in many genres of poetry and prose. He would defeat his nemesis not by trading satiric blow for satiric blow, but instead, just as Robinson Crusoe suggests, by trading "Satyr" for "Panegyrick," burying his satiric rage in a narrative apparently devoid of satire.

Defoe's Religion

Taking a churchman as a starting point also reopens the question of Defoe's theology. I have not attempted to trace Defoe's specific position-taking vis-à-vis well-known controversies among the dissenters, such as the Salters' Hall controversy, or within the Anglican Church, such as the controversy surrounding Benjamin Hoadley, the bishop of Bangor. Scholars sometimes use Defoe's responses to these conflicts to establish his theological position. Nor have I tried to pinpoint which sect of dissenting Christianity the sum total of Defoe's religious pronouncements most nearly resembles. From the perspective opened by Defoe's confrontation with Leslie, the Bangorian and Salters' Hall controversies appear to be debates about much the same thing, as Paula Backscheider has already observed:

> The Salters' Hall controversy was in many ways a variant on the Bangorian controversy. It arose over the ordination of Hubert Stogdon of Devon, who held unorthodox views of the Trinity. The General Body of London meeting at Salters' Hall quickly agreed that there were some errors of doctrine so serious as to disqualify a person from the ministry. The dispute rose over the test of the truth of whatever doctrine might be at issue. One group of representatives insisted the Bible alone should be used, while the other wanted the confessions of faith as well as the Bible. For some the idea of using the confessions of faith implied that scripture alone was inadequate. Scriptural authority carried by four votes, and a group of ministers withdrew from the meeting. . . . [They] insisted upon the subscription to the doctrine of the Trinity as stated in the fifth and sixth answers to the 1643 Westminster shorter catechism and the first article of the creed of the Church of England.[8]

The question for a history of this kind is whether this more granular treatment of religious controversy contributes to the *literary* part of the history. For Backscheider, the Salters' Hall controversy foretells *Robinson Crusoe* in a direct way: "*Robinson Crusoe* dramatizes Defoe's position on the very recent Salters' Hall controversy. His novel illustrates deliberately and in great detail that scripture and revelation without dogma are sufficient. . . . Since boyhood he had heard sermons that taught, 'True Religion is more Affection and Practice, than Doctrine, or Notion, and is seated more in the heart than in the head.' It is no coincidence that at the height of the Salters' Hall debate, Crusoe finds his way to God while alone on an island and then converts Friday."[9] In this sense, Defoe's religious commitments, as expressed in his writings about the Bangorian and Salters' Hall controversies, reinforce a religious reading of *Robinson Crusoe*.[10] But in light of what constant are the Bangorian and Salters' Hall controversies variations on the same theme? Both involve a perceived attack on the Trinity, Bangor splitting Anglicanism against itself, and Salters' Hall splitting the dissenters. The constant that foments crises within Anglicanism and Protestant dissent appears to be the threat deism posed to all of Trinitarian Christianity. If the evidence points to an adversary who deserves the title of nemesis, did

Defoe secretly go to the extreme of countering Leslie's strict Trinitarianism with an anti-Trinitarianism of form? I have addressed form on the level of sign (the footprint), on the level of genre (the two Jonahs coding for allegory and counter-allegory), on the level of character (the torn figure of a *Kreutznaer*), and thematics (Providence, conversion, the noble savage), and at every point Defoe appears to have been quite willing to go to any extreme to root out this enemy, albeit under cover of plausible fiction. That cover becomes less recognizably deistical and more recognizably Protestant, as the transformation of satire into panegyric reaches its completion in *The Life and Strange Surprizing Adventures of Robinson Crusoe*.

Defoe remains irreducible. Judge him by what he wrote against libertine deists and freethinkers, coupled with the wholesome homilies of his moral-didactic catechisms, and we get one answer: he could not have been a deist in his life or his art. Maximillian Novak holds that Defoe was an anti-deist from early to late: "In his early works, he seldom missed an opportunity of attacking John Toland's unmysterious Christianity. . . . Writing under the name 'Orthodox' in *Applebee's Journal* of 18 March 1721, he argued: 'Freethinkers are profane, and Free-Actors also; for,—erasing the Awe of God in their Hearts, they plead immediately, and of Course, for a Freedom in all Manner of Vice,—using the Pretence of Liberty for a Justification of a Crime, as if the Liberty God gave to Man of being a free Agent, disengaged him entirely from all the restraint of Laws, whether Human or Divine.'"[11] As this passage suggests, textual support for Novak's conclusion is abundant. The section of *Serious Reflections* titled "Of Atheistical and Prophane Discourse" reads closer to Charles Leslie than to Charles Blount, mocking the deism of which *Robinson Crusoe* stands accused: "Now, I am not in this Discourse entring into any of the Arguments of these grand Questions on one side or the other, that would make this Work a Collection of Polemicks; nor am I Casuist enough for such a Work; but I am observing or remarking upon the Wickedness of the treating these Subjects with Levity and Ignorance in the common Road of Conversation."[12] Written in 1720, this is Defoe's rebuttal to Gildon's charge that "*Ludere cum Sacris* is what he has not at all scrupl'd."[13] The same text continues with a condemnation of libertine deists and freethinkers. The narrator of *Serious Reflections* ranks these sinners below those who simply profane and blaspheme God's name because they dilute and dissipate God's authority, fashioning God in their own image, as refined and morally weak, a gentleman instead of a deity:

> Below these we have a Sort of People who will acknowledge a God, but he must be such a one as they please to make him; a fine well bred

good natur'd Gentleman like Deity, that cannot have the Heart to damn any of his Creatures to an Eternal Punishment, nor could not be so weak as to let the *Jews* crucify his own Son; these Men expose Religion, and all the Doctrines of Repentance, and Faith in Christ, with all the Means of a Christian Salvation, as matter of Banter and Ridicule. The Bible they say is a good History in most Parts, but the Story of our Saviour they look upon as a meer Novel, and the Miracles of the New Testament as a Legend of Pristcraft. . . .

Further, besides these we have *Arians* and *Socinians,* the Disciples of an ancient Heretick . . . *These are Iniquities,* as *Job* said, *should be punished by the Judges.* . . . and these are the Things which have given such a Stroke to the Ruin of the Nation's Morals; for no Method can be so direct to prepare People for all Sorts of Wickedness, as to perswade them out of a Belief of any supreme Power to restrain them; make a Man once cease to believe a God, and he has nothing left to limit his Appetite but meer Philosophy.[14]

If these direct denunciations of deists were not enough, Defoe adds personal insult against known deists such as Toland, about whom Defoe wrote in *Reformation of Manners: A Satyr on Himself* (1702):

Socinian T[olan]d's his dear Ghostly Priest,
And taught him all Religion to digest.
Took prudent Care he shou'd not much profess,
And he was ne're addicted to Excess.
And yet he *Covets* without Rule or End,
Will sell his Wife, his Master, or his Friend.
To boundless Avarice a constant Slave,
Unsatisfy'd as Death, and greedy as the Grave.[15]

Who would suspect Defoe of deist leanings given this ad hominem attack on a known deist?

But judge Defoe by how far he went to defeat a religious thinker who styled himself the great harrasser of Unitarians, Quakers, Presbyterians, deists, Jews, Muslims, and all things cosmopolitan, and could name the principle uniting them, and we arrive at a different answer. Where Defoe could have leapt to the defense of his own denomination of dissenting Protestants in the face of Leslie's scorched-earth assault on all dissenters, he did otherwise. He leapt to the defense of the Quakers. Why? This investigation provides a plausible account of the motives behind Defoe's Quaker writings. The Quaker disguise is a reference point because it is continuous from 1703 to 1724. I have presented evidence of an alliance between Defoe and William Penn to bring down Charles Leslie and, through analysis of Defoe's defense of the Quakers, have identified proto-deistical arguments meant to oppose Leslie's orthodox Trinitarianism as fundamentally as possible. The disguise he adopts as a Quaker minister is one among many, but it coheres with subsequent decisions to compose genres of cosmopolitan fiction derived from Classical, Eastern, Continental, and English sources. Rather than read *Robinson Crusoe* as a break from this cosmopolitan past, I see it as continuous with these failed experiments—continuous with their cosmopolitanism, their skepticism, and their preoccupation with philosophical and theological questioning.

Not only does the confrontation with Leslie direct us to an ideological struggle; it makes sense of Defoe's decades-long apprenticeship in the art of the modern novel through the adaptation of genres of the cosmopolitan fantastic. Once we overcome the antipathy to handling failures, these works gain new interest. If they are failures, there is every reason to assume Defoe was aware of their faults and strove not to repeat them. Even as failures they contain disconnected elements of the masterpiece: the construction of a singular character, the sustaining of an ironic narrative voice, the mixing of incongruous genres so their combination seems natural, the bonding together of serious ethical and political reflection with vividly realized human situations that grab and hold the reader, the weaving in of what I have called deist scenarios, the deployment of "shimmering" (as opposed to typological) signs, and the transformation of satire into what Robinson Crusoe calls his book, "Panegyrick"—all of these aspects of *Robinson Crusoe* make sense as part of a more general pattern of opposition. Thus, I regard the vehemence of Defoe's condemnation of deists and freethinkers as protective cover meant to obscure his *formal* proximity to them.

As an *Ansatzpunkt*, then, the hint about a nemesis directs attention to a larger context previously absent from theories of the rise or origin of the novel—namely, the deist controversy of 1680–1750, occurring not exclusively, but especially, in England. These dates, 1680–1750, are coterminus with the generally accepted timeframe during which the modern, realist novel emerged in English. Yet why these events overlap remains an unasked and unanswered question. In Defoe himself, in his apprenticeship as an author of long prose fiction, deism and the eventual form of the novel coincide. Yet Defoe presents himself so often and so vehemently as an enemy of freethinking libertines, among whom he lumps the deists, that it has been easy to overlook the fact that Defoe's earlier experiments in prose fiction imitated genres publicly associated with deism. My reading of *Robinson Crusoe* suggests continuity with these earlier cosmopolitan works, a pattern that did not cease with *Robinson Crusoe*. If, indeed, *Madagascar; or, Robert Drury's Journal* (1727) is a work by Defoe—and its content, style, and necessarily anonymous publication suggest Defoe's hand—then a strong but submerged line of literary cosmopolitanism persists through the Crusoe trilogy into the late *Madagascar*.[16]

The preface of that work defends the author from the charge that he has introduced readers to a deistical natural religion as an *"Inclination of his own,"* when *"the most to-be-suspected Part of the Account of this Religion is Fact, as related by Drury;* and particularly the remarkable Conference with Deaan Murnanzack, *his ridiculing of* Adam's Rib, God's talking with Men, making the World in six Days, and resting the seventh, his taking these Things for childish Notions of Drury's, and more especially saying and repeating they were old Women Stories, are no other than this Prince's own Words."[17] The fact that Drury left England a Church of England man and that "ever since he came home he has firmly adher'd to the same, even to Bigotry" must mean that he has no personal inclination to deism and merely reports what he observed or has heard about from explorers to the uncolonized parts of Africa. Refuting Hobbes, the narrator states that ethnographic observation of primitive peoples suggests that their first instinct is to love their mates and children, and, when banded into collectives, to pass simple laws to preserve society and promote security. The narrator, now a "Transcriber," grows defensive: "it wou'd be a Weakness to imagine he was able or willing to invent any such Thing, which might favour Free thinking or Natural Religion, in Opposition to Reveal'd; since they were Matters he scarce ever troubl'd himself to enquire after. And in all those places where Religion is touch'd on, or the Original of Government, the Transcriber is only answerable for putting some Reflections in the Author's Mouth."[18] Here is Defoe at his devious best, sounding for all the world like the innocent translator of *A Continuation of Letters Written by a Turkish Spy,* or the editor of *Moll Flanders,* or the pilloried ventriloquist who complains, "Thus a poor Author has ventur'd to have all Mankind call him a Villain and Traytor to his Country and Friends, for making other Peoples thoughts speak in his Words."[19] Whenever Defoe nears the topic of the origin of the novel, he spins out fictitious webs of concealment. "*I can but just touch on these Things,*" writes Robert Drury in his journal, "*yet these Hints, tho hasty, and undigested, may open a Door to such a Discovery of the Original of practical Religion as well reveal'd as natural, as is little expected.*"[20] The discovery would be "little expected" because rendered in a fictionalized ethnographic account of the rites and rituals of an indigenous culture. If you are waiting for the next part of the explanation, you will have to keep waiting, because as might be expected there will be no explication of what Drury means by the Original of practical Religion: "We have exceeded the Number of Sheets design'd for this Book, and too long delay'd the Publication; so that on no Account, can I at present examine Authors proper to be consulted; but am oblig'd, unwillingly to leave this agreeable Enquiry; yet not without Thoughts of reassuming it."[21] Resuming what? One supposes: the "Inquiry into the Original of practical Religion as well reveal'd as natural." But the narrator has suddenly run out of time. "On no Account, can I at present examine Authors proper to be consulted." Which authors are those? They are the ones who have come to light in this investigation—Herbert, Spinoza, Blount, Toland, Shaftesbury—who make up the undisclosed deist background for Defoe's conscious discovery of the form and content of *Robinson Crusoe*. Just as Defoe had no intention of offering any "nearer Explication of the Matter" of his nemesis, so here he withholds "this agreeable Enquiry; yet not without Thoughts of reassuming it," which he never does.

Why, then, did Defoe embrace deism in art when he appears to oppose it in theology and in life? In Defoe's *The Political History of the Devil*, deism and Satan coincide in this playful retelling of the Fall: "But to come back to the Method of Satan's tempting her, *viz.* by whispering to her in her sleep; 'twas a cunning Trick, that's the Truth of it, and by that means he certainly set her Head a madding after *Deism,* and to be made a Goddess, and then back'd it by the subtle talk he had with her afterward." Pretending outrage at this nighttime violation of Eve through her ear, Defoe elaborates on the seduction, likening it to a bedroom trick that works on women and men alike: "I am the more Particular on this Part, because, however the Devil may have been the first that ever practiced it, yet I can assure him the Experiment has been tried upon many a Woman since, to the wheedling her out of her Modesty, as well as her Simplicity; and the Cunning Men tell us still, that if you can come at a Woman when she is in deep sleep, and Whisper to her close to her Ear, she will certainly Dream of the Thing you say to her, and so will a Man too."[22] If Charles Gildon is right, Defoe is tempting his audience the same way. His novels serve as critique of and conduit for a despised republican deism. With rare exception, scholars have heard the critique but ignored the conduit.[23] Yet this notion of the novel as a medium for deism to enter the cultural mainstream helps explain one of the oddest features of the dual history of the novel and deism: that as the novel dominates, deism recedes. The novel reshapes popular culture, and deism loses its charm, in both senses. Overshadowed by the religious revivals of the late eighteenth and nineteenth centuries, disproved by methodical works such as Leslie's, transformed into less risky forms, such as nineteenth-century agnosticism, deism is neither a popular alternative nor a major threat in England by 1760 and in America by 1820. Yet the notion of a public religion based on the fewest possible principles, and not punishing citizens even for lacking these—the paradoxical idea of a natural or universal religion that accepts the first principle, that God exists, but downplays any single way of knowing this to be true—these deist impulses take flight in Defoe's novel. "I shall not pretend to invade the Province of the Learned," the narrator of *Serious Reflections* promises, "nor offer one Argument from Scripture or Providence; for I am supposed to be talking to Men that doubt or deny them both. Divinity is not my Talent, nor ever like to be my Profession . . . in a word, talking Scripture is out of Fashion."[24]

Biographers, critics, and editors who assert that Defoe's religious views are conventional and hostile to deism focus on the homiletic works and the closing essay of the trilogy, *A Vision of the Angelick World*, because they appear to express some of Defoe's most direct Christian moralism. Yet even in these texts, Defoe's irony sometimes interposes between art and doctrine. In *A New Family Instructor* (1727), a father figure describes the pedagogical sequence of religious education he recommends for the young. A child must be sufficiently mature to comprehend "the disputed Points, especially such as related to Idolatry, to *Socinian* Errors, and to all the Modern Heresies of the Times; such as to Deism, Scepticism, and Atheism, and with all our Free-thinking Errors, &c."[25] Yet when the catechism plays out in a fictional scene between father and son, we find an exchange reminiscent of the opening of *Robinson Crusoe*. The father issues his stern warning: "really it was the most dangerous Thing in the World for a young Gentleman, sober and virtuous, to venture into *Italy*, till he was thoroughly grounded in Principle, and had fixt his Mind immoveably in Matters of Religion; for that nothing was more ordinary, than for such, either to be seduc'd, by the Subtlety of the Clergy, to embrace a false Religion, or by the Artifice of a worse Enemy, to give up all Religion, and sink into *Scepticism and Deism*, or, perhaps, *Atheism*." And the son issues his ambivalent response: "The young Gentleman listen'd with respect to his Father's Discourse, especially to the first Part; and gave him many Assurances, that he would have all possible regard to his Instructions. . . . As to the last Part, relating to Religion, he seem'd to wave it only with a kind of common Notice, signifying, that he would take Care of himself as much as was possible."[26] Was Defoe aware of the audible echo between the *Notitiae Communes* (Common Notions) of the deists and the "kind of common Notice" with which the son hears his father's warnings? The "young Gentleman" hardly chimes in with his father's attack on deism and freethinking, promising only "that he would take Care of himself as much as was possible," a declaration of freedom from the father's pre- and proscriptions—and a strong statement that his duty is to himself, not to divine will.

A Vision of the Angelick World

Scholars who read *Robinson Crusoe* as an allegory of Protestant spiritual awakening also like to point to the placement of *A Vision of the Angelick World* as the final work in Defoe's trilogy. Because its purpose is apparently to confirm communication between human beings and the divine, *A Vision* would seem an ideal conclusion for a novel that does the same. Rodney Baine made this case in 1968: "The popular portrait of Defoe as the worldly London merchant and political time-server is best corrected by a study of his occult works, especially of his views of angelic ministry. 'A Vision of the Angelick World' was a serious attempt in an increasingly skeptical age to advance angelology as a handmaid to religion. . . . [T]his tract was certainly free from any meretricious appeal."[27] Seldom countered in criticism and therefore deemed accurate, this argument informs G. A. Starr's edition of *Serious Reflections*. According to Starr's hypothesis, Defoe placed *A Vision* last because it sums up the moderate Protestant faith expressed in *Robinson Crusoe* and looks forward to future acts of piety. Thus, *Serious Reflections* and its closing statement become "a fascinating draft of a significant body of writing that Defoe produced in the later 1720s . . . that explores deviations from, and threats to, sound belief."[28]

There are a number of problems with this view, starting with chronology. As Paul Dottin and others have pointed out, the *Serious Reflections during the Life and Surprising Adventures of Robinson Crusoe* was likely written during the composition of that work, or even before. It "consists mainly of old essays which Defoe had long kept in his papers, and which he tried to adopt to his story,"[29] Starr himself observes, "At one point he tells us in a rather startling footnote ([on] p. 112), '*This was all Written in* King William's Reign and refers to that Time' . . . He lifts large passages bodily from his previously published works . . . In fact there are a number of poetical 'Excursions' of some length that are almost certainly Defoe's, and were probably composed decades earlier."[30] This makes it difficult to say whether *Serious Reflections* and its closing essay follow from or precede *Robinson Crusoe*. Defoe possibly composed much of the last section first, at time that his theological convictions were far from clear, if, indeed, they ever became clear. A careful reading of *A Vision of the*

Angelick World reveals a far more playful attitude toward religion than Defoe's apologists allow.

What are we to make, for instance, of the narrator's offhand statement that "the Maxim I have laid down to my self for my Conduct in this Affair is in a few Words, that we should not lay too great stress upon Dreams, and yet not wholly neglect them"?[31] Is this serious or a joke? Is Crusoe aware of how contradictory he sounds? Surely Defoe is. Dreams occupy a middle territory between the mundane and spiritual worlds. The text seems preoccupied with filling in this rhetorical terrain, as if its author were seeking to expand a religious vocabulary that did not yet exist. At one point Defoe's narrator repeats "a long Dispute . . . carried on between two Persons of my Acquaintance upon this very Subject . . . one a Layman, the other a Clergyman."[32] The dialogue, whether it anticipates *Robinson Crusoe* or follows it, captures a familiar tension between realism and allegory. The Layman holds that "if Dreams were from the Agency of any prescient Being, the Notices would be more direct, and the Discoveries clear; not by Allegories and emblematick Fancies, expressing things imperfect and dark."[33] The Layman expresses a series of rational arguments against the spiritual efficacy of dreams, before the Clergyman responds. The narrator, standing, one supposes, for Defoe himself, observes that the "Clergyman gave distinct Answers to all these Objections, and to me, I confess, very satisfactory"—satisfactory as well to generations of Defoe's biographers, critics, and editors, who equate Defoe's own convictions with those of his Clergyman. "Dreams," the Clergyman asserts, "were often allegorick and allusive, when they were evidently from God."[34] After the Clergyman answers each of the Layman's objections, Defoe again appears to decide the case between them: "I thought it would be much to the Purpose to remark this Opinion of another Man, because it corresponded so exactly with my own."[35] What justification can there be for taking this statement at face value? When does Defoe sincerely align his convictions with those of any of his fictional creations?

The next turn in this winding text takes us back to the topic of chapter 2, reenacting (or, if this text was written in the 1690s, preparing the way for) Defoe's lunar voyage and attendant inquiry into the plurality of worlds: "I had one Day been conversing so long with him [the Clergyman] upon the common received Notions of the Planets being habitable, and of a Diversity of Worlds, that I think verily, I was for some Days like a Man transported into these Regions myself."[36] The narrator observes that his experiences in the lunar regions threatened him with a kind of lunacy, reminiscent of a famous scene in *Don Quixote:* "the Swiftness of the Motion these Ideas come in with, occasions a Commotion in Nature, the Understanding is mobb'd with them, disturb'd. . . . Indeed, I can liken it to nothing so well as the Wheels of a Wind-mill, which if the Sails or Wings are set, and the Wind blow a Storm, run round so fast, that they will set all on Fire, if a skillful Hand be not ready to direct and manage it."[37] Here Robinson Crusoe repeats his admission, "I had an invincible inclination to travel," only now the statement takes in space *and* sea voyages, *The Consolidator* and *Robinson Crusoe*. Travel produces adventure but also a detached perspective: "When first my fancy rais'd me up in the Confines of this vast Abyss, and having now travelled thro' the misty Regions of the Atmosphere could look down as I mounted, and see the World below me, tis scarce possible to imagine, how little, how mean, how despicable every Thing look'd; let any Man try this Experiment of himself, and he shall certainly find the same Thing."[38]

As we saw in chapter 2, this detached perspective is as conducive to a secular as a religious view; however, Crusoe immediately draws the religious lesson: "could we always look upon the Things of Life with the same Eyes, as we shall do when we come to the Edge of Time, when one Eye can as it were look back on the World, and the other look forward into Eternity, we should save ourselves the Trouble of much Repentance." Rising up into the *Aether*, Crusoe asserts that "the Reason of the Creation of such immense bodies as the Sun, Stars, Planets, and Moons . . . is far from being to be found in the Study of Nature, on the Surface of our Earth . . . the God of Nature has form'd an infinite Variety which we know nothing of, and that all the Creatures are a Reason to one another for their Creation."[39] Are these Defoe's final conclusions? There is good reason to answer yes and no. Crusoe unphilosophically brackets the other conclusion that seventeenth-century libertine authors such as Cyrano de Bergerac drew from the Lucianic and lunar voyage traditions: "I saw perfectly the Emptiness of our modern Notions, that the Planets were habitable Worlds."[40] And how does Crusoe disprove the possibility of life on other planets? He claims to have studied all of the candidates in our solar system, declaring each too cold or too hot to sustain life. Crusoe's smug confidence ignores the threat that the plurality of worlds posed to any universal system of religion invented by people on Earth. The philosophical question takes in not only the planets revolving around *our* sun, but those circling *any* star in any solar system. What follows is a long section on the spirits Crusoe encountered on his flights, and especially the devil, which ends, "You will ask me, how I came to know all this? I say, ask me no Questions, till the Elevation of your Fancy carries you to the outer Edge of the Atmosphere, as I tell you mine did," a playful appeal to empiricism that echoes Defoe's boast at the end of *The Consolidator*: "But if any one shall scruple the Matter of Fact as I have here related it, I freely give him leave to do as I did, and go up to the Moon for a Demonstration; and if upon his return he does not give ample Testimony to the Case in every part of it, as here related, I am content to pass for the Contriver of it my self, and be punish'd as the Law shall say I deserve."[41]

Scholars who take these sentiments as Defoe's own convictions pass over what our confused narrator declares a few paragraphs later: that "all Visions, or propounded Visions either of Heaven or Hell, are meer Delusions of the Mind, and generally are Fictions of a waking bewildered Head."[42] In place of mystical visions, Crusoe champions intimations, dreams, trances, hints, experiences that suggest some kind of supernatural involvement in human affairs, without committing to claims of direct experience of spiritual essences. He recounts anecdotes of individuals seized with the strong impulse to go somewhere, who heeded the impulse and received great rewards, or who ignored these intimations and received great hurt: "I seriously advise all sober thinking Persons not to disregard those powerful Impulses of the Mind." The discourse is scattershot, heavy-handed, and philosophically obtuse, closer in style and substance to Defoe's early failures than to his eventual success. Crusoe defends the reality of spiritual communication and the next moment states, "I would be far from prompting the crazy Imaginations of Hypocondriac Distemper'd Heads, which run Men out to so many Extravagancies."[43] He mocks those who "think they are talk'd to from the invisible World, by the Howling of every Dog, or the Screeching of every Owl."[44] Of the reality of apparitions, Defoe—or his narrator—expresses equal parts certainty and ambivalence. His approach to these problems veers toward psychology and away from divinity. Defoe focuses on the good or bad effects that certain forms of belief have on human beings. Casting doubt on the apparitions themselves, he jumps to the other extreme and rejects "the very ill use of the general Notion, that there are no Apparitions, nor Spirits at all," for such denial may lead to the persuasion that "there are no Spirits at all, either in the visible or invisible World, and carrying it on further, they next annihilate the Devil . . . the next Thing is, and they soon come to it. *That there is no God,* and so Atheism takes its rise in the same Sink, with a Carelessness about Futurity."[45] Fully persuaded that these words carry Defoe's stamp of approval, Starr adds this editorial note: "The sequence of denials sketched in these two paragraphs represents Defoe's version of a contemporary Atheist's Progress: his defenses of the existence of apparitions, spirits and the devil in various works of the 1720s . . . should be seen . . . as his way of buttressing their [the readers'] belief in God."[46]

The last plot turn in *A Vision* begins, "I have no Mind to enter upon an Argument to prove the being of our Maker. . . . But I have a mind to conclude this Work with a short History of some Atheists, which I met with many Years ago."⁴⁷ This history involves a series of anecdotes and dialogues that follow the travails of a young atheist who appears suspiciously like Gildon, before he fell under Charles Leslie's spell.⁴⁸ This young man, "though as *he afterwards said,* he was rather persuaded to be *among them,* than to be *one of them,* he had however too much yielded to their Delusions."⁴⁹ On his way to a meeting of "their hellish Society," he is overtaken by a fierce storm. "A great Flash of Lightning more than ordinarily surpriz'd him," as the sudden death of Blount did Gildon, scaring him into self-accusation and regret: "*Where am I going? What am I doing about! What is it has stopt me thus! Why are these Thunders, these Rains, and this Lightening thus Terrible? . . . What if there should be a God!*"⁵⁰ He returns home sick, and—a second coincidence—just then a "near Relation of his, a pious good Man, who had often used to speak very plainly to him of the horrid Sin he was guilty of, happened to come to visit him." This coincidence leads to a third, when another member of the atheistical club arrives, hoping, to accompany his friend to "the usual Meeting of their dreadful Society." Hearing the knock, and recognizing the visitor through a little Grate in the door, the near relation impersonates the voice of the first atheist and tells his friend to go away: "*Beseech them all to repent; for depend upon it, There is a* GOD."

This repulse drives the second atheist away, and the same storm that caused the first lightning strike forces him into a bookseller's shop, where there "happens to be sitting in the Shop reading a Book, a Gentleman of his Acquaintance, though far differing from him in his principles, being a very sober, studious, religious young Man." This sober young man calls the man just come in from the storm an "*atheistical Wretch*" and proceeds to catechize him of his errors. The dialogue continues for the next ten pages, which mark the end of the trilogy. Defoe has this theology student take the atheist's pulse as he reads the words "*There may be a God*":

Stud. Did you feel no Motion within you, when you read those Words, *There may be a God?*
Ath. What Motion? What do you talk of?
Stud. Come do not deny it, for I am a Witness against you.
Ath. Witness for what? I have kill'd no Body, I have robb'd no Body; if you should turn Informer, I value not your Evidence.
Stud. No, no. I shall not turn Informer of that Kind, but I am a Witness in your Maker's behalf.
Ath. What can you Witness?

Stud. I'll tell you what I can Witness, I can testify, that your own Conscience is against you, in your impious denying the Existence of that God that gave you Life; you could not conceal it, I tell you I *felt it*.⁵¹

The dialogue continues until the theology student convinces the atheist that "there is something more than common, in every Thing that has happened to me to Day!" With this, the atheist declares, "There must be A GOD or A DEVIL in Being."⁵²

Here, then, is the conclusion of the third part of the trilogy—unless it was written before part 1 and tacked on to shield the work from Gildon's accusation that *Robinson Crusoe* promulgates a freethinking attitude toward religion. I share Christopher Hill's skepticism about this concluding section of the novel: "The disagreements of the commentators show how difficult it is to interpret the novel as a consistent allegory; and it seems to me very unlikely that Defoe's (or Crusoe's) remarks in *Serious Reflections* were part of his original plan"—unless the original plan was to explore the psychological need for belief rather than belief itself by confabulating a vocabulary of dreams, trances, noises, voices, hints, impulses, and apparitions, not for what they tell us about the beyond, but instead for what they tell us about human fragility and the need for faith.⁵³ Why else would Defoe or his narrator sum up the concluding anecdote of atheists undergoing conversion this way: "Many an Apparition related with a great deal of Certainty in the World, and of which good Ends have follow'd, has been no more than such a serious Mistake as this."⁵⁴ A "serious Mistake"? Starr assures readers of his edition that Defoe "laughs more gently at those who believe too much (especially if they are fellow Protestants), than at those who believe too little."⁵⁵ This does not appear to have been the case with *The Shortest Way with the Dissenters,* and there is some question whether the zealous friend who takes the young atheist's pulse to catch him in a lie escapes Defoe's mockery. Nor is it merely what Starr calls a "grim joke" when Crusoe recalls the naïve question the Indians in America asked the missionaries when told of the Future State, the Resurrection of the Dead, and Eternal Felicity in Heaven: they "enquir'd where the *Spaniards* went after Death, and if any of them went to Heaven? And being answered in the Affirmative, shook their Heads, and desired they might go to Hell then."⁵⁶

The effort to paint the closing section of the trilogy as an affirmation of Defoe's steadfast faith and *Robinson Crusoe*'s status as a religious allegory ignores a great deal of evidence to the contrary. I have foregrounded such evidence throughout this study; it exists in *A Vision* as well. The opening sections adopt a quasi-scientific tone, admitting that "the Understanding or Sense of a Brute may act upon visible Objects, but Matter cannot act upon immaterial Things, and so the Eye of a Beast cannot see a Spirit, or the Mind of a Brute act upon Futurity, Eternity, and the sublime Things of a State to come."[57] In the same vein, when Crusoe looks back on his experiences on the island, he has to admit that the place was not exactly teeming with disembodied spirits: "I had an abundance of strange Notions of my seeing Apparitions there . . . it was all Hypochondriack Delusion."[58] Defoe has Crusoe admit that the remarkable experiences that first struck him as apparitional—he instances the footprint in the sand, the dying old goat, and the feeling of dead weight on his leg after a palsy at night—can all be explained in psychological or physical terms. "But I return to the Article of the Impulses of the Mind," says Crusoe, "for I lay greater Weight upon these than upon any of the other Discoveries of the Invisible World."[59] This admission leaves Defoe and the reader with a paradox: if spirits are a projection of human psychology, we nevertheless appear to need them. They therefore exist and do not exist, are true and false at the same time. To the theologian and the theologically minded critic, this paradox must be disproved. To the freethinking novelist, however, the paradox is true to life. How might fiction sustain the reader in this paradoxical relation to divinity? This, I believe, is the question that animates Defoe's *A Vision of the Angelick World*. It is the sort of problem he had to solve before he wrote *Robinson Crusoe*.

I am distinguishing, therefore, between a religious skepticism implicit in the *way* Defoe writes and the theological views he articulates in his diatribes against libertines, deists, freethinkers, and the like. Defoe's enemies did the same. In this respect, I follow Auerbach's approach in *Mimesis*, in the famous closing lines of chapter 8 on Dante. Auerbach makes no attempt to account for the preponderance of evidence suggesting Dante's conventional acceptance of Catholic doctrine (the sort of acceptance that leads him to assign figures whom he loves and admires to various rungs of Hell). Instead, Auerbach isolates moments in the *Inferno* where humane and realistic depictions of suffering characters exceed the framework of allegory. He writes, "By virtue of this immediate and admiring sympathy with man, the principle, rooted in the divine order, of the indestructibility of the whole historical and individual man turns *against* that order, makes it subservient to its own purposes, and obscures it. The image of man eclipses the image of God. Dante's work made man's Christian-figural being a reality, and destroyed it in the very process of realizing it. The tremendous pattern was broken by the overwhelming power of the images it had to contain."[60] One can imagine scholars versed in Dante's professed theology taking issue with this conclusion and drawing attention to passages—in the *Commedia* and elsewhere—that suggests more conventional views of Catholicism and literary form. Nevertheless, Auerbach noticed something important about Dante's art, if not his life. Defoe presents a similar case. Of him, too, it could be said that the image of man—and woman—eclipses the image of God. "We know practically nothing of the particular reasons responsible for Defoe's turning away from a theological career at the end of his education at Newington Green," wrote Rudolph G. Stamm in 1936.[61] Here is a solution: his ambitions as an artist started early and lasted his entire life. Attend to his statements of faith and distaste for freethinking libertines and Defoe seems a stickler for religious orthodoxy; attend to the decisions he makes as a writer—his experiments with cosmopolitan genres before Crusoe and the effect his novels have on readers worldwide—and he seems a deist in allegorical disguise, a shape-shifter extraordinaire.

"A Strange Capitalist"

If traditional Protestant readings of Defoe's life and works provide one way to discount the evidence presented in this book, a critical stance that reduces Defoe's texts to refined propaganda provides another. I have described Defoe's irony as both a political and aesthetic force—political for its ability to intervene in public life, aesthetic for its holding the key to a mode of free-indirect discourse in first-person narrative that becomes the mainstay of his famous novels. Still, in the view of many scholars, the quaint humanist trope of irony cannot and should not survive the laser light of ideological analysis. J. A. Downie's conclusion is direct and representative: "I would argue, *Robinson Crusoe* and *Captain Singleton*, as well as *Moll Flanders* and *Colonel Jack,* involve imperialist propaganda to promote his schemes of trade and colonization. That they do not nakedly state a thesis is a mark of the subtlety with which Defoe approaches the subject, not an argument against such an interpretation of his novels. In the final analysis, I would suggest, imperialism informs both the structure and content of, say, *Robinson Crusoe,* as much as the stimulus supplied by moral didacticism. Further, the two are linked."[62] Downie realizes that there are impediments to viewing *Robinson Crusoe* as a brief for capitalist and colonialist ideologies. Indeed, he admits that Crusoe himself makes an odd poster child for colonialism: "Crusoe is a strange capitalist.... When we read his admission that 'trade was none of my element', our view of Crusoe as *homo economicus* must be severely qualified.... He founds a small colony on his island in the mouth of the Orinoco which he leaves to decay. This hardly seems a good advertisement for colonization . . . A capitalist does not scorn advantages, a colonist does not ramble. . . . Crusoe, then, is not meant to be an advertisement for empire, but *Robinson Crusoe* is imperial propaganda for all that."[63] For all that what? Well, the answer is for all that *irony,* which needs to be ignored or reduced to yet another propagandistic tool.

Such a reduction of irony to little or nothing is a common feature of attempts to isolate the ideology of the novel, as this example from Michael McKeon's *Origins of the English Novel* illustrates:

> *Robinson Crusoe* at times emits the aura of irony because, like all ideology, it is dedicated to the instrumental disclosure—in Defoe's case with unparalleled penetration and candor—of a complex of contradictions that it is simultaneously dedicated to mediating and rendering intelligible. The central and recurrent form of this contradiction can be expressed, as we have seen, in the notion of the human internalization of divinity, and it is precisely because Defoe "still" seeks to understand the problem of mediation in the awesome terms of a Christian culture that we, who have long since stopped trying, are sometimes distracted from the profundity to the absurdity of the effort.[64]

Here irony becomes an especially pure instance of ideology, so that the critic who sees through it gains insight into the dialectical contradictions that actuate the system. The underlying explanation remains the same—that of Defoe's Protestant reconciliation of material and spiritual realms, now viewed from a post-theological distance that renders all such attempts absurd. With this, irony becomes a shadow of what it meant to Defoe and his enemies—namely, a double-edged rhetorical device over which Defoe exercised supreme control, a weapon capable of bringing church and state to full attention.

Many critics come up against this limitation of Defoe's actual language even as they seek and find underlying attitudes toward race, gender, class, economics, and theology. Ideological analysis at some point has to downplay the formal characteristics of a text designed to frustrate just such reduction to a set position. Evidence of Defoe's success in this regard includes the debates among modern scholars who isolate one aspect of Defoe's cultural complicity—race, for instance—and try to specify his bias in this area. They begin to disagree among themselves, and their interpretations range from calling Defoe a pernicious colonialist to celebrating an enlightened openness to difference. "What we find in Defoe's novel," writes Rebecca Bullard, "is not, however, the articulation of any single, particular political doctrine, but rather a polyphony of political ideas, which sometimes combine harmoniously but more often clash dissonantly with one another."[65]

What difference does this indifference to irony make? It blunts the interpretation of the best moments in *Robinson Crusoe*, even those related to economic themes. Take the famous passage that caught Marx's attention. After his catastrophe, Crusoe swims back to the wrecked ship and finds a satchel of money. This occasions the following meditation: "I smil'd to my self at the Sight of this Money, O Drug! Said I aloud, what art thou good for, Thou art not worth to me, no not the taking off of the Ground, one of those Knives is worth all this Heap, I have no Manner of use for thee, e'en remain where thou art, and go to the Bottom as a Creature whose Life is not worth saving. However, upon Second Thoughts I took it away; and wrapping all this in a Piece of Canvas, I began to think about making another Raft."[66] Here, one might argue, the disappearance of the author achieves artistic perfection. Defoe commits fully to Crusoe's point of view, even as the castaway's thoughts shift and change. He realizes that money is useless to him on the island, but he does not entirely despair of escaping. The "upon Second Thoughts" is delicious, but the end of that sentence is key: "I began to think about making another raft." A raft to escape. A raft to return to a place where that money will be valuable. The irony is in the shift in tone from an Ecclesiastical vanity, vanity, all is vanity to practicality—thoughts of building another raft. Yet this passage also grounds an economic analysis of the book. In the span of a single lifetime, as in the span of a single tortured sentence, Crusoe appears to be living through the transformation from one economic system, ruled by the antecedent idea of use value, typical of an agrarian, communalist economy, to another economic system ruled by abstract notions of exchange, credit, and commodity. The passage therefore invites this conclusion: "Crusoe's mental flip-flopping bears the ideological traces of a vast reconfiguration of social relations at the dawn of the eighteenth century that would eventuate in the automization and naturalization of the economy as the primary determinant of human value over and against the inherited hierarchies of monarchal and religious power structures."[67] Here irony does not even retain an aura. For something to bear the ideological traces of a vast reconfiguration of social relations, that something must work powerfully in a symbolic context. Yet the soft language of bearing a trace also relieves specificity. Once economy becomes "the primary determinant of human value," it goes without saying that economics must have been more important to Defoe than religion.

Ignoring Defoe's irony runs another risk. The manner of reading required of arguments that transform *Robinson Crusoe* into ideology bears a strong resemblance to the mode of interpretation that transforms *Robinson Crusoe* into a Christian catechism. Whether by way of accusation or praise, an allegorical or typological hermeneutic prevails. For Crusoe, read apologist for nascent capitalism and imperialism; for Crusoe, read Christian pilgrim. This substituting logic makes of *Robinson Crusoe* an allegory. Writes Laura Doyle in *Freedom's Empire*, "Defoe offers a parable for the way an Anglo-Protestant identity took shape and its imperial wealth accrued by way of these Atlantic encounters, while he also unwittingly displays how narrative and governance work together to reserve these benefits for Anglo-Atlantic subjects *only*."[68] Doyle calls Defoe unwitting because a larger ideology—of white Anglo-Saxon world domination—takes over, transforming every textual encounter, especially those with Friday, into a parable of "the faithless and profiteering logic, of the Anglo-Saxons' relation to Africans on the Atlantic."[69]

Such ideologically driven interpretations ignore the counter-allegorical dimensions of *Robinson Crusoe*. If the effective politics of the text are bound up in this counter-allegory, and irony is instrumental to it, then an ideological critique that dissolves Defoe's irony misses the key point—the point Defoe's enemies understood: he was as dangerous for the way he wrote as for what he wrote. These ideological readings of Crusoe also avoid a question occasioned by *Robinson Crusoe*'s immediate and enduring worldwide popularity. How does a criticism that reduces Defoe's text to a simple moral or economic parable explain the phenomenon of *Robinson Crusoe* as an early instance of "world literature"? Were readers of all times and cultures enthralled by the book because its story of Christian Providence and conversion struck a universal chord? Did readers everywhere take delight in the exploitation of oppressed races and the triumph of Anglo-Saxon whites? More likely, Defoe was drawn to literary deism, despite his personal antagonism toward deists, because he aspired to write an epic for the world, not a Calvinist allegory for his time and place. In deism he discovered the key philosophical principles and artistic models for the modern novel.

The Disappearing Author

Defoe's reticence to reveal his motives does not keep him from celebrating his achievement, although he does so discreetly. Defoe celebrates in 1720 when, at the start of *Serious Reflections,* he tweaks Gildon and likens his mentor, Leslie, to the commander of the Spanish Armada. He celebrates when he has Friday shoot the wolf and bear. And he celebrates by inserting a character into his own fiction, the "antient Gentlewoman" of *Serious Reflections,* who all but confirms his enemies' worst fears about the book. Secure behind his gift for sincere ventriloquism, Defoe even, on occasion, celebrates more directly:

> There even yet remains a Question, whether the Instruction of these Things will take place, when you are supposing the Scene, which is placed so far off, had its Original so near Home.
> But I am far from being anxious about that, seeing I am well assur'd, that if the Obstinacy of our Age should shut their Ears against the just Reflections made in this Volume, upon the Transactions taken Notice of in the former, there will come an Age, when the Minds of Men shall be more flexible, when the Prejudices of their Fathers shall have no Place, and when the Rules of Vertue and Religion justly recommended, shall be more gratefully accepted than they may be now, that our Children may rise up in Judgment against their fathers, and one Generation be edified by the same Teaching, which another Generation had despised.[70]

Should we hear the moralist insisting on the piety of his teachings or the radical admitting his book is as bad as his enemies say but reveling in the charge and predicting future vindication? Should we hear simple self-defense or a complex reflection on the way literature works, by representing far-off things for the imagination to bring home? Defoe provides no Fieldingesque justification for the form his novel takes. Instead, scattered throughout his less successful fiction—the lunar voyage and spy novel, as well as parts 2 and 3 of a trilogy known only for its first part—Defoe leaves fragments of a theory of the novel that, because of its proximity to an illicit cosmopolitan deism, must remain disconnected and disavowed. Threat foments fiction, which preserves and transforms the threat.

Toward the end of *Farther Adventures,* Crusoe's party, trekking overland in China, makes it to the Great Wall, where Crusoe stands for an hour in contemplation. It is another moment that drew the attention of Dumoulin (see fig. 16):[71]

> I stood still an Hour to look at it on every Side, near, and far off, I mean, that was within my View; and the Guide of our Caravan, who had been extolling it for the Wonder of the World, was mighty eager to hear my Opinion of it; I told him it was a most excellent Thing to keep off the *Tartars;* which he happened not to understand as I meant

DEFOE, DEISM, AND THE NOVEL / 231

Figure 16. Plate no. 139, Crusoe before the Great Wall of China. From François Aimé Louis Dumoulin, *Collection de cent-cinquante gravures . . . des voyages et aventures surprenantes de Robinson Crusoé*, [1810] 1962. (Courtesy of Harvard University, Houghton Library)

it, and so took it for a Compliment, but the old Pilot laugh'd: O Seignior *Inglese*, says he, you speak in Colours; in Colours, *said I*, what do you mean by that? Why, you speak what looks like white *this Way*, and black *that Way*; gay *one Way*, and dull *another Way*; you tell him it is a good Wall to keep out *Tartars*; you tell me *by that*, it is good for nothing but to keep out *Tartars,* or it will keep out none but *Tartars;* I understand you, Seignior *Inglese;* I understand you, says he, but Seignior *Chinese,* understood you his own way.⁷²

For the Great Wall of China, substitute a sprout of barley, a footprint in the sand, the name Kreutznaer, the noble savage, a dying old goat, the appeal to Providence. Defoe "speaks in Colours" and learned to do so by speaking under threat. This is the violent side of the origin of the novel, quite distinct from the contest between Samuel Richardson and Henry Fielding over whether Pamela is or is not a conniving hussy. This is the part of the history where authors have secret friends whose names they dare not mention, where state and church tribunals pillory, imprison, torture, burn, and hang writers for their words. This is not a popularity contest, although hearts and minds are ultimately at stake. This is more a matter of attacking while evading detection (on Defoe's part) and chasing down a dangerous author (on the part of his enemies). Perversely, these enemies had the best vantage point from which to view Defoe's motives and strategies.

Defoe wears masks so well that discerning the author's face behind the many visages is next to impossible. In a prose writer adopting a voice of confession and personal testimony to plumb the depths of character, this detachment from and immersion in character remains remarkable. Broad satire or collapsing sentimentalism awaits the writer who fails or never tries to reconcile distance and intimacy, satire and sentiment, in narrative. Austen is Defoe's great disciple in this regard. In early works she struggles to discover, and in later works effortlessly sustains a narrative poise between intimacy and detachment, the inner consciousness of character and the quick incisive commentary of narrator. Defoe did not achieve this balance overnight. *Robinson Crusoe* is the hard-won and successful conclusion of a series of narrative experiments, beginning with *The Shortest Way with the Dissenters.* Defoe the literary bandit and ventriloquist moves from pamphlets to a cosmopolitan space voyage modeled on Lucian and an Oriental spy novel modeled on Marana. These works failed. They did not survive their historical moment. They even annoy scholars. Gradually, Defoe refined these cosmopolitan efforts, donning the mask of spiritual autobiography and the castaway narrative, and, with Robinson Crusoe, found a voice and a life he could fully inhabit. This is the book that made Defoe's name—and the book in which Defoe disappears.

Virginia Woolf writes about *Robinson Crusoe,* "Our first task, and it is often formidable enough, is to master his perspective. . . . [A]ll alone we must climb on the novelist's shoulders and gaze through his eyes." As a reader, Woolf is eager to see the world through Crusoe's eyes, but she denigrates the scholarly attempt to see the world through a novelist's eyes. "Nobody who has any slight acquaintance with English literature needs to be told how many hours can be spent and how many lives have been spent in tracing the development of the novel and in examining the chins of the novelists," she writes, with obvious disdain for chin examiners, or biographers. "Only now and then, as we turn from theory to biography and biography to theory, a doubt insinuates itself . . . [whether] we should suck an ounce of additional pleasure from *Robinson Crusoe* or read it one whit more intelligently."[73] In Defoe's case, however, chins turn out to be very important: Defoe's hostility toward Charles Leslie led him to expose his chin, and risk his neck. The pillory was one result; *Robinson Crusoe* another. While Woolf holds that "learning whom he loved and why" is irrelevant, in this case learning whom Defoe hated most and what he did about it brings us, just as Robinson Crusoe promised, to the origin of *Robinson Crusoe*.

Notes

1. Lessons of the Pillory

1. This impressive string of invective is quoted in J. A. Downie, "Mr. Review and His Scribbling Friends: Defoe and the Critics, 1705–1706," *Huntington Library Quarterly* 41, no. 4 (1978): 355.

2. Raymond F. Howes, "*Robinson Crusoe:* A Literary Accident," *English Journal* 16, no. 1 (1927): 31–35.

3. Paula R. Backscheider, *Daniel Defoe: His Life* (Baltimore: Johns Hopkins University Press, 1989), 139, 349. Debates about the Defoe canon roil Defoe studies. Some of the key bibliographical reference points in this debate are John Robert Moore, *A Checklist of the Writings of Daniel Defoe*, 2d ed. (Hamden, CT: Archon Press, 1971); P. N. Furbank and W. R. Owens, *Defoe De-attributions: A Critique of J. R. Moore's Checklist* (London: Hambledon Press, 1994); P. N. Furbank and W. R. Owens, *The Canonization of Daniel Defoe* (New Haven, CT: Yale University Press, 1988); P. N. Furbank and W. R. Owens, *A Critical Bibliography of Daniel Defoe* (London: Pickering and Chatto, 1998); Ashley Marshall, "Beyond Furbank and Owens: A New Consideration of the Evidence for the 'Defoe' Canon," *Studies in Bibliography* 59 (2015): 131–90. I have taken note of disagreements about attribution throughout this study.

4. Daniel Defoe, "Robinson Crusoe's Preface," in *Serious Reflections during the Life and Surprising Adventures of Robinson Crusoe: With His Vision of the Angelick World. Written by Himself* (London: W. Taylor, 1720), sig. a2r; Daniel Defoe, *Serious Reflections during the Life and Surprising Adventures of Robinson Crusoe, with his Vision of the Angelick World,* in *The Novels of Daniel Defoe*, vol. 3, ed. G. A. Starr (London: Pickering and Chatto, 2008), 51. Hereafter, citations of *Serious Reflections* that provide two page numbers refer first to the 1720 edition (which is available at Eighteenth-Century Collections Online), then to the Pickering and Chatto edition of 2008. I follow this approach throughout this book, but for the principal prose fictions only, since Furbank and Owens have deattributed several of the works I discuss in this study. For the first

citation of each of the major works, I indicate which set and volume of the Pickering Masters edition contains the text in question. When referring the the editorial notes of any edition, I use only one page number, keyed to the edition in question.

5. Defoe, "Robinson Crusoe's Preface," in *Serious Reflections,* sig. a2r-a3r/51–52.

6. Cervantes scholars have indeed identified the Ducado *de Medina Sidonia,* the oldest hereditary duchy of Spain, and its current occupant, the seventh Duke *de Medina Sidonia,* Don Alonzo Pérez de Guzmán (1550–1615), commander of the ill-fated Armada, as one of several satiric targets Cervantes had in mind. None to my knowledge has argued that *all* of *Don Quixote* is "an emblematic History of, and a just Satyr upon" this one man. Defoe represents this view as common knowledge among the cognoscenti of his time.

7. The person Robinson Crusoe will not name is actually a composite. Maximillian Novak describes half of the figure of the "malicious, but foolish Writer." He traces the insinuation that *Robinson Crusoe* is Quixote-like to a phrase that Thomas Cox used when defending himself against charges brought by Defoe's publisher, W. Taylor, after a cheap pirated edition of *Robinson Crusoe* surfaced. Cox wrote in the *Flying Post* of October 29, 1719, "If Mr. Taylor, or the author of Crusoe's Don Quixotism, should make any farther steps to insinuate that I was the proprietor of that Abridgment, I assure the public, in justice to myself, I shall publish some secrets as yet unknown to the world; and prove that there is as little sincerity and honesty in exposing me, both in bookseller and author, as there is truth in Robinson Crusoe": see Maximillian E. Novak, *Daniel Defoe, Master of Fictions* (Oxford: Oxford University Press, 2001), 537–38. But Cox's use of the word "quixotism" is not directly relevant to its meaning in the passage, which points to the other half of the figure of the foolish malicious Critick, Charles Gildon. It was Gildon who, in 1719, delivered the first and to this day the most scathing review of Parts 1 and 2 of *Robinson Crusoe*.

8. Defoe, *Serious Reflections,* sig. a3v/52.

9. Novak notes the odd reference to the Duke *de Medina Sidonia;* yet because *Robinson Crusoe* does not read as a satire, he dismisses the clue: "notwithstanding moments of satire in volumes one and two, no one would find such passages sustained enough to argue that they shift the essential genre of the work.... *The Life and Strange Surprizing Adventures*... is a combination of fictional spiritual autobiography and adventure novel, while *Farther Adventures*... is essentially a novel of travel and adventure. [Moreover] most modern commentators... think that very little of Cervantes's contempt for Sidonia found its way into *Don Quixote*": Maximillian E. Novak, *Transformations, Ideology, and the Real in* Robinson Crusoe *and Other Narratives* (Newark: University of Delaware Press, 2015), 88–89. But this ignores the question of why Defoe raises the subject in the first place, overstating *Don Quixote*'s reputation as a disguised satire, and raising only to deny Gildon's charge that *Robinson Crusoe* is a polemical work targeting a known adversary.

10. On the harshness of Defoe's sentence, see John Robert Moore, *Defoe in the Pillory and Other Studies* (New York: Octagon Books, 1973), 3–7. Moore calls the sentence "the most severe of its kind in English literary history, *and it was not meant to punish but to destroy.*" The wording of Defoe's sentence, "to remain in prison till all be

performed," amounted to "a pleasant locution for life imprisonment." The sentence to stand for three hours in the pillory "was the most humiliating punishment known to English law." Defoe stood in the pillory before the Royal Exchange on July 29, 1703; in Cheapside on July 31; and again at Temple Bar on the same day. His incarceration in Newgate Prison lasted, with brief intermission before his trial, from July 7, 1703, until the first week of November the same year.

11. Backscheider, *Daniel Defoe*, 118.

12. John Richetti, *The Life of Daniel Defoe* (Malden, MA: Blackwell, 2005), 20–21.

13. Maximillian E. Novak, "*Robinson Crusoe* and Defoe's Career as a Writer," in *The Cambridge Companion to "Robinson Crusoe,"* ed. John Richetti (Cambridge: Cambridge University Press, 2018), 33.

14. Moore, *Defoe in the Pillory and Other Studies*, 3.

15. Ibid. The question is based on an interrogative posed by W. P. Trent.

16. On February 25, 1703, Secretary of State Daniel Finch, the second Earl of Nottingham, "brought a formal complaint before the House of Commons, who resolved that 'this book being full of false and scandalous Reflections on this Parliament, and tending to promote Sedition, be burnt by the hands of the common Hangman, tomorrow in New Palace Yard'": Novak, *Daniel Defoe*, 180.

17. James Sutherland provides the animal explanation: "He had the animal courage of active folks. . . . He was full of restless and audacious energy," making his punishment for publishing *The Shortest Way* an accidental byproduct of his impetuous behavior: "He was certainly very unlucky to be ruined by one of the cleverest things he ever did. . . . It is more than likely that his martyrdom has been accidental": James Sutherland, *Daniel Defoe* (Philadelphia: J. B. Lippincott, 1938), 82. Novak adds, "Defoe was a gambler and could not resist the perverse pleasure of approaching the edge of the abyss": Novak, *Daniel Defoe*, 177. Joseph Hone supplies the political explanation, describing *The Shortest Way with the Dissenters* as "agitprop in the battle for the general elections" and "a clandestine polemic designed to alarm moderates away from Tory policy": Joseph Hone, *Literature and Party Politics at the Accession of Queen Anne* (Oxford: Oxford University Press, 2017), 157. A similarly political account appears in D. N. DeLuna, "Ironic Monologue and 'Scandalous *Ambo-dexter* Conformity' in Defoe's *The Shortest Way with the Dissenters*," in *British Literature, 1640–1789: A Critical Reader*, ed. Robert DeMaria Jr. (Malden, MA: Blackwell, 1999), 126–41. Richetti calls *The Shortest Way* a rhetorical blunder: "the pamphlet was, notoriously, a failed parody that became a successful and thereby disastrous hoax": Richetti, *The Life of Daniel Defoe*, 47.

18. Daniel Defoe, *A Brief Explanation of a Late Pamphlet Entitled, The Shortest Way with the Dissenters* (London: s.n., 1703), 2. The pamphlet is four pages long, written by all appearances to exonerate individuals still held under suspicion of collaboration with Defoe. Defoe and his publisher tried to avoid trouble in a subsequent edition by altering the title page to read, "The Shortest Way with the Dissenters [Taken from Dr. Sach-ll's Sermon. and Others]." Hone argues that Defoe is lying and that his principal motive for writing *The Shortest Way with the Dissenters* was to influence the political debate about a Tory/High Church bill to forbid occasional conformity: Hone, *Literature and Party Politics at the Accession of Queen Anne*, 157.

19. Defoe, *A Brief Explanation of a Late Pamphlet Entitled, The Shortest Way with the Dissenters*, 2.
20. Howard D. Weinbrot, *Literature, Religion, and the Evolution of Culture, 1660–1780* (Baltimore: Johns Hopkins University Press, 2013), 67.
21. Novak, *Daniel Defoe*, 177. Hone quotes a letter from Defoe to Harley that likewise singles out Sacheverell as Defoe's principal target, "As Defoe later put it in a letter to Harley explaining his part in the controversy, *The Shortest Way* was a response to the 'use' that Sacheverell and his colleagues made of her [the Queen's] first speech": Hone, *Literature and Party Politics at the Accession of Queen Anne*, 157. The publication date of December 1, 1702, "was ideal timing for maximum political impact, coming after the occasional conformity bill was passed by the Commons and just one day before it was sent to the Lords. The tract would not have had the same effect if it had been published a week or two later": Hone, *Literature and Party Politics at the Accession of Queen Anne*, 158. That Defoe's troublesome pamphlet provoked commentary for years after the debate on the occasional conformity bill had ended provides reason to question this conclusion.
22. Daniel Defoe, *The Present State of the Parties in Great Britain* (London: J. Baker, 1712), 24. Also quoted in Novak, *Daniel Defoe*, 173. Novak supplies parallel passages from Sacheverell's *The Political Union: A Discourse Shewing the Dependence of Government on Religion in General* (London: Leonard Lichfield, 1702) to reveal the extent of Defoe's mimicry. Backscheider also identifies Sacheverell as Defoe's target while noting a more immediate source, an anonymous pamphlet titled *The Establishment of the Church, the Preservation of the State: Shewing the Reasonableness of a Bill against Occasional Conformity*: Backscheider, *Daniel Defoe*, 95.
23. Defoe, *The Present State of the Parties in Great Britain*, 18–19.
24. J. C. D. Clark, *English Society, 1688–1832: Ideology, Social Structure and Political Practice during the Ancien Regime* (Cambridge: Cambridge University Press, 1985), 298.
25. Mary Astell, *A Fair Way with the Dissenters and Their Patrons. Not Writ by Mr. L——y, or Any Other Furious Jacobite, whether Clergyman or Layman; but by a Very Moderate Person and Dutiful Subject to the Queen* (London: R. Wilkin, 1704).
26. Clark, *English Society 1688–1832*, 282.
27. For more than a century, Leslie's *A Short and Easie Method with the Deists* enjoyed remarkable success in England, Scotland, Ireland, and America. Editions of the work appeared in Dublin (1709); Boston (1719 and 1723, causing the arrest and trial of its publisher); Williamsburg, Virginia (1733); Edinburgh (1745); and London (1698, 1699, 1701, 1711, 1712, 1715, 1723, 1726, 1727, 1799). The mid-century hiatus is deceptive, since Leslie's *Short and Easie* was repackaged as *Deism Refuted; or, The Truth of Christianity Demonstrated*, published in London in 1755 and Dublin in 1758. Based on the success of this title, Leslie started to produce spin-off short and easies written against other enemies, especially the Jews: Charles Leslie, *A Short and Easie Method with the Jews*, 3d ed. (London: Geo. Strahan, 1715), with editions and reprints in 1726, 1727, and 1737; *The Case of the Jews Considered with Respect to Christianity* (London: s.n., 1755), redacted from other works and published posthumously in 1755, no doubt

in response to the passage and immediate repeal of the Jewish Naturalization Act in 1753–54. The editors of the Pickering Masters edition observe that Leslie's *The New Association of Those Called, Moderate-Church-Men* (London: s.n., 1702), "provoked the *Shortest Way*," but they say little about the impact of his *A Short and Easie Method with the Deists*, a far more important and influential work.

28. Defoe, *A Brief Explanation of a Late Pamphlet Entitled, The Shortest Way with the Dissenters*, 3.

29. On Leslie's creation of *The Rehearsal* to counter Defoe's *The Review*, see Downie, "Mr. Review and His Scribbling Friends," 350. Leslie's purpose in creating *The Rehearsal* was "to contradict the opinions of 'Tutchin, Defoe, and the rest of the *Scandalous Club*. Their Books have been solidly and sincerely Answer'd, But their *Papers* have been neglected, that is, their *weekly penny papers,* which go through the Nation like *News-Papers*.'"

30. Defoe argues that "to Conform to the Church of *England*, and receive the Sacrament, meerly to Qualify for a Civil Employment, is a scandalous Practice, a Reproach to Religion, and Offensive to all good Christians . . . 'tis a Sin in a Dissenter to Conform to the Church of *England*": Daniel Defoe, *The Sincerity of the Dissenters Vindicated, from the Scandal of Occasional Conformity* (London: s.n., 1703), sig. a2r–a2v.

31. See Robert D. Cornwall, "Charles Leslie," in *The Oxford Dictionary of National Biography*, online ed., ed. David Cannadine (Oxford: Oxford University Press, 2004), https://doi.org/10.1093/ref:odnb/16484. Cornwall captures the man and his mission: "Leslie's published works included dozens of political and religious tracts and books, with a strong connection between his political and theological writings. Rooting his thought in the patriarchalism of Robert Filmer, he offered an antidote to the contractualism of John Locke and his followers, including Benjamin Hoadly and Daniel Defoe. As Filmer's most prominent interpreter, Leslie insisted that God ordained a hierarchical political structure for all aspects of society, whether civil, religious, or familial. Fathers reigned supreme in the home, bishops in the church, and the monarch in national government. The revolution of 1688 which brought the eviction of James II and the ascendancy of William and Mary was, therefore, a humanly designed abrogation of this divinely ordered society. Sacred and civil governments, in Leslie's perspective, stood in two parallel lines, and though remaining distinct and separate they should protect and support each other. If one took liberties regarding the church then it seemed logical that one would take seditious attitudes toward the state." See also the notes on Leslie throughout W. R. Owens and P. N. Furbank, eds., *The Complete Works of Daniel Defoe*, 63 vols. (London: Pickering and Chatto, 2000–2009). The editors acknowledge Leslie's importance to Defoe and cite numerous instances of direct confrontation between the two men.

32. Thomas Babington Macaulay, *The History of England*, 5 vols. (London: Longman, Brown, Green, and Longmans, 1855–63), 4:456.

33. Richetti, *The Life of Daniel Defoe*, 49–50.

34. James Boswell, *The Life of Samuel Johnson, LL.D.*, 4 vols. (London: A. Baldwin and Son, 1799), 4:302. Leslie once published a polemic called, *The Best Answer Ever Was*

Made, and to Which No Answer Will Ever Be Made (London: John Morphew, 1709). Johnson's simultaneous toast and roast captures the spirit of this title.

35. Clark, *English Society*, 187.

36. Daniel Defoe, *The Dissenter's Answer to the High Church Challenge* (London: s.n., 1704), 36.

37. Cornwall, "Charles Leslie."

38. Jonathan Swift, *The Examiner*, no. 15. November 16, 1710, reprinted in Jonathan Swift, *Political Tracts by the Author of Gulliver's Travels* (London: C. Davis, 1738), 93.

39. Quoted in Downie, "Mr. Review and His Scribbling Friends," 350.

40. Charles Leslie, *A View of the Times, Their Principles and Practices*, 4 vols. (London: s.n., 1708–1709), vol. 4, no. 34, February 5, 1708. Hereafter referred to in the text as *The Rehearsal*.

41. P. N. Furbank and W. R. Owens, *A Political Biography of Daniel Defoe* (London: Pickering and Chatto, 2006), 57–60.

42. Robert Joshua Leslie, *The Life and Writings of Charles Leslie, M.A.: Nonjuring Divine* (London: Rivingtons, 1885), 89.

43. Charles Leslie, *A Short and Easie Method with the Deists*, 3d ed. (London: C. Brome, W. Keblewhite, E. Poole, Geo. Strahan, 1701), 1. I quote from the third edition to emphasize the work's visibility at the time Defoe wrote his version of the short and easy.

44. Ibid., 2–3.

45. Ibid., A2

46. Ibid., 53.

47. See Michael Hunter, "'Aikenhead the Atheist': The Context and Consequences of Articulate Irreligion in the Late Seventeenth Century," in *Atheism from the Reformation to the Enlightenment*, ed. Michael Hunter and David Wootton (Oxford: Oxford University Press, 1992), 221–54. See also Michael F. Graham, *The Blasphemies of Thomas Aikenhead: Boundaries of Belief on the Eve of the Enlightenment* (Edinburgh: Edinburgh University Press, 2008), along with Justin Champion, "Review of *The Blasphemies of Thomas Aikenhead*," July 2009, http://www.history.ac.uk/reviews/review/781.

48. Defoe, *The Present State of the Parties in Great Britain*, 20–21.

49. Novak, *Daniel Defoe*, 178.

50. Bonamy Dobrée, "Some Aspects of Defoe's Prose," in *Pope and His Contemporaries: Essays Presented to George Sherburn*, ed. James L. Clifford and Louis A. Landa (Oxford: Oxford University Press, 1949), 175. See also Maximillian E. Novak, "Defoe's *Shortest Way with the Dissenters*: Hoax, Parody, Paradox, Fiction, Irony, and Satire," *Modern Language Quarterly* 27 (1966): 402–17; Maximillian E. Novak "Defoe's Uses of Irony," in *The Uses of Irony: Papers on Defoe and Swift Read at a Clark Library Seminar, April 2, 1966* (Los Angeles: William Andrews Clark Memorial Library, 1966). Richard West contrasts Defoe's *Shortest Way* and Swift's *Modest Proposal*, the satire with which it is often compared, writing that, whereas "the very outrageousness of his title is a signal from Swift to even the stupidest readers that what they are going to enjoy is a satire that should not be taken literally. . . . *The Shortest Way with [the] Dissenters* never gives any

indication that it is not in earnest": Richard West, *Daniel Defoe: The Life and Strange Surprising Adventures* (New York: Carroll and Graf, 1998), 73.

51. Sutherland, *Daniel Defoe*, 31.

52. See also Paul K. Alkon, "Defoe's Argument in *The Shortest Way with the Dissenters*," *Modern Philology* 73, no. 4 (1976): S12–23. Especially relevant is Alkon's observation that "since nothing in *The Shortest Way* explicitly discloses Defoe's answer [or position], it takes some casuistical skill to detect the sophistry. Readers without a position must formulate one in order to define their relation to the argument. But it is easiest to assume the wrong answer because a progression of analogical and metaphoric arguments leading to and coming after the most explicit statement increase confusion about what is being proposed": ibid., S18.

53. Defoe, *The Shortest Way with the Dissenters*, 18–19.

54. Defoe, *The Shortest Way with the Dissenters*, 15. On Defoe's rhetorical training at Morton's Academy, see Novak, *Daniel Defoe*, esp. 40–50; Backscheider, *Daniel Defoe*, esp. 13–20. Novak states, "If anyone mastered the art of writing taught at Newington Green, it was Defoe, and there could have been no better training in the creation of character and fictional content than the kind of exercises given by Morton," 43. On Morton's pedagogy, see also Lew Girdier, "Defoe's Education at Newington Green Academy," *Studies in Philology* 50, no. 4 (1953): 573–91.

55. Ibid., 4.

56. *The Shortest Way with Whores and Rogues; or, A New Project for Reformation, Dedicated to Mr. Daniel de Foe, Author of the Shortest Way with the Dissenters* (London: s.n., 1703), sig. a3r, a5v, a6v. The work is sometimes attributed to John Dunton.

57. *The Fox with His Fire-Brand Unkenell'd and Insnar'd; or, A Short Answer to Mr. Daniel Foe's Shortest Way with the Dissenters* (London: s.n., 1703), 4. Farnaby refers to Thomas Farnaby (1575–1647), whose textbooks in grammar, syntax, and rhetoric were popular in Defoe's day.

58. Defoe, *A Brief Explanation of a Late Pamphlet, Entitled, The Shortest Way with the Dissenters*, 217.

59. *The Fox with His Fire-Brand Unkenell'd and Insnar'd*, 3–5. This author describes *The Shortest Way* as a libel, linking it to "Fitz Harris' Libel," which proved such a fatal irony that Fitz Harris was "hang'd for it in good earnest," a fate the author wishes for Defoe, as well.

60. Ibid., 4.

61. Charles Leslie, *The Wolf Stript of His Shepherd's Cloathing* (London: s.n., 1704), 74.

62. *The Reformer Reform'd; or, The Shortest Way with Daniel D'Fooe* (London: T. Everat, 1703), 4.

63. Edward Ward (attrib.), *The Secret History of the Calves Head Club; or, The Republican Unmask'd*, 2d ed. (London: s.n., 1703).

64. *The Reformer Reformed*, 6.

65. Charles Shadwell, "Prologue to *Rotherick O'Connor, King of Connaught, or the Distress'd Princess, A Tragedy*," in *Five New Plays* (London: A Bettesworth, 1720), "The Prologue by Colonel Allen," separated from the play and unpaginated.

66. *The Shortest Way with Whores and Rogues*, Or a New Project for Reformation Dedicated to Mr. Daniel de Foe, Author of the Shortest Way with Dissenters (London: 1703), "The Dedication," sig. 6.

67. Charles Gildon, *The Life and Strange Surprizing Adventures of Mr. D—— de F——, of London, Hosier, Who Has Liv'd above Fifty Years by Himself, in the Kingdoms of North and South Britain. The Various Shapes He Has Appear'd in, and the Discoveries He Has Made for the Benefit of His Country* (London: J. Roberts, 1719), iii–iv. I return to Gildon's critique of *Robinson Crusoe* in chapter 4.

68. Leslie, *A View of the Times, Their Principles and Practices* (London: 1708–09), vol. 1. The four volumes of this text bring together the separately published issues of Leslie's *The Rehearsal*, whose primary purpose was to respond to John Tutchin's *Observator* and Defoe's *Review*. The issue of *The Rehearsal* containing this quotation appeared as no. 10, September 30–October 7, 1704.

69. Leslie, *A View of the Times, Their Principles and Practices*, vol. 1, no. 18, November 25–December 2, 1704.

70. Charles Leslie, *The Case of the Church of England's Memorial Fairly Stated* (London: s.n., 1705), 7.

71. Charles Leslie, *The Wolf Stript of His Shepherd's Cloathing*, 74.

72. Robert Joshua Leslie, *The Life and Writings of Charles Leslie, M.A.*, 89.

73. Scholars who wish to keep Defoe free and clear of deism emphasize his repudiation of Toland in *The Reformation of Manners* and downplay the significance of Toland's involvement in distributing *The Shortest Way with the Dissenters*. They point out that Toland may have been working only at the publisher's behest, leaving Defoe in the dark as to his active support for the text. The most thorough investigation of this question reaches a more nuanced conclusion. "To have had access to the number of copies distributed by him in Holland, so recently after its publication on 1 December 1702, Toland must have been associated at least with the publisher of *The Shortest Way*. Moreover, Toland at this time was not a man of means; he was hardly in a position to distribute numerous copies of the pamphlet gratis on his own account. This strongly implies that his connection to *The Shortest Way* extended some way beyond the publisher": J. D. Alsop, "Defoe, Toland, and *The Shortest Way with the Dissenters*," *Review of English Studies* 43, no. 170 (1992): 245–47.

74. Defoe, *A Brief Explanation of a Late Pamphlet, Entitled, The Shortest Way with the Dissenters*, 215.

75. *Oxford English Dictionary*, s.v., "irony" (E. Reyner, *Rules Govt. Tongue* 227, 1656), https://en.oxforddictionaries.com/definition/irony.

76. Daniel Defoe, *The Genuine Works of Mr. Daniel Defoe*, vol. 1 (London: 1721), sig. a4r.

77. Quoted in Lee Sonstang Horsley, "Contemporary Reactions to Defoe's Shortest Way with Dissenters," *Studies in English Literature, 1500–1900* 16, no. 3 (1976): 419. Horsley's source is Defoe, *The Present State of the Parties in Great Britain*, 24.

78. This is a short way of suggesting a much longer literary tradition in which Defoe participates—that of ancient philosophical and literary skepticism, descending

to the eighteenth century through new publishing ventures such as Thomas Stanley's *The History of Philosophy*, 3d ed. (London: W. Battersby, 1701), as well as new English translations of Lucian, Petronius, and the humanist literary skeptics, Erasmus and Montaigne.

79. William Minto, *Daniel Defoe* (London: Macmillan, 1879), 169.

80. Horsley, "Contemporary Reactions to Defoe's *Shortest Way with Dissenters*," 409.

81. See chapter 2, "Madness, Extirpation, and Defoe's *Shortest Way with the Dissenters*," in Weinbrot, *Literature, Religion, and the Evolution of Culture*, 21–102. The argument about incompetent readers appears in Novak, "*Robinson Crusoe* and Defoe's Career as a Writer," 35. William Hazlitt's comment on this topic is worth noting here. He wrote, "Strange to tell, no one, either among those he wrote for, or among those he wrote against, had wit enough to comprehend it, and yet one cannot peruse *The Shortest Way with the Dissenters* at this distance of time without being astonished with the extent of their stupidity": William Hazlitt, *The Works of Daniel De Foe, with a Memoir of his Life and Writings* (London: John Clements, 1811), xxiii–xxiv.

82. Defoe, *The Dissenter's Answer to the High Church Challenge*, 37–38.

83. Novak, *Daniel Defoe*, 184.

84. Quoted in Alsop, "Defoe, Toland, and *The Shortest Way with the Dissenters*," 247. The source of Alsop's information is a secret communiqué sent from Holland to the English government, which "firmly suggests that there was an orchestrated attempt to disseminate the publication as widely as possible."

85. "I shall Never for the Future Think my self Injur'd if I am Call'd a Coward," Defoe wrote in reference to his appeals for mercy: quoted in Novak, *Daniel Defoe*, 183.

86. Daniel Defoe, *A Hymn to the Pillory*, 2d ed. (London: s.n., 1703), 23.

87. Daniel Defoe, *A Dialogue between a Dissenter and the Observator* (London: s.n., 1703), 3–4. On "Bellamy," see Novak, *Daniel Defoe*, 179–80: "On 29 December [1702] Nottingham issued a warrant for Edward Bellamy, an agent of Whig propaganda. Taken into custody on 2 January, Bellamy admitted to carrying the manuscript to the printer, George Croome. On 3 January Nottingham ordered that Defoe be taken into custody and his papers seized, and that he should be brought before him for examination."

88. Sutherland, *Daniel Defoe*, 88.

89. William Pittis, *The True-Born Hugonot; or, Daniel de Foe, a Satyr* (London: s.n., 1703), 10. Pittis was another of Defoe's inveterate political enemies. For more on this Tory polemicist, see Theodore F. M. Newton, "William Pittis and Queen Anne Journalism," *Modern Philology* 33, no. 2 (1935): 169–86. Pittis answered Defoe's *Dyet of Poland* with his own *The Dyet of Poland: A Satyr Considered Paragraph by Paragraph* (London: Benjamin Bragg, 1705).

90. Pittis, *The True-Born Hugonot*, 12.

91. On the source of Defoe's *The Shortest Way*, see also Novak, *Daniel Defoe*, 177, who observes that there were many previous examples of his hoax: "It should be pointed out that the *Poems on Affairs of State*, which appeared after the end of the

Licensing Act in 1695, were filled with works using a mask or persona to establish a paradoxical position. . . . [Defoe] grew up during the seventeenth century, when the 'skeptical' method of argument through paradox was considered to be more convincing because less dogmatic."

92. Pittis, *The True-Born Hugonot*, 20.

93. Miriam Leranbaum, "'An Irony not Unusual': Defoe's 'Shortest Way with Dissenters," *Huntington Library Quarterly* 37, no. 3 (May 1974): 246–48.

94. Dario Pfanner's article on Blount in *The Oxford Dictionary of National Biography* rejects (without saying why) both Macaulay's and Leranbaum's account of Blount's intentions and the effect of his pamphlet. "It was probably not, as previously thought, deliberately written to discredit Bohun and had only a small role in the demise of the Licensing Act," Pfanner writes. "Its arguments, however, proved highly controversial": Dario Pfanner, "Charles Blount (1654–1693)," in *The Oxford Dictionary of National Biography*, ed. David Cannadine (Oxford: Oxford University Press, 2004), https://doi-org/10.1093/ref:odnb/2684. Mark Goldie also expressed skepticism about Blount's intentions without denying the extraordinary effect the pamphlet had on Bohun himself: "Conquest theory was a deeply conservative style of argument associated, in different forms, with Hobbes, Grotius, and with the Tory historian Robert Brady. It nullified the concept of consent as the foundation of political society and when applied to the revolution of 1689 avoided the conclusion that William had been nominated to the throne by the people. This juxtaposition of Blount and conquest creates the curious paradox of a Whig in Tory clothing": Mark Goldie, "Charles Blount's Intentions in Writing *King William and Queen Mary Conquerors*," *Notes and Queries* 223 (1978): 527–28. This is the same curious paradox that Defoe created in *The Shortest Way with the Dissenters*. "It would be unnecessary to discuss Macaulay's story but for the fact that almost every scholar who has given Blount or Bohun or the history of press freedom any attention has copied it. Nevertheless, it is almost certainly untrue": ibid. Despite Goldie's confident conclusion, Defoe's use of Blount is a good measure of Blount's "intentions."

95. Macaulay, *The History of England*, 4:355–56.

96. Goldie notes in passing Blount's previous efforts to end press censorship. These works, drawing heavily from the arguments of Milton's *Areopagitica* (1644), were Charles Blount, *A Just Vindication of Learning and Liberty of the Press; or, An Humble Address to the High Court of Parliament in Behalf of the Liberty of the Press* (London: s.n., 1679; repr. 1695), and Charles Blount, *Reasons Humbly Offered for the Liberty of Unlicens'd Printing, to Which Is Subjoin'd the Just and True Character of Edmund Bohun, the Licenser of the Press* (London: s.n., 1693). How could it not have remained his "intention" to attack the Licensing Act with *King William and Queen Mary Conquerors*?

97. Macaulay, *The History of England*, 4:355–56.

98. While it is reasonable to suggest that these two ways of dying are quite different, casting doubt on the suicide itself, the story has long circulated that Blount killed himself for love of his deceased wife's sister, after the church refused to permit their marriage, and she refused to have him without the church's permission. This study identifies at least two men who were overjoyed to see Blount dead: Charles Leslie and Edmund Bohun.

99. Quoted in Sutherland, *Daniel Defoe*, 93.

100. Daniel Defoe, *An Appeal to Honour and Justice . . . Tho It Be of His Worst Enemies . . . Being an Account of His Conduct in Publick Affairs* (London: J. Baker, 1715), 9.

101. The quotation comes from Harold Love's informative article about Roger L'Estrange in *The Oxford Dictionary of National Biography,* https://doi.org/10.1093/ref: odnb/16514 (revised and submitted October 4, 2007).

102. Leslie, *A Short and Easie Method with the Deists,* 2d ed. (London: C. Brome, W. Keblewhite, H. Hindmarsh, E. Poole, 1699), xii–xiv.

103. Ibid., xi.

104. Charles Blount, *The First Two Books of Philostratus, Concerning the Life of Apollonius Tyaneus: Written Originally in Greek, and Now Published in English: Together with Philological Notes upon Each Chapter* (London: Nathaniel Thompson, 1680). The "Philological Notes" were deemed so anti-Christian that even Pierre Bayle, while appropriating portions of Blount's notes for his own article on Apollonius of Tyana in the *Dictionnaire historique et critique,* felt compelled to distance himself from the deist by mangling the account of his suicide in an uncharitable and cowardly footnote. Thanks to such efforts, Blount is better known today for his sad and suspicious demise than for being what his German biographer calls him—England's *Frühaufklärer:* Karl-Josef Walber, *Charles Blount (1654–1693) Frühaufklärer* (Frankfurt am Main: Peter Lang, 1988).

105. Leslie, *A Short and Easie Method with the Deists,* 2d ed. (London: C. Brome, W. Keblewhite, H. Hindmarsh, E. Poole, 1699), sig. a3r.

106. *Reflections upon a Late Scandalous and Malicious Pamphlet Entitul'd, The Shortest Way with the Dissenters* (London: s.n., 1703), "The Preface," iii. There is some disagreement about the authorship of this pamphlet. Novak holds that it may have been written by Defoe. Hone follows Novak even to the threshold of certainty, writing, "Defoe himself may have been among the first to attack *The Shortest Way*—albeit in a different narrative persona—in *Reflections upon a Late Scandalous and Malicious Pamphlet*": Hone, *Literature and Party Politics at the Accession of Queen Anne,* 160. At least one contemporary assumed Leslie was the author, and Leslie clearly suffered public humiliation at the hands of Defoe.

107. *Reflections upon a Late Scandalous and Malicious Pamphlet,* iii–iv.

108. *The Fox with His Fire-Brand Unkenell'd and Insnar'd,* 12.

109. There seems to be some confusion about whether Penn involved himself *only* to help Defoe avoid the pillory or whether, these efforts failing, he next tried to gain Defoe's release from Newgate Prison. John Robert Moore settled this matter in 1971 when he wrote, "In 1703 the great Quaker William Penn (together with his son William) exerted himself to secure Defoe's release from Newgate": John Robert Moore, "Defoe's Persona as Author: The Quaker Sermon," *Studies in English Literature, 1500–1900* 11, no. 3 (1971): 511. Defoe wrote a letter to Penn thanking him for his help, which postdates his time in the pillory, suggesting that Penn's efforts continued even after Defoe's public shaming. In a letter to William Penn dated April 18, 1704, Defoe referred to "those many and kind visits you bestowed on me in a house of bondage and affliction." Novak observes that Penn himself "had been acquitted in a [similar] case by a jury that refused to follow the instructions of the prosecution [which] suggests that Defoe had some awareness of

the legal history of such cases": Novak, *Daniel Defoe*, 188. The idea that Penn would involve himself only to help Defoe avoid the pillory, then discontinue his efforts on his behalf once he was pilloried, is absurd.

110. Defoe, *An Appeal to Honour and Justice . . . Tho It Be of His Worst Enemies . . . Being an Account of His Conduct in Publick Affairs* (London: J. Baker, 1715), 11–12.

111. Backscheider quotes Defoe's letter to Harley upon his release. "I think my Self bound to Own you as the Principall Agent of this Miracle": Backscheider, *Daniel Defoe*, 124.

112. Defoe, *An Appeal to Honour and Justice*, 12.

113. Ibid.

114. Daniel Defoe, *The Letters of Daniel Defoe*, ed. George Harris Healey (Oxford: Clarendon Press, 1955), 7–8. The letter has also been reproduced in Richard S. Dunn and Mary Maples Dunn, eds., *The Papers of William Penn, Volume 4: 1701–1718* (Philadelphia: University of Pennsylvania Press, 1987), 289. Portions of the letter appear in Novak, *Daniel Defoe*, 184, and in *The Friend: Religious and Literary Journal* 76, no. 1 (1902): 2.

115. Defoe, *An Appeal to Honour and Justice*, 16. The context is Defoe's description of work he did for Queen Anne as a secret agent in Scotland. The lines hold equally for Defoe's protection of his accomplices in the episode of *The Shortest Way with the Dissenters*.

116. Furbank and Owens repeat consensus opinion that William Penn "was not personally known to Defoe," a conclusion apparently drawn from Defoe's own statements, even though he had every reason to lie. This leads them to conclude that Defoe "recognized Leslie as an important adversary" only after 1704, when Leslie "launched a new journal, *The Rehearsal*, with the direct purpose of skirmishing with John Tutchin, author of the Whiggish *Observator*, and Defoe, the author of the *Review*": Furbank and Owens, *A Political Biography of Daniel Defoe*, 23, 58. The evidence presented here suggests that (1) Defoe was aware of Leslie's vicious attacks on Penn and the Quakers; and (2) he undertook an assault on Leslie with this larger Quaker context in mind, a context that predates 1704 by nearly two decades.

117. *The Friend: Religious and Literary Journal* 76, no 1. (1902): 2.

118. Defoe, *A Hymn to the Pillory*, 24.

119. Daniel Defoe, *The Fortunes and Misfortunes of the Famous Moll Flanders*, 2d ed. (London: John Bretherton, 1722), 352; Daniel Defoe, *The Fortunes and Misfortunes of the Famous Moll Flanders* (1721), in *The Novels of Daniel Defoe*, vol. 6, ed. Liz Bellamy (London: Pickering and Chatto, 2009), 266.

120. Daniel Defoe, *A Tour through the Whole Island of Great Britain*, 4 vols. (London: J. and F. Rivington, 1769), 2:312.

121. David Manning, "Accusations of Blasphemy in English Anti-Quaker Polemic, 1660–1701," *Quaker Studies* 14, no. 1 (2009): 35, https://online.liverpooluniversitypress.co.uk/doi/pdf/10.3828/quaker.14.1.27.

122. Whereas later Leslie would advertise new works as "by the author of the *Short and Easie* Method," at first he foregrounds his authorship of the anti-Quaker tract. He subtitles *An Essay Concerning the Divine Right of Tythes* (London: Charles

Brome, 1700) as "by the author of The Snake in the Grass"; Leslie's *Five Discourses by the Author of The Snake in the Grass* (London: Charles Brome, 1700) makes the same boast, as do his *Primitive Heresie Revived in the Faith and Practice of the People called Quakers . . . to Which Is Added a Friendly Expostulation with William Penn . . . by the Author of The Snake in the Grass* (London: Charles Brome, 1698) and *Satan Dis-rob'd from His Disguise of Light; or, The Quakers Last Shift to Cover Their Monstrous Heresies . . . by the Author of The Snake in the Grass* (London: C. Brome, W. Keblewhite, H. Hindmarsh, 1697). The pace and ferocity of Leslie's publishing on this topic alone give some idea of what Defoe was up against when he challenged Leslie in 1702.

123. Charles Leslie, *The Snake in the Grass; or, Satan Transformed into an Angel of Light* (London: Charles Brome, 1696), viii–ix. The linking of Quakers and Jews (Pharisees) was routine during this period. Leslie imposes the same "happy Necessity" of conversion on both groups. The necessity is happy because freely embraced as the fruit of superior reason and thus far uncompelled.

124. Charles Leslie, *A Reply to a Book Entitul'd Anguis Flagellatus; or, A Switch for the Snake* (London: Charles Brome, 1702), 107.

125. Ibid., 5.

126. Francis Bugg, *A Quaker Catechism: To Which Is Added The Shortest Way with Daniel De-Foe* (London: H. Hills, 1706).

127. See Henry J. Cadbury, "Daniel Defoe and William Penn," *Journal of the Friends Historical Society* 14, no. 4 (1917): 172–73; Juliet Reeve, "Daniel Defoe and Quakers," *Friends' Intelligencer* 103, no. 18 (1946): 282–84.

128. Francis Bugg, *The Quaker's Infallibility Shaken All to Pieces* (London: R. Wilkin, 1711), iii, 599. A Laodicean is someone who has an indifferent attitude toward religion.

129. Leslie, *Deism Refuted*, 34–35.

130. For an excellent study of the political history of this attempt to associate unlike positions into an "atheist cabal," see Roger Lund, "Guilt by Association: The Atheist Cabal and the Rise of the Public Sphere in Augustan England," *Albion* 34, no. 3 (2002): 391–421. Lund points out that there was a perceived theological bond among Whigs, Latitudinarians, Dissenters, and Deists, justifying the view of the High Church that they were complicit in the same plot. Lund quotes a passage from Swift stating that it was common knowledge that out of one hundred deists and atheists, ninety-nine would be Whigs.

131. Charles Leslie, *The Second Part of The Wolf Stript of his Shepherd's Cloathing* (London: s.n., 1707), 3. The wolf in this text and its predecessor is Defoe. This shoving of moderation down the slippery slope to radicalism benefited from the fiery prose Sacheverell supplied. He described the character of a Low-Church-Man as "a Man, so far from being given to *Superstition*, that he believ'd nothing at all in Religion, and that he should be ready to satisfie the Country, if they would be so kind as to Chuse him, that he wou'd be a *Deist, Socinian, or Republican*, or anything to promote Their, and His, and the Churches interest, and in a Word, a *Thorough-Pac'd and Season'd Low-Church-Man*": Henry Sacheverell, *The Character of a Low-Church-Man* (London: s.n., 1702), 27.

132. Manning, "Accusations of Blasphemy in English Anti-Quaker Polemic," 28. A specific provision of the Clarendon Code referred to as the Quaker Act of 1662 targeted the Quakers by forcing them to swear an oath of allegiance to the King of England. (Quakers did not swear oaths.)

133. See Ethyn Williams Kirby, "The Quakers' Efforts to Secure Civil and Religious Liberty: 1660–96," *Journal of Modern History* 7, no. 4 (1935): 401–21. The rebuff of one effort to ameliorate the Quakers' condition they blamed on "inimical pamphleteers, who were busy sending forth eloquent tracts, accusing them of heresy and Jacobitism. Prominent among these writers were the eminent nonjuror Charles Leslie and an ex-Quaker, Francis Bugg, who possessed both an amazing repertoire of unpleasant tales about the Quakers and a vivid style": ibid., 416–17.

134. Leslie, "The Preface," in *Five Discourses by the Author of The Snake in the Grass*, n.p.

135. Charles Leslie, *The Charge of Socinianism against Dr. Tillotson Considered . . . Wherein Likewise Charles Blount's* Great Is Diana Is *Considered* (Edenburgh [sic]: s.n., 1695), 26.

136. William Penn, *The Sandy Foundation Shaken* (London: s.n., 1668), 12–13.

137. David Hume, *Essays, Moral and Political* (Edinburgh: A. Kincaid, 1742), 151.

138. Another title by Patrick Smith reads. *A Preservative against Quakerism, or, A Complication of Deism, Enthusiasm, and divers other Ancient and Modern Dangerous Errors and Heresies* (London: C. Rivington, 1732).

139. "I remember to have asked some considerable Whigs, whether it did not bring a Disreputation upon their Body, to have the whole Herd of Presbyterians, Independents, Atheists, Anabaptists, Deists, Quakers and Socinians, openly and universally Listed under their Banners?" *The Examiner*, no. 29, February 22, 1710, in Swift, *Political Tracts by the Author of Gulliver's Travels* 2 vols. (London: C. Davis, 1738), I, 200.

140. Richard Smallbroke, *A Vindication of the Miracles of Our Blessed Saviour, in Which Mr. Woolston's Discourses on These Are Particularly Examin'd*, 2 vols. (London: James and John Knapton, 1729–31), II, v–vi. The same passage appears in Alexander Arscott, *Some Considerations Relating to the Present State of the Christian Religion*, 3d ed. (London: J. Phillips, 1779), 247.

141. *The Review*, June 12, 1708, quoted in Ezra Kempton Maxfield, "Defoe and the Quakers," *PMLA* 47, no. 1 (1932): 182. Defoe refers here to the Bugg we have already met, calling him a writer "who has done more by raving at them to make any Man turn Quaker, than all the Authors I have met with."

142. This use of the Quaker persona to add authority to Defoe's appeal continues through the next decade in two related works: *The Secret History of the Secret History of the White Staff* (London: S. Keimer, 1715), and *An Appeal to Honour and Justice*. Both of these works construct fictional death-bed scenes to settle old scores, and the recipient of the dying man's relation is in each case a Quaker. See Moore, "Defoe's Persona as Author."

143. Currently, the only article-length treatment of this topic is Maxfield, "Daniel Defoe and the Quakers."

144. Ibid., 182.

145. Moore, "Defoe's Persona as Author," 511.

146. Daniel Defoe, *A Review of the Affairs of France,* December 13, 1705, in *A Review of the Affairs of France,* vol. 2, pt 2, 1705, ed. John McVeagh (London: Pickering and Chatto, 2004), 793–94. These volumes appear in the bibliography under *Defoe's Review,* ed. John McVeagh, 9 vols. (London: Pickering and Chatto, 2003–11).

147. An Act for Preventing Mischiefs and Dangers That May Arise by Certain Persons called Quakers and Others Refusing to Take Lawful Oaths, commonly known as the Quaker Act of 1662, "made it illegal for Quakers to worship together. . . . The Quaker Act also made it illegal for people to refuse to swear the Oath of Allegiance to the Church of England. Two years after the Quaker Act was passed, the English Parliament passed the Conventicle Act, which restated that no other religious meetings could take place except those carried out by the Official Church of England. Parliament passed another Conventicle Act in 1670. These three Acts resulted in the arrests, punishments, and imprisonments of thousands of Friends in England. Parliament passed the Five Mile Act in 1665, which prevented Quakers from forming their own townships. Parliament was not only targeting Quakers, but also others in the Nonconformist Movement": Katherine Ellison, "English Quakers Campaign for Freedom of Religion, 1647–1689," Global Nonviolent Action Database, n.d., https://nvdatabase.swarthmore.edu/content/english-quakers-campaign-freedom-religion-1647-1689. See also John Miller, "'A Suffering People': English Quakers and Their Neighbors c. 1650–c.1700," *Past and Present* 188, no. 1 (2005): 71–103; Kirby, "The Quakers' Efforts to Secure Civil and Religious Liberty." Charles F. Mullet explains that "the Blasphemy Act of 1698 imposed a 3 year imprisonment for denying the Trinity": Charles F. Mullett, "The Legal Position of English Dissenters, 1689–1767," *Virginia Law Review* 23, no. 4 (1937): 396. "Quakers and Unitarians were excepted from the concession made to the majority, because they respectively refused to take oaths and denied the Trinity."

148. Defoe, *The Review,* December 13, 1705. In McVeagh, *Defoe's Review,* 2:2:796.

149. Daniel Defoe, *A Sharp Rebuke from One of the People Call'd Quakers to Henry Sacheverell, the High-Priest of Andrew's Holbourn* (London: S. Keimer, 1715), 17.

150. Daniel Defoe, *A Friendly Epistle by Way of Reproof from One of the People Called Quakers to Thomas Bradbury, a Dealer in Many Words,* 6th ed. (London: S. Keimer, 1715), 6.

151. Quoted in Maxfield, "Daniel Defoe and the Quakers," 183. Maxfield finds Defoe's embrace of the Quakers ill-informed, opportunistic, and insincere. But see Ami Hicken King, "Daniel Defoe and the Quakers: A Study in Captain Singleton and Roxana" (PhD. diss., Arizona State University, Tempe, 1998). King discovered that members of the Defoe family who settled in America were avowed Quakers who claimed that Defoe attended Quaker meetings.

152. Manning, "Accusations of Blasphemy in English Anti-Quaker Polemic," 32.

153. Even on the question of whether Defoe had a minor stroke or apoplexy in 1715, the biographers disagree. "For a dying author," Furbank and Owens observe, "he remained remarkably productive": Furbank and Owens, *A Political Biography of Daniel Defoe,* 147. John Robert Moore has it both ways: "The story of Defoe's apoplexy has been doubted by both Defoe's contemporaries and modern biographers . . . The stroke

of apoplexy which the publisher gave as an excuse for the author's abrupt conclusion was exaggerated, but it was probably not fictitious": Moore, *A Checklist of the Writings of Daniel Defoe*, (257).

154. Defoe, *A Sharp Rebuke from One of the People Call'd Quakers to Henry Sacheverell*, 36.

155. Manning observes that "it was the Quaker's ability to convince the authorities of a consensual belief in the doctrine of the Trinity that helped them rescue legal toleration in 1689": Manning, "Accusations of Blasphemy in English Anti-Quaker Polemic," 32.

156. The Eighteenth Century Collections Online catalog lists Defoe as the author and notes that Juliet Reeve attributed the work to Defoe in 1945.

157. Daniel Defoe (attrib.), *A Defence of the People Call'd Quakers, Wherein from the Fundamental Principles of the New Testament, They Are Shown to Be the True, Primitive, Apostolical Christians* (London: W. Boreham, 1720), 4.

158. Charles Blount, *Religio Laici, Written in a Letter to John Dryden, Esq.* (London: R. Bentley and S. Magnes, 1683), 1.

159. Defoe, *A Defence of the People Call'd Quakers*, 4.

160. See esp. Defoe, *The Dissenter's Answer to the High Church Challenge*, written expressly against Charles Leslie, in which the topic of "things indifferent" constitutes the fundamental point of disagreement between dissenters and the High Church.

161. Manning observes, "From the very inception of the Quaker movement, the theology of the light within was undermined by a perception, embellished by the law, that it was inherently and self-evidently blasphemous": Manning, "Accusations of Blasphemy in English Anti-Quaker Polemic," 34.

162. Defoe, *A Defence of the People Call'd Quakers*, 4–5.

163. Ibid., 7.

164. Ibid., 5.

165. Quoted in Manning, "Accusations of Blasphemy in English Anti-Quaker Polemic," 37.

166. *D' Foe's Answer to the Quakers Catechism; or, A Dark Lanthorn for a Friend of the Light* (London: s.n., 1706), 5, 9, 8.

167. Ibid., 8.

168. For the instant popularity of *The Isle of Pines*, see Gaby M. Mahlberg, "Authors Losing Control: The European Transformation of Henry Neville's *The Isle of Pines* (1668)," *Book History* 15 (2012): 1–25. For the work's risqué reputation, see A. Owen Aldridge, "Polygamy in Early Fiction: Henry Neville and Denis Veiras," *PMLA* 65, no. 4 (1950): 464–72. See also Daniel Carey, "Henry Neville's *Isle of Pines:* Travel, Forgery and the Problem of Genre," *Angelaki* 1 (1996): 23–40.

169. Henry Neville, *The Isle of Pines; or, A Late Discovery of a Fourth Island of Terra Australis Incognita* (London: Allen Banks and Charles Harper, 1668), 8.

170. On the relation of polygamy to deism, see Alfred Owen Aldridge, "Polygamy and Deism," *Journal of English and Germanic Philology*, 40, no. 3 (1948): 343–60.

171. I return to this received understanding of Defoe's religion in chapters 4 and 5.

172. G. A. Starr, ed., *Christianity Not as Old as the Creation: The Last of Defoe's Performances* (London: Pickering and Chatto, 2012).

173. Geoffrey Sill, "Christianity Not as Old as the Creation," ed. G. A. Starr, *Scriblerian and the Kit-Cats* 46, no. 1 (2013): 45–46.

174. John McVeagh, *Defoe's Review*, vol. 2, pt. 2, 1709–10, November 8, 1709, 466. Quoted in Sutherland, *Daniel Defoe*, 141 note.

175. K. R. P. Clark, "Defoe, Dissent, and Early Whig Ideology," *Historical Journal* 52, no. 3 (2009): 598. For a concurring view, see John Robert Moore, "Defoe's Religious Sect," *Review of English Studies* 17, no. 68 (1941): 461–467. Katherine Clark bases her argument on Defoe's assumed Trinitarianism: "a number of studies have located Defoe's fiction in the context of various Puritan genres, this is the first text to emphasize one key aspect of Defoe's religion, his Trinitarianism, the eschatology that this entailed, the centrality of Defoe's Christology for understanding his works, both fictional and nonfictional, and his emerging historical vision": Katherine Clark, *Daniel Defoe: The Whole Frame of Nature, Time, and Providence* (Houndmills, U.K.: Palgrave Macmillan, 2007), 2. In *A Challenge of Peace*, Defoe tries to convince Queen Anne of the political and religious loyalty of the dissenters: "*And among those who Dissent, they whose Principles are Honest, have always regarded the Church of England, with a Temper of both Charity and Respect; and 'tis to them a matter of no difficulty to entertain a Proposal of Union in Affection and Interest, and to give all the Deference and Distinction in Government, to the Establish'd Church*": Daniel Defoe, *A Challenge of Peace Address'd to the Whole Nation* (London: s.n., 1703), sig. a3r.

176. Novak, "*Robinson Crusoe* and Defoe's Career as a Writer," 46.

177. Furbank and Owens, *A Political Biography of Daniel Defoe*, 31. "It would certainly be no disgrace for his biographers to have been hoodwinked by him," Furbank and Owens add.

178. Daniel Defoe, *The Political History of the Devil, as Well Ancient as Modern* (London: T. Warner, 1726), 105.

179. Yet even in these works, an undercurrent of deism is sometimes evident. *The Family Instructor* uses its imagined audience of young children to justify trimming theology of its unnecessary accretions, and while this was a move completely compatible with a Puritan outlook, its extreme, as Leslie foresaw, became the deist's stripped down Common Notions. Defoe writes, "The observing Reader will see here, that the Author to observe a just Equality between all Opinions, and in order to make this work generally useful and acceptable to all Denominations of Christians, and to all among them who seriously apply themselves to the great Business of their Eternal Salvation, has kept himself in the Answers to this little Child's enquiry, to the plain general Principles of the Christian Religion, wherein he has neither prescribed himself in Method or in Words to the Catechisms of either the Church of England, the Assembly's Catechism, or any other; but laid down the Principles of Religion consonant to them all, as plainly as he could, as they are deduc'd from the Holy Scriptures, and as they agree with the several Confessions of Faith and Doctrinal Articles as well of the Church of *England*, as of all the Protestant Churches and Congregations in *Europe*, who profess the same Faith, believe the same God, and hope for eternal Life thro' Faith in the same ever Blessed Intercessor and Redeemer": Daniel Defoe, *The Family Instructor in Three Parts*, 2d ed., 2 vols. (London: E. Matthews, 1715), 1:37. To be sure,

this is not deism, but the same method of finding a common denominator among the denominations of Christianity might be applied—as the deists were applying it—to an averaging of all world religions, in search of some "Principles of Religion consonant to them all." These moments of possible critique are few and far between in Defoe's didactic theological works for youth. The entire purpose of another catechism, *Religious Courtship* (London: E. Matthews, 1722), as the subtitle states, is to demonstrate "the necessity of marrying religious husbands and wives only," and not only that, but the importance of marrying someone of the same religion. Achieving a sound relation to Christianity and preserving Christian faith in families and among married couples are the constant concerns of this long didactic work.

180. Defoe, *The Dissenter's Answer to the High Church Challenge*, 47.

181. See P. N. Furbank and W. R. Owens, *A Political Biography of Daniel Defoe* (London: Pickering and Chatto, 1998), 39, and G. A. Starr's editorial notes to the Pickering Masters edition of Defoe's *The Consolidator*, which identify at least a dozen individuals who earned Defoe's lifelong enmity, among them Admiral Sir George Rooke, against whom Defoe conducted "a possible vendetta" after Rooke's "bungled expedition to Cadiz." Some might consider Nottingham a more potent enemy than Leslie, assuming that threats against the body are more significant than threats against the mind, although Leslie made threats against Defoe's body, as well. Defoe would "bear a long lasting grudge against Nottingham and what he regarded as his harsh and deceitful treatment, and would pursue him over the years in a long sequence of savage gibes and blackenings of his reputation": Furbank and Owens, *A Political Biography of Daniel Defoe*, 23.

182. Furbank and Owens, *A Political History of Daniel Defoe*, 57–58.

183. Daniel Defoe, *The Protestant Jesuite Unmask'd in Answer to the Two Parts of Cassandra . . . With my Service to Mr. Lesley* (London: s.n., 1704). I have quoted only a portion of the text's direct attack on Leslie, who "has a fling at the *Shortest Way with [the] Dissenters*. But what is there spoke in a kind of *Irony* he has passionately express'd with abundance of Sincerity": ibid., 50. Wilson, Lee, Trent, Hutchins, Moore, and Novak attribute this work to Defoe, and Leslie (*Rehearsal*, March 17–24, 1705) also thought Defoe was the author.

184. Defoe, *The Secret History of the White Staff* (Dublin: S. Grierson, 1714), 6.

185. Defoe, *An Appeal to Honour and Justice*, 13.

186. Defoe, *The Protestant Jesuite Unmask'd*, 41.

187. Leslie, *The Wolf Strip of His Shepherd's Cloathing*, 48.

188. Defoe, *The Dissenter's Answer to the High Church Challenge*, 3–4.

189. Leslie, *A View of the Times, their Principles and Practices*, vol. 2, no. 35, February 7, 1707.

190. Charles Leslie, *Now or Never; or, A Project under God, to Secure the Church and Monarchy of England* (London: J. Baker, 1710), 11–12.

2. Defoe's Lunar Voyage

1. Paula R. Backscheider, *Daniel Defoe: His Life* (Baltimore: Johns Hopkins University Press, 1989), 139. Defoe displayed his ironic style in texts not discussed here, including frankly political interventions such as the *Minutes of the Negotiations of Monsr. Mesnager at the Court of England* (London: S. Baker, 1711). On the *Minutes of Mesnager* see P. N. Furbank, "Defoe's Minutes of Mesnager: The Art of Mendacity," *Eighteenth-Century Fiction* 16, no. 1 (2003): 1–12.

2. Arthur Wellesley Secord, *Studies in the Narrative Method of Defoe* (New York: Russell and Russell, 1963), 9.

3. The notes to the Stoke Newington edition explain that *The Consolidator* "was published only once in Defoe's lifetime. It first appeared on 26 March 1705 and continued to be advertised in Defoe's *Review* through October 1705 as 'Lately Published.' The so-called Second Edition—actually the original sheets with a cancelled but updated title page—appeared . . . on 17 November 1705": Daniel Defoe, *The Consolidator; or, Memoirs of Sundry Transactions from the World in the Moon*, in *The Stoke Newington Daniel Defoe*, ed. Michael Seidel, Maximillian E. Novak, and Joyce D. Kennedy (New York: AMS Press, 2001), xv. Subsequent references to Seidel's editorial notes to *The Consolidator* refer to this 2001 Stoke Newington edition. In 1710 and again in 1715 pamphlets appeared advertising "Books Printed for John Marshall at the Bible-in-Grace-Street," which included *Defoe's Consolidator; or, Memoirs of Sundry Transactions from the World in the Moon, Price Bound 3s.*

4. Ibid., 10, 18.

5. Ibid., 22.

6. Ashley Marshall, "Fabricating Defoes: From Anonymous Hack to Master of Fictions," *Eighteenth-Century Life* 36, no. 2 (2012): 7.

7. Ibid., 25

8. Ibid.

9. Ibid.

10. For an exception to this focus on success, see Gavin Jones, *Failure and the American Writer: A Literary History* (New York: Cambridge University Press, 2014).

11. Walter Benjamin, *The Origins of German Tragic Drama*, trans. John Osbourne (London: Verso, 1977), 58.

12. Daniel Defoe, *The Consolidator; or, Memoirs of Sundry Transactions from the World in the Moon*, 2d ed. (London: B. Bragge, 1705), 43; Daniel Defoe, *The Consolidator; or, Memoirs of Sundry Transactions from the World in the Moon*, in *Satire, Fantasy and Writings on the Supernatural*, vol. 3, ed. Geoffrey Sill (London: Pickering and Chatto, 2003), 32. Hereafter, citations of *The Consolidator* that provide two page numbers refer first to the 1705 edition then to the Pickering and Chatto edition of 2003. Throughout this chapter I refer to the notes by the editors of the two modern editions: Michael Seidel (in *The Consolidator*, 2001) and Geoffrey Sill (in *The Consolidator*, 2003).

13. James Sutherland, *Daniel Defoe* (Philadelphia: J. B. Lippincott Co, 1938), 135–38. "Whether this man was the innocent victim of High Church persecution, as

Defoe claimed, or whether, as his opponents maintained, he was a scandalous imposter, it is now impossible to tell": ibid., 135. With his defense of Gill, Defoe solidified his reputation, according to Sutherland, as a "'scurrilous prostitute pen . . . an infamous, stigmatized incendiary, one who lives by defamation, and by writing to the level and capacity of the mob . . . a bold impetuous popular demagogue, and the admired oracle of the people": ibid., 137–38. Defoe used the same strategy in *The Dissenter's Answer to the High Church Challenge*, where he reports the fate of Thomas Delaune (d 1685), "a Man whose Learning and Temper were Conspicuous to all the Learned World. . . . [He accepts] this Challenge [to defend the Dissenters in print], and writes down his Reasons for Nonconformity; and as the Doctor had printed his Sermon . . . [they] took immediate Care to suppress the Book, by seizing the Copy at the Printer's; and this was followed by seizing the Author for writing a Seditious Libel, put him in Prison, fined him *Ultra Tenementum*, and were hardly prevail'd upon to vouchsafe him the Favour to excuse him the Pillory, which they told him in Court was only remitted in respect to his Learning. Here was a true Church-Conquest; and this Gentleman was persecuted with so much true Church Zeal, that he lay in Newgate for his Fine, till he, his Wife, and Children died there, to the eternal Scandal of both the Church-man and the Dissenters": Daniel Defoe, *The Dissenter's Answer to the High Church Challenge* (London: s.n., 1704), 14–15. The Gill controversy continued into 1707, when Defoe reissued his *Experiment* under a new title, *The Honesty and Sincerity of Those Worthy Gentlemen Commonly Called High-Church Men: Exemplified in a Modern Instance* (London: Benj. Bragg, 1707), which drew an angry response from Hugh James in *An Answer to a Late Pamphlet, Entitled, The Experiment; or, The Shortest Way with Dissenters Exemplified* (London: J. Morphew, 1707).

14. Defoe, *The Consolidator*, 68–69/54.

15. The pillory and Newgate were as traumatic as they were generative. Seidel observes, "Daniel Defoe published *The Consolidator* in 1705 when he was still recovering from the shock of having been imprisoned and pilloried": Defoe, *The Consolidator* (2001), xiii. Sara Landreth adds that "Defoe wrote *The Consolidator* just months after the fallout from the publication of *The Shortest Way with the Dissenters* (1702) landed him in prison. It is not surprising, then, that he chose to deliver much of *The Consolidator*'s political critique from behind the mask of a contradictory narrator who is at best 'hot headed' and at worst stark raving mad": Sara Landreth, "Defoe on Spiritual Communication, Action at a Distance, and the Mind in Motion," in *Mind, Body, Motion, Matter: Eighteenth-Century British and French Literary Perspectives*, ed. Mary Helen McMurran and Alison Conway (Toronto: University of Toronto Press, 2016), 151.

16. The controversy over Gill was another flashpoint that found Leslie and Defoe at each other's throats. Seidel states that "from the *Review* of Tuesday, 3 February 1708 to the *Review* of Saturday, 19 February 1709, [Defoe] kept up a quarrelsome exchange with Leslie's *Rehearsal* over the case": Defoe, *The Consolidator* (2001), 235. As a specimen of Defoe's willingness to call out named and code-named rivals, consider his comment on Joseph Addison: "Ad—son may tell his Master my Lord—the reason from Nature, why he would not take the Court's Word, nor write the poem call'd

The Campaign, till he had 200*l per Annum* secur'd to him, since 'tis known they have but one Author in the Nation that writes for 'em for nothing, and he is laboring very hard to obtain the Title of Blockhead": Defoe, *The Consolidator*, 27/39, 27. And as an example of his attack on an entire community, consider the ill will he still bore the dissenters in general, who failed to come to his defense when he was in jail. "*When I saw* this, it forc'd me to reflect upon Affairs in our own Country; *Well*, said I, 'tis happy for *England* that our *Dissenters* have not this Spirit of *Union*, and Largeness of Heart among them; for if they were not a *Narrow,* mean-*Spirited*, short-*Sighted*, self-*Preserving, friend-Betraying, poor-Neglecting People,* they might ha' every way as Safe, as Considerable, as Regarded and as Numerous as the *Crolians* in the *Moon*": Defoe, *The Consolidator*, 270–71/127.

17. Defoe, *The Consolidator*, 223–24/90.

18. Ibid., 124/74.

19. Paul Dottin, *The Life and Strange Surprising Adventures of Daniel Defoe*, trans. Louise Ragan (New York: Macaulay, 1929), 135. It is an open question who stole more from whom—Defoe from *A Tale of a Tub* in 1705 or Swift from Defoe's *Consolidator* in the third voyage of *Gulliver's Travels* in 1726: see John Robert Moore, "A New Source for *Gulliver's Travels*," *Studies in Philology* 38, no. 1 (1941): 66–80.

20. The quotation is from Novak's introduction in Joseph Browne, *The Moon-Calf; or, Accurate Reflections on The Consolidator* (1705), ed. Maximillian Novak, Augustan Reprints no. 269 (New York: AMS Press, 1996). Horsley shares this negative assessment, writing, "Defoe's *Consolidator*, a three hundred and sixty page book, was one of the longest satiric fictions published during the reign of Anne. The idea of travelling to the world in the Moon was 'very diverting,' and imposed few limitations on the contrivance of parallels. Even in the *Consolidator*, however, it cannot be said that Defoe sustained his central fiction, or that he went beyond, or intended to go beyond, slightly disguised 'Reflections upon a Party'": Lee Sonstang Horsley "'Of all Fictions the Most Simple': Swift's Shared Imagery," *Yearbook of English Studies* 5 (1975): 99. Browne may have drawn the title and image of *The Moon-Calf* from a ninety-page poem by Michael Drayton (1563–1631) called "The Moone Calf," published in *The Battaile of Agincourt Fought by Henry the Fifth, King of Scotland* (London: William Lee, 1631). Of the Moone-Calf, Drayton writes,

> The birth is double, and grows side to side,
> That humane hand it never can divide;
> And in this wonderous sort as they be Twins;
> Like Male and Female they be *Androgines,*
> The Man is partly Woman, likewise Shee
> Is partly Man, and in face they bee,
> Full as prodigious, as in parts; the Twinne.

21. Browne, *The Moon-Calf*, iv.

22. Marjorie Hope Nicolson describes *The Consolidator* as "a full-length 'novel' or 'romance'—you may call it what you will": Marjorie Hope Nicolson, *Voyages to*

the Moon (New York: Macmillan, 1948), 183; Paula Backscheider calls *The Consolidator* "a static dialogue rather than a fictional travel book": Backscheider, *Daniel Defoe*, 146. Michael Seidel calls *The Consolidator* an "allegorical lunar voyage narrative": "The Man Who Came to Dinner: Ian Watt and the Theory of Formal Realism," *Eighteenth-Century Fiction* 12, nos. 2–3 (2000): 211. Ashley Marshall gives *The Consolidator* two brief mentions in her book on satire and calls it "a 364-page fantasy narrative attack on the High Church position": Ashley Marshall, *The Practice of Satire in England, 1658–1770* (Baltimore: Johns Hopkins University Press, 2013), 19; Jason Pearl defines *The Consolidator* as "a lunar voyage that doubled as an allegorical satire": Jason H. Pearl, *Utopian Geographies and the Early English Novel* (Charlottesville: University of Virginia Press, 2014), 96. Narelle Shaw, in one of the few scholarly studies of *The Consolidator* as an independent work, calls the book "an allegory pertaining to political events during the period 1660–1705": Narelle L. Shaw, "Ancients and Moderns in Defoe's *Consolidator*," *Studies in English Literature, 1500–1900* 28, no. 3 (1988): 391. Richard West mislabels *The Consolidator* "one of the lucrative verse satires Defoe continued to write": Richard West, *Daniel Defoe: The Life and Strange Surprising Adventures* (New York: Carroll and Graf, 1998), 110. See also Rodney M. Baine, "Daniel Defoe's Imaginary Voyage to the Moon," *PMLA* 81, no. 5 (1966): 377–80.

23. Paul Alkon, "The Invisible Man Returns: New Defoe Editions," *Eighteenth-Century Fiction* 14, no. 2 (2002), 210. Alkon explains that *The Consolidator* "is a failure in the mode of fantasy and science fiction because it does not depict a futuristic world or situation that is sufficiently accounted for in its own terms . . . to be grasped intellectually and imaginatively entered by readers for the duration of the reading experience": ibid., 210–11. Geoffrey Sill also admits that the "disappointment that permeates *The Consolidator* together with its sprawling length, its looping redundancies and its plaintive tone, makes it a difficult book to read": *The Consolidator* (2003), 13.

24. *Tom Tell-Truth's Letter to a Dissenter in Vindication of the L—s against the Tackers* (London: s.n., 1705), 2. The great tacking debate had to do with a move to forbid the practice of Occasional Conformity by tacking a bill forbidding it onto a spending bill that would be difficult for legislators to reject. Furbank and Owens, Seidel, Hone, and Sill all take the tacking debate and the bills to outlaw Occasional Conformity as the immediate provocation for Defoe's *Consolidator*. Furbank and Owens relate the word "consolidator" to a "consolidated bill," in which "two or more bills are 'tacked' together. . . . Defoe's recriminations against the High Church Tories would take the form of savage satire of the 'Tackers'": P. N. Furbank and W. R. Owens, *A Political Biography of Daniel Defoe* (London: Pickering and Chatto, 2006), 42–43.

25. William Pittis, *The Dyet of Poland: A Satyr Considered Paragraph for Paragraph* (London: Benjamin Bragge, 1705), sig. a3r.

26. Ibid., sig. a3v, a4r. Pittis's title page promises "a Key to the Whole with the Names of the Author, and the Nobility and Gentry, that are scandalously pointed at, in it."

27. Daniel Defoe, *The Dyet of Poland: A Satyr* (Dantzick [London]: Ben. Bragg, 1705), sig. a2r.

28. Browne, *The Moon-Calf*, 12. As Seidel's notes to the Stoke Newington edition indicate, it is possible to supply correspondences between nearly every Chinese and

lunar reference and its counterpart in English political history from the civil wars to the early reign of Queen Anne.

29. Defoe, *The Dyet of Poland*, sig. a2r.

30. Ibid.

31. Defoe, *The Consolidator*, 337/150.

32. See Andrew McKendry, "'No Parallels from Hebrew Times': Troubled Typologies and the Glorious Revolution in Daniel Defoe's Williamite Poetry," *Eighteenth-Century Studies* 50, no. 1 (2016): 82.

33. See McKendry, "No Parallels from Hebrew Times," 82. On the more general history of typology in early modern England, see Paul Korshin, *Typologies in England 1650–1820* (Princeton, NJ: Princeton University Press, 1982). There were likely political and artistic reasons for this ambivalence. As Korshin and McKendry have shown, typology as sign and allegory as genre led a troubled existence in the early modern period. Defoe's situation as a supporter of William and the Revolution Settlement made this trouble even more pronounced. McKendry focuses exclusively on Defoe's poetry; this study locates a similar ambivalence toward typology and allegory in Defoe's prose.

34. Defoe, *The Consolidator* (2003), 25.

35. Ibid., 14.

36. Seidel calls Swift's *A Tale of a Tub* "the main literary inspiration of *The Consolidator*," adding that Defoe was "obsessed with the impact of Swift's work": Defoe, *The Consolidator* (2001), xii, xix. Novak asserts that the problem with *The Consolidator* was that Defoe admired Swift's satire too much. He writes, that the "major cause of this failure was Defoe's admiration for Swift's *Tale of a Tub*": Browne, *The Moon-Calf*, iv.

37. For an analysis of the Swift-Defoe hostilities focusing on class rivalry, see John Frederic Ross, *Swift and Defoe: A Study in Relationship* (Berkeley: University of California Press, 1941), esp. 33–37, in which Ross discusses Swift's dismissive quip and *The Consolidator*.

38. Jonathan Swift, *A Letter from a Member of the House of Commons of Ireland to a Member of the House of Commons in England, Concerning the Sacramental Test* (London: John Morphew, 1709), 5–6. This letter is reprinted in Jonathan Swift, *The Works of J.S, D.D, D.S.P.D in Six Volumes* (Dublin: George Faulkner, 1728), 4:3–4. Swift compares Defoe to the author of *The Observator*, John Tutchin (1660/64–1707). Stealing both the title and the dialogic form of Roger L'Estrange's Tory *Observator* (1681–1704), Tutchin, a radical Whig, was "farther gone" than Defoe in Swift's eyes because his expressions of republican and democratic sympathy were less guarded. The poem that brought his arrest and incarceration, "The Foreigners," although a notorious piece of xenophobia, also included these lines: "When no Successor to the Crown's in sight, / This Crown is certainly the People's Right. / If Kings are made the People to enthrall, / We had much better have no King at all." Quoted in J. A. Downie, "John Tutchin," in *The Oxford Dictionary of National Biography*, ed. David Cannadine (Oxford: Oxford University Press, 2004), https://doi.org/10.1093/ref:odnb/27899. Defoe attacked Tutchin for his xenophobia in *The True-Born Englishman;* did he also disagree with his radical republicanism? Not according to Swift. Like Defoe, Tutchin had joined Monmouth's

Rebellion, but where Defoe escaped the Bloody Assizes relatively unscathed, Tutchin was ordered fined, jailed, and "whipped through all the market towns of Dorset once a year." Where Defoe's *Shortest Way* cost him a surety for seven years' good behavior, Tutchin's *Observator* brought a trial for seditious libel in 1704 (he was found guilty and escaped prison on a technicality), and a surety of good behavior for the rest of his life, which was not long. Downie explains that "the Duke of Marborough did not take kindly to *The Observator*'s outspokenness. 'If I can't have justice done me,' Marlborough wrote to Harley, 'I must find some friend that will break his and the printer's bones' (Bath, MSS, I. 105)." Tutchin's death at the age of 43 "is thought to have occurred on 23 September 1707 in the London queen's bench prison after he had been beaten up."

39. The note from Lord Orrery appeared in Jonathan Swift, *The Works of Jonathan Swift, D.D., Dean of St. Patricks, Dublin*, 6 vols. (London: C. Bathurst, 1755), 2:122. Orrery's remark about Defoe first appeared in John Boyle, fifth Earl of Orrery, *Remarks on the Life and Writings of Dr Jonathan Swift* (London: A. Millar, 1752), 134.

40. Defoe, *The Consolidator*, 61–62/51–52.

41. Both Michael Seidel and Geoffrey Sill downplay the connection between Defoe's lunar voyage and Lucianic imitations and translations known for their religious freethinking. Thus, both attribute the name "Moor" to the Cambridge Platonist Henry More (1614–87), asserting that it alludes to More's poem *In Somnium Philosophicum* (1647), "in which More, borrowing from Kepler's *Somnium* (1647), enjoys a trance-like cosmic voyage to a 'massie Sphaer' similar to Kepler's": Defoe, *The Consolidator* (2001), 192. David Russen's *Iter Lunare* (1703), which I discuss later, references Thomas Moor (More) in connection with the lunar voyage tradition. Defoe may well have had both Mores in mind, as well as the Islamic Moors, whose principal god, Shiva, is known by a crescent moon on his head.

42. All quotations from Swift's *A Tale of a Tub* and *A Discourse Concerning the Mechanical Operation of the Spirit* refer to the second corrected edition of *A Tale of a Tub, Written for the Universal Improvement of Mankind* (London: John Nutt, 1704). *A Tale of a Tub* was in its fourth edition when Defoe published *The Consolidator*, which did not outlive its first. The quoted passage is from the start of sec. 8, p. 146, in this edition.

43. Ibid., 148.

44. Ibid., 290.

45. Ibid., 308.

46. Ibid., 309–310. Banbury was a Puritan stronghold and Quaker center in the seventeenth century. It was famous for having destroyed its crosses in 1600 and gravitating toward the most extreme expressions of Puritanism. "In the late 16th century Banbury's inhabitants were recorded as being 'far gone in Puritanism'. Consequently the ruling clique of the council ordered that at least two of the town's crosses, the High Cross and the Bread Cross, be destroyed": Eunice Harradine, "Banbury History," 2005, http://www.banbury-cross.co.uk/banhistory.htm. In *The Banbury Apes*, the narrator attacks the citizens of Banbury for welcoming Sacheverell: Daniel Defoe, *The Banbury Apes; or, A Chattering to the Magpye*, 6th ed. (London: R. Mawson, 1710). Moore and Novak attribute this work to Defoe; Furbank and Owens deattribute it.

47. Ibid., 312.

48. Ibid., 320. Another misogynistic passage appears in Swift, *A Tale of a Tub*, sec. 8, 153–54, where we learn that the ancient oracles "were frequently managed and directed by *Female* Officers, whose Organs were understood to be better disposed for the Admission of those Oracular *Gusts,* as entering and passing up thro' a Receptacle of greater Capacity, and causing also a Pruriency by the way, such as with due Management hath been refined from a Carnal into a Spiritual Extasie." Swift proceeds to a coded attack on the Quakers, our *modern AEolists,* who keep up the tradition of female priests.

49. Ibid., 319.

50. Ibid., 318–19.

51. The hierarchical distinction between low- and high-norm satire is central to the discussion in Northrop Frye, *Anatomy of Criticism* (Princeton, NJ: Princeton University Press, 1957), 234–36.

52. *A Discourse Concerning the Mechanical Operation of the Spirit,* in Swift, *A Tale of a Tub,* 288.

53. In 1714, Defoe again turned his thoughts to Swift and the question of how to write past him: "In pursuing an Enemy, that has neither acted the Gentleman or the Christian, methinks no Man ought to expect our keeping any Rules. . . . The Question will be, What way to deal with this Man-Monster, and with what Weapons we must fight him? It is usually esteem'd the most Honourable way of fighting, to beat a Man, as they call it, at his own Weapons; that is, to take the same Arms which his Enemy is most Master of; but I must be depriv'd of that Honour; it can't be practic'd here; for the Adversary begins with *LYING,* a Weapon, at which I acknowledge myself no match for him." Defoe, *The Scots Nation and Union Vindicated from the Reflections Cast on Them* (London: A. Bell and J. Baker, 1714), 3-4. Defoe may pretend to be no match for Swift as a liar, but the truth is he is no match for him as a *satirist.* The passage again suggests Defoe's awareness of Swift as an artistic rival.

54. Daniel Defoe, *An Elegy on the Author of the True-Born English-man* (London: s.n., 1704), "Preface to the Elegy."

55. Sutherland highlights this passage but goes on to say that Defoe probably meant it in jest. He writes, "If he was a revolutionary, it was not because he wanted to see a complete change in the social order, but rather because he liked to make intellectual play with new and startling ideas, and had an awkward way of following them to their conclusion. He loved to meddle with topics of whose existence more discreet men were conscious, but which they preferred, because they were discreet, to leave alone": Sutherland, *Daniel Defoe,* 143. Defoe's enemies did not think he meant it in jest.

56. The omission of Lucian from the standard biographies is striking. Lucian's name does not appear in the index to the biographies by Sutherland, Dottin, West, Novak, Backscheider, Furbank and Owens, and Richetti. The critical studies by Moore (*Defoe in the Pillory and Other Studies* [New York: Octagon Books, 1973]), Novak (*Realism, Myth, and History in Defoe's Fictions* [Lincoln: University of Nebraska Press, 1983]), and Merrett (*Daniel Defoe, Contrarian* [Toronto: University of Toronto Press, 2013]) also omit Lucian. Sill notes that Defoe was "clearly familiar"

with the earlier moon voyages, and Seidel observes that "Defoe's description of gravitational phenomena is characteristic of moon voyage literature before Newton. . . . Lucian's traveler in *Icaromenippus* also looks down upon the earth from the moon, once the mist has cleared, and sees the cities of the world and their inhabitants": Defoe, *The Consolidator* (2001), 187–88, 192.

57. Francis Hickes, *Certain Select Dialogues of Lucian Together with His True History, Translated from the Greek into English . . . Whereunto Is Added The Life of Lucian, Gathered out of His Own Writings* (London: Richard Davis, 1663); Ferrand Spence, *Lucian's Works Translated from the Greek, To Which Is Prefixt, The Life of Lucian* (London: Henry Clark, 1684).

58. See C. J. Betts, *Early Deism in France: From the So-Called Deistes of Lyon (1564) to Voltaire's Lettres Philosophique (1734)*, Archives Internationales d'Histoire des Idees (Leiden: Martinus Nijhoff, 1984).

59. Margaret C. Jacob, *Strangers Nowhere in the World: The Rise of Cosmopolitanism in Early Modern Europe* (Philadelphia: University of Pennsylvania Press, 2006), 1–12.

60. On the lunar voyage tradition and Defoe's relation to it, see Nicolson, *Voyages to the Moon*, 14. Portions of this book appear in Marjorie Hope Nicolson, "Cosmic Voyages," *English Literary History* 7, no. 2 (1940): 83–107. See also Baine, "Daniel Defoe's Imaginary Voyages to the Moon"; Scott L. Montgomery, *The Moon and the Western Imagination* (Tucson, AZ: University of Arizona Press, 1999); David Cressy, "Early Modern Space Travel and the English Man in the Moon," *American Historical Review* 111, no. 4 (2006): 961–82.

61. John Calvin, *The Institution of the Christian Religion* (London: Reinolde Wolfe and Richarde Harison, 1561), 208.

62. Johannes Brenz, *Newes from Ninive to Englande brought by the Prophet Jonah* (London: Henrie Denham, 1570), 443.

63. Richard Harvey, *A Theological Discourse of the Lamb of God* (London: John Windet, 1590), 87.

64. Roger Ascham, *The Scholemaster; or, Plaine and Perfite Way of Teaching Children* (London: John Daye, 1570), 43.

65. John Dryden, ed., *The Works of Lucian, Translated from the Greek, by Several Eminent Hands*, 4 vols. (London: Sam. Briscoe, 1710–11), "Epistle Dedicatory."

66. "The Life of Lucian," in Lucian, *Certain Select Dialogues of Lucian Together with His True History*, trans. Francis Hickes (London: Richard Davis, 1663), b3r. This text is a reissue of the original edition published at Oxford by William Turner in 1634.

67. Ibid., sig. b2v.

68. Francis Bacon, *The Essays, or Councils, Civil and Moral, of Sir Francis Bacon, Lord Veralum* (London: Sam. Smith and Benj. Walford, 1701), 43.

69. The well established sequence from Hume to Popper is summarized in Leah Henderson, "The Problem of Induction," *Stanford Encyclopedia of Philosophy*, March 21, 2018, http://plato.stanford.edu/entries/induction-problem. Thomas Stanley transmits Pyrrho in *The History of Philosophy*, 3d ed. (London: W. Battersby, 1701), pt. 12, sec. 1, 470–72.

70. Dryden, *The Works of Lucian*, 1:25–26. For an informative discussion of Dryden's take on Lucian, see Hardin Craig, "Dryden's Lucian," *Classical Philology* 16, no. 2 (1921): 141–63. Craig points out that "Lucian . . . was until the seventeenth century a person of small importance, compared, let us say, to Ovid. One principal reason for this in that he was popularly regarded as an enemy to Christianity and a renegade from the faith . . . The deists possibly found use for him in their attack upon theism in the Age of Dryden": ibid., 142.

71. An especially snarling version of this story appears in Jean de Chassanion's *The Theatre of God's Judgments*. "There is a notable example of *Lucian*, who having professed Christianity for a season under Emperour Trajan, fell away afterwards, and became so profane and impious, as to make a mocke at religion and divinity, whereupon his sirname was called *Atheist*. This wretch, as hee barked out (like a foule mouthed dog) bitter taunts against the religion of Christ, seeking to rent and abolish it: so he was himselfe in Gods vengeance torne in pieces and devoured of dogs": Jean de Chassanion, *The Theatre of God's Judgment; or, A Collection of Histories out of Sacred, Ecclesiastical, and Prophane Authors*, trans. Thomas Beard (London: Adam Islip, 1597), 78.

72. John Dryden, "The Life of Lucian," in Dryden, *The Works of Lucian*, I, 13.

73. Ibid., 29.

74. Ibid., 34.

75. Ibid., "The Epistle Dedicatory," sig. a3v.

76. On the domestication of Menippean satire, see Howard D. Weinbrot, *Menippean Satire Reconsidered* (Baltimore: Johns Hopkins University Press, 2005).

77. Ilya Kliger and Boris Maslov, eds., *Persistent Forms: Explorations in Historical Poetics* (New York: Fordham University Press, 2016), 369–370.

78. A. Georgiadou and D. H. J. Larmour, "Lucian's 'Verae Historiae' as Philosophical Parody," *Hermes* 126, no. 3 (1998): 310–11.

79. Dryden, *The Works of Lucian*, I, 50.

80. Defoe, *The Consolidator*, 29/39.

81. Nicolson, *Voyages to the Moon*, 14.

82. Cyrano de Bergerac, *Selenarhia; or, The Government of the World in the Moon: A Comical History*, trans. Thomas St. Serf (London: J. Cottrel, 1659), sig. b3r-v.

83. Ibid., sig. b3v.

84. Nicolson ("Cosmic Voyages," 99–100) calls Defoe "the most remarkable of my prophets of the future . . . His originality—so far as it has any—lies in anticipation of scientific inventions for which England was still seeking."

85. Defoe, *The Consolidator*, 37–38/42. Seidel and Sill both identify this tallest feather with Robert Harley, then Speaker of the House of Commons, an attribution that is difficult to square with their recognition that Defoe uses the Consolidator as a figure for High Fliers.

86. Ibid., 51/47.

87. Ibid., 46/46.

88. Ibid., 337–38/151.

89. Scholars who study the lunar voyage tradition in its pan-European context emphasize its mixture of realism and fantasy. Eric MacPhail notes "the tension between

the marvelous and the verisimilar" that marks Cyrano's *L'autre monde* and refers to the work as a "lunatic novel." He writes, "The paradox of literary truth, particularly as it informs the genre of the novel, is one of the most intricate mechanisms at work in *L'autre monde*.... At the same time as he parodies biblical miracles, Cyrano also targets an opposite literary tendency, that of realism or verisimilitude": MacPhail, "Cyrano's Machines," 37, 40.

90. Defoe, *The Consolidator*, 63–64/52. Scholars of the lunar voyage in the European tradition are alert to the genre's radical openness to cultural diversity: see Ann T. Delehanty and Tyler Blakeney, "Textual Engagement with the Other in Cyrano de Bergerac's *L'Autre Monde*," *French Studies* 68, no. 3 (2014): 313–27. The authors use the word "singularity" to refer to the ethical representation of culturally diverse characters who retain their independent natures in and through sympathetic (non-colonial) depictions. I take up the question of "singularity" in the representation of character in chapter 3 on Defoe's *Continuation of Letters Written by a Turkish Spy at Paris*.

91. Defoe, *The Consolidator*, 65/53.

92. Ibid., 68/54.

93. Bergerac, *The Comical History of the States and Empires of the Worlds of the Moon and Sun*, trans. A. Lovell (London: Henry Rhodes, 1687), 2–3. The narrator's openness to the possibility of life on other planets continues. He says, "I believe the Planets are Worlds about the Sun, and that the fixed Stars are also Suns, which have Planets about them, that's to say, Worlds, which because of their smallness, and that their borrowed light cannot reach us, are not discernable by Men in this World," 13–14. This reciprocity between Earth and moon worked in two different ways. It created a parallelism that fostered allegorical satire, but it also provided a context for a deistical leveling of cultural differences and thus a critique of religious zealotry. The editorial notes to the Stoke Newington and Pickering Masters editions stress only the former of these two interpretations of form. Commenting on a similar moment of reciprocity between the Earth traveler and the man in the moon in Wilkins's *A World in the Moone* (1640), Seidel observes, "Bishop Wilkins heads his eleventh proposition: 'That as their World is our Moone, so our World is their Moone,'" and he identifies the same "trope" in both Godwin and Cyrano, but he discounts the theological threat posed by the theory of a plurality of worlds, highlighting Wilkins' assurance that the "plurality of worlds contradicts neither reason nor faith": Defoe, *The Consolidator* (2001), xxxvii.

94. "The original edition of 1657 was mutilated by the efforts of Cyrano's friend Le Bret to exempt the work from censure. As a result of his solicitous cutting, the unexpurgated text was lost for over 250 years": Joan E. DeJean, "Method and Madness in Cyrano de Bergerac's *Voyage dans la Lune*," *French Forum* 2, no. 3 (1977): 224. Noting the unusual use of first-person narrative in this and other lunar voyages, DeJean adds, "The narrative structure of the *Voyage* prefigures in many ways the development of French prose in the eighteenth century": ibid., 224. See also Alexandra Torrero-Ibad, *Libertinage science et philosophie, dans le materialisme de Cyrano de Bergerac* (Paris: Honoré Champion, 2009).

95. Defoe, *The Consolidator*, 13–14/33. Both Seidel and Sill describe Defoe's attitude toward Chinese learning as critical, much as G. A. Starr does in "Defoe and China,"

Eighteenth-Century Studies 43, no. 4 (2010): 435–54. "From the evidence assembled here," Starr concludes, "it should be clear Defoe has a low opinion of what he takes to be China's system of governance and its religion . . . Defoe perceives China as a monitory example. What poses a threat, in his opinion, is the perverse Western appetite for Chinese goods, beliefs, and practices": Starr, "Defoe and China," 445. Sill concurs: "His contempt for Chinese civilization is only equaled by his scorn for the 'divine right' theory of monarchy, which he satirizes a few pages later": Defoe, *The Consolidator* (2003), 216. This seems to me a misreading of the role that China and the Chinese play in *The Consolidator*.

96. Defoe, *The Consolidator*, 14/33–34.

97. Implicated in the Rye House Plot, Algernon Sidney (1623–1683) was beheaded after a trial presided over by Lord Chief Justice Jeffreys, of the "Bloody Assizes," in which no second witness could be produced, as required in a case of treason. Jeffreys ruled that selected passages from the manuscript that became Sidney's posthumous *Discourses Concerning Government* (London: s.n., 1698), could be introduced as the second witness against their author. Jeffrey's infamous ruling was *scribere est agere* (to write is to act). He was right in a way: Sidney's *Discourses Concerning Government* became a blueprint for Jefferson and the architects of the American system. In conjunction with Sidney, "Argyll" refers to Archibald Campbell, the ninth Earl of Argyll, who, after also being implicated in the Rye-House-Plot, led an invasion of Scotland supporting Monmouth's Rebellion in 1685. He was captured, tried in the field, and beheaded on the "maiden," the English version of the guillotine.

98. Defoe, *The Consolidator*, 90/62. Sill's gloss on "the Great Eye of the World" acknowledges likely deist associations before bracketing them. He writes, "Defoe accepted many of the premises of natural theology, but insisted on revelation from Scripture as well": Defoe, *The Consolidator* (2003), 223. Seidel is somewhat closer to the mark when he glosses the "one Great Eye" passage with reference to Spinoza and the deists. "Spinoza, an extremely important philosopher for later Deists such as John Toland, Thomas Woolston, Matthew Tindal, William Wollaston, and Samuel Clarke, theorizes in *Tractatus theologico-politicus* (1670), that God and nature are the same: to explain the former is to know the latter": Defoe, *The Consolidator* (2001), 190. Nevertheless, Seidel joins Starr and Sill in denying any possible sympathy on Defoe's part for the deism implied by his choice of literary form and some choice passages in the text. Defoe may have accepted some aspects of the rational Christianity of Locke and Boyle, Seidel argues, but his Great Eye is finally nothing more than "Defoe's satiric emblem for demonstrative science. . . . Toland's is the Deist position, and Defoe would disagree violently" Defoe, *The Consolidator* (2001), 189.

99. On the origin and definition of English deism, see Michael B. Prince, "Religio Laici v. Religio Laici: Dryden, Blount, and the Origins of English Deism," *Modern Language Quarterly* 74, no. 1 (2013): 29–66. While we lack a cultural history of English deism from Lord Herbert of Cherbury to George Eliot, contributions to this history include John Orr, *English Deism: Its Roots and Its Fruits* (Grand Rapids, MI: William B. Eerdmans, 1934); James A. Herrick, *The Radical Rhetoric of the English Deists: The Discourse of Skepticism, 1680–1750* (Columbia, SC: University of South Carolina

Press, 1997); Wayne Hudson, *The English Deists* (London: Pickering and Chatto, 2009); Jeffrey R. Wigelsworth, *Deism in Enlightenment England: Theology, Politics, and Newtonian Public Science* (Manchester: Manchester University Press, 2009); Peter Byrne, *Natural Religion and the Nature of Religion: The Legacy of Deism*, Routledge Library Editions: Philosophy of Religion, vol. 5 (London: Routledge, 1989). See also J. A. Leo Lemay, *Deism, Masonry, and the Enlightenment: Essays Honoring Alfred Owen Aldridge* (Newark: University of Delaware Press, 1987); Wayne Hudson, Diego Lucci and Jeffrey R. Wigelsworth, eds., *Atheism and Deism Revalued: Heterodox Religious Identities in Britain, 1650–1800* (Burlington, VT: Ashgate, 2014).

100. Francis Wilson, "The Dark Side of Utopia: Misanthropy and the Chinese Prelude in Defoe's Lunar Journey," *Comparative Critical Studies* 4, no. 2 (2007): 193–207.

101. Defoe, *The Consolidator*, 6/31.

102. Ibid., 98–99/65.

103. Ibid., 94–95/63–64.

104. Ibid., 29/39.

105. Browne, *The Moon-Calf*, 3–4.

106. Ibid. "Robin Hog" appears to have been a depreciative name for a messenger for the press. The *Oxford English Dictionary* cites its use in Samuel Clarke's *New Description of the World* (1689): "Could I have added to this Bill of Fair, Booksellers and Printers, the World might have taken this Monster for a meer Robin Hog." It cites another instance in 1705, the same year as Browne's *The Moon-Calf*, in Edmund Hickeringill's *The Vindication of the Character of Priest-craft*: "Calling upon the Jaylors, the Sumners, the Rascals, the Robin Hogs, and Bumbailiffs, to help you to smother a Book, and stop it in the Press." The role of the "Brute-Tenders," then, is to stifle Defoe's *Consolidator*.

107. Browne, *The Moon-Calf*, 5, 11.

108. Ibid., 11.

109. Ibid.

110. Cressy, "Early Modern Space Travel and the English Man in the Moon," 974, n46.

111. Simon Tyssot de Patot, *The Travels and Adventures of James Massey*, trans. Stephen Whatley (London: John Watts, 1733), 114.

112. On Defoe's theory of fiction, or lack thereof, see Maximillian E. Novak, "Defoe's Theory of Fiction," *Studies in Philology* 61, no. 4 (1964): 650–68; Kevin Seidel, "*Robinson Crusoe* as Defoe's Theory of Fiction," *Novel* 44, no. 2 (2011): 165–85.

113. Defoe, *The Consolidator*, 30/40. Defoe uses the phrase again, referring to "the Chamber of the Emperor's Rarities": ibid., 16/31.

114. Seidel and Sill both hold that Defoe shares Swift's skepticism toward modern science and therefore view his engines and machines as derivative of Swift's satire against the moderns. Writes Sill, "Defoe's persistent mockery of such mechanistic aids, particularly when used as a substitute for revelation, suggests that the Cogitator is an ironic statement about the limits of such aids to knowledge (and about the narrator's credulity for admiring them)." Defoe, *The Consolidator* (2003), 227. Seidel calls *A Tale of a Tub* "in many ways the model for Defoe's attack on modern science,"

adding that Defoe "conveys something of Swiftean irony toward modern science": Defoe, *The Consolidator* (2001), 164, n3, 165. This view leads both editors to overlook Defoe's personal attack on Swift and miss the degree to which *The Consolidator* departs from the substance and style of *A Tale of a Tub*. I share Nicolson's view that Defoe's contraptions reveal not so much a critique of science as a fascination with new inventions, especially those that depict cognitive processes associated with independent thinking and writing. Backscheider emphasizes Defoe's lifelong interest in science, inspired by the teaching of Charles Morton, writing, "Defoe retained his lively interest in science, and Morton's theories can be found in works from the early *Storm* to the very late *General History of Discoveries and Improvements*": Backscheider, *Daniel Defoe*, 16.

115. For another view of these cognitive machines, see Landreth, "Defoe on Spiritual Communication." Landreth finds in Defoe's machines evidence of his belief in the communication of spirits and bases her discussion on that belief.

116. Defoe, *The Consolidator*, 18/35.

117. Ibid., 93–94/63.

118. Ibid., 109/69.

119. Ibid., 111/70.

120. John Locke, *An Essay Concerning Human Understanding, in Four Books*, 2 vols, 7th ed. (London: J. Churchill and S. Manship, 1715–16), book 3, secs. 2–3, b3r.

121. Ibid., book 3, chap. 2, sec. 1, 4.

122. Seidel, "The Man Who Came to Dinner," 211. Seidel astutely calls the Elevators in *The Consolidator* "an expansive symbol—its design assumes the dimensions and incorporates, literally, the strategies of the narrative." Defoe, *The Consolidator* (2001), xix.

123. Defoe, *The Consolidator*, 9/32.

124. "*L'Autre Monde* lays bare the machinery of fiction, exposing the mechanisms whereby the literary text solicits our belief": MacPhail, "Cyrano's Machines," 40.

125. Defoe, *The Consolidator*, 22/36–37.

126. For a response to Russen's attack on the Anabaptists, see Joseph Stennett, *An Answer to Mr. David Russen's Book Entitul'd Fundamentals without a Foundation, or a True Picture of the Anabaptist* (London: D. Brown, S. Crouch, J. Baker, 1704).

127. David Russen, *Iter Lunare; or, A Voyage to the Moon, Containing Some Considerations on That Planet* (London: J. Nutt, 1703), 40. This work is reproduced in David Russen, *The Female Critick; or, Letters in Drollery from Ladies to Their Humble Servants and Iter Lunar; or, A Voyage to the Moon*, ed. Michael F. Shugrue (New York: Garland, 1972): Russen's complaint applies to both seventeenth-century translations of Cyrano's *L'autre monde*, Thomas St. Serf's of 1659 and A. Lovell's of 1687, which use the phrase "Comical History" in their title and subtitle respectively (see Bibliography). While criticism of this little-known work is scarce, and there has been no attempt to demonstrate its relevance to Defoe, astute comments relevant to the text are found in Aaron Parrett, *The Translunar Narrative in the Western Tradition* (Aldershot, U.K.: Ashgate, 2004); Riccardo Capoferro, *Empirical Wonder: Historicizing the Fantastic, 1660–1760* (Bern, Switzerland: Peter Lang, 2010); MacPhail, "Cyrano's Machines";

John Cartwright, Brian Bowen, and Mary Elizabeth Bowen, "Introduction," in David Russen, *Iter Lunare,* ed. John Cartwright, Brian Bowen, and Mary Elizabeth Bowen (Boston: Gregg Press, 1976); Laura Torp, "'So Strange Things So Probably Told': Epistemic Consequences of Scientific Discourse in Lunar Travel Narratives," University of Michigan (BA honors thesis, University of Michigan, Ann Arbor, 2013), https://lsa.umich.edu/content/dam/english-assets/migrated/honors_files/TORP%20Final.pdf. The thesis was directed by Marjorie Levinson.

128. Russen, *Iter Lunare,* 3. Despite its title, Russen's *Iter Lunare* is not a moon voyage but instead an apology for Cyrano de Bergerac's lunar voyage.

129. See Benjamin Wardhaugh, *Poor Robin's Prophecies* (Oxford: Oxford University Press, 2012).

130. Russen, *Iter Lunare,* 141–42.

131. Cyrano de Bergerac, *The Comical History of the States and Empires of the Worlds of the Moon and Sun,* trans. A. Lovell (London: Henry Rhodes, 1687), sig. b2r-v.

132. See Guido Giglioni, "Girolamo [Geronimo] Cardano," in *Stanford Encyclopedia of Philosophy,* https://plato.stanford.edu/entries/cardano.

133. Russen, *Iter Lunare,* 15.

3. Cosmopolitan Defoe

1. "Now rare. The prow of a ship. From Middle French prore": *Oxford English Dictionary Online.*

2. Defoe's *A Continuation of Letters Written by a Turkish Spy at Paris* appeared on August 20, 1718. The first part of *Robinson Crusoe* appeared on April 25, 1719. Although P. N. Furbank and W. R. Owens describe the text as "probably" by Defoe, most scholars accept that the attribution is certain: see P. N. Furbank and W. R. Owens, *A Critical Bibliography of Daniel Defoe* (London: Pickering and Chatto, 1998), 182–83. Joseph Tucker quotes private correspondence he had with Defoe's biographer, John Robert Moore, who states, "The evidence for Defoe's authorship is solely internal, but it is quite sufficient. The book is unusually *thin* for him, but it is certainly his. And it does not involve what Dottin calls 'contributions' to a 'miscellany.' It is a perfectly coherent work, very similar to another quasi-Oriental book of Defoe's in the previous year: *The Conduct of Christians made the Sport of Infidels in a Letter from a Turkish Merchant at Amsterdam to the Grand Mufti at Constantinople*": Joseph E. Tucker, "On the Authorship of the 'Turkish Spy': An 'État Présent,'" *Papers of the Bibliographical Society of America* 52, no. 1 (1958): 38.

3. "A Letter from a Gentleman in the Country, to His Friend in London," in *Denmark Vindicated: Being an Answer to a Late Treatise Called An Account of Denmark, as It Was in the Year 1692* (London: Tho. Newborough and Ed. Mory, 1694), sig. a6r-v.

4. Srinivas Aravamudan, *Enlightenment Orientalism: Resisting the Rise of the Novel* (Chicago: University of Chicago Press, 2012), 24–25, 63–64.

5. Ibid., 3.

6. Ibid., 3.

7. On the modern invention of the category called religion, see, Peter Harrison, *"Religion" and the Religions in the English Enlightenment* (Cambridge: Cambridge University Press, 2010).

8. Admittedly, not all deists drew this lesson of respect and toleration from their own method. Shaftesbury and Voltaire are notorious examples of deist anti-Semites who thought that their skepticism toward religion justified attacks on Judaism. The deists opposed religious dogmas and ceremonials; Judaism, which they considered rife with such rigmarole, therefore fell under their censure. On the history of deist anti-Semitism, see esp. Léon Poliakov, *The History of Anti-Semitism*, vol. 3 (Philadelphia: University of Pennsylvania Press, 2003).

9. Aravamudan, *Enlightenment Orientalism*, 8–15.

10. Ibid., 63.

11. This is the argument of my first book and the constant teaching of the scholar to whom this book is dedicated, Ralph Cohen: see Michael Prince, *Philosophical Dialogue in the British Enlightenment* (Cambridge: Cambridge University Press, 1997).

12. On the immediate popularity of the *Turkish Spy*, see Jacob Crane, "The Long Transatlantic Career of the Turkish Spy," *Atlantic Studies* 10, no. 2 (2013): 228–46.

13. Throughout this chapter I rely on the few but excellent bibliographical and critical studies of the origin of Marana's spy novel. In addition to the sources discussed later, see, for the French context, Béatrice Guion, "L'espion du Grand-Seigneur; ou, L'invention du roman épistolaire oriental," *Littératures Classiques*, no. 71 (2010–2011): 187–202. For a perceptive argument linking the popularity of Marana's spy novel to state surveillance of private individuals, see Aleksandra Porada, "Giovanni Paulo Marana's Turkish Spy and the Police of Louis XIV: The Fear of Being Secretly Observed by Trained Agents in Early Modern Europe," *Altre Modernità/Otras Modernidades/Autres Modernités/Other Modernities*, no. 11 (2004), https://riviste.unimi.it/index.php/AMonline/article/view/4046/4142. Porada points out that "Marana was involved in the conspiracy of Rafaello della Torre against the government of Genoa in 1672," which resulted in his imprisonment for four years and eventual escape to Paris. Porada argues that despite its fawning praise of Louis XIV, Marana's *L'espion du Grand-Seigneur* became known as a vehicle of covert literary deism.

14. William H. McBurney, "The Authorship of the Turkish Spy," *PMLA* 72, no. 5 (1957): 917.

15. Quoted in French in Tucker, "On the Authorship of the 'Turkish Spy,'" 36: "Les plaintes qu'on me fait de toutes parts, de ce que suivant ma promesse, je ne donne pas au public la continuation de mon *Espion du Grand Seigneur*. . . . Les difficultez que j'y ay recontrées, soit par la lenteur de ceux qui me font l'honneur de traduire les relations de Mahmut Arabe, soit par les longeurs ordinaires des réviseurs de livres, soit enfin par d'autres obstacles secrets, sont cause que depuis trois ans, environ une douzaine de petits volumes qui sont achevez en ma langue, ne le sont pas encore in la vôtre."

16. Guion and McBurney cite documents indicating that the censor, François Charpentier, forced Marana to agree in writing to remove four offensive passages. Signing this document made Marana culpable for the contents of all 102 letters and, presumably, for any other letters that found their way into print.

17. Quoted in Tucker, "On the Authorship of the 'Turkish Spy,'" 37.

18. McBurney, "The Authorship of the Turkish Spy," 928. Although this manuscript has never been located, that has not kept scholars from writing as if it existed. C. J. Betts holds that the "assumption that Marana is the author of the whole series, which is difficult to rebut in the light of arguments advanced by Guido Almansi, is based on similarities between the letters and other works by Marana, on the internal coherence of the whole series . . . and on external evidence such as Marana's own statements. . . . [There is] little plausibility in other suggestions made [such as] a bewildering variety of minor English writers, who, had they written so successful a work, would certainly have made their claims public": C. J. Betts, *Early Deism in France: From the So-Called Deistes of Lyon (1564) to Voltaire's Lettres Philosophique (1734)*, Archives Internationales d'Histoire des Idees (Leiden: Martinus Nijhoff, 1984), 98.

19. McBurney, "The Authorship of the Turkish Spy," 934.

20. Henry Hallam, "Literary History of the Turkish Spy," *Gentlemen's Magazine*, series 2, vol. 15, March 1841, 149, https://babel.hathitrust.org/cgi/pt?id=pst.000068790561;view=1up;seq=165;size=125. Tucker observes, "Marana is certainly not the author of the entire undertaking": Tucker, "On the Authorship of the 'Turkish Spy,'" 34.

21. Hallam, "Literary History of the Turkish Spy," 151.

22. Joseph E. Tucker, "The Turkish Spy and Its French Background," *Revue de Littérature Comparée* 32 (1958): 75–76. Tucker observes, "Marana is certainly not the author of the entire undertaking."

23. Daniel Defoe, *L'espion turc dan les cours des princes chrétiens*, vol. 7, 15th ed. (London: Aux Dépens de la Companie, 1742). This volume is a close French translation of Defoe's English text. The few changes in order appear to respond to Defoe or his publisher's note before the second Letter XII in Book III, where the reader is instructed to transpose two misplaced letters. In that the French edition carries out these orders, we see again the dependence of the French on the "original" English volumes.

24. Daniel Defoe, *The Family Instructor in Two Parts* (London: E. Matthews, 1718), 2:i, iv.

25. The Bangorian controversy was a bitter ideological struggle within the Church of England, centered on the figure of the Bishop of Bangor, Benjamin Hoadley (1676–1761). His attack on non jurors such as Leslie went to the extreme of denying ecclesiastical authority over private conscience, igniting a fierce polemical struggle between 1716 and 1721, in which Defoe participated.

26. Daniel Defoe, *Satires, Fantasy and Writings on the Supernatural*, in *The Works of Daniel Defoe*, vol. 5, ed. David Blewett (London: Pickering and Chatto, 2005), 7–8.

27. Isaac D'Israeli, *Curiosities of Literature. Consisting of Anecdotes, Characters, Sketches, and Observations, Literary and Historical*, 2 vols. (London: Murray and Highley, 1798), 2:122–23.

28. See Daniel Defoe, *A Continuation of Letters Written by a Turkish Spy at Paris*, in *Satire, Fantasy and Writings on the Supernatural*, vol. 5, ed. David Blewett (London: Pickering and Chatto, 2005), 19–22.

29. Daniel Defoe, *A Continuation of Letters Written by a Turkish Spy* (London: W. Taylor, 1718), vii–viii/47. Hereafter, citations to this work that provide two page

numbers refer first to the 1718 edition, then to the Pickering and Chatto edition of 2005.

30. Defoe, *Continuation* (2005), 281.

31. Ibid., 282.

32. Matthew Morgan, *Eugenia; or, "An Elegy upon the Death of the Honourable Madam—"* (Oxford: Leonard Lichfield, 1694), 22.

33. The *Traité des trois imposteurs* is usually attributed to John Toland. For Ochino's relation to Catholicism and Protestant reform, see Michele Camaioni, "Bernardino Ochino and the German Reformation: The Augsburg Sermons and Flugschriften of an Italian Heretic (1543–1560)," in *Fruits of Migration: Heterodox Italian Migrants and Central European Culture 1550–1620,* ed. Cornel Zwierlein and Vincenzo Lavenia (Leiden: Brill, 2018), 126–46.

34. John Edwards, *A Brief Vindication of the Fundamental Articles of the Christian Faith* (London: J. Robinson and J. Wyat, 1697), 63.

35. Charles de Secondat, Baron de Montesquieu, *Persian Letters,* trans. Flloyd, 2 vols., 4th ed. (London: J. and R. Tonson, 1762), 1:v–vi.

36. Ibid.

37. Ibid.

38. Ibid., vii–ix.

39. This is the seventh definition provided by the *Oxford English Dictionary.*

40. *Richard Baxter's Answer to Dr. Stillingfleet's Charge of Separation* (London: Nevil Simmons, 1680), 15.

41. Joseph Addison and Richard Steele, *The Tatler,* ed. George A. Aitken, 4 vols. (New York: Hadley, 1899), 3:166 (April 29–May 2, 1710). An electronic copy of these volumes can be found at https://catalog.hathitrust.org/Record/009032917.

42. Samuel Richardson, *The History of Sir Charles Grandison,* 7 vols. (London: S. Richardson, 1754), 6:181.

43. John Flavel, *The Fountain of Life Opened; or, A Display of Christ in His Essential and Mediatorial Glory* (London: Rob. White, 1693), 83.

44. Thomas Starkey (c. 1498–1538), *A Dialogue between Pole and Lupset* (in manuscript about 1538). Definition from *Oxford English Dictionary.*

45. Mary Astell, *A Serious Proposal to the Ladies* (London: R. Wilkin, 1697), 5–6.

46. Commenting on Montesquieu's *Lettres Persanes,* Aravamuden writes, "The brilliant innovations of the epistolary form of *Lettres persanes* radicalize incipient qualities that had been exploited by previous exponents [of spy fiction (i.e., Marana)]. The multiple correspondents and recipients who produce and read the 161 letters within Montesquieu's fiction demand a secularizing and skeptical framework of interpretation. The sequencing of the letters violates chronology. A metanarrative emerges behind them, leaping over the temporal hiatuses and made visible": Aravamudan, *Enlightenment Orientalism,* 77–78. For "metanarrative" I would substitute a *chaîne secrete* revealing and concealing a deist cosmopolitanism expressed in complex prose fiction.

47. Giovanni Paulo Marana, *Letters Writ by a Turkish Spy, Who Lived Five and Forty Years Undiscovered, at Paris: Giving an Impartial Account to the Divan at Constantinople,*

of the Most Remarkable Transactions of Europe; and Discovering Several Intrigues and Secrets of the Christian Courts, (Especially of France) from the Year 1637, to the Year 1682 (London: J. Leake, 1687), sig. a2r.

48. Ibid.

49. Ibid.

50. Ibid., sig. a3v.

51. Giovanni Paulo Marana (attrib.), *The Second Volume of Letters Writ by a Turkish Spy* (London: J. Leake, 1691), sig. a3r. This volume is significant because it begins the expansion of Marana's original 102 letters into the eventual eight-volume set of 644 letters by 1694. The volumes appeared separately between 1691 and 1694, with frequent reissues: vol. 1 (101 letters: the English translation of Marana's original, minus one letter complimentary of the Stuarts): 1687, 1691, 1692, 1693, 1694; vol. 2 (94 letters): 1691, 1692, 1693, 1694; vol. 3 (83 letters): 1691, 1692, 1693, 1694; vol. 4 (77 letters): 1692, 1694; vol. 5 (75 letters): 1692, 1693, 1694; vol. 6 (79 letters): 1693, 1694; vol. 7 (65 letters): 1694; vol. 8 (70 letters): 1694: Giovanni Paulo Marana, *The Eight Volumes of Letters Writ by a Turkish Spy* (London: Joseph Hindmarsh and Richard Sare, 1694).

52. Maximillian E. Novak, *Daniel Defoe, Master of Fictions* (Oxford: Oxford University Press, 2001), 529.

53. Penn's comment on Saltmarsh is quoted in Geoffrey Nuttall, *The Holy Spirit in Puritan Faith and Experience* (Oxford: Blackwell, 1946), 13. Gwynn's comment on Saltmarsh appears in Douglas Gwyn, "John Saltmarsh, Quaker Forerunner," presidential address given during the Britain Yearly Meeting of the Society of Friends, London, May 4, 2003, journals.sas.ac.uk/fhs/article/download/3410/3362.

54. "Mr. Saltmarsh's Letter," September 9, 1690, in Marana, *The Second Volume of Letters Writ by a Turkish Spy*, 2.

55. Ibid.

56. Giovanni Paulo Marana (attrib.), *The Eighth and Last Volume of Letters Writ by a Turkish Spy* (London: J. Hindmarsh and Richard Sare, 1694), sig. a3r-v.

57. Ibid., sig. a3v-4r.

58. John Edwards, *The Socinian Creed; or, A Brief Account of the Professed Tenents [sic] and Doctrines of the Foreign and English Socinians* (London: J. Robinson and J. Wyat, 1697), 248.

59. Defoe, *Continuation*, v/46.

60. See John Toland, *Nazarenus: or Jewish, Gentile, and Muslim Christianity* (London: J. Brotherton and A. Dodd, 1718).

61. Defoe, *Continuation*, vi/46–47.

62. Ibid., iii–iv/45.

63. Ibid., v/46.

64. Marana, *Letters Writ by a Turkish Spy*, A8.

65. Defoe, *L'espion turc dans les cours des princes Chrétiens*, vol. 7, 15th ed. (London: Aux Dépens de la Companie, 1742), 306.

66. Defoe, *Continuation*, book 4, letter 4, 270–71/219.

67. Ibid., 271/219.

68. Beyazit H. Akman, "The Turk's Encounter with Defoe," *Archives of Digital Defoe: Studies of Defoe and his Contemporaries*, n.d., http://english.illinoisstate.edu/digitaldefoe/encounters/index.shtml.

69. Defoe, *Continuation*, 271/219.

70. Ibid., 272/219.

71. In their editorial notes to the Pickering Masters editions, Blewett and Starr downplay Defoe's apparent sympathy for Quietism. Starr notes that "quietism is faulted [in *Serious Reflections*] for reducing religion to an entirely private matter—'wrapp'd up in . . . Internals, conceal'd in the Cavities and dark Parts of the Soul'—and thus divorced from outward observance and social practice": Daniel Defoe, *Serious Reflections* (2008), 356. He grants, however, that the view of Quietism expressed in Defoe's *Continuation* is "somewhat more sympathetic." Blewett also alludes to the negative appraisal of Quietism in Defoe's *Serious Reflections*, which he calls "belittling," and summarizes Defoe's attitude as ambivalent. Defoe, *Continuation of Letters Written by a Turkish Spy* (2005), 275n13.

72. Betts, *Early Deism in France*, 108.

73. Robert Barclay's defense of the Quakers is titled *An Apology for the True Christian Divinity, as the Same Is Held Forth and Preached by the People Called, in Scorn, Quakers* (London: s.n., 1678).

74. David Blewett observes that "Quietism has affinities with Protestant forms of piety such as Quakerism": Defoe, *Continuation* (2005), 275.

75. Defoe, *Continuation*, 273–74/220–21.

76. Ibid., 132/136.

77. Ibid., 68/100.

78. Ibid., 6–7/62.

79. See Arthur J. Weitzman, "Editor's Introduction," in Giovanni Paulo Marana, *Letters Writ by a Turkish Spy (Selections)*, ed. Arthur J. Weitzman (London: Routledge and Kegan Paul, 1970), xiv. According to Weitzman's reading, the plot of the original *Turkish Letters* finds Mahmut abandoning aspects of Islam for deism. He writes that Mahmut "begins to doubt the efficacy of Muslim ritual and even sees some advantages to Christianity under the impact of the new tolerant attitudes. In the course of the letters, however, the doubts give way to scorn of organized religion and especially the Roman Catholic clergy, who receive tremendous abuse, for which reason the letters were placed on the Church's *Index* soon after they appeared. As a result of his contact with Western religion and philosophy, the spy turns to deism. The deists, Mahmut explains, 'deserve the Title of *Philosophers* or Lovers of Wisdom and Truth. And 'tis from them I have learn'd this unwillingness to be impos'd on in Matters of Religion'. . . . The attitude towards religion in *The Turkish Spy* foreshadowed the main developments of eighteenth-century religious liberalism": ibid., xiv–xv. Blewett makes the same point while avoiding the question of why Defoe associated himself with a genre linked to deism and the Enlightenment: "The *Turkish Spy* is the most important early expression in a popular form of the Enlightenment aspirations of Marana's contemporaries Boyle and Fontenelle in France and Locke and other members of the Royal Society in England": Defoe, *Continuation* (2005), 18.

80. Joseph Jacob, *The Fewness of the Faithful; or, A Discourse Shewing the Paucity of True Believers* (London: A. Baldwin and S. Drury, 1703), v.

81. Benjamin Andrewes Atkinson, *Christianity not Older than the First Gospel-Promise. In Answer to a Book, Entitled Christianity as Old as the Creation* (London: Richard Ford, 1730), v.

82. William Abernethy-Drummond, *A Candid Examination of that Celebrated Piece of Sophistry, Entitled, Heaven Open to All Men. In a Letter to a Gentleman in Town* (London: s.n., 1752), 5–6.

83. See esp. Akman, "The Turk's Encounter with Defoe," 204–7; Tucker, "On the Authorship of the 'Turkish Spy,'" 75–77.

84. Marana, *The Eight Volumes of Letters Writ by a Turkish Spy*, 8:355–56.

85. Ibid., 8:356.

86. Defoe, *Continuation*, vii/47.

87. Ibid., 1–3/59–60.

88. Ibid., 268–69/217–18.

89. The passage echoes Psalms 12, 35, and 119 and 2 Corinthians 1:3–5.

90. Defoe, *Continuation*, 269/218.

91. Ibid., 269/218.

92. Ibid., 266–67.

93. Maximillian E. Novak, "'The Sum of Human Misery'? Defoe's Ambiguity towards Exile," *Studies in English Literature, 1500–1900* 50, no. 3 (2010): 601–23. Novak stops the quotation before reaching the reference to Mahmut's Jewish friend and does not discuss the Jewish or cosmopolitan dimensions of the passage.

94. Thomas Stanley, *The History of Philosophy*, 3d ed. (London: W. Battersby, 1701), pt. 12, chap. 26, 487.

95. Defoe, *Continuation*, 83/108.

96. Mahmut claims Job as proof of the Arab origin of the great monotheisms. "Now *Job*, by all the Descriptions that can be given, was an Inhabitant in the Land of *UZ*: This *UZ* is, according to their own Doctors, a Country denominated from *UZ*, the Grandson of *Noah*, by the eldest son of *SHEM;* whose Posterity multiplying after their coming out of the Ark, extending themselves *Southward* into the most fruitful Countries of *Asia; such as India, Persia,* and *Westward* into *Syria, Damascus* and *Arabia*, justly called the happy; and their happy Posterity are feared to this Day, abounding in Wisdom and Knowledge, and consummated in the great Lawgiver, our sublime Prophet": ibid., 84-85/109.

97. Ibid., 83–84/108.

98. Ibid., 84/109.

99. Ibid., 253/208.

100. Ibid., 255/209.

101. Katherine Clark, *Daniel Defoe: The Whole Frame of Nature, Time, and Providence* (Hampshire, U.K.: Palgrave Macmillan, 2007), 118.

102. Defoe, *Continuation*, 110/125.

103. Ibid., 72/102.

104. Ibid., 75/104.

105. Ibid., 135/138.
106. Ibid., 22/71.
107. Ibid., 13/66.
108. Marana (attrib.), "A General Preface to the Whole," in *The Eight Volumes of Letters Writ by a Turkish Spy*, 1:sig. A2–A2 verso.
109. Ibid., sig. a2r-v.
110. This is the title of the eighteenth-century English translation by Simon Oakley. However, the work goes under a number of names in English and Latin, usually shortened to "Ibn Tufayl" or "the Hayy." The work's foremost modern translator and editor, Lenn E. Goodman, gives the title as *Ibn Tufayl's Hayy Ibn Yaqzān: A Philosophical Tale*. Goodman's introduction and notes provide detailed context and commentary on this important work: see Ibn Tufayl, *Ibn Tufayl's Hayy Ibn Yaqzān: A Philosophical Tale*, ed. and trans. Lenn E. Goodman (Chicago: University of Chicago Press, 2003).
111. Srinivas Aravamudan, "East-West Fiction as World Literature: The Hayy Problem Reconfigured," *Eighteenth-Century Studies* 47, no. 2 (2014): 219. Pope also noted the likely connection between the Hayy and *Robinson Crusoe:* see Alexander Pope, *The Correspondence of Alexander Pope*, 5 vols., ed. George Sherburn (Oxford: Clarendon Press, 1956), 2:13, n.3. The text can be found at https://catalog.hathitrust.org /Record/001022663. For scholarship on the connection, see Mahmoud Baroud, *The Shipwrecked Sailor in Arabic and Western Literature: Ibn Tufayl and His Influence on European Writers* (London: I. B. Tauris, 2012), esp. chap. 2.
112. Maximillian E. Novak, "Robinson Crusoe's Fear and the Search for Natural Man," *Modern Philology* 58, no. 4 (1961): 239. Novak refers to A. C. R. Pastor in *The Idea of Robinson Crusoe* (Watford, UK: Góngora Press, 1930), 1. Novak thinks that *Robinson Crusoe* is the reverse of the Hayy because fear controls Crusoe, revealing the state of nature to be not nurturing and supportive but brutalizing and productive of madness and suicide when human beings are truly exposed.
113. Samar Attar, "The Vital Roots of European Enlightenment: Ibn Tufayl's Influence on Modern Western Thought," in *Robinson Crusoe: Myths and Metamorphoses*, ed. Lieve Spaas and Brian Stimpson (New York: St. Martin's Press, 1996), 81. This essay appears also in Samar Attar, *The Vital Roots of European Enlightenment: Ibn Tufayl's Influence on Modern Western Thought* (Lanham, MD: Lexington Books, 2007), chapter 2. Attar draws attention to the Quakers' interest in the Hayy, noting that George Keith also translated the Hayy into English. Attar writes, "It is likely that his [Defoe's] Quaker friends may have introduced him to the *Hayy Ibn Yaqzan*, in which they saw a confirmation of their doctrine of inner light": Attar, "The Vital Roots of European Enlightenment," 93n 6.
114. Ibn Tufayl, *The Improvement of Human Reason, Exhibited in the Hai Ebn Yokdhan: Written in Arabick above 500 Years Ago, by Abu Jaafar Ebn Tophail*, trans. Simon Ockley (London: Edm. Powell and J. Morphew, 1708), title page.
115. Ibid., "The Bookseller to the Reader."
116. See Attar, *The Vital Roots of European Enlightenment*, 20. The English Short Title Catalog lists this translation as "ascribed" to George Keith.
117. Barclay, *An Apology for the True Christian Divinity*, 126.

118. Ibn Tufayl, *The Improvement of Human Reason*, app., 168.

119. "A Dialogue between Mahmut and Androgio ben Yokhdan," in *Memoirs for the Curious; or, An Account of What Occurs That's Rare, Secret, Extraordinary, Prodigious or Miraculous, through the World; whether in Nature, Art, or Learning*, 2 vols. (London: R. Janeway, 1701), 2:47–48.

120. Ibid., 48.

121. Ibid.

122. Ibid.

123. Ibid., 49.

124. Ibid., 49–50.

125. Defoe had evident interest in such thought experiments, especially when they could be shown to happen in reality. Attributed to Defoe by Chalmers, Wilson, Lee, Trent, Hutchins, Moore, and Novak and deattributed by Furbank and Owens, and appearing the same year as Crusoe, was a report on just such a case: Daniel Defoe, *The Dumb Philosopher; or, Great Britain's Wonder* [London: Tho. Bickerton, 1719].

4. Defoe's Deist Masterpiece

1. Checkley's intervention first appeared as *The Religion of Christ the Only True Religion; or, A Short and Easie Method with the Deists*, 7th ed. (Boston: T. Fleet, 1719). Checkley next published what he called the eighth edition of Leslie's *Short and Easie Method with the Deists* (Boston: J. Applebee, 1723). On Checkley's charisma, see Edmund F. Slafter, who describes Checkley as "the figure who more than any other man of the period of controversy and inquiry about the Church, occupied the popular mind": Edmund F. Slafter, *John Checkley; or, The Evolution of Religious Tolerance in Massachusetts Bay Boston*, 2 vols. (Boston: Prince Society, 1897) 1:3–4.

2. John Checkley, *The Speech of John Checkley upon His Tryal, at Boston in New England, for Publishing The Short and Easy Method with the Deist* (London: J. Wilford, 1730), 13–14. A second edition of this text appeared in 1738.

3. Francis Atterbury, *The Voice of the People, No Voice of God; or, The Mistaken Arguments of a Fiery Zealot* (London: John Baker, 1710), 24.

4. See the opening of chap. 9 of *Eight Cousins*, in Louisa May Alcott, *Work; Eight Cousins; Rose in Bloom; Stories and Other Writings* (New York: Library of America, 2014).

5. Charles Leslie, *Now or Never; or, A Project under God, to Secure the Church and Monarchy of England* (London: J. Baker, 1710), 11–12.

6. Daniel Defoe, *The Life and Strange Surprizing Adventures of Robinson Crusoe, of York, Mariner*, 2d ed. (London: W. Taylor, 1719), 222; Daniel Defoe, *The Life and Strange Surprizing Adventures of Robinson Crusoe, of York, Mariner*, in *The Novels of Daniel Defoe*, vol. 1, ed. G. A. Starr (London: Pickering and Chatto, 2008), 195. Hereafter, citations to *Robinson Crusoe* that provide two page numbers refer first to the 1719 edition from the British Library, which is reproduced in Eighteenth Century Collections Online and contains 375 pages, then to the Pickering and Chatto edition of 2008.

7. Jonathan Swift, *Travels into Several Remote Nations of the World*, 2 vols. (London: Benj. Motte, 1726), 1:153.

8. Philip Skelton articulates this view of private conscience in 1751 in his attack on deists such as Shaftesbury. While mocking their position, he captures it in terms that recall Crusoe's experience on his island, writing, "Here is a law . . . written on the heart of every man in capital letters. Place a man in what circumstances you please, and those circumstances shall suggest his duty to him. The whole creation is his teacher, and the relations and fitnesses of things are his standing monitors. He thinks for himself, and becomes his own casuist, divine, and priest, without either expense or trouble. The virtue of individuals, and the peace and happiness of societies, are not built by this system on a mere belief of future rewards and punishments, but on rewards enjoyed, and punishments inflicted, by the conscience of every man, immediately upon doing a good or evil action": Philip Skelton, *Deism Revealed; or, The Attack on Christianity Candidly Reviewed in Its Real Merits*, 2 vols. (London: A. Millar, 1751), 1:35–36.

9. See Paul Dottin's "The Life of Charles Gildon," at the start of *Robinson Crusoe Examin'd and Criticis'd: A New Edition of Charles Gildon's Famous Pamphlet*, ed. Paul Dottin (London: J. M. Dent and Sons, 1923), 5–46. Dottin draws attention to the popularity of Gildon's attack, which appeared in a first and second London edition and a third Dublin edition, all in 1719. His life offers a vivid account of Gildon's literary biography but says little about the deism that Gildon chose to promulgate with Charles Blount in 1693, in *The Oracles of Reason*. Indeed, Dottin's purpose in this book is in part to exonerate Defoe from Gildon's charge of covert literary deism in *Robinson Crusoe*. He explains Gildon's adherence to deism by writing, "Tempted by the doctrines of his new friends, and irresistibly drawn by the desire—frequent among young writers—to shock the bourgeois mind, Gildon became one of the pupils and admirers of Blount; he was soon chosen as the secretary and historiographer of the deistical club": Dottin, "The Life of Charles Gildon," 9. He also "published with pious care the posthumous works of Mrs. Behn."

10. Chapter 1 details Defoe's appropriation of Blount's *King William and Queen Mary Conquerors* (London: Richard Baldwin, 1693), the work credited with bringing down the Licensing Act in 1695. It was a work of perfectly disguised ventriloquism that led the Tory licensor not only to approve the work for publication but *to wish he had written it*. Edmund Bohun, the licensor, was ruined by the hoax, the same stunt Defoe pulled at Charles Leslie's expense with *The Shortest Way with the Dissenters*. Blount died at the age of 39 in 1693. The received account is that he shot himself in despair after the church refused to sanction his proposed marriage to his deceased wife's sister, a ruling that ran directly counter to Jewish legal tradition, as Blount explained in a learned essay published in the posthumous *The Miscellaneous Works of Charles Blount, Esq., to Which Is Prefixed the Life of the Author, and an Account and Vindication of His Death*, ed. Charles Gildon (London: s.n., 1695). Blount is supposed to have written a learned treatise comparing Jewish and Christian legal authorities on the question and then killed himself when he lost the argument. "Though not a very young man, he was possessed by an insane passion for the sister of his deceased wife," wrote Macaulay in *The History of England*, 5 vols. (London: Longman, Brown, Green, and Longmans, 1855), 4:362.

11. Macaulay, *The History of England*, 4:362n. Macaulay cites Pope's note on Blount in the *Epilogue to the Satires I*.

12. Charles Leslie, *A Short and Easie Method with the Deists*, 2d ed. (London: C. Brome, W. Keblewhite, H. Hindmarsh, E. Poole, 1699), xiv.

13. Charles Gildon, *The Deist's Manual; or, A Rational Enquiry into the Christian Religion* (London: A. Roper, Fran Coggan, and Geo. Strahan, 1705), sig. a7v. This quotation begins the preface.

14. Gildon republished his congratulatory letter from Charles Leslie in "A Letter from the Author of the Short Method with the Deists and Jews, appended to the Deists Manual," in ibid., 1. The editor of *The Theological Works of the Reverend Mr. Charles Leslie* refers to the "glorious success" of the "*Short Method with the Deists*, which convinced one of their most celebrated Writers, and persuaded him not only to make a publick retraction of his error, but to write against it in defence of the truth": Charles Leslie, *The Theological Works of the Reverend Mr. Charles Leslie*, 2 vols, (London: W. Bowyer, 1721), 1:198.

15. Dottin points out that at the time Gildon replied to the first two parts of *Robinson Crusoe* he was nearly blind and had to have an amanuensis read each volume to him and write down his criticism of each paragraph. His response appeared on September 28, 1703, only a month after part 2 of *Robinson Crusoe* appeared, on August 20, 1719.

16. Alexander Pope, *The Dunciad Variorum with the Prolegomena of Scriblerus* (London: John Wright for A. Dod, 1729), 21, Remarks to Verse 250.

17. Gildon's most notable attempt at sustained prose fiction was a work that appeared in 1692, received a second edition in 1706, and was reissued the same year as *Robinson Crusoe: The Post-boy Robb'd of His Mail; or, The Pacquet Broke Open* (London: A. Bettesworth and R. Rivington, 1719). It begins when two friends discover packets of letters stolen from a mail coach and left on the road. Dottin (9-10) describes it as written in part "after the manner of Lucian."

18. Charles Gildon, *The Life and Strange Surprizing Adventures of Mr. D—de F—, of London, Hosier, Who Has Liv'd above Fifty years by Himself, in the Kingdoms of North and South Britain. The Various Shapes He Has Appear'd in, and the Discoveries He Has Made for the Benefit of His Country* (London: J. Roberts, 1719), iii–iv.

19. Ibid., 32–33.

20. Paula R. Backscheider, *Daniel Defoe: His Life* (Baltimore: Johns Hopkins University Press, 1989), 418.

21. Martin J. Greif, "The Conversion of Robinson Crusoe," *Studies in English Literature, 1500–1900* 6, no. 3 (1966): 551–52.

22. Michael McKeon, *The Origins of the English Novel, 1600–1740* (Baltimore: Johns Hopkins University Press, 1987), 336. Elsewhere, McKeon writes that "*Robinson Crusoe* can be seen in rather close proximity to the preoccupations of Protestant soteriology in general and spiritual autobiography in particular. . . . [T]he peculiar coexistence of historicity and subjectivity in *Robinson Crusoe* [exemplifies] the obvious indebtedness of Defoe's work to the formal procedures of spiritual autobiography": ibid., 317–18.

23. Gildon, *The Life and Strange Surprizing Adventures of Mr. D—de F—*, 33. Gildon's attack on Defoe was hardly unprovoked. In 1703 Defoe turned these lines on Gildon:

G———Writes Satyrs, rails at Blasphemy,
And his next Page Lampoons the Deity;
Exposes his *Darinda*'s Vitious Life,
But keeps six Whores, and starves his modest Wife;
Sets up for a Reformer of the Town,
Himself a First Rate *Rake* below Lampoon.
(Daniel Defoe, *More Reformation: A Satyr upon Himself* [London: s.n., 1703], 10)

24. Gildon, *The Life and Strange Surprizing Adventures of Mr. D——de F——*, 2.
25. Ibid., 2.
26. Ibid., viii–ix.
27. Ibid., 24.
28. Ibid., 25.
29. "1619: Lucilio Vanini, aka Giulio Cesare," ExecutedToday.com, February 9, 2010, http://www.executedtoday.com/2010/02/09/1619-lucilio-vanini-aka-giulio-cesare.
30. An instructive example of this practice of issuing warnings by recounting the violent deaths of freethinkers is the book by Nicholas Chewny (1609–1685) called *Anti-Socinianism; or, A Brief Explication of Some Places of Holy Scripture, for the Confutation of Certain Gross Errours, and Socinian Heresies* (London: H. Twiford and T. Dring, 1656). The closing section provides *"also a brief description of the lives, and a true relation of the death, of the authors, promoters, propagators, and chief disseminators of this Socinian heresie, how it sprung up, by what means it spread, and when and by whom it was first brought into England, that so we be not deceived by it."* A similar work appeared in London in two volumes between 1719 and 1720 under the title *The History of King-Killers; or, The Fanatick Martyrology* (London: S. Redmayne and T. Jauncy, 1720), promising a short and easy life of "three hundred and sixty five hellish saints of that crew . . . being one for every day in the year."
31. For a review of secular approaches to Defoe, see John Richetti, "Secular Crusoe: The Reluctant Pilgrim Revisited," in *Eighteenth-Century Genre and Culture: Serious Reflections on Occasional Forms, Essays in Honor of J. Paul Hunter*, ed. Dennis Todd and Cynthia Wall (Newark: University of Delaware Press, 2001), 58–78. See also Ilse Vickers, "The Influence of the New Science on Defoe's Habit of Mind," *Man and Nature/L'Homme et la Nature* 7 (1988): 67–78; Ilse Vickers, *Defoe and the New Science*, Cambridge Studies in Eighteenth-Century Literature and Thought, no. 32 (New York: Cambridge University Press, 1997).
32. Dottin, *Robinson Crusoe Examin'd and Criticis'd*, 131.
33. Gildon, *The Life and Strange Surprizing Adventures of Mr. D——de F——*, 2.
34. The question of the order of composition of parts 1, 2, and 3 and their relationship, or lack thereof, remains a scholarly mystery. The book appeared as a trilogy, with the famous part 1 followed in 1719 and 1720 by two continuations, one fictional and the other discursive. Part 1 is the book we now know as *Robinson Crusoe*, which Defoe called *The Life and Strange Surprizing Adventures of Robinson Crusoe*; part 2, although included with part 1 for much of the eighteenth and nineteenth centuries, dropped out of currency after World War I. At the start of *Serious Reflections* (part 3), Defoe as much as admits that he was writing part 3 all along. Jeffrey Hopes argues that some of

part 3 was likely written in the 1690s: see Jeffrey Hopes, "Real and Imaginary Stories: *Robinson Crusoe* and *Serious Reflections*," *Eighteenth-Century Fiction* 8, no. 3 (1996): 314. For a detailed reception history of the trilogy in the nineteenth century, see Melissa Free, "Un-erasing 'Crusoe': 'Farther Adventures' in the Nineteenth Century," *Book History* 9 (2006): 89–130.

35. Daniel Defoe, *Serious Reflections during the Life and Surprising Adventures of Robinson Crusoe, with his Vision of the Angelick World* (London: W. Taylor, 1720), 120; Daniel Defoe, *Serious Reflections during the Life and Surprising Adventures of Robinson Crusoe, with His Vision of the Angelick World*, in *The Novels of Daniel Defoe*, vol. 3, ed. G. A. Starr (London: Pickering and Chatto, 2008), 129. Hereafter, citations of *Serious Reflections* that provide two page numbers refer first to the 1720 edition, then to the Pickering and Chatto edition of 2008.

36. Ibid., 120/130.
37. Ibid., 121/130.
38. Ibid.
39. Ibid., 123/130–31.
40. Ibid., 123/131–32.
41. Ibid., 124/132
42. Ibid., 125/132. Starr acknowledges that this entire dialogue brings in the question of deism, but he rejects any sympathy on Defoe's part for the Old Gentlewoman's ideas. His editorial note explains that "Defoe holds (as did most earlier divines) that human reason and 'the Light of Nature' are sufficient to lead all mankind to believe that God exists, and *that* he should be worshipped, But he differs from contemporary deists in holding that reason and nature cannot teach man *how* God should be worshipped; for this purpose (and for others), revelation is necessary. This position is summarized well by the author of *Christianity Not as Old as the Creation*," whom Starr believes is Defoe: *Serious Reflections* (2008), 341.

43. Defoe, *Serious Reflections*, 125/133.

44. Crusoe's assertions of colonial and Christian world domination become more frequent and vehement by the end of *Serious Reflections*, justifying his own ridiculous attack on the Muscovite idol. Laying down a general law, he asserts, "In Case any [native] rejected the Instruction of religious Men, and adher'd obstinately to his Idolatry, and would not be reclaimed by gentle and christian Usage, suitable Methods are to be taken with such, that they might not make a religious Faction in the Country, in order to recover their Liberty, as they call it to serve their own Gods, that is to say Idols; for it must be for ever as just, not to permit them to go back to Idolatry by Force, as it was to pull them from it by Force . . . This is my *Cruisado*": ibid., 267/218.

45. Robert James Merrett arrives at the opposite conclusion. Regarding *Serious Reflections* as "an apology for fiction," he writes, "*Serious Reflections* manifests a cognitive and aesthetic sensibility that enhances appreciation of Christian hermeneutics": Robert James Merrett, *Daniel Defoe: Contrarian* (Toronto: University of Toronto Press, 2013), 74. In a similar vein, G. A. Starr views *Serious Reflections* as "a legitimate and worthy sequel to *Robinson Crusoe*" because it captures the book's grounding in Protestant

casuistry: G. A. Starr, "*Robinson Crusoe* and Its Sequels: *The Farther Adventures* and *Serious Reflections*," in *The Cambridge Companion to "Robinson Crusoe,"* ed. John Richetti (Cambridge: Cambridge University Press, 2018), 67. "What these works have in common is that they are all arguing for the same set of beliefs, and arguing against the same versions of unbelief, or against what he takes to be threats to it. . . . Defoe sees the same connectedness among the objects of his hostility: thus he does not simply identify Deism, freethinking, and skepticism, but he does regard them all as leading to (if not disguises for) atheism": Starr, "*Robinson Crusoe* and Its Sequels." 79.

46. Defoe, *Serious Reflections during the Life and Surprising Adventures of Robinson Crusoe,* 125/133.

47. Ibid., 125–26/133.

48. Maximillian Novak speaks for many readers when he observes that "Crusoe's entire narrative is based on the assumption that God is continually punishing him for his original sin": Maximillian E. Novak, "Crusoe's Original Sin," *Studies in English Literature, 1500–1900* 1, no. 3 (1961): 25.

49. Greif, "The Conversion of Robinson Crusoe," 551.

50. Benjamin Keach, *Gospel Mysteries Unveil'd,* 2 vols. (London: R. Tookey, 1701), I, 61.

51. Benjamin Whichcote, *Several Discourses Concerning the Shortness of Humane Charity,* 4 vols. 2d ed. (London: James Knapton, 1701), 1:6.

52. Ibid., 1:8.

53. Increase Mather, *The Voice of God, In Stormy Winds, Considered in Two Sermons, Occasioned by the Dreadful and Unparallel'd Storm in the European Nations, November 27, 1703* (Boston: Benjamin Eliot, 1704), 65.

54. Ibid., 8.

55. Ibid., 1:10–11.

56. Whichcote, *Several Discourses,* 26.

57. Greif, "The Conversion of Robinson Crusoe," 567. Greif writes, "*Jonah's* being three *Days* and *Nights* in the Belly of a *Whale* was a *Sign* of *Christ's* being so long in the Heart of the *Earth.* Christ himself makes the Allusion. Matth. xii, 40."

58. Ibid., 574.

59. All references to *Characteristicks* are to an edition Defoe might have seen and the one Shaftesbury had a hand in revising before his untimely death in 1713: Anthony Ashley Cooper, Third Earl of Shaftesbury, *Characteristicks of Men, Manners, Opinions, Times,* 3 vols., 2d ed. (London: John Darby, 1714). The cited passage comes from the last essay in the collection, "Miscellaneous Reflections": ibid., vol. 3, misc. 2, 122.

60. Jonah 4, 9–11.

61. Shaftesbury, "Miscellaneous Reflections," in *Characteristicks of Men, Manners, Opinions, Times,* vol. 3, misc. 2, 122. This passage relates not only to Jonah but to Shaftesbury's assessment of the general style of the Hebrew Bible. "In the antienter Parts of Sacred Story," writes Shaftesbury, "where the Beginning of things, and Origin of human Race are represented to us, there are sufficient Instances of the *Familiarity of Style, this popular and pleasant Intercourse,* and Manner of Dialogue between God and

Man: *I might add even between* Man *and* Beast; and what is still more extraordinary, between GOD and SATAN."

62. Ibid., 118.
63. Ibid., 119.
64. Ibid., 122.
65. Daniel Defoe, *A Continuation of Letters Written by a Turkish Spy* (London: W. Taylor, 1718), 84/108–09.
66. Defoe, *Robinson Crusoe*, 15–16/66–67.
67. Ian Watt, *The Rise of the Novel: Studies in Defoe, Richardson, and Fielding* (Berkeley: University of California Press, 1957).
68. Defoe, *Robinson Crusoe*, 1/57.
69. Robert W. Ayers, "Allusive Allegoric History," *PMLA* 82, no. 5 (1967): 404–5, n.28. Most commentary follows this reasoning. W.R. Owens's editorial note suggests that Kreutznaer "might mean 'near the Cross', 'Cross-fool' or 'nourished by the Cross'": Daniel Defoe, *The Life and Strange Surprizing Adventures of Robinson Crusoe, of York, Mariner,* in *The Novels of Daniel Defoe*, vol. 1, ed. G. A. Starr (London: Pickering and Chatto, 2008), 288. See also Arthur Wellesley Secord, "Studies in the Narrative Method of Defoe," *Studies in Language and Literature* 9, no. 1 (1924): esp. 32–33, 42–43. This work is also available in digital reprint at https://catalog.hathitrust.org/Record/006156853.
70. Ayers, "Allusive Allegoric History," 404–5, n.2
71. David Marshall, "Autobiographical Acts in *Robinson Crusoe,*" *English Literary History* 71, no. 4 (2004), 902.
72. "Two names of his fellow students stand out—Timothy Cruso and Samuel Wesley. The former must surely have suggested the name of his greatest masterpiece. The latter was the father of the founder of Wesleyanism": A. J. Shirren, *Daniel Defoe in Stoke Newington* (London: Stoke Newington Public Libraries Committee, 1960), 3.
73. Roger D. Lund, "Strange Complicities: Atheism and Conspiracy in *A Tale of a Tub*," in *British Literature, 1640–1789: A Critical Reader,* ed. Robert DeMaria Jr. (Malden, MA: Blackwell, 1999), 155.
74. Daniel Defoe, "Verses to Mr. Campbell," in *The History of the Life and Adventures of Mr. Duncan Campbell*, 2d corrected ed. (London: E. Curll, 1720), 7–8. Chalmers, Wilson, Lee, Trent, Hutchins, and Novak all attribute this work to Defoe with varying degrees of certainty. (Some indicate that William Bond had a hand in it.) Furbank and Owens dispute the attribution. A note to the word "Gabalis" in these lines reveals the author's familiarity with both Pope's poem and the history of the Rosicrucians: "See *The History of the Count de Gabalis,* from whence he has taken the Machinery of his Rape of the Lock." The book referred to is Abbé N. de Montfaucon de Villars (Nicolas-Pierre-Henri, 1635–73), *The Count of Gabalis, Being a Diverting History of the Rosicrucian Doctrine of Spirits viz. Sylphs, Salamanders, Gnomes, and Daemons* (London: B. Lintot and E. Curll, 1714).
75. William Hazlitt, "The Life of Defoe," in *The Works of Daniel De Foe, with a Memoir of his Life and Writings* (London: John Clements, 1811), xxx. This page and the entire text can be accessed online at https://archive.org/details/worksdanieldefooohazlgoog/page/n43.

76. Eugenius Philalethes (pseud.), *The Fame and Confession of the Fraternity of R:C: Commonly, of the Rosie Cross*, trans. Thomas Vaughn (London, John Macock, 1652), 11. This work is a translation of the original German, *Fama Fraternitatis, oder, Entdeckung der Brüdershafft des Löblichen Ordens des Rosenkreuzes*, attributed to Johann Valentin Andreä.

77. Quoted in Francis Yates, *The Rosicrucian Enlightenment* (London: Routledge, 1972), 265.

78. A Freemason who renounced his radical principles may have aroused Defoe's disdain late in life, since Crassley, Trent, Hutchins, Moore and Novak all attribute *The Purjur'd Free Mason Detected* (London: J. Warner, 1730) to Defoe. Furbank and Owens deattribute the work, reasoning that because he wrote other texts that attack the Freemasons, such as *An Essay on the History and Reality of Apparitions* (1727) and *Second Thoughts Are Best* (1729), he could not be the author of a work that expressed sympathy for Freemasonry. Yet adopting the mask of the Freemason fits the pattern we have observed throughout this study, beginning with Defoe's impersonation of Quaker personas. On deism and Freemasonry, see J. A. Leo Lemay, ed., *Deism, Masonry, and the Enlightenment: Essays Honoring Alfred Owen Aldridge* (Newark: University of Delaware Press, 1987); Margaret C. Jacob, *Living the Enlightenment: Freemasonry and Politics in Eighteenth-Century Europe* (New York: Oxford University Press, 1991).

79. Andrea Walkden, "Parallel Lives and Literary Legacies: Crusoe's Elder Brother and Defoe's Cavalier," *English Literary History* 77, no. 4 (2010): 1061–62.

80. O. F. W. Fernsemer, "Daniel Defoe and the Palatine Emigration of 1709: A New View of the Origin of Robinson Crusoe," *Journal of English and Germanic Philology* 19, no. 1 (1920): 108. Fernsemer sums up the situation by writing, "Defoe's schemes for home colonization were not adopted, probably because the feeling of the English working classes had grown to a dangerous degree of aversion toward the foreigners, and partly because the Palatines themselves had expressed their disappointment at not being sent to the colonies right away. Neither was the Christian advice of a certain High Churchman, who suggested sending them all to Scotland where they could starve to death, followed. With the exception of those who had been taken in by private individuals and had found satisfactory employment, they were dispatched in the course of the following months to New York and North Carolina. . . . [M]ore than a thousand died in the encampment at Black Heath, and nearly half that number was to perish on the seas on their way to America." Defoe's possible authorship of *A Brief History of the Poor Palatine Refugees* (London: J. Baker, 1709) is relevant. Moore and Novak attribute the work to Defoe; Furbank and Owens deattribute it.

81. Fernsemer, "Daniel Defoe and the Palatine Emigration of 1709," 107. Defoe's "understandable sympathy for them [the Palatine immigrants] was not only based on the fact that they were brethren in faith, but on his extensive and first-hand knowledge of their history and civilization": ibid., 101.

82. *Gulliver Decypher'd; or, Remarks on a Late Book, Intitled Travels into Several Remote Nations of the World* (London: J. Roberts, 1727), 16–17.

83. Coetzee was aware of Swift's play at Defoe's expense. Rewriting *Robinson Crusoe* as *Foe* (1986), Coetzee introduces a Susan Barton, in lieu of Mary Burton, who washes

up on Robinson Cruso's island and becomes his second subject, after the now mute Friday.

84. Swift, *Travels into Several Remote Nations of the World in Four Parts*, 2 vols. (London: Benj. Motte, 1726), v.

85. See "Banbury: Introduction," in Christina Colvin, Janet Cooper, N. H. Cooper, P. D. A. Harvey, Marjory Hollings, Judith Hook, Mary Jessup, Mary D. Lobel, J. F. A. Mason, B. S. Trinder, and Hilary Turner, *A History of the County of Oxford: Volume 10, Banbury Hundred*, ed. Alan Crossley (London: Oxford University Press 1972), 5–18, British History Online, http://www.british-history.ac.uk/vch/oxon/vol10. For the centrality of Banbury during the Civil War, see Edward Hyde, Earl of Clarendon, *The History of the Rebellion and Civil Wars in England*, 2 vols. (Oxford: The Theater, 1703), book 6.

86. When Francis Bugg renewed his attack on the Quakers in 1702, he addressed himself to a Mr. Vivers and advised him "that on Monday the 21st of September *next* I purpose (God willing) to be at this town of Banbury with my Books": Francis Bugg, *Distinct Advice on Two Different Heads Given to the People Call'd Quakers* (London: 1 J. Taylor and R. Wilkins, 702), 6.

87. Richard Braverman, "Politics in Jewish Disguise," *Studies in Philology* 90, no. 4 (1993): 347–70. "The word 'Jews' had served as a byword for saintly Puritans. This identification was still very much alive at the time of the Revolution": ibid., 347.

88. W. C. Hazlitt, comp., *English Proverbs and Proverbial Phrases Collected from the Most Authentic Sources* (London: Reeves and Turner, 1907), 1; *Notes and Queries*, 5th ser., ix, 168, 7th ser., iii, 402–4.

89. *Defoe's Review*, ed. John McVeagh, 9 vols. (London: Pickering and Chatto, 2003-11), 6, 427.

90. In the *Oxford English Dictionary*, the source listed is Richard Corbet, "Iter Boreale," in *Certain Elegant Poems* (London: R. Cotes, 1647), 11.

91. From "The Little Jest of Robin Hood" (1500), to the *Renowned Robin Hood; or, His Famous Archery Truly Related with the Worthy Exploits He Acted before Queen Katherine, He Being an Out-Law Man* (1630), and the innumerable ballad broadsheets of the seventeenth century, to more ambitious collections, such as *The Noble Birth and Gallant Atchievements of that Remarkable Outlaw, Robin Hood . . . in Twelve Several Stories* (1690), Robin Hood was a cultural icon in Defoe's day.

92. The remainder of this chapter features plates from François Aimé Louis Dumoulin's *Collection de cent-cinquante gravures représentant et formant une suite non interrompue des voyages et aventures surprenantes de Robinson Crusoé* (Vevey, Switzerland: Loertscher et Fils, 1810; rprt. Paris: Club Français du Livres, 1962). An endnote accompanying each plate provides a translation of the French inscription. The inscription for plate no. 58 (The footprint in the sand), reads: Having gone down to check the canoe he left in the creek, Robinson notices a bare human footprint on the sand, which alarms him.

Considered the first graphic novel version of *Robinson Crusoe* and an early serial cartoon, Dumoulin's *Collection* retells the story of *Robinson Crusoe* in a continuous series of 150 finely etched plates. In a brief introduction, Dumoulin confesses an early fascination with *Robinson Crusoe*, which made him seek out work and adventure in the West Indies. He lived in Granada between 1773 and 1782, in time for the American Revolutionary War. Dumoulin's graphic re-creation highlights odd but telling moments in the narrative. He devotes four plates to the killing of the wolf and the bear at the end of part 1; Friday's inglorious death, seldom visualized or discussed, receives a vivid plate. Dumoulin captures Crusoe's discovery of barley growing as if by Providence near his door; he pictures Crusoe's tobacco- and rum-fueled dream of the "angelick spirit" and devotes two plates to Crusoe's ill-advised slashing and destruction of the Muscovite idol. David Blewett calls Dumoulin's *Collection* "the first attempt on a large scale to *replace* the text with a series of pictures sufficiently detailed and complete to tell a story that could be followed in the pictures alone. . . . [The] 150 etchings possess in embryo the action that was eventually to develop into the modern motion picture": David Blewett, *The Illustration of Robinson Crusoe 1719–20* (Gerrards Cross, U.K.: Colin Smythe, 1995), 40. An electronic edition can be found at http://www.gutenberg.org /files/24915/24915-h/24915-h.htm.

93. Quoted in Richard West, *Daniel Defoe: The Life and Strange Surprising Adventures* (New York: Carroll and Graf, 1998), 244.

94. Ibid., 244.

95. Robert M. Maniquis and Carl Fisher, eds., *Defoe's Footprints: Essays in Honour of Maximillian E. Novak* (Toronto: University of Toronto Press, 2009).

96. Homer O. Brown, "The Displaced Self in the Novels of Daniel Defoe," *English Literary History* 38, no. 4 (1971): 571.

97. Defoe, *Robinson Crusoe*, 181–82/170.

98. Robert Folkenflik, "Robinson Crusoe and the Semiotic Crisis of the Eighteenth Century," in *Defoe's Footprints: Essays in Honour of Maximillian E. Novak*, ed. Robert M. Maniquis and Carl Fisher (Toronto: University of Toronto Press, 2009).

99. Folkenflik, "Robinson Crusoe and the Semiotic Crisis of the Eighteenth Century," 99.

100. Leslie, *A Short and Easie Method with the Deists . . . to which is Added a Second Part to the Jews*, 2d ed. (London: Charles Brome, 1699), title page.

101. Charles Leslie, *A Short and Easie Method with the Jews*, 3d ed. (London: Geo. Strahan, 1715), 40.

102. The influence of Shaftesbury on Moses Mendelssohn has been well documented. See: Alexander Altman, *Moses Mendelssohn, A Biographical Study* (Philadelphia, PA: The Jewish Publication Society, 1973), 109–12. (Mendelssohn's first literary project was a translation of Shaftesbury's *The Moralists*.) "Deism was accepted by younger representatives of the [Jewish] movement for enlightenment [Haskala] such as Lazarus Bendavid, and, in a more popular form, by David Friedländer. . . . In the 19th cent. Also deism was the prevailing form of thought in large groups, especially in the educated middle-class": Isaac Landman, ed., *The Universal Jewish Encyclopedia*, 10 vols. (New York: Universal Jewish Encyclopedia, 1948), 3:516.

103. On deist philo-Semitism, see the work of Diego Lucci, especially "Judaism and Natural Religion in the Philosophy of William Wollaston," *Journal for Eighteenth-Century Studies* 30 (2007): 363–87, and "Judaism and the Jews in the British Deists' Attacks on Revealed Religion," *Hebraic Political Studies* 3 (2008): 177–214. See also Luisa

Simonutti, "Deism, Biblical Hermeneutics, and Philology," in *Atheism and Deism Revalued: Heterodox Religious Identities in Britain, 1650–1800,* ed. Wayne Hudson, Diego Lucci, and Jeffrey R. Wigelsworth (Burlington, VT: Ashgate, 2014), 45–62; Jonathan Karp and Adam Sutcliffe, *Philosemitism in History* (Cambridge: Cambridge University Press, 2011); Gertrude Himmelfarb, *The People of the Book: Philosemitism in England from Cromwell to Churchill* (New York: Encounter, 2011). Additional book-length studies that explore the complex relation of deism and Judaism are Adam Sutcliffe, *Judaism and Enlightenment* (Cambridge: Cambridge University Press, 2003); David B. Ruderman, *Jewish Enlightenment in an English Key: Anglo-Jewry's Construction of Modern Jewish Thought* (Princeton, NJ: Princeton University Press, 2000).

104. Charles Blount, *Miracles, No Violation of the Laws of Nature* (London: Robert Sollers, 1683), is largely a translation of chapter 6 of Spinoza's *Tractatus Theologico-Politicus. Treatise Partly Theological, and Partly Political,* a complete English translation of Spinoza's *Tractatus,* was published in London in 1689 and is thought to have been translated by Blount.

105. Robert Fleming, *The Rod, or The Sword. The Present Dilemma of the Nations of England, Scotland, and Ireland,* 2d ed. (London: Tho. Parlehurst, 1701), 74–75.

106. John Breuhowse, *The Highland Spectator; or, Observations on the Inhabitants of Various Denominations in London and Westminster* (London: J. Robinson, 1744), 89.

107. William Law, *An Appeal to All Who Doubt, or Disbelieve the Truth of the Gospel, Whether They Be Deists, Arians, Socinians, or Nominal Christians,* 3d ed. (London: Robinson and Roberts, 1768), 329.

108. Robert Adam, *The Religious World Displayed; or, A View of the Four Grand Systems of Religion,* 3 vols. (Philadelphia: Moses Thomas, 1818), iii, 455.

109. Robert Joshua Leslie, *The Life and Writings of Charles Leslie, M.A.: Nonjuring Divine* (London: Rivingtons, 1885), 88–89. The Jewish Naturalization Act passed Parliament in 1753 but was repealed the following year after a wave of anti-Semitic protest. Leading that charge was Charles Leslie, though dead since 1722. His *A Short and Easie Method with the Jews,* already in its third edition in 1715, was revised as *The Case of the Jews Considered with Respect to Christianity* (London: s.n., 1755).

110. Charles Leslie, *A Short and Easie Method with the Deists,* 3d ed. (London: C. Brome, W. Keblewhite, H. Hindmarsh, E. Poole, Geo. Strahan, 1701), 36–39.

111. Charles Leslie, *The Truth of Christianity Demonstrated* (London: B. Bragg, E. Pool, G. Strahan, 1711), 163.

112. Ibid., 82.

113. Ibid., 109.

114. Ibid., 121.

115. Ibid., 99.

116. Ibid., 126–27.

117. Leslie, *A Short and Easie Method with the Jews,* 2.

118. Charles Leslie, *Deism Refuted; or, The Truth of Christianity Demonstrated* (London: s.n., 1755), 26.

119. Charles Leslie, *The Charge of Socinianism against Dr. Tillotson Considered . . . Wherein Likewise Charles Blount's Great Diana is Considered* (Edenburgh [sic]: s.n., 1695), 25–26.

120. Leslie, *A Short and Easie Method with the Jews*, 16.

121. Published in 1938 in Italy, Auerbach's essay "Figura" presents the theoretical blueprint for *Mimesis* in that it provides an apparently neutral historical excavation of the meaning of "Figura" from the Greeks through early Christianity. It is in this essay that Auerbach first exposes the hermeneutic instability of typology; that same instability energizes the historical narrative of *Mimesis*: see Erich Auerbach, "Figura," in *Scenes from the Drama of European Life* (Minneapolis: University of Minnesota Press, 1984), 11–78.

122. Erich Auerbach, *Mimesis: The Representation of Reality in Western Literature*, trans. Willard R. Trask (Princeton, NJ: Princeton University Press, 2003), 48.

123. Ibid., 119–20.

124. On this topic see Andrew McKendry, "'No Parallels from Hebrew Times': Troubled Typologies and the Glorious Revolution in Daniel Defoe's Williamite Poetry," *Eighteenth-Century Studies* 50, no. 1 (2016): 81–99. I discuss this article in chapter 1.

125. In *More Reformation, A Satyr Upon Himself* (London: 1703), 22, Defoe as much as versifies Leslie's argument:

> For *Law* and *Gospel* were the very same,
> From one Divine Original they came:
> *Law* was but *Gospel* under *Types* conceal'd,
> And *Gospel* was those *Types* and *Laws* reveal'd
> The Sacred Institution only dy'd,
> Because the thing was come it signifi'd;
> The Types and Figures could no more remain,
> Because the Substance made the Shadows plain;
> The meaning of the Law was not destroy'd,
> Only the Gospel made th' Occasion void;
> The Sacred Substance still remain'd alive,
> *In its Eternal Representative.*

126. Daniel Defoe, "A Vision of the Angelick World," in Defoe, *Serious Reflections during the Life and Surprising Adventures of Robinson Crusoe*, 11/227. In the original 1720 edition, pagination starts over with "A Vision."

127. Defoe, "Robinson Crusoe's Preface," in *Serious Reflections*, sig. a2v/51.

128. Travel, too, can be read through a double optic and reveals diametrically opposed meanings, depending on whether Crusoe is read through a cosmopolitan-deist or Protestant-colonialist frame. John Gascoigne finds that narratives of Pacific exploration often serve an implicit deism, since they foreground, sometimes sympathetically, non-Western religious practices, as in the case of Friday: John Gascoigne, "Pacific Exploration as Religious Critique," *Parergon* 27, no. 1 (2010): 143–62.

129. Gildon, *The Life and Strange Surprizing Adventures of Mr. D—de F—*, 8. The editor of the Pickering Masters edition of *The Consolidator*, Geoffrey Sill, states, "Defoe believed that the actions of Providence were expressions of God's will": Defoe, *The Consolidator* (2003), 231. Starr shares this view, writing, "In much of *Robinson Crusoe*, a belief in Providence serves to offset the hero's sense of abandonment: his seemingly forlorn plight is overseen by an agency that possesses total power, and uses it to preserve and sustain him": Defoe, *Serious Reflections during the Life and Surprising Adventures of Robinson Crusoe* (2008), 43.

130. For an explanation of the meaning of Providence in *Robinson Crusoe* that finds nothing unusual in these vacillations since they can be comprehended under the Protestant distinction between general and particular Providence, see J. Paul Hunter, "Genre, Nature, *Robinson Crusoe*," in *The Cambridge Companion to "Robinson Crusoe,"* ed. John Richetti (Cambridge: Cambridge University Press, 2018), 8–11. Hunter follows established Defoe scholarship in asserting Defoe's ultimate faith in providential oversight.

131. Defoe, *Robinson Crusoe*, "The Preface," sig. a1v/55.

132. Ibid., 43/84–85.

133. Ibid., 72/103.

134. Christopher Hill, *God's Englishman: Oliver Cromwell and the English Revolution* (New York: Harper Torchbooks, 1970), 221.

135. Defoe, *Robinson Crusoe*, 153/153.

136. Gildon, *The Life and Strange Surprizing Adventures of Mr. D—de F—*, A2.

137. For scholarship on the converse of spirits and empirical apparitions in Defoe, see Daniel J. Johnson, "*Robinson Crusoe* and the Apparitional Eighteenth-Century Novel," *Eighteenth-Century Fiction* 28, no. 2 (2015–16): 239–61; Katherine Ellison, "Mediation and Intelligence in Defoe's *Vision of the Angelick World*," in *Topographies of the Imagination: New Approaches to Daniel Defoe*, ed. Katherine Ellison, Kit Kinkade, and Holly Faith Nelson (New York: AMS Press, 2014). Kevin Seidel focuses on the last section of *Serious Reflections* because *A Vision of the Angelick World* appears explicitly theological and representative of Crusoe's outlook on his island: Kevin Seidel, "Beyond the Religious and the Secular in the History of the Novel," *New Literary History* 38, no. 4 (2007): 637–47.

138. *The Farther Adventures of Robinson Crusoe; Being the Second and Last Part of His Life, and of the Strange Surprizing Accounts of His Travels Round Three Parts of the Globe* (London: W. Taylor, 1719), 72 (this text is available through ECCO based on the copy held in the British Library and has 382 pages); *The Farther Adventures of Robinson Crusoe; Being the Second and Last Part of His Life, and of the Strange Surprizing Accounts of His Travels round Three Parts of the Globe*, in *The Novels of Daniel Defoe*, 10 vols., ed. W. R. Owens and P. N. Furbank (London: Pickering and Chatto, 2008), 2:46.

139. Ibid., 223/129.

140. Ibid., 4/7.

141. Ibid., 12/11–12.

142. Ibid., 330/192–93.

143. Ibid., 331/193.

144. Ibid., 332/193.

145. Ibid., 338/197. The English translation of Dumoulin's caption for plate no. 146 reads: Destruction of Cham-Chi-Taungu, idol of the Tangut Tartars under Russian domination, by Robinson, aided by some of his companions from the caravan.

146. Homer O. Brown, *Institutions of the English Novel: from Defoe to Scott* (Philadelphia: University of Pennsylvania Press, 1997), 80; quoted approvingly in Johnson, "Robinson Crusoe and the Apparitional Eighteenth-Century Novel," 258.

147. *De Veritate*, trans. Meyrick H. Carre (Bristol, UK: J.W. Arrowsmith, Ltd., 1937).

148. Charles Blount, *Religio Laici, Written in a Letter to John Dryden, Esq.* (London: R. Bentley and S. Magnes, 1683), 49–50.

149. The advertisement to Dryden comes from the title page of *A Summary Account of the Deists Religion, in a Letter to That Excellent Physician, the late Dr. Thomas Sydenham* (London: s.n., 1745). The essay credited to Dryden reprints "Of Natural, as Opposed to Divine Revelation," in Charles Blount, *The Oracles of Reason* (London: s.n., 1693), 195–209. A note to this text in Eighteenth Century Collections Online reads, "The essay here attributed to John Dryden is in fact by Charles Blount and is entitled 'An Essay on Natural Religion, as Opposed to Divine Revelation.'"

150. Ibid. Pagination begins anew at 1, with the "Essay on Natural Religion." The same text is in Blount, *The Oracles of Reason*, 197.

151. Benjamin Franklin, "Letter to Ezra Stiles, March 9, 1790," in Benjamin Franklin, *Writings*, vol. 37 (New York: Library of America, 1987), 1179.

152. The translation for Dumoulin's caption for plate no. 29 reads: Robinson is astonished to see ears of corn, wheat, and rice growing outside his castle, not remembering that he shook out there several bags filled with leftovers and scraps.

153. Defoe, *Robinson Crusoe*, 91/115.

154. Ibid., 91–92/115.

155. Ibid., 248–49/212.

156. Ibid., 248–49/212. The Athanasian Creed says, "Whosoever will be saved, before all things it is necessary that he hold the catholic faith. Which faith except everyone do keep whole and undefiled, without doubt he shall perish everlastingly. And the catholic faith is this: That we worship one God in Trinity, and Trinity in Unity, neither confounding the persons, nor dividing the substance": "Athanasian Creed (AD 500)," Christian Apologetics and Research Ministry website, n.d., https://carm.org/athanasian-creed-500-ad.

157. Leah Orr, "Providence and Religion in the Crusoe Trilogy," *Eighteenth-Century Life* 38 (2014): 8.

158. Harry F. Robbins, "How Smart Was Robinson Crusoe?" *PMLA* 67, no. 5 (1952): 782–89. But see West, *Daniel Defoe*, 244: "Defoe's advice on planting corn, making a spade from iron wood, baking bread, fortifying one's home and building a dug-out canoe could serve as a manual for pioneers and mountain men in any part of America."

159. Defoe, *Serious Reflections during the Life and Surprising Adventures of Robinson Crusoe*, 256/211.

160. Orr, "Providence and Religion in the Crusoe Trilogy," 11.//
161. Gildon, *The Life and Strange Surprizing Adventures of Mr. D—de F—*, 18.
162. A Latin edition of the *Colloquies* appeared in 1706. An English translation appeared in 1711 as Erasmus, *Twenty-two Select Colloquies Out of Erasmus Roterodamus* (London: Daniel Brown et al., 1711). This edition moves "The Shipwreck" to the first dialogue in the collection. Versions of the shipwreck scenario appear in both *Robinson Crusoe* and *Roxana*.
163. Defoe, *Robinson Crusoe*, 109/126.
164. The translation of Dumoulin's caption for plate no. 33 reads: Very ill with fever, Robinson tries various ways to cure himself, including tobacco, which he burns on hot charcoal, taking the smoke into his mouth.
165. Ibid., 109–10/126.
166. Ibid., 110/126.
167. Ibid., 110–11/127.
168. Ibid., 112/127–28.
169. Ibid., 286/235. The famous passage that begins, "My Island was now peopled, and I thought myself very Rich in Subjects," concludes, "It was remarkable too, we had but three Subjects, and they were of three different Religions. My Man *Friday* was a Protestant, his Father was a *Pagan* and a *Cannibal*, and the *Spaniard* was a Papist: However, I allowed Liberty of Conscience throughout my Dominions."
170. Michel de Montaigne, *Essays of Michael Seigneur de Montaigne*, trans. Charles Cotten, 3 vols., 4th ed. (London: J. Nicholson, R. Wellington, B. Tooke [and seven others], 1711), 1:287.
171. William Carroll, "A Preliminary Discourse," in *Spinoza Reviv'd* (London: J. Morphew, 1709), sig. a5v.
172. For another argument drawing attention to the deist implications of Friday's catechism, see Gascoigne, "Pacific Exploration as Religious Critique." "By and large in Britain any Deistic capital to be derived from the Pacific voyages was expressed in a muted and not very confrontational form": ibid., 152. Again, the suggestions of deistical implication run counter to the dominant view of Defoe and his novel. Richetti concludes that *Robinson Crusoe* forms part of Defoe's lifelong polemic against secular philosophy. But that religious purpose proved fruitful for Defoe's "conception of character": John Richetti, *The Life of Daniel Defoe* (Malden, MA: Blackwell, 2005), 54.
173. Defoe, *Robinson Crusoe*, 252/214.
174. Ibid.
175. Ibid., 256/217.
176. Ibid., 256–57/217.
177. Ibid., 257/217–18.
178. Ibid., 258–59/218.
179. Ibid., 259/218.
180. Defoe, *Robinson Crusoe* (2008), 316–17. Glossing an ambiguous passage in Defoe's novel with an unambiguous passage in a catechism suggests a determination to read the novel along doctrinally predetermined lines.

181. Starr, *Defoe and Casuistry,* 4–5.
182. *The Farther Adventures of Robinson Crusoe* (1719), 161–62; *The Farther Adventures of Robinson Crusoe* (2008), 95.
183. Ibid., 162/96.
184. Ibid., 184/108. William Atkins's wife delivers something close to the deists' Common Notions in her broken English.
185. Timothy C. Blackburn, "Friday's Religion: Its Nature and Importance in *Robinson Crusoe*," *Eighteenth-Century Studies* 18, no. 3 (1985): 370–71.
186. Defoe, *Serious Reflections during the Life and Surprising Adventures of Robinson Crusoe*, a4v/52.
187. Defoe, *Robinson Crusoe* (2008), 323.
188. The translation for Dumoulin's caption for plate no. 91 reads: Having arrived in Pamplona, Robinson's small caravan was increased by twelve cavaliers and their valets, who were confined in the city by the great snowfall in the Pyrenees. Leaving alone and before the others, their guide was attacked by two famished wolves. Friday rushed to his cries and killed one of the wolves with a pistol shot; the other escaped.
189. Ibid., 346–47/274.
190. Defoe, *The Dissenter's Answer to the High-Church Challenge*, 54. We have already taken note of Defoe's wolf-obsessed attack on Leslie in *The Consolidator*, whom he labels "a mighty Stickler for the Doctrin of *absolute Subjection*. This Man draws *the most monstrous Picture of a Crolian* that could be invented, he put him in a *Wolf's Skin* with long *Asses Ears,* and hung him all over full of *Associations, Massacres, Persecutions, Rebellions,* and *Blood.* Here the People began to *stare* again, and a Crolian cou'd not go along the Street but they were always looking for the *long Ears,* the *Wolf's Claws* and the like": Defoe, *The Consolidator,* 223–24/110. "Wolf's Skin. A reference to Charles Leslie's pamphlet, *The Wolf Strip of His Shepherd's Cloathing* (1704)," note the editors of the Stoke Newington edition. *The Consolidator* (2001), 233.
191. Charles Leslie, *Salt for the Leach: In Reflections upon Reflection* (London: Charles Brome, 1712).
192. Charles Leslie, *The Finishing Stroke, Being a Vindication of the Patriarchal Scheme of Government* (London: s.n. 1711), 25–26.
193. Daniel Defoe, *The Protestant Jesuite Unmask'd in Answer to the Two Parts of Cassandra . . . with My Service to Mr. Lesley* (London: s.n., 1704), 41, 51.
194. Defoe, *Robinson Crusoe,* 348/275.
195. Defoe, "The Preface," in *More Reformation,* sig. a2v.
196. Daniel Defoe, *The Quaker's Sermon; or, A Holding-Forth concerning Barabbas* (London: s.n., 1711). Moore attributes the work to Defoe; Furbank and Owens dispute the claim, observing that the author identifies himself on page 19 as the author of the Pasquin of Rome letters in *The Tatler,* no. 187: P. N. Furbank and W. R. Owens, *Defoe De-attributions: A Critique of J. R. Moore's Checklist* (London: Hambledon Press, 1994), 47. Defoe, however, refers to Pasquin in *The Consolidator* and had every motive to disguise the source of this sneak attack on Sacheverell. My analysis shows how the work (1) fits the pattern of Defoe's other Quaker writings; (2) suggests a parallel between the

legal treatment of Defoe and Sacheverell; and (3) repeats Defoe's frequent gesture of comparing himself to Christ. If Defoe did not write it, a sound-alike did.

197. Defoe, *The Quaker's Sermon*, 3.

198. Ibid., 6. On Sacheverell, see Geoffrey Holmes, *The Trial of Doctor Sacheverell* (London: Eyre Methven, 1973).

199. Ibid., 7. Of Sacheverell, Defoe wrote in his *Review*, "Upon the whole, I think the roaring of this beast ought to give you no manner of disturbance. You ought to laugh at him," quoted in Geoffrey Holmes, *The Trial of Doctor Sacheverell*, 76.

200. The translation for Dumoulin's caption for plate no. 92 reads: In the mountains a bear appeared. Friday asked Robinson for permission to amuse the caravan at the animal's expense, which was granted. Friday spoke to the bear, drawing close. But the bear ignored him, so Friday threw a rock at the bear to provoke it.

The translation for Dumoulin's caption for plate no. 93 reads: The bear, finding himself affronted, pursued Friday, who climbed up a tree, the bear warily following him onto a long bending branch, upon which Friday began to dance and leap, which obliged the bear to assume such awkward postures to avoid falling that it much amused the company.

The translation for Dumoulin's caption for plate no. 94 reads: Friday, having amused the company at the bear's expense, let himself sink to the ground by the end of the branch; the Bear, wishing to follow him, descended the tree rearwards. As his feet touched the ground, Friday discharged a gunshot into the bear's ear and killed him in an instant.

201. Defoe, *Robinson Crusoe*, 349/275.

202. Sacheverell went out on a limb twice in 1709, first with his Assize Sermon at Derby on August 15, 1709, and then with his St. Pauls sermon on November 5, 1709, actions that led to his famous trial. In his *Review* for Thursday, December 8, 1709, Defoe calls Sacheverell "this wild Man, unweigh'd, hot, and furious—see how he flies, champs, foams and stinks": quoted in Defoe, *The Consolidator* (2001), 169.

203. Defoe, *Robinson Crusoe*, 351/277.

204. Ibid., 352/277.

205. Gildon, *The Life and Strange Surprizing Adventures of Mr. D——de F——*, vii.

206. In his *New Association* (1702), one of the texts that precipitated Defoe's *The Shortest Way with the Dissenters*, Leslie expresses admiration for Sacheverell, writing, "And speaking of one of them [members of 'the violent Party'], Mr. S——against whom they Write, they say, *that he ought never to be endur'd in a well order'd State.* Why? [Because] he joyns these *Moderate-Church Men* and the *Dissenters* together. This indeed was Provoking! For it discovers the *Plot!* But then again, he gives them both hard Words. He calls the Former, *false and perfidious Members, Shuffling, Treacherous Latitudinarians*, &c. And the latter, *Swarm of Sectaries, Propagators of Schism, Sharers in Villany and Rebellion*, &c. That is, he calls a *Spade*, a *Spade*": Charles Leslie, *The New Association of Those Called, Moderate-Church-Man* (London: s.n., 1702), 4. Defoe appears to have viewed these men as a pair, and brought them together in violent metamorphoses at the end of *The Life and Strange Surprizing Adventures of Robinson Crusoe*.

207. *Farther Adventures*, 205/119.

208. Ibid., 207/120.

209. Ibid., 207–08/120–21.

210. The translation for Dumoulin's caption for plate no. 129 reads: Friday, pierced by three arrows, dies after trying to negotiate with a great number of savages who had attacked Robinson's vessel from their canoes as it lay at anchor in calm waters and in sight of land.

211. Ibid., 208/121.

212. Ibid., 211–12/123.

213. Ibid., 210/122. Gildon was alert to this off-handed way of dispatching Friday. In his fictional dialogue, he has Friday complain: "Have injure me, to make me such a Blockhead, so much contradiction, as to be able to speak *English tolerably well* in a Month or two and not to speak it better in Twelve Years after: to make me go out to be kill'd by the Savages, only to be Spokesman to them, tho' I did not know, whether they understood one Word of my Language; for you must know, Father D——n that almost ev'ry Nation of us *Indians* speak a different Language": Gildon, *The Life and Strange Surprizing Adventures of Mr. D—de F—*, ix. Commenting on this passage, Dottin leaps to Defoe's defense, writing, "But Crusoe might reasonably have hoped Friday could have made himself understood by men of a neighboring tribe, even if their language was not exactly the dialect spoken by his own": Dottin, *Robinson Crusoe Examin'd and Criticis'd*, 137.

5. Defoe, Deism, and the Novel

1. Erich Auerbach, "Philology and '*Weltliteratur*,'" trans. Maire and Edward Said, *Centennial Review* 13, no. 1 (1969): 8.

2. Ibid., 16.

3. Ibid., 13–14.

4. Ibid., 11.

5. Ibid., 16. In a letter to Martin Hellweg, Auerbach expanded on this point, offering scholarly advice to a former student. "I would be very happy if you continued your work, and especially if you would use a technique that starts out not from a general problem but from a well-chosen, specific phenomenon [*Einzelphänomen*] that is easy to get a grip on; perhaps a history of a word or an interpretation of a passage. The specific phenomenon cannot be small and concrete enough, and it should never be a concept introduced by us or other scholars but rather something the subject matter itself presents": Erich Auerbach, Martin Elsky, Martin Vialon and Robert Stein "Scholarship in Times of Extremes: Letters of Erich Auerbach (1933–46), on the Fiftieth Anniversary of his Death," *PMLA* 122, no. 3 (2007): 755–56.

6. Francis Bacon, "Nemesis; or, The Vicissitude of Things," in *The Essays, or Councils, Civil or Moral, of Sir Francis Bacon* (London: Sam. Smith and Benj. Walford, 1701), 62–63.

7. Dante Alighieri, *La Vita Nuova/The New Life*, trans. Dante Gabriel Rossetti (London: Ellis and Elvey, 1899), 121.

8. Paula R. Backscheider, *Daniel Defoe: His Life* (Baltimore: Johns Hopkins University Press, 1989), pp. 401–2. Backsheider's note replicates the creedal language of Protestant Trinitarian faith.

9. Ibid., 417.

10. This controversy alone occupies articles and books. For a detailed synthesis of the primary documents, see Roger Thomas, "The Non-Subscription Controversy among Dissenters in 1719: The Salters' Hall Debate," *Journal of Ecclesiastical History* 4, no. 2 (1953): 162–86.

11. Maximillian E. Novak, "Defoe, the Occult, and the Deist Offensive During the Reign of George I," In *Deism, Masonry, and Enlightenment: Essays Honoring Alfred Owen Aldridge*, ed. J. A. Leo Lemay (Newark: University of Delaware Press, 1987), 94.

12. Daniel Defoe, *Serious Reflections during the Life and Surprising Adventures of Robinson Crusoe*, 100/117.

13. Charles Gildon, *The Life and Strange Surprising Adventures of D—de F—*, of London, Hosier, 24.

14. Defoe, *Serious Reflections*, 101–2/118.

15. Daniel Defoe, *Reformation of Manners: A Satyr on Himself* (London: s.n., 1702), 12.

16. With regard to authorship of *Madagascar*, Trent, Hutchins, Moore, and Novak attribute the work to Defoe; Furbank and Owens predictably deattribute this quasi-deistical work.

17. Daniel Defoe, "The Preface," in *Madagascar; or, Robert Drury's Journal, during Fifteen Year's Captivity on That Island* (London: W. Meadows, J. Marshall, W. Worrall, 1729), v–vi.

18. Ibid., vi.

19. Daniel Defoe, *A Brief Explanation of a Late Pamphlet Entitled, The Shortest Way with the Dissenters* (London: s.n., 1703), 217.

20. Defoe, *Madagascar*, xii.

21. Ibid., xii.

22. Daniel Defoe, *The Political History of the Devil, as Well Ancient as Modern* (London: T. Warner, 1726), 105.

23. For a rare exception, see Christopher Hill, "Robinson Crusoe," *History Workshop Journal* 10, no. 1 (1980): 22: "The democratic revolution, defeated in politics, triumphed in the novel."

24. Defoe, *Serious Reflections*, 94/113–14.

25. Daniel Defoe, *A New Family Instructor, in Familiar Discourses between a Father and His Children* (London: T. Warner, 1727), 5–6.

26. Ibid., 17.

27. Rodney M. Baine, *Daniel Defoe and the Supernatural* (Athens: University of Georgia Press, 1968), 12.

28. Defoe, *Serious Reflections* (2008), 1.

29. Paul Dottin, *The Life and Strange Surprising Adventures of Daniel Defoe*, trans. Louise Ragan (New York: Macaulay, 1929), 60. Jeffrey Hopes points out that the "relationship between the essays [in *Serious Reflections*] and the narrative [of parts 1 and 2] can appear, and indeed sometimes is, tenuous; one section on the Immorality of Conversation is said by Defoe to have been written in the 1690s. The final added section, 'A Vision of the Angelick World,' bears no immediately apparent relationship to *Robinson*

Crusoe whatsoever": Jeffrey Hope, "Real and Imaginary Stories: *Robinson Crusoe* and the *Serious Reflections*," *Eighteenth-Century Fiction* 8, no. 3 (1996): 314.

30. Defoe, *Serious Reflections* (2008), 8.
31. Defoe, *Serious Reflections*, 19–20/232. Pagination begins at 1 in the original edition of "A Vision."
32. Ibid., 20/232.
33. Ibid.
34. Ibid., 22/233.
35. Ibid., 24/234.
36. Ibid., 24/235.
37. Ibid., 25/235. The next sentence begins, "But not to enter upon this whimsical Description of Lunacy."
38. Ibid., 26/236
39. Ibid., 28/237.
40. Ibid., 29/238.
41. Defoe, *The Consolidator*, 338/151.
42. Defoe, *Serious Reflections*, 45/248.
43. Ibid., 58/255.
44. Ibid.
45. Ibid., 63/259–60.
46. *Serious Reflections* (2008), 423.
47. *Serious Reflections*, 63/260.
48. Starr speculates that the young man in question may be George Duckett (1684–1732), whom Defoe mentions in a letter to Harley in 1705: Defoe, *Serious Reflections* (2008), 423, n. 140. Dottin's description of Gildon as "the secretary and historiographer of the deistical club" points to a different suspect for Defoe's frightened atheist. See above, 275n9.
49. Defoe, *Serious Reflections*, 66/261.
50. Ibid., 67/262.
51. Ibid., 71/265.
52. Ibid., 75/267.
53. Hill, "Robinson Crusoe," 8.
54. Defoe, *Serious Reflections*, 83/272.
55. *Serious Reflections* (2008), 12.
56. *Serious Reflections*, 266/217.
57. Ibid., 60/256.
58. Ibid., 6/223–24.
59. Ibid., 5/251.
60. Erich Auerbach, *Mimesis: The Representation of Reality in Western Literature*, trans. Willard R. Trask (Princeton, NJ: Princeton University Press, 2003), 202.
61. Rudolph G. Stamm, "Daniel Defoe: An Artist in the Puritan Tradition," *Philological Quarterly* 15, no. 3 (1936): 227.
62. J. A. Downie, "Imperialism, and the Travel Books Reconsider'd," *Yearbook of English Studies* 13 (1983), 74.

63. Ibid., 76.

64. Michael McKeon, *The Origins of the English Novel, 1600–1740* (Baltimore: Johns Hopkins University Press, 1987), 332–33.

65. Rebecca Bullard, "Politics, History, and the *Robinson Crusoe* Story," in *The Cambridge Companion to "Robinson Crusoe,"* ed. John Richetti (Cambridge: Cambridge University Press, 2018), 87.

66. Daniel Defoe, *The Life and Strange Surprizing Adventures of Robinson Crusoe*, 66/99.

67. David Hollingshead, "Daniel Defoe and the Abandoned Life," *Studies in the Novel* 49, no. 1 (2017): 2.

68. Laura Doyle, *Freedom's Empire: Race and the Rise of the Novel in Atlantic Modernity, 1640–1940* (Durham, NC: Duke University Press, 2008), 190.

69. Ibid., 188.

70. "Robinson Crusoe's Preface," in Defoe, *Serious Reflections*, sig. a6v-a7r/54.

71. The translation for Dumoulin's caption for plate no. 139 reads: In China, Robinson and his crew join a caravan of Muscovites and Poles to return to Europe through Great Tartary. The caravan passes by the Great Wall of China.

72. Defoe, *Farther Adventures*, 313/183.

73. Virginia Woolf, "Robinson Crusoe," in *The Second Common Reader* (New York: Harcourt Brace, 1932), chap. 4. See the opening paragraphs.

Bibliography

The bibliography lists all works cited as by or attributed to Daniel Defoe. I have noted questions about attribution in the previous chapters but have not repeated these qualifications in the bibliography.

Abernethy-Drummond, William. *A Candid Examination of That Celebrated Piece of Sophistry, Entitled, Heaven Open to All Men. In a Letter to a Gentleman in Town.* London: s.n., 1752.

Adam, Robert. *The Religious World Displayed; or, A View of the Four Grand Systems of Religion*, 3 vols. Philadelphia: Moses Thomas, 1818.

Addison, Joseph, and Richard Steele. *The Tatler*, ed. George A. Aitken, 4 vols. New York: Hadley, 1899. An electronic copy of these volumes can be found at https://catalog.hathitrust.org/Record/009032917.

Akman, Beyazit H. "The Turk's Encounter with Defoe." *Archives of Digital Defoe: Studies of Defoe and His Contemporaries.* http://english.illinoisstate.edu/digitaldefoe/encounters/akman.pdf.

Alcott, Louisa May. *Work; Eight Cousins; Rose in Bloom; Stories and Other Writings.* New York: Library of America, 2014.

Aldridge, Alfred Owen. "Polygamy and Deism." *Journal of English and Germanic Philology* 40, no. 3 (1948): 343–60.

———. "Polygamy in Early Fiction: Henry Neville and Denis Veiras." *PMLA* 65, no. 4 (1950): 464–72.

Alkon, Paul K. "Defoe's Argument in *The Shortest Way with the Dissenters*." *Modern Philology* 73, no. 4 (1976): S12–S23.

———. "The Invisible Man Returns: New Defoe Editions." *Eighteenth-Century Fiction* 14, no. 2 (2002): 199–213.

Alsop, J. D. "Defoe, Toland, and *The Shortest Way with the Dissenters*." *Review of English Studies* 43, no. 170 (1992): 245–47.

Altman, Alexander. *Moses Mendelssohn, A Biographical Study.* Philadelphia: The Jewish Publication Society, 1973.

Andreä, Johann Valentin. *Fama Fraternitatis, oder, Entdeckung der Brüderschoft des Löblichen Ordens des Rosenkreuzes.* Kassel: Wilhelm Wessell, 1614.
Aravamudan, Srinivas. "East-West Fiction as World Literature: The Hayy Problem Reconfigured." *Eighteenth-Century Studies* 47, no. 2 (2014): 195–231.
———. *Enlightenment Orientalism: Resisting the Rise of the Novel.* Chicago: University of Chicago Press, 2012.
Arscott, Alexander. *Some Considerations Relating to the Present State of the Christian Religion*, 3d ed. London: J. Phillips, 1779.
Ascham, Roger. *The Scholemaster; or, Plaine and Perfite Way of Teaching Children.* London: John Daye, 1570.
Astell, Mary. *A Fair Way with the Dissenters and Their Patrons. Not Writ by Mr. L———y, or Any Other Furious Jacobite, whether Clergyman or Layman; but by a Very Moderate Person and Dutiful Subject to the Queen.* London: R. Wilkin, 1704.
———. *A Serious Proposal to the Ladies.* London: R. Wilkin, 1697.
Atkinson, Benjamin Andrewes. *Christianity not Older than the First Gospel-Promise. In Answer to a Book, Entitled Christianity as Old as the Creation.* London: Richard Ford, 1730.
Attar, Samar. "The Vital Roots of European Enlightenment: Ibn Tufayl's Influence on Modern Western Thought." In *Robinson Crusoe: Myths and Metamorphoses*, ed. Lieve Spaas and Brian Stimpson. New York: St. Martin's Press, 1996.
———. *The Vital Roots of European Enlightenment: Ibn Tufayl's Influence on Modern Western Thought.* Lanham, MD: Lexington Books, 2007.
Atterbury, Francis. *The Voice of the People, No Voice of God; or, The Mistaken Arguments of a Fiery Zealot.* London: John Baker, 1710.
Auerbach, Erich. "Figura." In *Scenes from the Drama of European Life*, 9–76. Minneapolis: University of Minnesota Press, 1984.
———. *Mimesis: The Representation of Reality in Western Literature*, trans. Willard R. Trask. Princeton, NJ: Princeton University Press, 2003.
———. "Philology and 'Weltliteratur,'" trans. Maire and Edward Said. *Centennial Review* 13, no. 1 (1969): 1–17.
Auerbach, Erich, Martin Elsky, Martin Vialon, and Robert Stein. "Scholarship in Times of Extremes: Letters of Erich Auerbach (1933–46), on the Fiftieth Anniversary of His Death." *PMLA* 122, no. 3 (2007): 742–62.
Ayers, Robert W. "Allusive Allegorick History." *PMLA* 82, no. 5 (1967): 399–407.
Backscheider, Paula R. *Daniel Defoe: His Life.* Baltimore: Johns Hopkins University Press, 1989.
Bacon, Francis. *The Essays, or Councils, Civil and Moral, of Sir Francis Bacon, Lord Veralum.* London: Sam. Smith and Benj. Walford, 1701.
Baine, Rodney M. *Daniel Defoe and the Supernatural.* Athens, GA: University of Georgia Press, 1968.
———. "Daniel Defoe's Imaginary Voyages to the Moon." *PMLA* 81, no. 5 (1966): 377–80.
Bakhtin, Mikhail. "Satire." In Kliger, Ilya and Boris Maslov, eds. *Persistent Forms: Explorations in Historical Poetics.* New York: Fordham University Press, 2016.

Barclay, Robert. *An Apology for the True Christian Divinity, as the Same Is Held Forth and Preached by the People Called, in Scorn, Quakers*. London: s.n., 1678.
Baroud, Mahmoud. *The Shipwrecked Sailor in Arabic and Western Literature: Ibn Tufayl and His Influence on European Writers*. London: I. B. Tauris, 2012.
Benjamin, Walter. *The Origins of German Tragic Drama*, trans. John Osbourne. London: Verso, 1977.
Bergerac, Cyrano de. *The Comical History of the States and Empires of the Worlds of the Moon and Sun*, trans. A. Lovell. London: Henry Rhodes, 1687.
———. *Selenarhia; or, The Government of the World in the Moon: A Comical History*, trans. Thomas St. Serf. London: J. Cottrel, 1659.
Betts, C. J. *Early Deism in France: From the So-Called Deistes of Lyon (1564) to Voltaire's Lettres Philosophique (1734)*. Archives Internationales d'Histoire des Idees. Leiden: Martinus Nijhoff, 1984.
Blackburn, Timothy C. "Friday's Religion: Its Nature and Importance in *Robinson Crusoe*." *Eighteenth-Century Studies* 18, no. 3 (1985): 360–82.
Blewett, David. *The Illustration of Robinson Crusoe 1719–1720*. Gerrards Cross, U.K.: Colin Smythe, 1995.
Blount, Charles. *The First Two Books of Philostratus, Concerning the Life of Apollonius Tyaneus Written Originally in Greek, and Now Published in English: Together with Philological Notes upon Each Chapter*. London: Nathaniel Thompson, 1680.
———. *A Just Vindication of Learning and Liberty of the Press; or, An Humble Address to the High Court of Parliament in Behalf of the Liberty of the Press*. London: s.n., 1679.
———. *King William and Queen Mary Conquerors*. London: Richard Baldwin, 1693.
———. *Miracles, No Violation of the Laws of Nature*. London: Robert Sollers, 1683.
———. *The Miscellaneous Works of Charles Blount, Esq., to Which Is Prefixed the Life of the Author, and an Account and Vindication of His Death*, ed. Charles Gildon. London: s.n., 1695.
———. *The Oracles of Reason*. London: s.n., 1693.
———. *Reasons Humbly Offered for the Liberty of Unlicens'd Printing, to Which Is Subjoin'd the Just and True Character of Edmund Bohun, the Licenser of the Press*. London: s.n., 1693.
———. *Religio Laici, Written in a Letter to John Dryden, Esq*. London: R. Bentley and S. Magnes, 1683.
Boswell, James. *The Life of Samuel Johnson, LL.D*, 4 vols. London: A. Baldwin and Son, 1799.
Boyle, John, fifth Earl of Orrery. *Remarks on the Life and Writings of Dr. Jonathan Swift*. London: A. Millar, 1752.
Braverman, Richard. "Politics in Jewish Disguise." *Studies in Philology* 90, no. 4 (1993): 347–70.
Brenz, Johannes. *Newes from Ninive to Englande Brought by the Prophet Jonah*. London: Henrie Denham, 1570.
Breuhowse, John. *The Highland Spectator; or, Observations on the Inhabitants of Various Denominations in London and Westminster*. London: J. Robinson, 1744.

Brown, Homer O. "The Displaced Self in the Novels of Daniel Defoe." *English Literary History* 38, no. 4 (1971): 562–90.

———. *Institutions of the English Novel: From Defoe to Scott*. Philadelphia: University of Pennsylvania Press, 1997.

Browne, Joseph. *The Moon-Calf; or, Accurate Reflections on The Consolidator* (1705), ed. Maximillian E. Novak. Augustan Reprints no. 269. New York: AMS Press, 1996.

———. *State Tracts: Containing Many Necessary Observations and Reflections on the State of Our Affairs at Home and Abroad*, 2 vols. London: George Sawbridge, 1715.

Bugg, Francis. *Distinct Advice on Two Different Heads Given to the People Call'd Quakers*. London: J. Taylor and R. Wilkins, 1702.

———. *A Quaker Catechism: To Which Is Added The Shortest Way with Daniel De-Foe*. London: H. Hills, 1706.

———. *The Quaker's Infallibility Shaken All to Pieces*. London: R. Wilkin, 1711.

Bullard, Rebecca. "Politics, History, and the *Robinson Crusoe* Story." In *The Cambridge Companion to "Robinson Crusoe,"* ed. John Richetti, 84–96. Cambridge: Cambridge University Press, 2018.

Burlesa, Edward. *Grammatica Burlesa, or a New English Grammar Made Plain and Easie*. London: T.N., 1652.

Byrne, Peter. *Natural Religion and the Nature of Religion: The Legacy of Deism*. Routledge Library Editions: Philosophy of Religion, vol 5. London: Routledge, 1989.

Cadbury, Henry J. "Daniel Defoe and William Penn." *Journal of the Friends Historical Society* 14, no. 4 (1917): 172–73.

Calvin, John. *The Institution of the Christian Religion*. London: Reinolde Wolfe and Richarde Harison, 1561.

Camaioni, Michelle. "Bernardino Ochino and the German Reformation: The Augsburg Sermons and Flugschriften of an Italian Heretic (1543–1560)." In *Fruits of Migration: Heterodox Italian Migrants and Central European Culture 1550–1620*, ed. Cornel Zwierlein and Vincenzo Lavenia, 126–46. Leiden: Brill, 2018.

Capoferro, Riccardo. *Empirical Wonder: Historicizing the Fantastic, 1660–1760*. Bern, Switzerland: Peter Lang, 2010.

Carey, Daniel. "Henry Neville's *Isle of Pines:* Travel, Forgery and the Problem of Genre." *Angelaki* 1 (1996): 23–40.

Carroll, William. *Spinoza Reviv'd*. London: J. Morphew, 1709.

Champion, Justin. "*The Blasphemies of Thomas Aikenhead: Boundaries of Belief on the Eve of the Enlightenment,*" July 2009. https://reviews.history.ac.uk/review/781.

Chassanion, Jean de. *The Theatre of God's Judgments; or, A Collection of Histories out of Sacred, Ecclesiastical, and Prophane Authors*, trans. Thomas Beard. London: Adam Islip, 1597.

Checkley, John. *The Religion of Christ the Only True Religion; or, A Short and Easie Method with the Deists*, 7th ed. Boston: T. Fleet, 1719.

———. *The Speech of John Checkley upon His Tryal, at Boston in New England, for Publishing The Short and Easy Method with the Deists*. London: J. Wilford, 1730.

Chewny, Nicholas. *Anti-Socinianism; or, A Brief Explication of Some Places of Holy Scripture, for the Confutation of Certain Gross Errours, and Socinian Heresies.* London: H. Twiford and T. Dring, 1656.
Clarendon, Edward Hyde, Earl of. *The History of the Rebellion and Civil Wars in England*, 2 vols. Oxford: The Theater, 1703.
Clark, J. C. D. *English Society, 1688–1832: Ideology, Social Structure and Political Practice during the Ancien Regime.* Cambridge: Cambridge University Press, 1985.
Clark, K. R. P. "Defoe, Dissent, and Early Whig Ideology." *Historical Journal* 52, no. 3 (2009): 595–614.
Clark, Katherine. *Daniel Defoe: The Whole Frame of Nature, Time, and Providence.* Houndmills, U.K.: Palgrave Macmillan, 2007.
Coetzee, J. M. *Foe.* New York: Penguin Books, 1986.
Colvin, Christina, Janet Cooper, N. H. Cooper, P. D. A. Harvey, Marjory Hollings, Judith Hook, Mary Jessup, Mary D. Lobel, J. F. A. Mason, B. S. Trinder, and Hilary Turner. *A History of the County of Oxford: Volume 10, Banbury Hundred*, ed. Alan Crossley. London: Oxford University Press 1972. British History Online, http://www.british-history.ac.uk/vch/oxon/vol10.
Corbet, Richard. *Certain Elegant Poems.* London: R. Cotes, 1647.
Cornwall, Robert D. "Charles Leslie." In *The Oxford Dictionary of National Biography*, online ed., ed. David Cannadine. Oxford: Oxford University Press, 2004. https://doi.org/10.1093/ref:odnb/16484.
Craig, Hardin. "Dryden's Lucian." *Classical Philology* 16, no. 2 (1921): 141–63.
Crane, Jacob. "The Long Transatlantic Career of the Turkish Spy." *Atlantic Studies* 10, no. 2 (2013): 228–46.
Cressy, David. "Early Modern Space Travel and the English Man in the Moon." *American Historical Review* 111, no. 4 (2006): 961–82.
D'Israeli, Isaac. *Curiosities of Literature: Consisting of Anecdotes, Characters, Sketches, and Observations, Literary and Historical.* London: Murray and Highley, 1798.
Dante Alighieri. *The New Life (La Vita Nuova)*, trans. Dante Gabriel Rossetti. London: Ellis and Elvey, 1899.
Defoe, Daniel. *An Appeal to Honour and Justice . . . Tho It Be of His Worst Enemies . . . Being an Account of His Conduct in Publick Affairs.* London: J. Baker, 1715.
———. *The Banbury Apes; or, A Chattering to the Magpye*, 6th ed. London: R. Mawson, 1710.
———. *A Brief Explanation of a Late Pamphlet Entitled, The Shortest Way with the Dissenters.* London: s.n., 1703.
———. *A Brief History of the Poor Palatine Refugees.* London: J. Baker, 1709.
———. *A Challenge of Peace, Address'd to the Whole Nation.* London: s.n., 1703.
———. *A Collection of the Writings of the True-Born Englishman.* London: John How, 1703.
———. *The Conduct of Christians Made the Sport of Infidels in a Letter from a Turkish Merchant at Amsterdam to the Grand Mufti at Constantinople.* London: S. Baker, 1717.
———. *The Consolidator; or, Memoirs of Sundry Transactions from the World in the Moon*, 2d ed. London: B. Bragge, 1705.

———. *The Consolidator; or, Memoirs of Sundry Transactions from the World in the Moon.* In *The Stoke Newington Daniel Defoe Edition*, vol. 39, ed. Michael Seidel, Maximillian E. Novak, and Joyce D. Kennedy. New York: AMS Press, 2001.

———. *The Consolidator; or, Memoirs of Sundry Transactions from the World in the Moon.* In *Satire, Fantasy and Writings on the Supernatural*, vol. 3, ed. Geoffrey Sill, 27–158. London: Pickering and Chatto, 2003.

———. *A Continuation of Letters Written by a Turkish Spy at Paris. Giving an Impartial Account to the Divan at Constantinople of the Most Remarkable Transactions of Europe, and Discovering Several Intrigues and Secrets of the Christian Courts, Especially That of France; Continued from the Year 1687, to the Year 1693.* London: W. Taylor, 1718.

———. *A Continuation of Letters Written by a Turkish Spy at Paris.* In *Satires, Fantasy and Writings on the Supernatural*, vol. 5, ed. David Blewett, 42–240. London: Pickering and Chatto, 2005.

———. *A Defence of the People Call'd Quakers, wherein from the Fundamental Principles of the New Testament, They Are Shown to Be the True, Primitive, Apostolical Christians.* London: W. Boreham, 1720.

———. *Defoe's Review*, ed. John McVeagh. 9 vols. London: Pickering and Chatto, 2003–2011.

———. *A Dialogue between a Dissenter and the Observator.* London: s.n., 1703.

———. *The Dissenter's Answer to the High-Church Challenge.* London: s.n., 1704.

———. *The Dumb Philosopher; or, Great Britain's Wonder.* London: Tho. Bickerton, 1719.

———. *The Dyet of Poland: A Satyr.* Dantzick [London]: Ben. Bragg, 1705.

———. *An Elegy on the Author of the True-Born English-man.* London: s.n., 1704.

———. *The Experiment: Or The Shortest Way with the Dissenters Exemplified, Being the Case of Mr. Abraham Gill . . . Humbly Dedicated to the Queen.* London: B. Bragg, 1705.

———. *The Family Instructor in Three Parts.* London: E. Matthews, 1715.

———. *The Family Instructor in Three Parts*, 2d ed., 2 vols. London: E. Matthews, 1715.

———. *The Family Instructor in Two Parts.* London: E. Matthews, 1718.

———. *The Farther Adventures of Robinson Crusoe; Being the Second and Last Part of His Life, and of the Strange Surprizing Accounts of His Travels round Three Parts of the Globe.* London: W. Taylor, 1719.

———. *The Farther Adventures of Robinson Crusoe; Being the Second and Last Part of His Life, and of the Strange Surprizing Accounts of His Travels round Three Parts of the Globe* (1719). In *The Novels of Daniel Defoe*, vol. 2, ed. W. R. Owens. London: Pickering and Chatto, 2008.

———. *The Fortunate Mistress: Or, A History of the Life and Vast Variety of Fortunes of Mademoiselle de Beleau, Afterwards Call'd the Countess de Wintselsheim, in Germany, Being the Person Known by the Name of the Lady Roxana, in the Time of King Charles II.* London: T. Warner, 1724.

———. *The Fortunes and Misfortunes of the Famous Moll Flanders* (1721). In *The Novels of Daniel Defoe*, vol. 6, ed. Liz Bellamy. London: Pickering and Chatto, 2009.

———. *The Fortunes and Misfortunes of the Famous Moll Flanders*, 2d ed. London: John Bretherton, 1722.

———. *A Friendly Epistle by Way of Reproof from One of the People Called Quakers to Thomas Bradbury, a Dealer in Many Words*, 6th ed. London: S. Keimer, 1715.

———. *The Genuine Works of Mr. Daniel Defoe*, 2 vols. London: s.n., 1721.

———. *The History of the Life and Adventures of Mr. Duncan Campbell*, 2d corrected ed. London: E. Curll, 1720.

———. *The Honesty and Sincerity of Those Worthy Gentlemen Commonly Called High-Church Men: Exemplified in a Modern Instance*. London: Benj. Bragg, 1707,

———. *A Hymn to the Pillory*, 2d ed. London: s.n., 1703.

———. *L'espion turc dans les cours des princes chrétiens*, vol. 7, 15th ed. London: Aux Dépens de la Companie, 1742. [French translation of *A Continuation of Letters Written by a Turkish Spy at Paris*]

———. *The Letters of Daniel Defoe*, ed. George Harris Healey. Oxford: Clarendon Press, 1955.

———. *The Life and Strange Surprizing Adventures of Robinson Crusoe, of York, Mariner: Who Lived Eight and Twenty Years, All Alone in an Uninhabited Island on the Coast of America, near the Mouth of the Great River Oroonoque; Having been Cast on Shore by Shipwreck, wherein All the Men Perished but Himself*, 2d ed. London: W. Taylor, 1719.

———. *The Life and Strange Surprizing Adventures of Robinson Crusoe, of York, Mariner*. In *The Novels of Daniel Defoe*, vol. 1, ed. W. R. Owens. London: Pickering and Chatto, 2008.

———. *Madagascar; or, Robert Drury's Journal, during Fifteen Year's Captivity on That Island*. London: W. Meadows, J. Marshall, W. Worrall, 1729.

———. *Minutes of the Negotiations of Monsr. Mesnager at the Court of England*. London: S. Baker, 1711.

———. *More Reformation: A Satyr upon Himself*. London: s.n., 1703.

———. *The New Family Instructor, in Familiar Discourses between a Father and His Children*. London: T. Warner, 1727.

———. *The Political History of the Devil, as Well Ancient as Modern*. London: T. Warner, 1726.

———. *The Present State of the Parties in Great Britain*. London: J. Baker, 1712.

———. *The Protestant Jesuite Unmask'd in Answer to the Two Parts of Cassandra . . . with My Service to Mr. Lesley*. London: s.n., 1704.

———. *The Purjur'd Free Mason Detected*. London: J. Warner, 1730.

———. *The Quaker's Sermon; or, A Holding-Forth against Barabbas*. London: s.n., 1711.

———. *Reformation of Manners: A Satyr on Himself*. London: s.n., 1702.

———. *Religious Courtship*. London: E. Matthews, 1722.

———. *The Scots Nation and Union Vindicated from the Reflections Cast on Them, in an Infamous Libel, Entitled, The Public Spirit of the Whigs*. London: A. Bell and J. Baker, 1714.

———. *The Secret History of the Secret History of the White Staff*. London: S. Keimer, 1715.

———. *The Secret History of the White Staff*. Dublin: S. Grierson, 1714.

———. *Serious Reflections during the Life and Surprising Adventures of Robinson Crusoe, with His Vision of the Angelick World. Written by Himself*. London: W. Taylor, 1720.

———. *Serious Reflections during the Life and Surprising Adventures of Robinson Crusoe, with his Vision of the Angelick World*. In *The Novels of Daniel Defoe*, vol. 3, ed. G. A. Starr. London: Pickering and Chatto, 2008.

———. *A Sharp Rebuke from one of the People Called Quakers to Henry Sacheverell, the High-Priest of Andrew's Holbourn*. London: S. Keimer, 1715.

———. *The Shortest Way with the Dissenters; or, Proposals for the Establishment of the Church*. London: s.n. 1702.

———. *The Sincerity of the Dissenters Vindicated, from the Scandal of Occasional Conformity*. London: s.n., 1703.

———. *A Tour through the Whole Island of Great Britain*, 4 vols. London: J. and F. Rivington, 1769.

———. *The True-Born Englishman: A Satyr*. London: s.n., 1701.

D'foe's Answer to the Quakers Catechism; or, A Dark Lanthorn for a Friend of the Light. London: s.n., 1706.

DeJean, Joan E. "Method and Madness in Cyrano de Bergerac's *Voyage dans la Lune*." *French Forum* 2, no. 3 (1977): 224–37.

Delehanty, Ann T., and Tyler Blakeney. "Textual Engagement with the Other in Cyrano de Bergerac's *L'Autre Monde*." *French Studies* 68, no. 3 (2014): 313–27.

DeLuna, D. N. "Ironic Monologue and 'Scandalous Ambo-dexter Conformity' in Defoe's *The Shortest Way with the Dissenters*." In *British Literature, 1640–1789: A Critical Reader*, ed. Robert DeMaria Jr., 126–41. Malden, MA: Blackwell, 1999.

Denmark Vindicated: Being an Answer to a Late Treatise Called An Account of Denmark, As It Was in the Year 1692. London: Tho. Newborough and Ed. Mory, 1694.

Dobrée, Bonamy. "Some Aspects of Defoe's Prose." In *Pope and His Contemporaries: Essays Presented to George Sherburn*, ed. James L. Clifford and Louis A. Landa, 171–84. Oxford: Oxford University Press, 1949.

Dottin, Paul. *The Life and Strange Surprising Adventures of Daniel Defoe*, trans. Louise Ragan. New York: Macaulay, 1929.

———. "The Life of Charles Gildon." In *Robinson Crusoe Examin'd and Criticis'd: A New Edition of Charles Gildon's Famous Pamphlet*, ed. Paul Dottin, 5–46. London: J. M. Dent and Sons, 1923.

Downie, J. A. "Imperialism, and the Travel Books Reconsider'd." *Yearbook of English Studies* 13 (1983): 66–83.

———. "John Tutchin." In *The Oxford Dictionary of National Biography*, ed. David Cannadine. Oxford: Oxford University Press, 2004. https://doi.org/10.1093/ref:odnb/27899.

———. "Mr. Review and His Scribbling Friends: Defoe and the Critics, 1705–1706." *Huntington Library Quarterly* 41, no. 4 (1978): 345–66.

Doyle, Laura. *Freedom's Empire: Race and the Rise of the Novel in Atlantic Modernity, 1640–1940*. Durham, NC: Duke University Press, 2008.

Drayton, Michael. *The Battaile of Agincourt Fought by Henry the Fifth, King of Scotland*. London: William Lee, 1631.

Dryden, John, ed. *The Works of Lucian, Translated from the Greek, by Several Eminent Hands*, 4 vols. London: Sam. Briscoe, 1710–11.

Dumoulin, François Aimé Louis (Dessinées et Gravées). *Collection de cent-cinquante gravures représentant et formant une suite non interrompue des voyages et aventures surprenantes de Robinson Crusoé.* Vevey, Switzerland: Loertscher et Fils, 1810; rprt. Paris: Club Français du Livres, 1962. http://www.gutenberg.org/files/24915/24915-h/24915-h.htm.

———. *Collection de cent-cinquante gravures représentant et formant une suite non interrompue des voyages et aventures surprenantes de Robinson Crusoé.* Paris: Club Français du Livre, 1962.

Dunn, Richard S., and Mary Maples Dunn, eds. *The Papers of William Penn, Volume 4: 1701–1718.* Philadelphia: University of Pennsylvania Press, 1987.

Edwards, John. *A Brief Vindication of the Fundamental Articles of the Christian Faith.* London: J. Robinson and J. Wyat, 1697.

———. *The Socinian Creed; or, A Brief Account of the Professed Tenents [sic] and Doctrines of the Foreign and English Socinians.* London: J. Robinson, 1697.

Ellison, Katherine. "Mediation and Intelligence in Defoe's *Vision of the Angelick World.*" In *Topographies of the Imagination: New Approaches to Daniel Defoe,* ed. Katherine Ellison, Kit Kinkade, and Holly Faith Nelson, 93–116. New York: AMS Press, 2014.

Erasmus, Desiderius. *Twenty-two Select Colloquies Out of Erasmus Roterodamus.* London: Daniel Brown et al., 1711.

Fernsemer, O. F. W. "Daniel Defoe and the Palatine Emigration of 1709: A New View of the Origin of Robinson Crusoe." *Journal of English and Germanic Philology* 19, no. 1 (1920): 94–124.

Flavel, John. *The Fountain of Life Opened; or, A Display of Christ in His Essential and Mediatorial Glory.* London: Rob. White, 1693.

———. *Navigation Spiritualized, or a New Compass for Sea-Men,* London: Thomas Fabian, 1677.

Folkenflik, Robert. "Robinson Crusoe and the Semiotic Crisis of the Eighteenth Century." In *Defoe's Footprints: Essays in Honour of Maximillian E. Novak,* ed. Robert M. Maniquis and Carl Fisher, 98–125. Toronto: University of Toronto Press, 2009.

The Fox with His Fire-Brand Unkenell'd and Insnar'd; or, A Short Answer to Mr. Daniel Foe's Shortest Way with the Dissenters. London: s.n., 1703.

Franklin, Benjamin. "Letter to Ezra Stiles, March 9, 1790." In *Benjamin Franklin, Writings,* vol. 37, 1179. New York: Library of America, 1987.

Free, Melissa. "Un-Erasing 'Crusoe': 'Farther Adventures' in the Nineteenth Century." *Book History* 9 (2006): 89–130.

Frye, Northrop. *Anatomy of Criticism: Four Essays.* Princeton, NJ: Princeton University Press, 1957.

Furbank, P. N., "Defoe's *Minutes of Mesnager:* The Art of Mendacity." *Eighteenth-Century Fiction* 16, no. 1 (2003): 1-12.

Furbank, P. N., and W. R. Owens. *The Canonization of Daniel Defoe.* New Haven, CT: Yale University Press, 1988.

———. *A Critical Bibliography of Daniel Defoe.* London: Pickering and Chatto, 1998.

———. *Defoe De-attributions: A Critique of J. R. Moore's Checklist.* London: Hambledon Press, 1994.

———. *A Political Biography of Daniel Defoe.* London: Pickering and Chatto, 2006.

Gascoigne, John. "Pacific Exploration as Religious Critique." *Parergon* 27, no. 1 (2010): 143–62.
Georgiadou, A., and D. H. J. Larmour. "Lucian's 'Verae Historiae' as Philosophical Parody." *Hermes* 126, no. 3 (1998): 310–25.
Giglioni, Guido. "Girolamo [Geronimo] Cardano." In *Stanford Encyclopedia of Philosophy.* https://plato.stanford.edu/entries/cardano.
Gildon, Charles. *The Deist's Manual; or, A Rational Enquiry into the Christian Religion.* London: A. Roper, Fran Coggan, and Geo. Strahan, 1705.
———. *The Life and Strange Surprizing Adventures of Mr. D——de F——, of London, Hosier, Who Has Liv'd above Fifty years by Himself, in the Kingdoms of North and South Britain. The Various Shapes He Has Appear'd in, and the Discoveries He Has Made for the Benefit of His Country.* London: J. Roberts, 1719.
———. *The Post-boy Robb'd of His Mail; or, The Pacquet Broke Open.* London: A. Bettesworth and R. Rivington, 1719.
———. *Robinson Crusoe Examin'd and Criticis'd: A New Edition of Charles Gildon's Famous Pamphlet,* ed. Paul Dottin, London: J. M. Dent and Sons, 1923.
Girdler, Lew. "Defoe's Education at Newington Green Academy." *Studies in Philology* 50, no. 4 (1953): 573–91.
Godwin, Francis. *The Man in the Moone; or, A Discourse of a Voyage Thither by Domingo Gonsales, the Speedy Messenger.* London: John Norton, 1638.
Goldie, Mark. "Charles Blount's Intentions in Writing *King William and Queen Mary Conquerors.*" *Notes and Queries* 223 (1978): 527–32.
Graham, Michael F. *The Blasphemies of Thomas Aikenhead: Boundaries of Belief on the Eve of the Enlightenment.* Edinburgh: Edinburgh University Press, 2008.
Greif, Martin J. "The Conversion of Robinson Crusoe." *Studies in English Literature, 1500–1900* 6, no. 3 (1966): 551–74.
Guion, Béatrice. "L'espion du Grand-Seigneur; ou, L'invention du roman épistolaire oriental." *Littératures Classiques,* no. 71 (2010–11): 187–202.
Gulliver Decypher'd; or, Remarks on a Late Book, Intitled Travels into Several Remote Nations of the World. London: J. Roberts, 1727.
Gwyn, Douglas. "John Saltmarsh, Quaker Forerunner." Presidential address given during the Britain Yearly Meeting of the Society of Friends, London, May 4, 2003. journals.sas.ac.uk/fhs/article/download/3410/3362
Hallam, Henry. "Literary History of the Turkish Spy." *Gentlemen's Magazine,* series 2, vol. 15, March 1841, 149. https://babel.hathitrust.org/cgi/pt?id=pst.000068790561;view=1up;seq=165;size=125.
Harrison, Peter. *"Religion" and the Religions in the English Enlightenment.* Cambridge: Cambridge University Press, 2010.
Harvey, Richard. *A Theological Discourse of the Lamb of God.* London: John Windet, 1590.
Hazlitt, William. *The Works of Daniel De Foe, with a Memoir of His Life and Writings.* London: John Clements, 1811.
Herbert of Cherbury, Edward Herbert, Baron. *De Veritate,* trans. Meyrich H. Carré. Bristol, UK: J.W. Arrowsmith, Ltd., 1937.

———. *De veritate prout distinguitur a revelation, a verisimili, a possibili, et a falso,* 2d ed. London: s.n., 1633.

Herrick, James A. *The Radical Rhetoric of the English Deists: The Discourse of Skepticism, 1680–1750.* Columbia: University of South Carolina Press, 1997.

Hickes, Francis. *Certain Select Dialogues of Lucian Together with His True History, Translated from the Greek into English . . . Whereunto Is Added The Life of Lucian, Gathered out of His Own Writings.* London: Richard Davis, 1663.

Hill, Christopher. *God's Englishman: Oliver Cromwell and the English Revolution.* New York: Harper Torchbooks, 1970.

———. "Robinson Crusoe." *History Workshop Journal* 10, no. 1 (1980): 6–24.

Himmelfarb, Gertrude. *The People of the Book: Philosemitism in England from Cromwell to Churchill.* New York: Encounter Books, 2011.

The History of King-Killers; or, The Fanatick Martyrology. London: S. Redmayne and T. Jauncy, 1720.

Hollingshead, David. "Daniel Defoe and the Abandoned Life." *Studies in the Novel* 49, no. 1 (2017): 1–23.

Holmes, Geoffrey. *The Trial of Doctor Sacheverell.* London: Eyre Methuen, 1973.

Hone, Joseph. *Literature and Party Politics at the Accession of Queen Anne.* Oxford: Oxford University Press, 2017.

Hopes, Jeffrey. "Real and Imaginary Stories: *Robinson Crusoe* and the *Serious Reflections.*" *Eighteenth-Century Fiction* 8, no. 3 (1996): 313–28.

Horsley, Lee Sonstang. "Contemporary Reactions to Defoe's *Shortest Way with Dissenters.*" *Studies in English Literature, 1500–1900* 16, no. 3 (1976): 407–20.

———. "'Of All Fictions the Most Simple': Swift's Shared Imagery." *Yearbook of English Studies* 5 (1975): 98–108.

Howell, James. *Epistolae Ho-Elianae: Familiar Letters, Domestic and Foreign,* 7th ed. London: Thomas Guy, 1705.

Howes, Raymond F. "*Robinson Crusoe:* A Literary Accident." *English Journal* 16, no. 1 (1927): 31–35.

Hudson, Nicholas. "'Why God No Kill the Devil?' The Diabolical Disruption of Order in *Robinson Crusoe.*" *The Review of English Studies* 34, no. 156 (1988): 494–501.

Hudson, Wayne, Diego Lucci, and Jeffrey R. Wigelsworth, eds. *Atheism and Deism Revalued: Heterodox Religious Identities in Britain, 1650–1800.* Burlington, VT: Ashgate, 2014.

———. *The English Deists.* London: Pickering and Chatto, 2009.

Hume, David. *Essays, Moral and Political.* Edinburgh: A. Kincaid, 1742.

Hunter, J. Paul. "Genre, Nature, *Robinson Crusoe.*" In *The Cambridge Companion to "Robinson Crusoe,"* ed. John Richetti, 3–15. Cambridge: Cambridge University Press, 2018.

———. *The Reluctant Pilgrim: Defoe's Emblematic Method and Quest for Form in Robinson Crusoe.* Baltimore MD: The Johns Hopkins Press, 1966.

Hunter, Michael. "'Aikenhead the Atheist': The Context and Consequences of Articulate Irreligion in the Late Seventeenth Century." In *Atheism from the Reformation to the Enlightenment,* ed. Michael Hunter and David Wootton, 221–54. Oxford: Oxford University Press, 1992.

Ibn Tufayl. *An Account of the Oriental Philosophy . . . Showing . . . the Profound Wisdom of Hai Ebn Yokdan, both in Natural and Divine Things,* trans. George Keith. London: s.n., 1674.

———. *The History of Hai Eb'n Yockdan, an Indian Prince: or The Self-Taught Philosopher . . . Set Forth not Long Ago in the Original Arabick, with the Latin Version, by Edward Pococke 1671. And now Translated into English.* London: Richard Chiswell, 1686.

———. *Ibn Tufayl's Hayy Ibn Yaqzān: A Philosophical Tale,* ed. and trans. Lenn E. Goodman. Chicago: University of Chicago Press, 2003.

———. *The Improvement of Human Reason, Exhibited in the Hai Ebn Yokdhan: Written in Arabick above 500 Years Ago, by Abu Jaafar Ebn Tophail,* trans. Simon Ockley. London: Edm. Powell and J. Morphew, 1708.

———. *Philosophus autodidactus sive epistola Abi Jaafar, Ebn Tophail de Hai Ebn Yokdhan,* trans. Edward Pococke. Oxford: Joannes Owens, 1700.

Jacob, Joseph. *The Fewness of the Faithful; or, A Discourse Shewing the Paucity of True Believers.* London: A. Baldwin and S. Drury, 1703.

Jacob, Margaret C. *Living the Enlightenment: Freemasonry and Politics in Eighteenth-Century Europe.* New York: Oxford University Press, 1991.

———. *Strangers Nowhere in the World: The Rise of Cosmopolitanism in Early Modern Europe.* Philadelphia: University of Pennsylvania Press, 2006.

James, Hugh. *An Answer to a Late Pamphlet, Entitled, The Experiment; or, The Shortest Way with Dissenters Exemplified.* London: J. Morphew, 1707.

Johnson, Daniel J. "*Robinson Crusoe* and the Apparitional Eighteenth-Century Novel." *Eighteenth-Century Fiction* 28, no. 2 (2015–16): 239–61.

Jones, Gavin. *Failure and the American Writer: A Literary History.* New York: Cambridge University Press, 2014.

Karp, Jonathan, and Adam Sutcliffe. *Philosemitism in History.* Cambridge: Cambridge University Press, 2011.

Keach, Benjamin. *Gospel Mysteries Unveil'd,* vol. 1. London: R. Tookey, 1701.

King, Ami Hicken. "Daniel Defoe and the Quakers: A Study in Captain Singleton and Roxana." Ph.D. diss., Arizona State University, Tempe, 1998.

Kirby, Ethyn Williams. "The Quakers' Efforts to Secure Civil and Religious Liberty: 1660–96." *Journal of Modern History* 7, no. 4 (1935): 401–21.

Kliger, Ilya, and Boris Maslov, eds. *Persistent Forms: Explorations in Historical Poetics.* New York: Fordham University Press, 2016.

Korshin, Paul. *Typologies in England: 1650–1820.* Princeton, NJ: Princeton University Press, 1982.

Landman, Isaac, ed. *The Universal Jewish Encyclopedia,* 10 vols. New York: Universal Jewish Encyclopedia, 1948.

Landreth, Sara. "Defoe on Spiritual Communication, Action at a Distance, and the Mind in Motion." In *Mind, Body, Motion, Matter: Eighteenth-Century British and French Literary Perspectives,* ed. Mary Helen McMurran and Alison Conway, 139–69. Toronto: University of Toronto Press, 2016.

Law, William. *An Appeal to All That Doubt, or Disbelieve the Truth of the Gospel, Whether They Be Deists, Arians, Socinians, or Nominal Christians*, 3d ed. London: Robinson and Roberts, 1768.
Lemay, J. A. Leo, ed. *Deism, Masonry, and the Enlightenment: Essays Honoring Alfred Owen Aldridge*. Newark: University of Delaware Press, 1987.
Leranbaum, Miriam. "'An Irony not Unusual': Defoe's 'Shortest Way with the Dissenters." *Huntington Library Quarterly* 37. no. 3 (1974): 227-50.
Leslie, Charles. *The Best Answer Ever Was Made, and to Which No Answer Will Ever Be Made*. London: John Morphew, 1709.
———. *The Case of the Church of England's Memorial Fairly Stated*. London: s.n., 1705.
———. *The Case of the Jews Considered with Respect to Christianity*. London: s.n., 1755.
———. *The Charge of Socinianism against Dr. Tillotson Considered . . . Wherein Likewise Charles Blount's Great Is Diana Is Considered*. Edenburgh [*sic*]: s.n., 1695.
———. *Deism Refuted; or, The Truth of Christianity Demonstrated*. London: s.n., 1755.
———. *An Essay Concerning the Divine Right of Tythes*. London: Charles Brome, 1700.
———. *The Finishing Stroke, Being a Vindication of the Patriarchal Scheme of Government*. London: s.n., 1711.
———. *Five Discourses by the Author of The Snake in the Grass*. London: Charles Brome, 1700.
———. *The New Association of Those Called, Moderate-Church-Men*. London: s.n., 1702.
———. *Now or Never; or, A Project under God, to Secure the Church and Monarchy of England*. London: J. Baker, 1710.
———. *Primitive Heresie Revived in the Faith and Practice of the People Called Quakers . . . to Which Is Added a Friendly Expostulation with William Penn . . . by the Author of The Snake in the Grass*. London: Charles Brome, 1698.
———. *A Reply to a Book Entitul'd Anguis Flagellatus; or, A Switch for the Snake*. London: Charles Brome, 1702.
———. *Salt for the Leach. In Reflections upon Reflection*. London: Charles Brome, 1712.
———. *Satan Dis-rob'd from His Disguise of Light; or, The Quakers Last Shift to Cover Their Monstrous Heresies . . . by the Author of The Snake in the Grass*. London: C. Brome, W. Keblewhite, H. Hindmarsh, 1697.
———. *The Second Part of The Wolf Stript of his Shepherds Cloathing*. London: s.n., 1707.
———. *A Short and Easie Method with the Deists*. 2d ed. London and Edinburgh: John Reid, 1698.
———. *A Short and Easie Method with the Deists*, 2d ed. London: C. Brome, W. Keblewhite, H. Hindmarsh, E. Poole, 1699.
———. *A Short and Easie Method with the Deists*, 3d ed. London: C. Brome, W. Keblewhite, H. Hindmarsh, E. Poole, Geo. Strahan, 1701.
———. *A Short and Easie Method with the Deists*. Boston: J. Applebee, 1723.
———. *A Short and Easie Method with the Deists . . . to Which Is Added a Second Part to the Jews*, 2d ed. London: C. Brome, W. Koblewhite, H. Hindmarsh, E. Poole, 1699.

———. *A Short and Easie Method with the Jews*, 3d ed. London: Geo. Strahan, 1715.

———. *The Snake in the Grass; or, Satan Transformed into an Angel of Light*. London: Charles Brome, 1696.

———. *The Theological Works of the Reverend Mr. Charles Leslie*, 2 vols. London: W. Bowyer, 1721.

———. *The Truth of Christianity Demonstrated*. London: B. Bragg, E. Pool, G. Strahan, 1711.

———. *A View of the Times, Their Principles and Practices*, 4 vols. London: s.n., 1708–1709.

———. *The Wolf Stript of His Shepherd's Cloathing*. London: s.n., 1704.

Leslie, Robert Joshua. *The Life and Writings of Charles Leslie, M.A.: Nonjuring Divine*. London: Rivingtons, 1885.

Locke, John. *An Essay Concerning Human Understanding, in Four Books*, 2 vols., 7th ed. London: J. Churchill and S. Manship, 1715–16.

Love, Harold. "Sir Roger L'Estrange, 1616–1704." In *The Oxford Dictionary of National Biography*. https://doi.org/10.1093/ref:odnb/16514.

Lucci, Diego. "Judaism and Natural Religion in the Philosophy of William Wollaston." *Journal for Eighteenth-Century Studies* 30 no. 2 (2007): 363–87.

———. "Judaism and the Jews in the British Deists' Attacks on Revealed Religion." *Hebraic Political Studies* 3 (2008): 177–214.

Lucian of Samosata. *Certain Select Dialogues of Lucian Together with His True History*, trans. Francis Hickes. London: Richard Davis, 1663.

———. *Lucian's Works Translated from the Greek, to Which Is Prefixt, The Life of Lucian*, trans. Ferrand Spence. London: Henry Clark, 1684.

Lund, Roger D. "Guilt by Association: The Atheist Cabal and the Rise of the Public Sphere in Augustan England." *Albion* 34, no. 3 (2002): 391–421.

———. "Strange Complicities: Atheism and Conspiracy in *A Tale of a Tub*." In *British Literature, 1640–1789: A Critical Reader*, ed. Robert DeMaria Jr., 142–68. Malden, MA: Blackwell, 1999.

Macaulay, Thomas Babington. *The History of England*, 5 vols. London: Longman, Brown, Green, and Longmans, 1855–63.

MacPhail, Eric. "Cyrano's Machines: The Marvelous and the Mundane in L'Autre Monde." *French Forum* 18, no. 1 (1993): 37–46.

Mahlberg, Gaby M. "Authors Losing Control: The European Transformations of Henry Neville's *The Isle of Pines* (1668)." *Book History* 15 (2012): 1–25.

Maniquis, Robert M., and Carl Fisher, eds. *Defoe's Footprints: Essays in Honour of Maximillian E. Novak*. Toronto: University of Toronto Press, 2009.

Manning, David. "Accusations of Blasphemy in English Anti-Quaker Polemic, 1660–1701." *Quaker Studies* 14, no. 1 (2009): 27–56. https://online.liverpooluniversitypress.co.uk/doi/pdf/10.3828/quaker.14.1.27.

Marana, Giovanni Paulo (attrib.). *The Eighth and Last Volume of Letters Writ by a Turkish Spy*. London: J. Hindmarsh and Richard Sare, 1694.

———. *The Eight Volumes of Letters Writ by a Turkish Spy*. London: Joseph Hindmarsh and Richard Sare, 1694.

———. *Letters Writ by a Turkish Spy (Selections)*, ed. Arthur J. Weitzman. London: Routledge and Kegan Paul, 1970.

———. *Letters Writ by a Turkish Spy, Who Lived Five and Forty Years Undiscovered at Paris: Giving an Impartial Account to the Divan at Constantinople, of the Most Remarkable Transactions of Europe; and Discovering Several Intrigues and Secrets of the Christian Courts, (Especially of France) from the Year 1637, to the Year 1682*. London: J. Leake, 1687.

———. *The Second Volume of Letters Writ by a Turkish Spy*. London: J. Leake, 1691.

Marshall, Ashley. "Beyond Furbank and Owens: A New Consideration of the Evidence for the 'Defoe' Canon." *Studies in Bibliography* 59 (2015): 131–90.

———. "Fabricating Defoes: From Anonymous Hack to Master of Fictions." *Eighteenth-Century Life* 36, no. 2 (2012): 1–35.

———. *The Practice of Satire in England, 1658–1770*. Baltimore: Johns Hopkins University Press, 2013.

Marshall, David. "Autobiographical Acts in *Robinson Crusoe*." *English Literary History* 71, no. 4 (2004): 899–920.

Mason, William. *Arts Advancement, or the Most Exact, Lineal, Swift, Short, and Easie Method of Short-Hand-Writing Hitherto Extant*. London: William Mason, 1682.

Mather, Increase. *The Voice of God, in Stormy Winds. Considered in Two Sermons, Occasioned by the Dreadful and Unparallel'd Storm in the European Nations, November 27, 1703*. Boston: Benjamin Eliot, 1704.

Maxfield, Ezra Kempton. "Daniel Defoe and the Quakers." *PMLA* 47, no. 1 (1932): 179–90.

McBurney, William H. "The Authorship of the Turkish Spy." *PMLA* 72, no. 5 (1957): 915–35.

McKendry, Andrew. "'No Parallels from Hebrew Times': Troubled Typologies and the Glorious Revolution in Daniel Defoe's Williamite Poetry." *Eighteenth-Century Studies* 50, no. 1 (2016): 81–99.

McKeon, Michael. *The Origins of the English Novel, 1600–1740*. Baltimore: Johns Hopkins University Press, 1987.

Memoirs for the Curious; or, An Account of What Occurs That's Rare, Secret, Extraordinary, Prodigious or Miraculous, through the World; whether in Nature, Art, or Learning. London: R. Janeway, 1701.

Merrett, Robert James. *Daniel Defoe: Contrarian*. Toronto: University of Toronto Press, 2013.

Miller, John. "'A Suffering People': English Quakers and Their Neighbors c.1650–c.1700." *Past and Present* 188, no. 1 (2005): 71–103.

Minto, William. *Daniel Defoe*. London: Macmillan, 1879.

Montaigne, Michel de. *Essays of Michael Seigneur de Montaigne*, trans. Charles Cotton, 3 vols., 4th ed. London: J. Nicholson, R. Wellington, B. Tooke [and seven others], 1711.

Montesquieu, Charles de Secondat, Baron de. *Persian Letters*, trans. Mr. Ozell. London: J. Tonson, 1722.

———. *Persian Letters*, trans. Flloyd, 2 vols., 4th ed. London: J. and R. Tonson, 1762.

Montgomery, Scott L. *The Moon and the Western Imagination*. Tucson: University of Arizona Press, 1999.

Moore, John Robert. *A Checklist of the Writings of Daniel Defoe*, 2d ed. Hamden, CT: Archon Press, 1971.
———. *Defoe in the Pillory and Other Studies*. New York: Octagon Books, 1973.
———. "Defoe's Persona as Author: The Quaker Sermon." *Studies in English Literature, 1500–1900* 11, no. 3 (1971): 507–16.
———. "Defoe's Religious Sect." *Review of English Studies* 17 no. 68 (1941): 461–67.
———. "A New Source for *Gulliver's Travels.*" *Studies in Philology* 38, no. 1 (1941): 66–80.
Morgan, Matthew. *Eugenia; or, An Elegy upon the Death of the Honourable Madam.* Oxford: Leonard Lichfield, 1694.
Mullett, Charles F. "The Legal Position of English Protestant Dissenters, 1660–1689." *Virginia Law Review* 22, no. 5 (1936): 495–526.
———. "The Legal Position of English Protestant Dissenters, 1689–1767." *Virginia Law Review* 23, no. 4 (1937): 389–418.
Neville, Henry. *The Isle of Pines; or, A Late Discovery of a Fourth Island of Terra Australis Incognita*. London: Allen Banks and Charles Harper, 1668.
Newton, Theodore F. M. "William Pittis and Queen Anne Journalism." *Modern Philology* 33, no. 2 (1935): 169–86, 33, no. 2 (1935): 279–302.
Nicolson, Marjorie Hope. "Cosmic Voyages." *English Literary History* 7, no. 2 (1940): 83–107.
———. *Voyages to the Moon*. New York: Macmillan, 1948.
Novak, Maximillian E. "Crusoe's Original Sin." *Studies in English Literature, 1500–1900* 1, no. 3 (1961): 19–29.
———. *Daniel Defoe, Master of Fictions*. Oxford: Oxford University Press, 2001.
———. "Defoe, the Occult, and the Deist Offensive during the Reign of George I." In *Deism, Masonry, and Enlightenment: Essays Honoring Alfred Owen Aldridge*, ed. J. A. Leo Lemay, 93–108. Newark: University of Delaware Press, 1987.
———. "Defoe's *Shortest Way with the Dissenters:* Hoax, Parody, Paradox, Fiction, Irony, and Satire." *Modern Language Quarterly* 27 (1966): 402–17.
———. "Defoe's Theory of Fiction." *Studies in Philology* 61, no. 4 (1964): 650–68.
———. "Defoe's Uses of Irony." In *The Uses of Irony: Papers on Defoe and Swift Read at a Clark Library Seminar, April 2, 1966*, ed. Maximillian E. Novak and Herbert John Davis, 7–38. Los Angeles: William Andrews Clark Memorial Library, 1966.
———. *Realism, Myth, and History in Defoe's Fiction*. Lincoln: University of Nebraska Press, 1983.
———. "*Robinson Crusoe* and Defoe's Career as a Writer." In *The Cambridge Companion to "Robinson Crusoe,"* ed. John Richetti, 32–48. Cambridge: Cambridge University Press, 2018.
———. "Robinson Crusoe's Fear and the Search for Natural Man." *Modern Philology* 58, no. 4 (1961): 238–45.
———. "'The Sum of Human Misery'? Defoe's Ambiguity towards Exile." *Studies in English Literature, 1500–1900* 50, no. 3 (2010): 601–23.
———. *Transformations, Ideology, and the Real in* Robinson Crusoe *and Other Narratives*. Newark: University of Delaware Press, 2015.

Nuttall, Geoffrey. *The Holy Spirit in Puritan Faith and Experience.* Oxford: Blackwell, 1946.
Orr, Leah. "Providence and Religion in the Crusoe Trilogy." *Eighteenth-Century Life* 38 (2014): 1–27.
Owens, W. R., and P. N. Furbank, eds. *The Works of Daniel Defoe,* 63 vols. London: Pickering and Chatto, 2000–2009.
Parrett, Aaron. *The Translunar Narrative in the Western Tradition.* Aldershot, U.K.: Ashgate, 2004.
Pastor, A. C. R. *The Idea of Robinson Crusoe.* Watford, UK: Góngora Press, 1930.
Pearl, Jason H. *Utopian Geographies and the Early English Novel.* Charlottesville: University of Virginia Press, 2014.
Penn, William. *The Papers of William Penn, Volume 4: 1701–1718,* ed. Craig W. Horle, Allison Duncan Hirsch, Marianne S. Wokeck, and Joy Wittenburg. Philadelphia: University of Pennsylvania Press, 1987.
———. *The Sandy Foundation Shaken.* London: s.n., 1668.
Pfanner, Dario. "Charles Blount (1654–1693)." In *The Oxford Dictionary of National Biography,* ed. David Cannadine. Oxford: Oxford University Press, 2004. https://doi-org.10.1093/ref:odnb/2684.
Philalethes, Eugenius (pseud.). *The Fame and Confession of the Fraternity of R.C., Commonly, of the Rosie Cross,* trans. Thomas Vaughn. London: John Macock, 1652.
Pittis, William. *The Dyet of Poland: A Satyr Considered Paragraph for Paragraph.* London: Benjamin Bragg, 1705.
———. *The True-Born Hugonot; or, Daniel de Foe, a Satyr.* London: s.n., 1703.
Pocock, Edward, trans. *Philosophus autodidactus sive epistola Abi Jaafar, Ebn Tophail de Hai Ebn Yokdhan.* Oxford: Joannes Owens, 1700.
Poliakov, Léon. *The History of Anti-Semitism,* vol. 3. Philadelphia: University of Pennsylvania Press, 2003.
Pope, Alexander. *The Correspondence of Alexander Pope,* 5 vols., ed. George Sherburn. Oxford: Clarendon Press, 1956. https://catalog.hathitrust.org/Record/001022663.
———. *The Dunciad Variorum with the Prolegomena of Scriblerus.* London: John Wright for A. Dod, 1729.
Porada, Aleksandra. "Giovanni Paulo Marana's Turkish Spy and the Police of Louis XIV: The Fear of Being Secretly Observed by Trained Agents in Early Modern Europe." *Altre Modernità/Otras Modernité/Other Modernities,* no. 11 (2014). https://riviste.unimi.it/index.php/AMonline/article/view/4046/4142.
Prince, Michael B. *Philosophical Dialogue in the British Enlightenment.* Cambridge: Cambridge University Press, 1997.
———. "Religio Laici versus Religio Laici: Dryden, Blount, and the Origins of English Deism." *Modern Language Quarterly* 74, no. 1 (2013): 29–66.
Reeve, Juliet. "Daniel Defoe and Quakers." *Friends' Intelligencer* 103, no. 18 (1946): 282–84.
Reflections upon a Late Scandalous and Malicious Pamphlet Entitul'd, The Shortest Way with the Dissenters. London: s.n., 1703.
The Reformer Reform'd: or the Shortest Way with Daniel D'Fooe. London: T. Everat, 1703.

Richard Baxter's Answer to Dr. Stillingfleet's Charge of Separation. London: Nevil Simmons, 1680.

Richardson, Samuel. *The History of Sir Charles Grandison*, 7 vols. London: S. Richardson, 1754.

Richetti, John, ed. *The Cambridge Companion to "Robinson Crusoe."* Cambridge: Cambridge University Press, 2018.

———. *The Life of Daniel Defoe*. Malden, MA: Blackwell, 2005.

———. "Secular Crusoe: The Reluctant Pilgrim Revisited." In *Eighteenth-Century Genre and Culture: Serious Reflections on Occasional Forms, Essays in Honor of J. Paul Hunter*, ed. Dennis Todd and Cynthia Wall, 58–78. Newark: University of Delaware Press, 2001.

Robbins, Harry F. "How Smart Was Robinson Crusoe?" *PMLA* 67, no. 5 (1952): 782–89.

Rogers, Woodes. *A Cruising Voyage Round the World*. London: A. Bell and B. Lintot, 1712.

Ross, John Frederic. *Swift and Defoe: A Study in Relationship*. Berkeley: University of California Press, 1941.

Ruderman, David B. *Jewish Enlightenment in an English Key: Anglo-Jewry's Construction of Modern Jewish Thought*. Princeton, NJ: Princeton University Press, 2000.

Russen, David. *The Female Critick; or, Letters in Drollery from Ladies to Their Humble Servants and Iter Lunare; or, A Voyage to the Moon*, ed. Michael F. Shugrue. New York: Garland, 1972.

———. *Iter Lunare; or, A Voyage to the Moon, Containing Some Considerations on That Planet*. London: J. Nutt, 1703.

———. *Iter Lunare*, ed. John Cartwright, Brian Bowen, and Mary Elizabeth Bowen. Boston: Gregg Press, 1976.

Sacheverell, Henry. *The Character of a Low-Church-Man*. London: s.n., 1702.

———. *The Political Union: A Discourse Shewing the Dependence of Government on Religion in General*. London: Leonard Lichfield, 1702.

Secord, Arthur Wellesley. *Studies in the Narrative Method of Defoe*. University of Illinois Studies in Language and Literature 9. Urbana-Champaign: University of Illinois Press, 1924. https://catalog.hathitrust.org/Record/006156853.

Seidel, Kevin. "Beyond the Religious and the Secular in the History of the Novel." *New Literary History* 38, no. 4 (2007): 637–47.

———. "*Robinson Crusoe* as Defoe's Theory of Fiction." *Novel* 44, no. 2 (2011): 165–85.

Seidel, Michael. "The Man Who Came to Dinner: Ian Watt and the Theory of Formal Realism," *Eighteenth-Century Fiction* 12, nos. 2–3 (2000): 193–211.

Shadwell, Charles. *The Works of Mr. Charles Shadwell*, 2 vols. Dublin: George Rish and Joseph Leathley, 1720.

Shaftesbury, Anthony Ashley Cooper, Third Earl of. *Characteristicks of Men, Manners, Opinions, Times*, 3 vols., 2d ed. London: John Darby, 1714.

Shaw, Narelle L. "Ancients and Moderns in Defoe's *Consolidator*." *Studies in English Literature, 1500–1900* 28, no. 3 (1988): 391–400.

Shirren, A. J. *Daniel Defoe in Stoke Newington*. London: Stoke Newington Public Libraries Committee, 1960.
The Shortest Way with Whores and Rogues; or, A New Project for Reformation, Dedicated to Mr. Daniel de Foe, Author of the Shortest Way with the Dissenters. London: s.n., 1703.
Sidney, Algernon. *Discourses Concerning Government*. London: s.n., 1698.
Sill, Geoffrey. "Christianity Not as Old as the Creation," ed. G. A. Starr. *Scriblerian and the Kit-Cats* 46, no. 1 (2013): 45–46.
Simonutti, Louisa. "Deism, Biblical Hermeneutics, and Philology." In *Atheism and Deism Revalued: Heterodox Religious Identities in Britain, 1650–1800*, ed. Wayne Hudson, Diego Lucci, and Jeffrey R. Wigelsworth, 45–62. Burlington, VT: Ashgate, 2014.
Skelton, Philip. *Deism Revealed; or, The Attack on Christianity Candidly Reviewed in Its Real Merits*, 2 vols. London: A. Millar, 1751.
Slafter, Edmund F. *John Checkley; or, The Evolution of Religious Tolerance in Massachusetts Bay Boston*, 2 vols. Boston: Prince Society, 1897.
Smallbroke, Richard. *A Vindication of the Miracles of Our Blessed Saviour, in Which Mr. Woolston's Discourses on These Are Particularly Examin'd*, 2 vols. London: James and John Knapton, 1729–31.
Smith, Patrick. *A Preservative Against Quakerism, or a Complication of Deism, Enthusiasm, and Diverse other Ancient and Modern Dangerous Errors and Heresies*. London: C. Rivington, 1732.
Stamm, Rudolph G. "Daniel Defoe: An Artist in the Puritan Tradition." *Philological Quarterly* 15, no. 3 (1936): 225–45.
Stanley, Thomas. *The History of Philosophy*, 3d ed. London: W. Battersby, 1701.
Starr. G. A., ed. *Christianity Not as Old as the Creation: The Last of Defoe's Performances*. London: Pickering and Chatto, 2012.
———. *Defoe and Casuistry*. Princeton, NJ: Princeton University Press, 1971.
———. "Defoe and China." *Eighteenth-Century Studies* 43, no. 4 (2010): 435–54.
———. "*Robinson Crusoe* and Its Sequels: *The Farther Adventures* and *Serious Reflections*." In *The Cambridge Companion to "Robinson Crusoe,"* ed. John Richetti, 67–83. Cambridge: Cambridge University Press, 2018.
Stennett, Joseph. *An Answer to Mr. David Russen's Book Entitul'd Fundamentals without a Foundation; or, A True Picture of the Anabaptist*. London: D. Brown, S. Crouch, J. Baker, 1704.
A Summary Account of the Deists Religion, in a Letter to That Excellent Physician, the Late Dr. Thomas Sydenham. London: s.n., 1745.
Sutcliffe, Adam. *Judaism and Enlightenment*. Cambridge: Cambridge University Press, 2003.
Sutherland, James. *Daniel Defoe*. Philadelphia: J. B. Lippincott, 1938.
Swift, Jonathan. *A Letter from a Member of the House of Commons of Ireland to a Member of the House of Commons in England, Concerning the Sacramental Test*. London: John Morphew, 1709.
———. *Political Tracts by the Author of Gulliver's Travels*. London: C. Davis, 1738.
———. *A Tale of a Tub, Written for the Universal Improvement of Mankind*. London: John Nutt, 1704.

———. *Travels into Several Remote Nations of the World*, 2 vols. London: Benj. Motte, 1726.
———. *The Works of J.S, D.D, D.S.P.D in Six Volumes*. Dublin: George Faulkner, 1728.
———. *The Works of Jonathan Swift, D.D., Dean of St. Patricks, Dublin*, 6 vols. London: C. Bathurst, 1755.
Thomas, Roger. "The Non-subscription Controversy amongst Dissenters in 1719: The Salters' Hall Debate." *Journal of Ecclesiastical History* 4, no. 2 (1953): 162–86.
Toland, John. *Nazarenus; or, Jewish, Gentile, and Muslim Christianity*. London: J. Brotherton and A. Dodd, 1718.
Tom Tell-Truth's Letter to a Dissenter in Vindication of the L——s against the Tackers. London: s.n., 1705.
Torp, Laura. "'So Strange Things So Probably Told': Epistemic Consequences of Scientific Discourse in Lunar Travel Narratives." BA honors thesis, University of Michigan, Ann Arbor, 2013. https://lsa.umich.edu/content/dam/english-assets/migrated/honors_files/TORP%20Final.pdf.
Torrero-Ibad, Alexandra, *Libertinage science et philosophie, dans le materialisme de Cyrano de Bergerac*. Paris: Honoré Champion, 2009.
Tucker, Joseph E. "On the Authorship of the 'Turkish Spy': An 'État Présent.'" *Papers of the Bibliographical Society of America* 52, no. 1 (1958): 34–47.
———. "The Turkish Spy and Its French Background." *Revue de Littérature Comparée* 32 (1958): 74–91.
Tyssot de Patot, Simon. *Lettres choisies de Mr. Simon Tyssot de Patot*, 2 vols. La Haye: Matthieu Roguet, 1727.
———. *The Travels and Adventures of James Massey*, trans. Stephen Whatley. London: John Watts, 1733.
———. *Voyages et avantures de Jaques Massé*. Bourdeaux: Jacques L'Aveugle, 1710.
Vickers, Ilse. *Defoe and the New Science*. Cambridge Studies in Eighteenth-Century Literature and Thought, no. 32. New York: Cambridge University Press, 1997.
———. "The Influence of the New Science on Defoe's Habit of Mind." *Man and Nature/L'Homme et la Nature* 7 (1988): 67–78.
Villars, Abbé N. de Montfaucon de. *The Count of Gabalis, Being a Diverting History of the Rosicrucian Doctrine of Spirits viz. Sylphs, Salamanders, Gnomes, and Daemons*. London: B. Lintot and E. Curll, 1714.
Walber, Karl-Josef. *Charles Blount (1654–1693), Frühaufklärer: Leben und Werk*. Frankfurt am Main: Peter Lang, 1988.
Walkden, Andrea. "Parallel Lives and Literary Legacies: Crusoe's Elder Brother and Defoe's Cavalier." *English Literary History* 77, no. 4 (2010): 1061–86.
Ward, Edward (attrib.). *The Secret History of the Calves Head Club; or, The Republican Unmask'd*, 2d ed. London: s.n., 1703.
Wardhaugh, Benjamin, *Poor Robin's Prophecies*. Oxford: Oxford University Press, 2012.
Watt, Ian. *The Rise of the Novel: Studies in Defoe, Richardson, and Fielding*. Berkeley: University of California Press, 1957.
Weinbrot, Howard D. *Literature, Religion, and the Evolution of Culture, 1660–1780*. Baltimore; Johns Hopkins University Press, 2013.

———. *Menippean Satire Reconsidered.* Baltimore: Johns Hopkins University Press, 2005.

West, Richard, *Daniel Defoe: The Life and Strange Surprising Adventures.* New York: Carroll and Graf, 1998.

Whichcote, Benjamin. *Several Discourses Concerning the Shortness of Humane Charity,* 4 vols. 2d ed. London: James Knapton, 1701.

Wigelsworth, Jeffrey R. *Deism in Enlightenment England: Theology, Politics, and Newtonian Public Science.* Manchester: Manchester University Press, 2009.

Wilkins, John. *The Discovery of a World in the Moone. Or a Discourse Tending to Prove, that 'tis Probable There May Be Another Habitable World in That Planet.* London: Edward Griffin, 1638.

Wilson, Francis. "The Dark Side of Utopia: Misanthropy and the Chinese Prelude in Defoe's Lunar Journey." *Comparative Critical Studies* 4, no. 2 (2007): 193–207.

Woolf, Virginia. "Robinson Crusoe." In *The Second Common Reader,* chap. 4. New York: Harcourt Brace, 1932.

Yates, Francis. *The Rosicrucian Enlightenment.* London: Routledge, 1972.

Index

A. W., *Essay on Natural Religion*, 180, 287n149, 287n150
Abernethy-Drummond, William, *Candid Examination*, 116, 272n82
Act of Settlement, 158
Act of Toleration, 32, 36
Adam, Robert, *Religious World Displayed*, 164–65, 284n108
Addison, Joseph, 254–55n16; *Tatler*, 105, 269n41, 289n196
agnosticism, 218
Aikenhead, Thomas, executed for deism, 11, 240n47
Akman, Beyazit H., "Turk's Encounter with Defoe," 113, 271n68
Alcott, Louisa May, *Eight Cousins*, 136, 274n4
Aldridge, Alfred Owen, "Polygamy in Early Fiction," 250n168
Alighieri, Dante: *Inferno*, 225–26; *La Vita Nuova/The New Life*, 211, 291n7
Alkon, Paul: "Defoe's Argument in *The Shortest Way*," 12, 241n52; "Invisible Man Returns," 53, 256n23
allegory: biblical, 57, 149–50, 155–56; counter-, 154, 168–173, 225, 229; Defoe's complex relation to, 55–57, 120, 142, 184, 198, 213;

Jonah, Book of, 148–49, 154, 213; Kreutznaer as allegorical figure, 154–56; lunar, 52; political, 53, 55–57, 73–74; satirical, 54–57; *Tale of a Tub* as, 60–63; typology in, 168–71, 257n33. *See also individual works by Defoe*
Alsop, J. D., "Defoe, Toland, and *The Shortest Way with the Dissenters*," 20–21, 242n73, 243n84
Anabaptists, 60, 85, 114, 160, 248n139, 265n126
Anglican/Anglicanism, 8, 10, 33, 36, 51, 63, 66, 114, 117, 133, 149; Bangorian controversy in, 211–12; John Checkley and, 134; Church of England, 16, 42; High Church, 117; Charles Leslie and, 8
Anne (queen of England), 4, 20, 22, 28, 35, 44, 50, 200, 246n115, 251n175, 255n20
anti-Semite/anti-Semitic/anti-Semitism, 115, 123–24, 151, 164, 267n8, 284n109
Apollonius of Tyana, 27, 245n104
Appiah, Anthony Kwame, *Cosmopolitanism*, 88
Applebee's Journal, 213
Apuleius, *Golden Ass*, 71
Arabian Nights Entertainment, 127

Aravamudan, Srinivas: "East-West Fiction as World Literature," 127, 273n111; *Enlightenment Orientalism*, 92–94, 266n4, 267n9, 269n46
Argyll, 9th Earl, Archibald Campbell, 13, 77, 263n97
Arian/Arians/Arianism, 67, 117, 143, 164, 214, 284n107
Ascham, Roger, *Scholemaster*, 67, 260n64
Astell, Mary, 105; *Fair Way with the Dissenters*, 7, 238n25; *Serious Proposal to the Ladies*, 105, 269n45
Athanasian Creed, 183, 287n157
atheism/atheist/atheists, 16, 24, 47, 67–68, 70, 79, 88, 101, 109, 110, 124, 139, 143–44, 156, 164, 188, 213, 218, 222–24, 240n47, 247n130, 248n139, 261n71, 278–79n45, 293n48
Atkinson, Benjamin Andrewes, *Christianity not Older than the First Gospel-Promise*, 116, 272n81
Attar, Samar, "Vital Roots of European Enlightenment," 127–28, 273n113, 273n116
Atterbury, Francis, *Voice of the People, No Voice of God*, 135–36, 140, 274n3
Auerbach, Erich: *Ansatzpunkt* (point of departure), 208–10, 215; Dante's eclipse of allegory, 225–26; "Figura," figural interpretation, 167–70, 285n122; *Mimesis*, 169, 225–26, 226, 285n123, 293n60; "Philology and 'Weltliteratur'," 208–09, 210, 291n5; typology and literary history, 168–69
Augustine, Saint, 106
Ayers, Robert W., "Allusive Allegoric History," 156, 280n69, 280n70

Backscheider, Paula, *Daniel Defoe: His Life*, 1, 4, 29, 47, 140, 212, 235n3, 237n11, 238n22, 241n54, 246n111, 253n1, 256n22, 259n56, 265n114, 292n8
Bacon, Francis, 131; *The Essays, or Councils, Civil and Moral*, 260n68; "Nemesis; or, The Vicissitude of Things," 210–11, 291n6; "On Atheism," 68
Baine, Rodney, "Daniel Defoe and the Supernatural," 219, 256n22, 260n60
Bakhtin, Mikhail, satire, origins of, 70–71, 179
Banbury (Puritan and Quaker center), 60, 160, 258n46, 282n85, 282n86; Gulliver's family origins in, 160; reputation for storytelling, 160; "saints" mocked by Swift, 60–61, 160
Bangorian controversy, 97, 211–12, 268n25
Barabbas, New Testament thief, as figure for Sacheverell, 199–200, 290n196
Barclay, Robert, *Apology for the True Christian Divinity*, 129, 271n73, 273n117
Baroud, Mahmoud, *Shipwrecked Sailor in Arabic and Western Literature*, 273n111
Baxter, Richard, *Richard Baxter's Answer to Dr. Stillingfleet's Charge of Separation*, 105, 269n40
Bayle, Pierre, *Dictionnaire historique et critique*, 245n104
bears in Defoe, 14, 36, 44, 195–96, 198–204, 290n199, 290n202
Behn, Aphra: *Oroonoko, or the Royal Slave*, 64; translator of Fontenelle's *Les entretiens sur la pluralité des mondes*, 66; works preserved by Charles Gildon, 275n9
Bellamy, Edward, 21–22, 243n87
Benjamin, Walter, *Origins of German Tragic Drama*, 49–50, 57
Betts, C. J., *Early Deism in France*, 113, 260n58, 268n18, 271n72

Bible: Hebrew, renamed Old Testament, 166, 170; Job, Book of, 123, 272n96; Jonah, Book of, 149–52, 214; as literature, 20, 41, 143, 151, 185, 186, 187, 212, 214, 279–80n61; New Testament, 34, 121, 165–66, 167, 199, 214
Bickerstaff, Isaac, 105
Bickham, George, "Whig's Medley," 5
Bion, 68
Blackburn, Timothy C., "Friday's Religion," 194–95, 289n185
Blakeney, Tyler, "Textual Engagement with the Other," 262n90
Blewett, David: *A Continuation of Letters Written by a Turkish Spy*, (editor), 270n71, 271n74; *Illustration of Robinson Crusoe*, 27–30, 283n92
Bloody Assizes, 25, 258n38, 263n97
Blount, Charles: anathematized by Charles Leslie, 26, 285n119; chief deist, 135, 147, 194, 197, 217, 245n104, 263n99; Dryden's ingratitude toward, 71; philology of, 167–69; and the Quakers, 34; suicide of, 25, 26, 71, 138, 223, 244n98, 275n10; translator of Spinoza, 164, 284n104. Works: *First Two Books of Philostratus*, 26, 27, 245n104; *Great is Diana of the Ephesians*, 26, 167, 170, 248n135, 285n120; *Just Vindication of Learning and Liberty of the Press*, 244n96; *King William and Queen Mary Conquerors*, as model for Defoe's *Shortest Way*, 23–27, 31–32, 46, 100, 117, 244n94; *Miracles, No Violation of the Laws of Nature*, 164; *Miscellaneous Works*, 138; *Oracles of Reason*, 26, 135, 138–39, 180, 275n9, 287n149, 287n150; *Reasons Humbly Offered for the Liberty of Unlicensed Printing*, 244n96; *Religio Laici*, 38, 71, 93, 179–80; *Summary Account of the Deists Religion*, 180

Bohun, Edmund, 23–24, 27, 244n94, 244n96, 244n98, 275n10
Boswell, James, *Life of Samuel Johnson*, 8, 98
Bowen, Brian, 265n127
Bowen, Mary Elizabeth, 265n127
Boyle, John, 5th Earl of Orrery, 59, 258n39
Boyle, Robert, 263n98, 271n79
Bradbury, Thomas, 37
Bradshaw, William, 98
Braverman, Richard, "Politics in Jewish Disguise," 160, 282n86
Bremen (place), in *Robinson Crusoe*, 155–56, 158–60
Brenz, Johannes, *Newes from Ninive to Englande*, 67
Breuhowse, John, *Highland Spectator*, 164
Brown, Homer O.: "Displaced Self in the Novels of Daniel Defoe," 161; *Institutions of the English Novel*, 177, 287n146
Browne, Joseph: *Moon-Calf*, 55, 79–80, 255n20; *State Tracts*, 46
Bugg, Francis: antagonist of Penn and Defoe, 32, 34, 248n133, 248n141, 282n86; *Quaker Catechism*, 32; *Quaker's Infallibility Shaken All to Pieces*, 32
Bullard, Rebecca, "Politics, History, and the *Robinson Crusoe* Story," 228
Bunyan, John, *Pilgrim's Progress*, 141, 154, 187
Burles, Edward, *Grammatica Burlesa*, 10
Butler, James, 37
Byrne, Peter, *Natural Religion and the Nature of Religion*, 264n99

Caelicolae, 165
Calves'-Head Club, 15–16
Calvin, John, *Institution of the Christian Religion*, 60, 67
Calvinism/Calvinist, 64, 101, 175

Camaioni, Michele, "Bernardino Ochino and the German Reformation," 269n33
Capoferro, Riccardo, *Empirical Wonder*, 265n127
Cardano, Girolamo, 87
Carey, Daniel, "Henry Neville's Isle of Pines," 250n168
Carroll, William, *Spinoza Reviv'd*, 188
casuistry, 141, 191–92, 213, 278–79n45
Catholicism, 113, 114, 144, 191, 268n33
Celsus, 71
Cervantes, *Don Quixote*, 3–4, 41, 46, 49, 71, 86, 99, 208, 220, 236n6, 236n9
Champion, Justin, 240n47
Charles de Secondat, baron de Montesquieu. *See* Montesquieu, baron de, Charles-Louis de Secondat
Charles I (king of England), 16, 57
Charles II (king of England), 15, 56, 72
Chassanion, Jean de, *Theatre of God's Judgment*, 261n71
Checkley, John: Defoe labeled the deists' oracle, 134–35, 274n1, 274n2; *Discourse concerning Episcopacy*, 134; *Speech of John Checkley upon His Tryal*, 134–35
Cherbury, Lord Herbert. *See* Herbert, Edward, 1st Baron Herbert of Cherbury
Chewny, Nicholas, *Anti-Socinianism*, 277n30
China: as deist utopia in *Consolidator*, 34, 54, 75, 77–78; Great Wall of, 230–37, 294n71; satiric or "monitory" example, 262–63n95
Christian Neoplatonism, 211
Clarendon Code, 36, 248n132
Clark, J. C. D., *English Society, 1688–1832*, 7–9

Clark, John (illustrator), 154–55
Clark, K. R. P., "Defoe, Dissent, and Early Whig Ideology," 42
Clark, Katherine, *Daniel Defoe: The Whole Frame of Nature, Time, and Providence*, 124–25, 251n175
Clarke, Samuel, 263n98; *New Description of the World*, 264n106
Coetzee, J.M., *Foe*, 281–82n83
Cohen, Ralph, 267n11
Collins, Anthony, 147
Comber, Thomas, 40
Common Notions of deism (*notitiae communes*), 78, 93, 177, 179–80, 194, 218–19, 251n179, 289n184
Conventicle Act, 249n147
Corbet, Richard, "Iter Boreale," 161, 282n90
Cornwall, Robert D., "Charles Leslie," 9, 239n31
cosmopolitan/cosmopolitanism: condemned by Charles Leslie, 33; Defoe's apprenticeship, 35, 49, 91–92, 94, 116, 124, 215–16, 232, 269n46; deism in, 49, 65–66, 88, 93, 230; literary models of, 35, 48–49, 60, 65, 92, 109, 117, 130–32, 226; Lucian's influence on, 47, 65, 68–69, 87, 88, 106, 116, 204; openness to cultural difference, 66, 92; and philo-Semitism, 123; protagonists in, 102, 106, 115, 124–25, 176–77, 207; and skepticism, 123; as theory of the novel, 81, 110, 269n46; and travel, 68–69, 285n128
Cotton, Charles: *Burlesque upon Burlesque*, 64; translator of Montaigne's *Essays*, 188
counter-allegory. *See* allegory: counter-
Cox, Thomas, 236n7
Craig, Hardin, "Dryden's Lucian," 261n70
Crane, Jacob, *Long Transatlantic Career of the Turkish Spy*, 267n12

Cressy, David: "Early Modern Space Travel and the English Man in the Moon," 66, 80, 260n60, 264n10
Creutz, Johannes, 159
Cromwell, Oliver, 160, 165
Cruso, Timothy, 156
Cyrano de Bergerac, *Comical History of the World in the Moon*, 72–73, 74, 76, 80, 85–87, 221, 262n89, 262n93, 262n94

Dante. *See* Alighieri, Dante
Defoe, Daniel: description of, 13–14, 21–22, 233; his inscrutability, 1–4, 19, 232; his nemesis, or negative muse, 3, 4, 8, 30, 41, 43, 52, 148; object of attack, 1, 15, 49; reversions to the pillory, 50–52, 113; stroke of apoplexy, 37, 249–50n153
———, political views: colonialist ideology of, 226–29; Hanoverian, 117; a Leveler, 136; party attacks against, 1, 15, 49; republican, 15, 42, 77, 117, 134, 172, 217; Whig polemicist, 16, 20, 22, 29, 63, 117, 139, 159, 257n38; Williamite, 17, 20, 22, 25, 27, 56–7, 117, 257n33, 285n124
———, religious views: deists and freethinkers, attacks on, 42, 213–14; disguised deism of, 15, 35, 42, 43, 79, 94, 101, 117, 133, 135, 172, 213, 214, 226; homiletic works of Christian piety, 97, 140, 218–19, 251–52n179; Jews and Judaism, ambivalence towards, 171; Presbyterian, 42; Quakerism as screen and polemic, 28, 30–31, 35–36, 43, 215, 248n141; radicalism of, 15, 32, 38, 77, 100, 136, 158, 172, 281n78; Sacheverell, view of, 44, 198–200; "theologically orthodox dissent," 18, 42, 48, 144, 218–19, 251n174
———, about his writings: comic sublime in, 152–54; cosmopolitanism of, 90, 91, 94; editor, trope of, 109–12; extra-realism of early fictions, 94; genius of, 3, 232; compared to Homer, 139; "a great, a truly great liar" (Minto), 19; history-writing in, 2, 171, 213; literary deism of, 35, 47–48, 94, 153, 155–56, 161–62, 163, 167–68, 182, 185, 187, 190–91, 196, 200, 207; narrative style, 11–16, 18–20, 41, 46, 54, 57, 113–14, 121, 123–25, 133, 145, 149, 150, 154, 160, 172, 181, 182, 215, 220–21, 230–32; personas, use of, 35, 38, 76, 102, 112, 135, 147, 154, 213, 215; satire, abjures, 63; sequels, Defoe's view of, 97; Swift as artistic rival, 58–63, 259n53; translator, trope of, 110, 111, 216; transformation from brick manufacturer into novelist, 1, 41–42; typology in, 170–71; ventriloquist, 6, 14, 18, 25, 75, 216, 232, 275n10
Defoe, Daniel, works by or attributed to: *Appeal to Honor and Justice*, 25, 28, 30, 44, 248n142; *Banbury Apes*, 258–59n46; *Brief Explanation of a Late Pamphlet*, 6, 8, 14, 18, 216; *Brief History of the Poor Palatine Refugees*, 281n80; *Captain Singleton*, 30, 226; *Challenge of Peace Address'd to the Whole Nation*, 44, 251n175; *Christianity Not as Old as the Creation*, 42, 250n172, 278n42; *Colonel Jack*, 226; *Conduct of Christians Made the Sport of Infidels*, 97, 266n2; *Defence of the People Call'd Quakers*, 38, 39, 40; *Defoe's Review*, 8, 35–36, 45, 136, 290n199; *Dialogue between a Dissenter and the Observator*, 21, 22; *Dissenter's Answer to the High Church Challenge*, 9, 20, 43, 44, 250n160, 254n13; *Dumb*

Defoe, Daniel (*continued*)
Philosopher, 274n125; *Dyet of Poland*, 54–55; *Elegy on the Author of the True-Born English-man*, 6; *L'espion turc*, Defoe's volume in, 96–97; *Essay on the History and Reality of Apparitions*, 281n78; *Experiment, or the Shortest Way with Dissenters Exemplified*, 50; *Family Instructor in Two Parts*, 97, 140, 251–52n179; *Fortunes and Misfortunes of the Famous Moll Flanders*, 30, 81, 110, 127, 185, 226; *Friendly Epistle by Way of Reproof*, 37–38; *History of the Life and Adventures of Mr. Duncan Campbell*, 156–57; *Honesty and Sincerity of Those Worthy Gentlemen Commonly Called High-Church Men*, 254n13; *Hymn to the Pillory*, 11, 21, 30, 55; *Jure Divino*, 43, 100, 268n23; *Letter to William Penn*, July 12, 1703, 29–30; *Madagascar; or, Robert Drury's Journal*, 216–17, 292n16; *More Reformation*, 198, 276–77n23, 285n125; *New Family Instructor*, 218–19; *Perjur'd Free-Mason Detected*, 281n78; *Political History of the Devil*, 43, 217; *Present State of the Parties in Great Britain*, 6, 7, 11, 12; *Protestant Jesuite Unmask'd*, 43, 44, 198; *Quaker Sermon*, 199, 289n196; *Reformation of Manners*, 214; *Religious Courtship*, 251–52n179; *Review of the Affairs of France* (see *Defoe's Review*); *Robinson Crusoe* (see *Life and Strange Surprizing Adventures of Robinson Crusoe*); *Secret History of the Secret History of the White Staff*, 248n142; *Secret History of the White Staff*, 44; *Sharp Rebuke from One of the People Call'd Quakers*, 36–38; *Shortest Way to Peace and Union*, 17; *Tour through the Whole Island of Great Britain*, 30–31; *True Born Englishman*, 90, 131, 257–58n38
———, *Consolidator*, deism of, 77–78; Dryden, attack on, 72; failure of, 53–55, 72, 74, 253n3; as imitation of Lucian and lunar voyage tradition, 60–72, 92; polemic against High Church, 50–51; as political allegory, 52–53; republicanism of, 77; *Robinson Crusoe*, precursor of, 57, 75, 78, 82, 83, 84, 125, 221, 222; Swift, attack on, 58–65, 255n19; tacking controversy, 73
———, *Continuation of Letters Written by a Turkish Spy at Paris*, absorbed into *L'espion turc* in 1742, 96–97, 100; attacks Christianity, 114–15; degeneration of hero in, 115; difficulty classifying, 118; Enlightenment Orientalism of, 92, 109, 111, 113–15, 119–26; exile in, 119–20; editorial and formal problems of, 98–100, 118; failure of, 90–92, 117–19, 126; as imitation of Marana's *Letters Writ by a Turkish Spy*, its secret history, 95–100; Islamophilia of, 124; Jewish influence on, 122–24; narrative thread of, 112; as novel, 47; political satire, 126; *Robinson Crusoe*, precursor of, 126
———, *Farther Adventures*, 175–76, 193, 202–04; failure of, 204; Friday's death in, 204–07; Great Wall of China, 231
———, *Fortunate Mistress, or Roxana*, 31, 40, 110; Quaker friend in, 40, 127
———, *Life and Strange Surprizing Adventures of Robinson Crusoe*: accident, 1, 50, 91; allegory in, 2, 148, 154, 171–72, 213, 220, 225, 229; bear, its human analogue, 199–200; capitalism and, 226; casuistry in, 191–92; classic children's story, 136; colonialism

and, 172, 226, 229; comic sublime of, 154; conversions in, 139–41, 172, 184–94; cosmopolitanism of, 173, 177, 189, 202, 215, 216, 217, 230; Crusoe's naming, 154–56, 160–63; counter-allegory of, 154; deist thought experiment, 133; *Don Quixote*, 2–3, 49, 208; Friday's roles, 187–88, 191–92; frontispiece by Clark and Pine, 154–55; genres of, 154, 215; geography in, 159–60; hermeneutic problems in, 228; imperialism and, 226–27, 229; Jonah, Book of, 153–54; literary deism of, 136, 142, 144, 145, 147, 148, 172, 177, 189, 195, 202, 207, 216, 217, 218, 230; its narrative, 154; pillory and, 46, 50; as propaganda, 226–27; Protestant spiritual autobiography, 2, 42, 140–41, 148, 154, 156, 172–73, 189, 194, 219, 225–26, 229, 232–33; providence in, 141, 172–77, 181–83; racism in, 205; religious origin of, 160; realism of, 172, 220; religious crusade in, 278n44; revenge as motive for, 4, 27, 46, 195–204; romance in, 2, 140; as disguised satire, 3, 211; shimmering signs in, 171–72; *sortes Virgilianae* in, 143; as trilogy, 84, 91, 184; wolf, its human analogue, 196–97. *See also entries for other volumes of the trilogy*

———, *Serious Reflections during the Life and Surprising Adventures of Robinson Crusoe*, ancient gentlewoman in, 145–48, 188–89; apparitions in, 222–23, 225; conversions of atheists, 223–24; hermeneutic problems in, 224; lunar voyage in, 220–21; "Of Atheistical and Prophane Discourse," 213; part of original plan, 219, 224; "Robinson Crusoe's Preface," 2, 3, 27, 133, 157, 171, 184, 230, 235n4;

sequel or prequel, 144, 208, 219, 277–78n34; source of an overlooked clue, 1; testing ground and escape valve, 145–47; "*Vision of the Angelick World*," 170–71, 218–25

———, *Shortest Way with the Dissenters*, 1, 4–6, 10, 12–22; accomplices of, 20; aesthetic achievement of, 19, 25, 27, 28, 30, 31, 41, 44, 46, 50, 54; Defoe's commentary on, 18–20, 21–22; deists' approval of, 10, 17, 18; genre of, 12, 14–15, 19; narrative point of view, 12, 23–25, 27, 41; reception of, 6, 10–20, 22, 27; target(s) of, 7–8

D'Foe's Answer to the Quakers Catechism, 40, 250n166

deism/deists, 10, 17, 24, 31, 32, 33, 34, 38, 39, 43, 45, 46, 47, 48; absence from literary histories of the novel, 116; anthropology of religion, 92–93; anti-Semitism of, 93, 164, 267n8; Common Notions (*Notitiae Communes*) in, 93, 177, 179; controversy, 210, 215; cosmopolitanism, 80, 93–94, 102, 116, 124, 230; counter-allegory and, 168; as critical philology, 24, 93; Defoe an opponent of, 42–43, 79–80, 94, 213, 218, 242n73, 251–52n179, 263n98; and Enlightenment Orientalism (Aravamudan), 48, 106; and European Enlightenment, 48, 66; and Freemasonry, 158, 281n78; its irenic, or peace-loving intent, 177–79; Islamophilia of, 93–94; in *The Isle of Pines*, 40–41, 250n170; Judaism and, 164–65, 283n102, 283–84n103; literary disguises of, 47, 75, 76, 79, 92–93, 108–110, 112–18, 124–30, 135, 176–77, 188, 204–207, 271n79, 286n129; and the novel, 88, 133, 207, 215–18,

deism/deists (*continued*)
229, 232–33; origins of, 164–65, 179, 263n99; *Persian Letters* (Montesquieu), 102–05; philo-Semitic, 93, 283n101; polygamy in, 250n169; popularity of, 49, 92, 94, 116–17, 116–17, 135, 138–39; providence in, 177–80, 286n129; and Quietism, 113–14; as Satanic temptation, 43, 217; skeptical commonplaces in, 122–23; as theology, 77–78, 93; as threat against Christianity, 17, 20; typology and, 167. *See also* Socinian/Socinians; Arian/Arians/Arianism; Spinoza/Spinozism/Spinozist
Dejean, Joan E., "Method and Madness in Cyrano de Bergerac's *Voyage dans la lune*," 262n94
Delaune, Thomas, 254n13
Delehanty, Ann T., "Textual Engagement with the Other," 262n90
DeLuna, D. N., 237n17
Derrida, Jacques, 69
Descartes, 178
Diagoras, 68
Dialogue between Mahmut and Androgio ben Yokhdan, 130–32, 274n119
D'Israeli, Isaac, *Curiosities of Literature*, 97–98
dissenters, 8, 13, 15–16, 20–21, 25–27, 32–36, 39, 42, 50, 57, 60, 64, 66, 156, 159–60, 199–200, 211–14, 249n147, 250n160, 251n2, 254n13, 255n16
Divine right, 42, 57, 77, 147, 170, 179, 263n95
Dobrée, Bonamy, "Some Aspects of Defoe's Prose," 12
Dottin, Paul: *Life and Strange Surprising Adventures of Daniel Defoe*, 53, 144, 219, 259n56, 266n2, 275n9, 276n15; *Robinson Crusoe Examin'd*

and Criticis'd, 144, 291n211, 291n213, 293n48
Downie, J. A.: "Imperialism, and the Travel Books Reconsider'd," 226–27, 239n29; "John Tutchin," 257–58n38; "Mr. Review and His Scribbling Friends: Defoe and his Critics, 1705–1706," 1, 9, 235n1, 239n29, 240n39
Doyle, Laura, *Freedom's Empire*, 229
Drayton, Michael, *The Battaile of Agincourt Fought by Henry V*, 255n20
Dryden, John: *Absalom and Achitophel*, 57; *Conquest of Granada*, 135; deist work attributed to, 179–80, 287n149; *Hind and the Panther*, 72; *Life of Lucian* (in *Works of Lucian*), 65–67, 69–72, 261n70; *Works of Lucian*, 64, 65, 67
Dumoulin, François Aimé Louis, *Collection de cent-cinquante gravures . . . des voyages et aventures surprenantes de Robinson Crusoé*, iv, ix, 162, 177–78, 181–82, 186, 196–97, 200–203, 205–206, 231, 282–83n92, 287n145, 287n152, 288n164, 289n188, 290n200, 291n210, 294n71
Dunton, John, 98, 107, 241n56

Edwards, John: *Brief Vindication*, 102; *Socinian Creed*, 109
Elector of Hanover. *See* George I (king of England)
Ellison, Katherine, "English Quakers' Campaign for Freedom of Religion," 286n138
Enlightenment, the, 48, 92–94, 103, 116, 127, 130, 263–64n99, 271n79, 273n113; Jewish (Haskala), deism of, 164, 283n102, 283–84n103
Enlightenment Orientalism. *See* Aravamudan, Srinivas
epistolary novel, 95, 116, 269n46

equivalence, as skeptical commonplace, 122–23, 125
Erasmus, *Colloquies*, "The Shipwreck," 185, 288n162

failure: and Defoe's success, 50, 215; neglected topic in literary history, 49–50, 57, 58, 63, 65, 74, 89, 91, 95, 165, 204, 215, 222, 253n10, 257n36
Fame and Confession of the Fraternity of R:C:, 157, 281n76
Farnaby, Thomas (rhetorician), 14, 241n57
Fawkes, Guy, 15, 20
Fernsemer, O. F. W., "Daniel Defoe and the Palatine Emigration," 159, 281n80, 281n81
Fielding, Henry, 39, 184, 230, 232; *Joseph Andrews*, 81
Filmer, Robert, 77, 239n31
Five Mile Act, 249n147
Fisher, Carl (editor), *Defoe's Footprints*, 161, 283n95
Flavel, John: *Fountain of Life Opened*, 105, 269n43; *Navigation Spiritualized*, 105
Fleming, Robert, *Rod, or the Sword*, 164
Folkenflik, Robert, "Robinson Crusoe and the Semiotic Crisis," 163
Fontenelle, Bernard le Bovier de, *Entretiens sur la pluralité des mondes*, 66, 271n79
Forster, E. M., 5, 53
Fox with His Fire-Brand Enkennel'd and Ensnar'd, 14–15, 27, 241n57, 241n59, 245n108
Franklin, Benjamin: "Letter to Ezra Stiles, March 9, 1790," 180; *Poor Richard's Almanac*, 86
Free, Melissa, "Unerasing 'Crusoe'," 278n34
Freemasonry/Freemasons, 94, 158, 281n78; deism and, 158; Rosicrucianism and, 158

Friend: Religious and Literary Journal, 30
Frye, Northrop, *Anatomy of Criticism*, 62, 259n51
Furbank, F. N.: *Complete Works of Daniel Defoe*, 239n31; *Critical Bibliography of Daniel Defoe*, 266n2; *Defoe De-attributions*, 235n3, 235n4, 239n31, 259n46, 274n125, 281n78, 281n80, 289n196, 292n16; *Political Biography of Daniel Defoe*, 10, 43, 235n3, 239n31, 246n116, 249–50n153, 251n177, 252n181, 256n24

Gabalis, Count of, *History of the Count of Gabalis*, 157, 280n74
Gadamer, Hans-Georg, 179
Gascoigne, John, "Pacific Exploration as Religious Critique," 285n128, 288n172
Gassendi, Pierre, 178
genre/genres: allegorical satire, 54, 57; allegory versus history, 171–72, 204; cosmopolitan, 49, 94, 103, 117, 130–33, 215, 226; deist coded, 100, 215–16, 262n89, 262n90, 271n79; "essential genre of" (Novak), 236n9; indeterminate, 12, 14, 50, 54, 75, 87, 94, 99, 215; irony a genre, 18; Lucianic satire and the novel, 70–71; lunar, 71, 86, 261–62n89, 262n90; parable, 75; party coded, 57, 94; of *Robinson Crusoe*, 148–54, 172, 189, 191–92, 195, 211, 213; theory of, in Defoe, 81–82, 132–33
George I (king of England), 158
Georgiadou, A.: "Lucian's 'Vera Historia' as Philosophical Parody," 71
Giglioni, Guido, "Girolamo Cardano," 266n132
Gildon, Charles: critic of *Robinson Crusoe*, 3, 16, 135, 137–44, 140, 160, 172, 173, 175, 185, 192, 195, 203–204, 213, 217, 223, 224, 229, 236n7, 236n9, 275n9, 275n10,

Gildon, Charles (*continued*)
276n13, 276n14, 276n15, 276n17,
276–77n23, 291n213, 293n48;
Deist's Manual, 138; disciple of
Charles Leslie, 138–39, 143, 229,
276n13, 276n14; his Friday shoots
Defoe, 201–202; friend and editor
of Charles Blount, 138; *Life and
Strange Surprizing Adventures of
Mr. D———de F———*, 16, 139,
140–42, 144, 173, 175, 184,
185, 190, 201, 213, 214, 236n7,
291n213; literary failure of,
276n17; *Post-Boy Robb'd of His Mail*,
276n17
Gill, Abraham, 50–51, 254n13,
254–55n16
George I (king of England), 158
Godwin, Francis, *Man in the Moone*,
72, 74
Goldie, Mark, "Charles Blount's
Intentions," 244n94, 244n96
Goodman, Lenn E. (translator and
editor): *Ibn Tufayl's Hayy Ibn Yaqzān*,
273n110
Graham, Michael F., 240n47
Greif, Martin J.: "Conversion of
Robinson Crusoe," 140–41, 148,
150, 276n21, 279n57
Guion, Béatrice, *"L'espion du Grand
Seigneur*," 267n13, 267n16
Gulliver Decypher'd, 159, 281n82
Guzmán, Don Alonzo Pèrez de. *See
Sidonia*, Duke *de Medina*
Gwyn, Douglas, "John Saltmmarsh,
Quaker Forerunner," 107, 270n53

Halifax, 1st Earl, Charles Montagu, 25
Hallam, Henry, "Literary History of the
Turkish Spy," 96, 101
Hanover, Hanoverian, 117, 158
Harley, Robert, 1st Earl of Oxford, 28,
97, 238n21, 246n111, 258n38,
261n85, 293n48

Harradine, Eunice, "Banbury History,"
258n46
Harrison, Peter, *"Religion" and the
Religions in the English Enlightenment*,
267n7
Harvey, Richard, *Theological Discourse*,
67
Haskala. *See* Enlightenment: Jewish
(Haskala), deism of
hatred, and literary invention, 3–4, 9,
44, 49, 56, 148, 204, 211
Haywood, Eliza, *Love in Excess*, 66
Hazlitt, William (comp.): *English
Proverbs and Proverbial Phrases*,
160; "Life of Defoe," in *Works*, 157,
243n81, 280n75
Hellweg, Martin, 291n5
Henderson, Leah, "Problem of
Induction," 260n69
Herbert, Edward, 1st Baron Herbert
of Cherbury, 25, 38, 79, 146,
169, 178–79, 263n99; *De veritate*,
178–79; *Religio Laici*, 38
hermeneutic/hermeneutics, 57, 154,
163, 165, 172, 179, 210, 229,
278–79n45, 285n121
Herrick, James A.: *Radical Rhetoric of the
English Deists*, 263n99
heuristic, 191–92
Hickeringill, Edmund, *Vindication of the
Character of Priestcraft*, 264n106
Hickes, Francis, *Certain Select Dialogues
of Lucian*, 65, 67–68, 73
Hill, Christopher: *God's Englishman*,
174; "Robinson Crusoe," 224,
292n23
Himmelfarb, Gertrude, *People of the
Book*, 284n103
*History of King-Killers, Or, The Fanatick
Martyrology*, 277n30
Hoadley, Benjamin, Bishop of Bangor,
37, 211–12, 239n31, 268n25
Hobbes, Thomas, 25, 101; *Leviathan*,
130, 138, 146, 194, 216, 244n94

Hollingshead, David, "Daniel Defoe and the Abandoned Life," 228, 299n67
Homer, Defoe compared to, 16, 49, 139
Hone, Joseph, 237n17, 237n18, 245n106, 256n24
Hopes, Jeffrey, "Real and Imaginary Stories," 278n34, 292n29
Horace, 70
Horsley, L. S., "Contemporary Reactions to Defoe's Shortest Way," 18, 19, 242n77, 255n20
Howell, James, *Epistolae Ho-Elianae*, 90
Howes, Raymond F.: "Robinson Crusoe: A Literary Accident," 1, 235n2
Hudson, Wayne, 264n99, 284n103
Huguenots, 114
humanism/humanists, 60, 80, 87, 117, 131, 151, 161, 185, 226, 242–43n78
Hume, David: critique of induction, 69, 260n69; *Essays, Moral and Political*, 34, 145; religious skepticism, 171; viewed Quakers as deists, 34
Hunter, J. Paul: "Genre, Nature, *Robinson Crusoe*," 286n130; *Reluctant Pilgrim*, 7, 140
Hunter, Michael, "Aikenhead the Atheist," 240n47
Hyde, Edward, Earl of Clarendon, *History of the Rebellion*, 282n85
Hypsistarians, 165

Ibn Tufayl, Hai Ibn Yaqzān: compared to the Turkish Spy, 130–33; deist thought experiment, 128–29, 132; design of, 128–29; influence on *Robinson Crusoe*, 127; Quaker favorite, 41, 129. *See also* Pococke, Edward (translator), *Philosophus Autodidactus*; Ockley, Simon (translator of *Hai Ibn Yaqzān*), *The Improvement of Human Reason*
imperialism, Western appropriation of the East, 112–13
Independents, 36

Index Librorum Prohibitorum (Index of Forbidden Books), 95
induction, problem of, 68–69, 260n69
irony: Defoe's, 11–20, 25–26, 46, 56, 145, 218; downplayed in ideological critique, 227–28; and rise of the novel, 54, 226

J. D. (illus.), *French Lucian Made English*, 66
Jacob, Joseph, *Fewness of the Faithful*, 116
Jacob, Margaret C.: *Strangers Nowhere in the World*, 65; *Living the Enlightenment*, 281n78
Jacobite/Jacobitism, 8, 136
Jeffreys, George, 1st Baron Jeffreys, 263n97
James II (king of England), 15, 29, 33, 42, 239n31
James Francis Edward Stuart (James III, the Old Pretender), 55
James, Hugh, *Answer to a Late Pamphlet*, 254n13
Jesuits, 114
Jewish Naturalization Act (1753–54), 239n27, 284n109
Jews/Judaism, 10, 26, 40, 49, 107, 118–19, 122–24, 149, 152, 154, 160, 163–71, 214, 238–39n27, 247n123, 270n60, 272n93, 275n10, 282n87, 283n102, 283–84n103, 284n109
Johnson, Daniel J., "*Robinson Crusoe* and the Apparitional Eighteenth-Century Novel," 249n151, 286n137
Johnson, Samuel, 8–9
Jonah. *See* Bible: Jonah, Book of
Jones, Gavin, *Failure and the American Writer*, 253n10
Juvenal, 70

Keach, Benjamin, *Gospel Mysteries Unveil'd*, 149

Keith, George: *Account of the Oriental Philosophy*, 129; *Deism of William Penn and His Brethren Destructive*, 34
King, Ami Hicken, 249n151
Kincade, Kit, "Mediation and Intelligence," 286n137
Kirby, Ethyn Williams, "The Quakers' Effort to Secure Civil and Religious Liberty," 249n147
Kliger, Ilya (comp.), "Persistent Forms," 70–71
Korshin, Paul, *Typologies in England*, 256n32

Landreth, Sara, "Defoe on Spiritual Communication," 254n15
Larmour, D. H. J., "Lucian's 'Vera Historia' as Philosophical Parody," 71
Latitudinarian/Latitudinarians, 247n130, 290n206
Lavenia, Vincenzo (editor), *Heterodox Italian Migrants*, 269n33
Law, William, *Appeal to All Who Doubt*, 164
Lege, William, 45
Lemay, J. A. Leo, *Deism, Masonry, and the Enlightenment*, 264n99, 281n78
Leranbaum, Miriam, "'An Irony Not Unusual'," 23, 25, 244n93
Leslie, Charles: anathematizes Charles Blount, 26; attacks Defoe, 15, 17, 44–45, 136; attacks the Quakers, 31–34, 248n133; Defoe's nemesis, 6–11, 30, 31, 36, 38, 43, 44, 46, 50, 52, 73, 89, 208, 210–11, 233, 254–55n16; describes Defoe's "charm" on readers, 136; exiled, 45; inspires Defoe's poetry and prose, 43–44; Judaism, attack on, 163–65; popularity of, 238n27, 239n27; suspects a *Shortest Way* conspiracy, 20; takes Defoe's bait, 24–27; typology, defense of, 166—68. Works: *The Best Answer Ever Was Made*, 239–40n34; *Case of the Church of England's Memorial Fairly Stated*, 17; *Case of the Jews Considered*, 238n27, 284n109; *Charge of Socinianism against Dr. Tillotson Considered*, 167–68; *Deism Refuted*, 32, 33, 167, 238n27; *Finishing Stroke*, 196–97; *Five Discourses*, "Preface," 33–34; *Good Old Cause; or, Lying in Truth*, 45; *New Association*, 6, 8, 239n27, 290n206; *Now or Never*, 45, 136, 137; *Reflections upon a Late Scandalous and Malicious Pamphlet*, 27; *Rehearsal*, 8, 9, 45, 242n68; *Reply to a Book Entitul'd Anguis Flagellatus*, 31, 32; *Salt for the Leach*, 196–97; *Second Part of The Wolf Stript*, 33; *Short and Easie Method with the Deists*, 7, 8, 10, 11, 25–27, 58, 163, 165–67, 238n27; *Short and Easie Method with the Jews*, 164, 168; *Snake in the Grass*, 31, 33, 35, 246–47n122; *Theological Works*, 45, 276n14; *Truth of Christianity Demonstrated*, 166–67; *View of the Times, Their Principles and Practices*, 9, 16–17, 45; *Wolf Strip of Its Shepherd's Cloathing*, 9, 15, 44, 45, 196
Leslie, Robert Joshua: *The Life and Writings of Charles Leslie*, 10, 17, 45; equates deists and Jews, 165
"Letter from a Gentleman in the Country," 91
L'espion turc. See Defoe, Daniel, works by or attributed to: *Continuation of Letters Written by a Turkish Spy at Paris*, as imitation of Marana's *Letters Writ by a Turkish Spy*, its secret history; Marana, Giovanni-Paulo: *Letters Writ by a Turkish Spy*
L'Estrange, Roger, *The Poetical Observator*, 6, 23, 24, 25, 26, 27, 58, 167

libertinisme érudit, 64; and deism, 66
Licensing Act, 23–25, 243–44n91, 275n10
literary deism, 35, 47, 75–76, 80, 92; found manuscript in, 107–08, 116, 133, 135, 148, 216, 229; and rise of the novel, 229; translator, translation in, 110
literary history, method of, 4, 46–49, 208–11, 226–29. *See also* Auerbach, Erich
Locke, John, *Essay Concerning Human Understanding,* 83, 263n98
London riots, March 1, 1710, 200
Love, Harold, 245n101
Lucci, Diego: *Atheism and Deism Revalued,* 263n99; "Judaism and Natural Religion," 283n103
Lucian of Samosata: atheism of, 47, 67–68; Christian apologies for, 64–72; cosmopolitanism of, 64, 68–69; homosexuality of, 70; *Icaromenippus,* 72, 73; "Lucianic" as mode of satire, 66; Menippean satirist, 70–71; missing from Defoe studies, 259–60n56; model for the modern novel, 75; prose model in schools, 67; revival of in 17th century, 64–66; *Vera Historia [A True History],* 60, 261n78
lunar voyage, 47, 52, 53, 57, 59, 60, 71, 72, 73, 76, 80, 88, 135; Christian uses of, 85–86; and literary deism, 76–77, 79, 100, 116, 132–33, 220, 221, 230, 255–56n22, 258n41, 260n60, 261–62n89, 262n90, 262n94, 264n100; and the novel, 81–85; and plurality of worlds, 220; skeptical uses of, 71, 80, 94, 113
Lund, Roger D., "Strange Complicities," 156, 247n130
Luther, 61
Lutherans, 159
Luttrell, Narcissus, 4, 138

Macaulay, Thomas Babington: Blount's attack on Bohun, 23–24, 25, 138; Blount's suicide, 138, 244n94, 244n95, 275n10, 275n11; *The History of England,* 8
MacPhail, Eric, "Cyrano's Machines," 261–62n89, 265n124, 265n127
Mahometan/Mahometans, 108, 109–10, 116, 119, 128, 130. *See also* Muslim/Muslims
Mahlberg, Gaby M., "Authors Losing Control," 250n168
Maniquis, Robert M. (editor), *Defoe's Footprints,* 161
Manning, David, "Accusations of Blasphemy in English Anti-Quaker Polemic, 1660–1701," 31, 33, 37, 250n161
Marana, Giovanni-Paulo: authorship unknown, 95–98; censorship of, 95; cosmopolitanism of, 102; deism of, 102; *Eight Volumes of Letters Writ by a Turkish Spy,* 118, 119; *Eighth and Last Volume of Letters Writ by a Turkish Spy,* 108, 109; English origin, 96–99; "General Preface to the Whole," 126; genre(s) of, 102, 118; *Letters Writ by a Turkish Spy,* 89, 106–107; "Mr. Saltmarsh's Letter," 107, 108; popularity of, 109, 117; religious scandal, 109; *Second Volume of Letters Writ by a Turkish Spy,* 107
Marlborough, duchess, Sarah Churchill, 53
Marlborough, 1st duke, John Churchill, 258n38
Marshall, Ashley, "Fabricating Defoes," 48–49, 235n3, 255n22
Marshall, David, "Autobiographical Acts in Robinson Crusoe," 156
Maslov, Boris (comp.), *Persistent Forms,* 70, 71
Mather, Increase, *The Voice of God, In Stormy Winds,* 149–50

Maxfield, Ezra Kempton, "Daniel Defoe and the Quakers," 35, 37, 249n151
McBurney, William H., "The Authorship of the Turkish Spy," 95–96, 267n13
McKendry, Andrew, "No Parallels from Hebrew Times," 57, 285n122
McKeon, Michael, *Origins of the English Novel, 1600–1740*, 92, 141, 227, 276n22
McVeagh, John (editor), *Defoe's Review*, 42
Mendelssohn, Moses, 283n100
Merrett, Robert James, *Daniel Defoe, Contrarian*, 259n56, 278–79n45
metaphor, 54, 56
Midgley, Robert, 98
Miller, John, "A Suffering People," 249n147
Milton, John, 25; *Areopagitica*, 244n96
Minto, William, *Daniel Defoe*, 19
Molinos, Miguel de: founder of Quietist movement, 112–15; *Prayer of Quietude*, 113; *Spiritual Guide*, 113
Moll Flanders. See Defoe, Daniel, works by or attributed to: *Fortunes and Misfortunes of the Famous Moll Flanders*
Monmouth, 1st duke, James Scott, 13, 57
Monmouth's Rebellion, 25, 257n38, 263n97
Montaigne, "Of Cannibals," 187–88
Montesquieu, baron de, Charles-Louis de Secondat: and literary deism, 103–04, 105–06, 117; *Lettres persanes, Persian Letters*, 97–98; romance, 102; secret chain, 102
Montgomery, Scott L., *The Moon and the Western Imagination*, 260n60
Moore, John Robert, 29, 35, 48, 235n3, 236–37n10, 245n109, 251n174, 266n2, 289n194; *Checklist of the Writings of Daniel Defoe*,

249–50n153; *Defoe in the Pillory*, 5; "Defoe's Persona as an Author," 36, 248n142
More, Henry (Cambridge Platonist), 60, 258n41
More, Sir Thomas (Renaissance humanist), 59, 131; *Utopia*, 60, 86, 258n41
Morgan, Matthew, *Eugenia*, 101
Morning Chronicle and London Advertiser, 141
Morton, Charles, Morton's Academy, 13, 156, 241n54, 265n114
Mullett, Charles, "The Legal Position of English Dissenters," 249n147
Muslim/Muslims, 49, 96, 108–111, 112, 116, 119, 128, 130, 152, 214, 270n60, 271n79

narrative style, Defoe's. See under Defoe, Daniel: about his writings
natural religion, 177, 187; Friday as figure of, 135, 190, 193–94, 263n98
naturalism, as deist outlook, 165
Nazarene/Nazarenes, 110, 112, 114–15
Neville, Henry, *Isle of Pines*, 250n168, 250n169, 250n170
Newgate Prison, 4, 28–29, 63, 254n15
Nicolas-Pierre-Henri, abbe de Villars, *Count of Gabalis*, 157, 280n74
Nicolson, Marjorie Hope: "Cosmic Voyages," 73; *Voyages to the Moon*, 72–74, 76, 255–56n22, 264n114
noble savage, 188–89
Northrop Frye, *Anatomy of Criticism*, 62
notitiae communes. See Common Notions of deism (*notitiae communes*)
Nottingham, 2nd Earl, Daniel Finch, 20, 43, 44, 237n16, 243n87, 252n181
Novak, Maximillian: "Crusoe's Original Sin," 279n48; *Daniel Defoe: Master of Fictions*, 6, 12, 20, 53, 91, 107, 213, 236n7, 236n9, 237n16, 237n17,

238n4, 238n22, 240n50, 241n54, 243n81, 243n85, 243–44n91, 245n106, 245–46n109, 246n114, 252n183, 272n93, 274n125, 279n48, 280n74, 281n78; "Defoe, the Occult, and the Deist Offensive," 213; "Defoe's Theory of Fiction," 264n112; "Introduction" to Browne, *The Moon-Calf,* 53, 79, 91, 255n20, 257n36; "*Robinson Crusoe* and Defoe's Career as a Writer," 4, 6, 20, 42–43, 243n81; "Robinson Crusoe's Fear and the Search for Natural Man," 127, 273n112; "Sum of Human Misery?," 122, 272n93; "Transformations, Ideology, and the Real," 236n9
Nuttall, Geoffrey, *The Holy Spirit in Puritan Faith and Experience,* 107, 270n53

Observator. See Tutchin, John
Occasional Conformity, 6, 8, 16, 18, 35, 36, 42, 237n18, 239n30
Ochino, Bernardino, 101
Ockley, Simon (translator of *Hai Ibn Yaqzān*), *The Improvement of Human Reason,* 126, 128–30
Orientalism, 92; Saidian, 92; Enlightenment (Aravamudan), 92–94, 100, 103; literary, 35, 48, 49, 113, 127, 130, 215, 269n46. *See also* cosmopolitan/cosmopolitanism
Orr, John, *English Deism,* 263n98
Orr, Leah: "Providence and Religion in the Crusoe Trilogy," 182–84
Owens, W. R.: *Critical Bibliography of Daniel Defoe,* 266n2; *Defoe Deattributions,* 235n3, 239n31, 289n194; *Life and Strange Surprizing Adventures* (editor), 195–96, 239n31, 280n68; *Political Biography of Daniel Defoe,* 10, 43, 246n116, 249n153, 252n181, 256n24

Oxford English Dictionary, 18, 105, 161
Oxford, 1st Earl, Robert Harley. *See* Harley, Robert, 1st Earl of Oxford

Palatine/Palatines, 156, 158–59, 281n80
panegyrick, 3, 215
paradox, 19, 74–75, 80; aesthetic balance in, 192, 225; irony and, 54; skeptical commonplaces and, 123
Parrett, Aaron, *Translunar Narrative,* 265n127
party politics, 132. *See also* Tory/Tories; Whig/Whigs
Pasquin, 289n196
Pearl, Jason H., 256n22
Penn, William (Quaker): assists Defoe while in prison, 28–30, 46, 245n109; attacks on, 40; enemy of Charles Leslie, 30–32; *Sandy Foundation Shaken,* anti-Trinitarianism of, 34, 41
Petronius, *Satyricon,* 71, 242–43n78
Pfanner, Dario, "Charles Blount," 244n94
Philalethes, Eugenius (pseud.), *Fame and Confesssion of the Fraternity of R:C: Commonly, of the Rosie Cross,* 157–58
philology, deist, 93, 145, 167–69, 208–209
philo-Semitic/philo-Semitism, 123–24, 164, 283n101
picaresque, 81
Pidou de Saint-Olon, François, 95
Pilgrim's Progress, 141
pillory, 4–5, 11, 17, 18, 21, 28, 30, 35, 41, 51, 52, 54, 55, 59, 63, 198, 232, 233, 236–37n10, 243n85, 245n109, 254n13, 254n15
Pine, John (illustrator), 154–55
Pittis, William: *Dyet of Poland: A Satyr Considered Paragraph for Paragraph,* 54–55, 77, 243n89; *True-Born Hugonot,* 22–23, 25, 100

Plato, 131
plurality of worlds, 76–77, 85–86, 220–21, 262n93
Pocockc, Edward (translator), *Philosophus Autodidactus*, 129
Poliakov, Léon, *The History of Anti-Semitism*, 266n8
Pope, Alexander: on Blount's suicide, 25, 138; *Dunciad Variorum*, 139; Gildon, mockery of, 139; the Hayy linked to *Robinson Crusoe*, 273n111; Rosicrucian machinery in "Rape of the Lock," 156–58
Poor Robin's Almanac, 86, 265
Popper, Karl, 69
Porada, Aleksandra, "Giovanni Paulo Marana's Turkish Spy and the Police of Louis XIV," 267n13
Presbysterianism/Presbysterians, 36, 42, 58, 60, 105, 214, 248n139
Prince, Michael B.: *Philosophical Dialogue in the British Enlightenment*, 267n11; "Religio Laici versus Religio Laici," 263n99
Protestant/Protestantism, 36, 37, 42, 43, 60, 86, 113, 116, 133, 137, 184, 188, 191, 192, 194, 195, 212, 271n74, 286n129, 280n131; non-conformist, 37, 86, 116, 133, 137, 147, 154, 156, 213, 214, 219, 224, 226–27, 229, 251–52n179, 269n32, 276n22, 288n166, 288n170, 291–92n8; spiritual autobiography in, 189
Providence, 13; deist ambivalence toward, 81, 179–81; diverse meanings in *Robinson Crusoe*, 141–42, 144, 172–77, 181–82
Puritans/Puritanism, 60, 80, 117, 141, 251n175, 251n179, 258n46, 270n53, 282n87
Pyrrho: *Pyrrhôneioi Hypotyposeis (Outlines of Pyrrhonism)*, 68; Pyrrhonian skepticism, 68–70, 260n69

Quaker/Quakerism/Quakers, attacks on, 33, 42, 246n116, 246–47n122, 249n147, 250n155, 250n161; blasphemy of, 31–34, 37, 42; characters and personas in Defoe's writings, 30–31, 47, 248n142; Charles Leslie, principal antagonist of, 31–32, 246–47n122; controversy as impetus for *The Shortest Way with the Dissenters*, 246n115; Defoe's defense of, 28–35; as deism in disguise, 34–35, 38–39, 113–15; female equality in, 39; Judaism and, 247n123; legal restrictions against, 36, 248n132, 249n147; Quaker Act 1662, 248n147; Quaker theology, 31–40, 250n155; Quietism and, 112, 270n71; religious symbolism rejected by, 40–41; repudiation of Defoe by, 36–40; utopianism of, 40–41
Quietism/Quietists, 112, 270n71
Quincy, Thomas de, 158

realism, 57, 111, 121–22
Reformer Reform'd; or, The Shortest Way with Daniel D'Fooe, 15, 241n62
relativism, 75, 87, 116, 188
republican/republicanism, 15, 16, 24, 25, 42, 66, 77, 117, 134, 172, 217, 257n38
revenge, as motive for literary invention, 4, 45, 46, 72, 195, 199, 201, 204, 211
Revolutionary Settlement, 56
Richardson, Samuel: *Clarissa*, 81; female characters in, 39–40, 232; *History of Sir Charles Grandison*, 105
Richetti, John: *Life of Daniel Defoe*, 4, 8, 237n17, 288n172; "Secular Crusoe," 277n31
Robbins, Harry F., "How Smart Was Robinson Crusoe?," 183
Robin Hood, 161

Rogers, Woodes, *Cruising Voyage Round the World*, 156
Rooke, George, Sir (admiral), 252n181
Rosenkreuz, Christian, 156; resemblance to Robinson Crusoe, 157
Rosicrucian/Rosicrucianism, 156–58, 280n74
Ross, John Frederic, *Swift and Defoe*, 257n37
Roxana. *See* Defoe, Daniel, works by or attributed to: *The Fortunate Mistress, or Roxana*
royalist, 25, 57
Russen, David, *Iter Lunare*, 85–87, 258n41, 265n127
Rye House Plot, 15, 263n97

Sacheverell, Henry, 5–8, 12, 13, 36, 37, 43, 44, 238n22, 289n194, 290n204; "Character of a Low-Church Man," 247n131; "Perils of False Brethren," 198; *Political Union*, 6
Said, Edward, 92, 112
Salters Hall Controversy, 211–12
Saltmarsh, John, 107, 108, 270n53
satire: allegorical, 54, 56, 57, 60, 63, 64, 71, 74, 87, 255n20, 262n93; Defoe's, difficulty classifying, 63; high versus low norm (Frye), 62; Lucianic, 66, 67, 71, 74–76, 84, 85, 87, 88, 115, 258n41; Menippean, 70, 71, 81, 204; personal, 3; political, 53; Pyrrhonian, 70; Roman, 15, 71; secret, 2, 3, 137, 158, 212–13; Swiftean, 59, 61, 62, 87, 88; Tory, 57
Sault, Richard, 98, 107
Scholar Armed, 7
Secord, Arthur Wellesley, *Studies in the Narrative Method of Defoe*, 47, 280n69
Seidel, Kevin, "*Robinson Crusoe* as Defoe's Theory of Fiction," 264n112, 286n137

Seidel, Michael: *Consolidator* (editor), 254n15, 254–55n16, 256n22, 256n24, 256–57n28, 257n36, 258n41, 259–60n56, 261n85, 262n93, 263n98, 264–65n114; "The Man Who Came to Dinner," 84
semiotic crisis, 163
Seneca, 86; *Apocolocyntosis*, 71
Sextus Empiricus, 68
"Seven Voyages of Sinbad the Sailor," 127
Shadwell, Charles, prologue to *Rotherick O'Connor, King of Connaught*, 16
Shaftesbury, 1st Earl, Anthony Ashley Cooper, 13, 57
Shaftesbury, 3rd Earl, Anthony Ashley Cooper: anti-Semitism of, 266n8; attends Sacheverell's trial, 199; *Characteristicks*, praise of Jonah and style of the Hebrew Bible, 150–53, 279–80n60, 283n100; as deist, 93, 146, 150, 164, 194, 217, 275n8; influence on Mendelssohn, 283n102
Shaw Narelle L., 255–56n22
Shirren, A. J., *Daniel Defoe in Stoke Newington*, 280n72
Shortest Way with Whores and Rogues, 13–14, 16, 241n56, 242n66
Sidney, Algernon (republican martyr), 77; *Discourses concerning Government*, 263n97
Sidonia, Duke de Medina, 2, 3, 41, 208, 236n6, 236n9
Sill, Geoffrey: "Christianity Not as Old as the Creation" (review), 42; *Consolidator* (editor), 57, 256n23, 256n24, 259n56, 261n85, 262n95, 263n98, 264n114, 286n129
Simonutti, Luisa, "Deism, Biblical Hermeneutics, and Philology," 283–84n103
singularity, as concept of character, 102, 105–06, 262n90
Skelton, Philip, *Deism Revealed*, 275n8

skepticism, 123, 243n78; ancient, 80; in cosmopolitan fiction, 215; Defoe's hostility toward (Starr), 279n45; and "equivalence," 215; extreme, 68; Lucianic, 80; Pyrrhonian, 68, 69; religious, 215, 266n8; spy novel and, 116
Slafter, Edmund F., *John Checkley*, 274n1
Smallbroke, Richard, *Vindication of the Miracles of Our Blessed Saviour*, 34–35
Smith, Patrick, "Preservative against Quakerism," 248n138
Society of Friends. *See* Quaker/Quakerism/Quakers
Socinian/Socinians, 32, 34, 43; Socinian controversy, 33–34; Socinus, 117
Spence, Ferrand (translator of Lucian), 64–65
Spinoza/Spinozism/Spinozist, 25, 80, 164, 263n98, 284n104
Stamm, Rudolph G., "Daniel Defoe: An Artist in the Puritan Tradition," 226
Stanley, Thomas, *History of Philosophy*, 69, 123, 242n78
Starkey, Thomas, *Dialogue between Pole and Lupset*, 105, 269n44
Starr, G. A., 140; *Christianity Not as Old as the Creation* (editor), 42; *Consolidator* (editor), 252n181; *Defoe and Casuistry*, 191–92; "Defoe and China," 262n95; "Robinson Crusoe and Its Sequels," 278n45; *Serious Reflections* (editor), 219, 270n71, 278n42, 286n129, 293n48
state of nature, 188, 196–97
Steele, Richard, *Tatler*, 105
Stennett, Joseph, *Answer to Mr. Russen's Book*, 265n126
Sterne, Laurence: *Tristram Shandy*, 53; embarrassment to clockmakers, 142
Stevenson, Robert Louis, 161
Stiles, Ezra, 180
Stogdon, Hubert, 212

sublime, 111–12, 118, 121, 123, 128, 150–52, 153, 154, 225
Summary Account of the Deists Religion, 287n149
Sutherland, James, *Daniel Defoe*, 5–7, 12, 22, 25, 42, 50, 237n17, 259n55
Swift, Jonathan: attacks Defoe, 257n38; Defoe, his adversary, 63; Defoe's criticism of, 59; derivative of Defoe, 255n19; dissenters, attacks on, 60; misogyny of, 61, 259n48; as precursor of Defoe's lunar voyage, 58–61, 257n36; pretends to forget Defoe's name, 58–59; Quakers, attacks on, 34, 61, 259n48; Tory satire of, 62; Whigs and deists equated, 248n138. *Works*, 59; *Discourse Concerning the Mechanical Operation of the Spirit*, 58–61; *Examiner*, 9, 34; *Gulliver's Travels*, 53, 159–60, 204; *Letter from a Member of the House of Commons of Ireland to a Member of the House of Commons in England*, 58; *Modest Proposal*, 20; *Tale of the Tub*, 19, 87, 156, 264n114

tacking controversy, 256n24. *See also* Occasional Conformity
Test Act, 58
theocracy, theocratic state, 8, 51, 66, 93
theodicy, 190
theory of the novel: absent from Defoe, 1, 81; allegory and realism combined, 215; biblical elements of, 123–24; cognitive dimensions of, 81–84, 137; Defoe's, 45, 50, 81, 88, 92, 133, 210, 215, 230; deist thought experiments in, 129; genre in, 82, 86; hermeneutic context of, 169, 171–72, 215; lunar theory of representation, 71, 81, 83–84; a machine for automatic writing, 84; narrative dimensions of, 120–23;

scattered remains of a theory under threat, 94, 215–18, 231–32; translation and, 111–12, 216. *See also* failure; literary deism
Thirty-Nine Articles, 39
Thirty Years' War, 177
Thomas, Roger, "Non-Subscription Controversy," 291n10
Tindal, Matthew, 146, 263n98; *Christianity as Old as the Creation*, 42; *Rights of the Christian Church Asserted*, 188
Toland, John: Defoe's attack on, 213, 242n73, 263n98; deist, 43, 93, 110, 146–47, 164, 194, 214, 217, 263n98; distributor of *Shortest Way*, 18, 20–21, 243n84; *Traité des trois imposteurs* (attrib.), 101, 269n33
Tom Tell-Truth's Letter to a Dissenter, 54, 256
Torp, Laura, *So Strange Things So Probably Told*, 265n127
Torrero-Ibad, Alexandra, *Libertinage science et philosophie*, 262n90
Tory/Tories, 6, 16, 17, 20, 22, 23, 24, 25, 45, 54, 56, 62, 117, 139, 200, 237n17, 237n18, 243n89, 244n94, 256n24, 275n10
Traité des trois imposteurs, 101, 268n33
Trent, W. P., 237n15
Trinitarian/Trinitarianism/Trinity, 32–34, 36, 40, 42–43, 114, 125, 167, 171, 212–13, 212, 215, 249n147, 250n155, 287n156; anti-, 33–34, 42–43, 170–71, 183, 212–13
Tucker, Joseph E.: "On the Authorship of the 'Turkish Spy'," 95, 266n2, 267n15, 268n17, 268n20, 268n22, 272n83; "Turkish Spy and Its French Background," 96–97
Tufayl, Ibn. *See* Ibn Tufayl, Hai Ibn Yaqzān
Turkish Spy. *See* Defoe, Daniel, works by or attributed to: *Continuation of Letters Written by a Turkish Spy at Paris*, as imitation of Marana's *Letters Writ by a Turkish* Spy, its secret history; Marana, Giovanni-Paulo: *Letters Writ by a Turkish Spy*
Tutchin, John: death of, 258n38; "Foreigners," 257n38; *Observator*, 9, 17, 21–22, 58, 136, 239n29, 242n68, 246n116
Tyburn Tree/Three-leg'd Tree, platform for execution proposed for Defoe, 55, 77
typology, 165–71, 257n32, 257n33, 285n121; deist critique of, 167
Tyssot de Patot, Simon: *Lettres choisies*, 80; *Travels and Adventures of James Massey*, 80–81

Unitarian/Unitarians, 32, 33, 49, 94, 114, 214, 249n147
Universal Jewish Encyclopedia (editor, Landman), 283n102
Universalism, 79, 92, 131, 194
utopian fiction, 49, 59, 64–65, 92–93, 131, 172, 255–56n22

Vanini, Lucilio, *De admirandis naturae reginae deaeque mortalium arcanis*, 143
Varro, *Saturae Menippeae*, 71
Vaughn, Thomas (translator), *Fame and Confession of the Fraternity of R:C:*, 281n76
Vicar of Bray, 72
Vickers, Ilse, *Defoe and the New Science*, 277n31
Villars, abbé de. *See* Nicolas-Pierre-Henri, abbe de Villars, *Count of Gabalis*
Vico, Giambattista, 93
Voltaire, 93, 164, 267n8

Walkden, Andrea, "Parallel Lives and Literary Legacies," 158

Ward, Edward (attrib.), *Secret History of the Calves'-Head Club*, 16, 241n63

Wardhaugh, Benjamin, *Poor Robin's Prophecies*, 266n129

Watt, Ian: realism hypothesis, 92; *Rise of the Novel*, 154

Weinbrot, Howard D.: *Literature, Religion, and the Evolution of Culture*, 6, 20, 243n81; *Mennipean Satire Reconsidered*, 261n76

Weitzman, Arthur, "Editor's Introduction" in *Marana's Turkish Spy*, 115–16, 271n79

West, Richard, *Daniel Defoe: The Life and Strange Surprising Adventures*, 161, 240–41n50, 256n22, 259n56, 287n158

Whichcote, Benjamin, *Several Discourses Concerning the Shortness of Humane Charity*, 149–50

Whig/Whigs, 5, 6, 16, 17, 20, 22, 29, 33, 57, 63, 117, 139, 158–59, 243n87, 244n94, 246n116, 247n130, 248n139, 257n38

Whig's Medley. *See* Bickham, George, "Whig's Medley"

Wigelsworth, Jeffrey R., 263n99, 284n103

Wilkins, John, Bishop, *Discovery of a World in the Moone*, 59, 72, 80, 262n93

William III (king of England), 20, 22, 25, 27, 29, 33, 45, 101, 126, 219, 244n94

William of Orange. *See* William III (king of England)

Wilson, Francis, "Dark Side of Utopia," 78

wolves in Defoe, 36, 52, 196–98, 247n131, 289n190

Wollaston, William, 147, 164, 263n98

Woolf, Virginia, "Robinson Crusoe," 232–33

Woolston, Thomas, 194, 248n140, 263n98

Wootton, David, 240n47

Yates, Francis, *Rosicrucian Enlightenment*, 158, 281n77

Zwierlein, Cornel (editor), *Heterodox Italian Migrants*, 269n33

Recent winners of the Walker Cowen Memorial Prize

The Shortest Way with Defoe: Robinson Crusoe, Deism, and the Novel
Michael B. Prince

Public Vows: Fictions of Marriage in the English Enlightenment
Melissa J. Ganz

Citizens of Convenience: The Imperial Origins of American Nationhood on the U.S.-Canadian Border
Lawrence B. A. Hatter

Empiricist Devotions: Science, Religion, and Poetry in Early Eighteenth-Century England
Courtney Weiss Smith

Nationalizing France's Army: Foreign, Black, and Jewish Troops in the French Military, 1715–1831
Christopher J. Tozzi

Prose Immortality, 1711–1819
Jacob Sider Jost

The Evil Necessity: British Naval Impressment in the Eighteenth-Century Atlantic World
Denver Brunsman

Be It Ever So Humble: Poverty, Fiction, and the Invention of the Middle-Class Home
Scott R. MacKenzie

Backstage in the Novel: Frances Burney and the Theater Arts
Francesca Saggini, translated by Laura Kopp

The Nation's Nature: How Continental Presumptions Gave Rise to the United States of America
James D. Drake

Our Coquettes: Capacious Desire in the Eighteenth Century
Theresa Braunschneider

Virginians Reborn: Anglican Monopoly, Evangelical Dissent, and the Rise of the Baptists in the Late Eighteenth Century
Jewel L. Spangler

Ending the French Revolution: Violence, Justice, and Repression from the Terror to Napoleon
Howard G. Brown

Wild Enlightenment: The Borders of Human Identity in the Eighteenth Century
Richard Nash

www.ingramcontent.com/pod-product-compliance
Lightning Source LLC
Chambersburg PA
CBHW021341300426
44114CB00012B/1037